DOGS

BREEDING, NUTRITION, DIAGNOSIS AND HEALTH MANAGEMENT

DOGS

BREEDING, NUTRITION, DIAGNOSIS AND HEALTH MANAGEMENT

Dr. M.C. Sharma
B.V.Sc. & A.H., M.V.Sc., Ph.D.
Sr. Scientist (Medicine)
Officer-in-Charge Polyclinic, I.V.R.I.
Formerly Diplomatic Indian Expert (ITEC)
Vietnam.

Dr. N.N. Pathak
B.Sc., B.V.Sc. & A.H., M.V.Sc., Ph.D.
Sr. Scientist (Nutrition)
Formerly Diplomatic
Indian Expert & Project Leader (ITEC)
Vietnam

Prof. P.N. Bhat
M.V.Sc., M.Sc., Ph.D. (Purdue)
Former Director, IVRI,
Dy. Director General (AS) ICAR,
Animal Husbandry Commissioner
Govt. of India, New Delhi

CBS

CBS Publishers & Distributors Pvt. Ltd.

New Delhi • Bengaluru • Chennai • Kochi • Kolkata • Mumbai
Hyderabad • Nagpur • Patna • Pune • Vijayawada

ISBN: 81-239-0244-7

First Edition: 1993
Reprint: 2001, 2008, 2012, 2019

Published by **Satish Kumar Jain** and produced by **Varun Jain** for
CBS Publishers & Distributors Pvt. Ltd.,
4819/XI Prahlad Street, 24 Ansari Road, Daryaganj, New Delhi - 110002
delhi@cbspd.com, cbspubs@airtelmail.in • www.cbspd.com
Ph.: 23289259, 23266861, 23266867 • Fax: 011-23243014

Corporate Office: 204 FIE, Industrial Area, Patparganj, Delhi - 110 092
Ph: 49344934 • Fax: 011-49344935
E-mail: publishing@cbspd.com • publicity@cbspd.com

Branches:
- ***Bengaluru:*** 2975, 17th Cross, K.R. Road, Bansankari 2nd Stage, Bengaluru - 70 • Ph: +91-80-26771678/79 • Fax: +91-80-26771680 E-mail: cbsbng@gmail.com, bangalore@cbspd.com
- ***Chennai:*** No. 7, Subbaraya Street, Shenoy Nagar, Chennai - 600030 Ph: +91-44-26681266, 26680620 • Fax: +91-44-42032115 E-mail: chennai@cbspd.com
- ***Kochi:*** Ashana House, 39/1904, A.M. Thomas Road, Valanjambalam, Ernakulum, Kochi • Ph: +91-484-4059061-65 Fax: +91-484-4059065 • E-mail: cochin@cbspd.com
- ***Kolkata:*** 6-B, Ground Floor, Rameshwar Shaw Road, Kolkata - 700014 Ph: +91-33-22891126/7/8 • E-mail: kolkata@cbspd.com
- ***Mumbai:*** 83-C, Dr. E. Moses Road, Worli, Mumbai - 400018 Ph: +91-9833017933, 022-24902340/41 • E-mail: mumbai@cbspd.com

Representatives:

- Hyderabad: 0-9885175004
- Patna: 0-9334159340
- Jharkhand: 0-9811541605
- Nagpur: 0-9021734563
- Pune: 0-9623451994
- Uttarakhand: 0-9716462459

Printed at:
J.S. Offset Printers, Delhi (India)

FOREWORD

The dog, among all the animals, has proved to be the best friend and faithful companion of man because of its fidelity, loyalty, obedience and pleasant disposition. The dog, it is said, appeared on the earth about 20 million years ago. It is believed that its domestication started ten to fifteen thousand years ago in parts of the old world when man learnt to cultivate wild grains and started living in communities.

Dogs are believed to be the descendants of wolves. Several theories exist regarding origin of dogs, but there is little doubt about its contribution to the human civilization. It has established itself as a companion, guard and hunter, besides serving mankind in different areas. The unique quality of the dog to trace and identify smells as well as its own territorial field, has been exploited most widely by man. Over the years several breeds have come up with special traits.

The present-day dogs differ from their ancestors in appearance as a result of selective breeding over centuries. New breeds were developed to meet the varying requirements of man, viz. hunting, guarding flocks of sheep, draught in icy regions, as a guide to blind persons and for detecting crime and criminals. As a pet, dog provides great relief to human-beings from tension, and brings us close to nature.

In India, of late, interest in dog-keeping has increased greatly. It is becoming a symbol of status for some and succor for others. This has resulted in awareness for the scientific breeding of established breeds according to the demands from different classes of the society.

Industries relating to manufacture of appliances like collar, strap, chain, clothes and complete food for dogs have sprung up. This has had a positive affect on the employment generation. Today, all the drugs and biologicals used in providing health protection to pet dogs are produced in our country. This has reduced sufferings of the pet dogs and made their rearing easier.

There has been a great demand from dog-lovers for a book giving information on all aspects of dog keeping under Indian conditions. Dog keeping is also a subject of teaching in veterinary colleges. The authors, through their painstaking efforts, have compiled the scattered informations on dog management at one place. I hope that this book, containing valuable scientific and general information regarding dogs, will be of immense use to our graduate and post-graduate students, professionals as well as the dog owners across the country.

V.L. CHOPRA
Secretary, Govt. of India
(DARE) & Director General
Indian Council of Agricultural Research
Krishi Bhavan
New Delhi-110001.

PREFACE

Friendly association of dogs with man is known from time immemorial. With the passage of time the dog has changed itself in respect of its habits, behaviour and living pattern. At present it is a popular pet all over the world. In recent years there has been increasing interest particularly in urban areas, in dog keeping. Earlier pet dogs of exotic breeds were rare and considered a luxury and a symbol of status, but changing life style of today has made dog keeping a necessity. To meet the increasing demand for pet dogs, more and more breeding kennels are coming up. Today one finds dog breeding studs even in small towns. Most of the dog owners are ignorant about the habits and behaviour of dogs. Increasing importance of dogs has resulted in inclusion of specific courses on various aspects of dog management in the curriculum of veterinary education. World over scores of books and other literatures are available regarding the origin of dog, its developmental stages, breeding and feeding practices, management of different diseases alongwith their control, but most of them are not suited to the conditions prevailing in Indian sub-continent. This book has been specifically compiled to suit agro-climatic and socio-economic conditions in our country and satisfy the needs of dog owners of diversified classes. This book incorporates important topics like the dog's past and present, its breeding and reproductive performances, nutritional and feeding habits, management schemes required and various clinical diagnostic features of different infectious and non-infectious diseases, their treatment, control measures, commonly used surgical procedures in curing various diseases and various legal provisions in protecting the pet dog. The appendices include information regarding dog shows, insurance formalities, anatomical details of dogs, their health care, prescription writing and different pharmaceutical preparations along with their doses and schedule for the treatment of pet dogs. The authors invite comments, corrections, additions and criticism from their readers regarding this text so that the second edition may be more informative and useful. It has been our endeavour to provide up-to-date, complete and unbiased presentation of all materials related to dog rearing and practice.

We wish to acknowledge the assistance rendered by Kunwarani Prabha Kumari, U.P. Kennel Club, Lucknow, Smt. E. Negi, Communication Centre, IVRI, Izatnagar, Shri R.R. Lokeshwar, Editor and Smt. Aruna T. Kumar, Associate Editor, Animal Sciences, ICAR, New Delhi, Smt. Vijoy Laxmi Dhir, IARI, New Delhi, Dr. P.K. Malik, former A.A.O., United India Insurance Company Ltd., Lucknow, Smt. Rukmani Sudarshan, Secretary, Kennel Club of India, Madras, Shri Kundan Singh, Press Manager, IVRI, Izatnagar, Mr Thakur Das, Mr. Mohd. Saleem, Mr. P.K. Saxena, Mr Mohd. Waseem, Typists, Mr. G.C. Sinha, Artist and Mr B.K. Das, photographer. Shri Kailash Chandra, P.S. to Director, IVRI, Izatnagar. The authors sincerely acknowledge their gratitude to Dr. D.S. Balain, Director, IVRI for rendering his kind assistance time to time. The authors also express their thanks to all the dog owners who have rendered special assistance and made available information regarding dogs for this book. The authors are obliged to Er S.C. Tiwari, Superintending Air-Craft Engineer, Indian Air Lines and Chairman, Institute of Electronics & Telecommunication Engineers, Delhi Centre for his time to time inspiration in bringing out this manuscript. The authors would also like to thank their spouses and families for their patience and help during the period of preparation of this manuscript. Last but not the least, the authors offer their sincere gratitude to all those who have contributed to make this book a reality.

M.C. SHARMA
N.N. PATHAK
P.N. BHAT

CONTENTS

LIST OF PLATES

DOGS

BREEDING, NUTRITION, DIAGNOSIS AND HEALTH MANAGEMENT

1

DOG - PAST AND PRESENT

Dogs are perhaps closest to humans. Among all the domestic animals, dogs appeared on the earth about 20 million years ago. Their pleasing disposition, cooperative behaviour and natural instinct for affinity with human beings were the reasons for choosing them as domestic animals for companionship. Numerous folk tales relate the fidelity, loyalty, obedience and affinity of dogs to their master and his associates. Since the beginning of civilization, dogs have been selected and bred for different purposes like companionship, sports, protection against strangers and hunting. Dogs of small breeds are good companions, hounds are loved by hunters while shepherd dogs are maintained for managing farm animals on pastures and ranges. Polar dogs are used as draught animals for pulling sledge carts on the snow-covered ground of Tundra. In recent years, they are being used in several new fields. Selected breeds are used by the police, military, railways, prisons and blind homes to watch, search for missing, deserted or absconding persons, guide blind persons and assist humans in many other ways.

Dogs were domesticated in the prehistoric period in Denmark, Switzerland, Germany, Egypt, Indus Valley, Mesopotamia, Turkestan, Southeast Asian countries, China, Japan, Australia and several countries of Africa and America.

Although dogs were domesticated in the prehistoric period wild, feral and street dogs are still found in different countries. Wild dogs are considered to be very ferocious animals. They hunt for their prey in a well-formed design.

Wild dog: Varieties available today are the Dingoes of Australia, Pariah of South and West Asia, and wild dogs of India.

Feral dogs: Feral dogs are domesticated breeds that have returned to their wild habitat and have also regained their original habits. They are often found in the jungles of Asia, Africa and other parts of the world.

Pet dogs: Pet dogs are mostly pedigreed animals maintained under controlled management.

CLASSIFICATION OF DOG

Zoological Classification

The dog belongs to Class Mammalia, Subclass Metatheria, Order Carnivora, Family Canidae, Genus *Canis,* species *familiaris.*

Earliest domestication of dogs was around 10,000 BC. Evidence to this effect can be found from the Belt Cave in Persia. The modern breeds of dogs were developed through selection and/or interbreeding of different ancient varieties supposed to have descended from common Indian wolf, Dingo and Pariah. Some researchers also relate dogs to jackals. This view however is under dispute and needs detailed investigation. The following opinions are commonly held regarding the origin of domesticated dogs:

Direct descendants of wolf (particularly the Indian wolf); originated from the jackal; originated from the interbreeding of wolf and jackal; descendants of the wild Dingo; originated from the Indian wild dog or Dhole dog but this has been described as a separate genus *Cuon alpinus.*

Domestic dogs are considered to have descended from the wolf of northern Europe, Indian barking wolf and probably the jackal. Polar dogs and Alsatians are the descendants of northern wolf; shepherd dogs, hounds, grey hounds and Indian *dèsi* dogs are the descendants of the Indian barking wolf, Dingo, Pariah or their intercrosses; and Pomeranians and Terriers are supposed to be the descendants of the second group of wild ancestors of the jackal.

The popularity of dogs increased with the advancement of civilization in different countries. A large number of kennels were established in Europe and America for the breeding of dogs to meet the demands of human.

Modern breeds suited for maintaining as pet dogs are classified according to the British or American Kennel Club's classification. A widely accepted well-defined classification of Indian domestic dogs is not available. Most of the Indian breeds of dogs are known by different names. However, a tentative classification has been proposed to bring uniformity and easy identification. British and American Kennel Club's classifications are given in Annexures 1 and 2. Details of some important breeds found in India have been given in Annexure 3.

INDIAN CLASSIFICATION

In India, selection of dogs is based on their utility. Nomadic and settled tribes like *Banjara, Tharu, Bhatu, Cole, Bhil* and *Mundia* prefer fast-running breeds for hunting. Farmers like intelligent dogs to help them in guarding their household, farm animals and fields. These are mostly selected local breeds, well-adapted to the food habits and living conditions of the farmers. Among urban Indians dog keeping is a status symbol and they like to have rare specimens of dogs without any significant importance to their utility. Dogs are usually kept as companions in many families. Considering the large variations in the types of dogs, environment and types of owners, etc. the dogs in India are classified as given in the following paragraphs:

House dogs: These are strictly pet animals (which are taken out of doors only for exercise, defaecation and urination). They are kept in the house either loose or tied. House dogs are mostly exotic, Alsatian, Pomeranian, Labrador, Terriers and Spaniels. Selected specimens from local breeds are also kept as house dogs.

House yard dogs: People in villages keep selected local dogs, sometimes crosses of local and exotic dogs to serve as guards. These dogs are allowed freedom of movement and spend an equal time indoors and outdoors.

Yard dogs: These dogs are always kept outdoors and offered food 2 or 3 times daily. Yard dogs are companions of farmers, and assist them in guarding the standing crop in the fields and orchards. These dogs are almost exclusively local animals patronized by a family.

Nomad: These are selected dogs developed through semi-scientific breeding by the nomadic tribes. They are usually multipurpose utility animals and help owners in hunting and guarding their belongings in the camps. These dogs adapt easily to changed situations and do not have affinity for any other place other than their owner's camp.

Mongrels: Mongrels are stray dogs found in large numbers in the inhabitated rural and urban areas. These dogs like to live near the sources of food like slaughter places, meat shops and *halwai* shops. They feed on kitchen wastes, food shop rejects, garbage and dead carcasses. Usually mongrels steal food from the kitchen and shops and are a nuisance in that area.

Note: Specialized dog breeding has set in India. Some good breeds, developed earlier are the Rampur hound of Rampur Nawab, Poligar of Madras and Banjara hound or Tazi Kutta of northern India.

SELECTION OF A PET DOG

Before selecting a particular breed of dog as a pet, the following aspects should be considered:

Purpose of keeping: The selection of a dog depends on the purpose for which it will be kept. A fast-running long and slender dog is suitable for hunting. Heavy dogs are good guards and toy breeds are preferred as companions.

Housing: Ferocious heavy dogs need separate housing whereas mild dogs and toy breeds may be accommodated in any corner of the house.

Food habits of family: In a family of predominantly vegetarian members keeping heavy and hunting breeds should be avoided because once adapted to a vegetarian diet, they generally dislike hunting. Local dogs, working breeds and toy breeds can easily adapt themselves to milk and/or egg-supplemented vegetarian diets.

Interest in dog keeping: At least one member in the family, preferably with a flexible temperament should be interested in dogs and spare some time for the pet. Dogs need gentle treatment and should not be threatened or tortured frequently, otherwise they may acquire shyness and fear, or may become unruly. A family dog must know each member, close friends and relatives.

Procurement: A dog should be preferably procured from a registered kennel or established dog breeder maintaining pedigree and health record of the pet.

SELECTION OF A PUP

The following points should be considered for selecting a pup to be reared as a pet.

Breed: The pup should have the breed characters.

Pedigree: Pedigree is normally maintained up to 4 generations. Both parents should be registered with the kennel club of the place. The pup should be eligible for registration in a kennel club or dog breeders' association, otherwise the market value of the dog and its progeny may be less than of the registered dogs.

Clinical examination: Normally an experienced dog owner should possess adequate knowledge about the general signs of health. An inexperienced person can take the help of a veterinary doctor for selecting a healthy pup from the litter. The common apparent signs of health considered at the time of selection are as follows:

(i) The animal should be alert, active, lively and curious. Some pups may be shy but it should not be confused with sickness.
(ii) The eyes should be bright, clear and free from lachrymation and inflammation.
(iii) The nose should be clean and free from nasal discharge. It should also be carefully examined for fungal infection.
(iv) The ears should be clean, free from crusts and loss of hairs and should not emit a foul odour.
(v) Gums should be firm and pink.
(vi) The skin should not be dry and scaly, and there should not be any eruptions or inflammation on the open skin in the region of groin, axilla and ventral surface of the body.
(vii) Body coat should be lustrous, glossy, clean and free from the infestations of ectoparasites.
(viii) The claws, foot pad and grooves between the toes should be thoroughly examined for ticks and inflammation.

(ix) The dog's body should be examined thoroughly putting gentle pressure for the general body conditions. Sometimes air is injected subcutaneously for apparent improvement in body condition.

(x) Pulse, respiration and rectal temperature should also be recorded and examined.

(xi) Faeces and urine should be normal.

A healthy pup can be procured at any age after the feeding of dam's colostrum. Newborn pups should be allowed suckling as early as possible, and preferably within 12 hours postpartum. Colostrum feeding provides immunity against many diseases in early life since it is a rich source of immunoglobulins. It is always better to procure a pup after about 2 weeks of weaning and preferably at 4-5 months of age at which breed characteristics are quite visible.

Certain skills are required to familiarize the newly procured pup to its new home and family members.

The animal should be first given some rest and offered milk with bread or biscuits. After this its master who should be responsible for the care and management of the animal should be identified. The first duty of the master is to introduce the dog to all the family members and show him the place of rest, urination and defaecation. He should prepare a time-table for its walk, exercise, feeding, watering, urination, defaecation and grooming etc. A neck collar/shoulder belt can be introduced at an early age and the animal tied with a chain at the place fixed for its resting. A dog kept for guarding should be trained to take frequent rounds in the boundary and let loose at night and at a time when members of the family have gone out. Unknown persons should not be allowed in the vicinity of the pet dog.

Annexure-1

BRITISH KENNEL CLUB CLASSIFICATION OF DOMESTIC DOGS

Dogs have been classified into the following 6 main groups on the basis of body size, morphology, behaviour, place of breeding (origin) and utility:

1. Non-sporting Breeds (Working Group)

Alaskan Malamute
Alsatians (German Shepherd)
Anatolian (Karabash) Dog
Australian Kelpie
Bearded Collie
Beauceron
Belgian Shepherd Dog (Groenendael)
Belgian Shepherd Dog (Tervueren)
Bernese Mountain Dog
Bouvier De Flandre
Boxer
Briard
Bullmastiff
Cardigan Welsh Corgi
Great Dane
Hungarian Kuvasz
Hungarian Puli
Husky
Maremma Italian Sheep Dog
Mastiff
Newfoundland
Norwegian Buhund
Old English Sheepdog
Pembroke Welsh Corgi
Polish Sheepdog
Pyreneam Mountain Dog
Rottweiler
Rough Collie
St. Bernard
Samoyed
Shetland Sheepdog
Siberian Husky
Smooth Collie
Tibetan Mastiff

2. Non-sporting Breeds (Utility Group)

Boston Terrier
Bulldog
Canaan Dog
Chow Chow
Dalmatian
French Bulldog
Giant Schnauzer
Iceland Dog
Japanese Akita
Keeshond
Leonberger
Lhasa Apso
Mexican Hairless
Miniature Schnauzer
Poodle (Standard)
Poodle (Miniature)
Poodle (Toy)
Schipperke
Schnauzer
Shih Tzu
Tibetan Spaniel
Tibetan Terrier

3. Gun dogs

American Cocker Spaniel
Chesapeake Bay Retriever
Clumber Spaniel
Cocker Spanial
Curly Coated Retriever
English Setter
English Springer Spaniel
Field Spaniel
Flat Coated Retriever
German Longhair Pointer
German Shorthair Pointer
German Wirehair Pointer
Golden Retriever
Gordon Setter
Hungarian Vizsla
Irish Setter
Irish Water Spaniel
Italian Spinone
Labrador Retriever
Large Munsterlander
Pointer
Pointing Wire-Haired Griffon
Small Munsterlander
Sussex Spaniel
Weimaraner
Selsh Springer Spaniel

4. Hound Breeds

Basenji
Basset Hound
Basset Griffon Vendeen
Beagle
Bloodhound
Borzoi
Dachsbracke
Dachshund (Long Haired)
Dachshund (Miniature Long-Haired)
Dachshund (Smooth-Haired)
Dachshund (Miniature Smooth-Haired)
Dachshund (Wire-Haired)
Dachshund (Miniature Wire-Haired)
Deerhound
Elkhound
Finnish Spitz
Foxhound
Greyhound
Ibizan Hound
Irishi Wolfhound
Otterhound
Pharaoh Hound

Portuguese Warren Hound
Rhodesian Ridgeback
Saluki
Swedish Foxhound
Swiss Laufhund (Jura)

5. Toy Breeds

Affenpinscher
Bichon Frise
Cavalier King Charles Spaniel
Chihuahua (Long Coat)
Chihuahua (Smooth Coat)
Chinese Crested Dog
English Toy Terrier
(Black and Tan)
Griffon Bruxellois
Italian Greyhound
Japanese Chin
King Charles Spaniel
Lowchen
Maltese
Miniature Pinshcher
Papillon
Pekingese
Pomeranian
Pug
Silky Terrier
Yorkshire Terrier

6. Terrier Breeds

Airedale Terrier
Australian Terrier
Bedlington Terrier
Border Terrier
Bull Terrier
Cairn Terrier
Dandie Dinmont Terrier
Glen of Imaal Terrier
Irish Terrier
Kerry Blue Terrier
Lakeland Terrier
Manchester Terrier
Miniature Bull Terrier
Norfolk Terrier
Norwich Terrier
Scottish Terrier
Sealyham Terrier
Skye Terrier
Smooth Fox Terrier
Soft-Coated Wheaten Terrier
Staffordshire Bull Terrier
Welsh Terrier
West Highland White Terrier
Wire Fox Terrier

Annexure-2

AMERICAN KENNEL CLUB CLASSIFICATION OF DOGS

The American kennel club classification of dogs is somewhat different from the British Kennel Club classification. In this classification more emphasis has been given on the type of dogs which have been classified into the following 6 main classes:

1. Sporting Breeds

Griffon (Wire-Haired pointing)
Pointer
Pointer (German Short-Haired)
Pointer German (Wire-Haired)
Retriever (Chesapeake Bay)
Retriever (Curly-Coated)

Retriever (Flat-Coated)
Retriever (Golden)
Retriever (Labrador)
Setter (English)
Setter (Gordon)
Setter (Irish)
Spaniel (American Water)
Spaniel (Brittany)
Spaniel (Clumber)
Spaniel (Cocker)
Spaniel (English Cocker)
Spaniel (English Springer)
Spaniel (Field)
Spaniel (Irish Water)
Spaniel (Sussex)
Spaniel (Welsh Springer)
Vizsla
Weimaraner

2. Non-sporting Breeds

Boston Terrier
Bulldog
Chow Chow
Dalmatian
French Bulldog
Keeshond
Lhasa Apso
Poodle (miniature)
Schipperke

3. Working Breeds

Akita
Alaskan Malamute
Belgian Malinois
Belgian Sheepdog
Belgian Tervuren
Bernese Mountain Dog
Bouvier des Flandres
Boxer
Briard
Bull Mastiff
Collie
Dobermann Pinscher
German Shepherd Dog
Kuvasz
Mastiff
Newfoundland
Old English Sheepdog
Puli
Rottweiler
St. Bernard
Samoyed
Schnauzer (Giant)
Schnauzer (Standard)
Shetland Sheepdog
Siberian Husky
Great Dane
Great Pyreness
Komondor
Welsh Corgi (Cardigan)
Welsh Corgi (Pembroke)

4. Hound Breeds

Afghan Hound
Basenji
Basset Hound
Beagle
Bloodhound
Borzoi (or Russian Wolfhound)
Coonhound (Black-and-tan)
Dachshund
Deerhound (Scottish)
Foxhound (American)
Foxhound (English)
Greyhound

Terrier
Norwegian Elkhound
Otterhound
Rhodesian Ridgeback
Saluki
Shippet
Wolfhound (Irish)

5. Terrier Breeds

Airedale Terrier
Australian Terrier
Bedlington Terrier
Border Terrier
Bull Terrier
Cairn Terrier
Dandie Dinmont Terrier
Fox Terrier
Irish Terrier
Kerry Blue Terrier
Lakeland Terrier
Manchester Terrier
Norwich Terrier
Schnazuer (Miniature) Terrier
Scottish Terrier
Sealyham Terrier
Skye Terrier
Staffordshire Terrier
Welsh Terrier
West Highland White Terrier

6. Toy Breeds

Affenpinscher
Bichon Frise
Chihuahua
English Toy Spaniel
Griffon (Brussels)
Italian Greyhound
Japanese Spaniel
Maltese
Papillon
Pekingese
Pinscher (Miniature)
Pomeranian
Poodle (Toy)
Pug
Shih Tzu
Silky Terrier
Toy Manchester Terrier
Yorkshire Terrier

Annexure-3

BREED CHARACTERISTICS OF SOME SELECTED DOGS

S. No.	*Breed*	*Place of Origin*	*Characteristics*
1	2	3	4
1.	Afghan Hound	Afghanistan, Egypt	Hairy dogs of varied colour, moderate length, levelled back and well-muscled body; average height of adult male 67-70 cm and adult female 63-67 cm; body weight 23-28 kg; drooping, long, hairy ears, long and strong neck and low set tail with ring at the tapering end. (Fig. 1).
2.	Alsatian/German Shepherd dog	Germany	A double-coated animal; hair smooth and glossy; under-coat woolly and protects from cold; usually grey, dark tan and

		various shades of black and white; average height of male 60-70 cm and of female 55-60 cm; body weight 25-35 kg; ears erect and smooth; well-muscled, strong and long neck; long hairy tail slightly curved at the end, may extend up to the hock. (Fig. 2).
3. Basset Hound	France, Belgium	Body coat smooth, short, fine and black, white, tan and lemon, in any combination; average height 32-38 cm and body weight 10-20 kg; very long, drooping ears with velvety texture; tail long, strong and tapering. (Fig. 3).
4. Beagle	Obscure, England	Wide-domed head and straight muscular body; body coat smooth and usually tri-coloured; average height 32-38 cm and body weight 14-18 kg; tail thick and normally carried erect. (Fig. 4).
5. Blood Hound	Middle East	Body coat short, smooth and glossy; black and tan, red and tan or dark, interspersed with light or white hair; average height of adult male about 65 cm and of bitch about 60 cm; average body weight 40-45 kg and of bitch 35-50 kg; tail long and tapering. (Fig. 5).
6. Borzoi/Russian Wolfhound	Russia	Body long and slender, and covered with wavy or curled long silky body coat; hair well-feathered on the chest and tail; white, lemon-white, fawn, orange, red or blue markings; height 70-85 cm and body weight 25-30 kg; males heavier than females. (Fig. 6).
7. Boston Terrier	USA	Apparently looks like a bulldog; head short and square; face short and blunt like a bulldog; body short and compact; ears erect and triangular with pointed tip; tail short and coiled, and docking normally practised; body coat short and smooth; mostly black and white or/and white; average height about 45 cm and body weight 7-10 kg. (Fig. 7).
8. Boxer	Germany	A medium-sized sturdy dog with broad head, short nose and strong jaws; muscular body covered with smooth coat of red, fawn or brindle; tail placed high and docked leaving behind 4-5 cm stump; height 45-60 cm and body weight 25-30 kg; males slightly heavier than females. (Fig. 8).
9. Bull Dog	England	A low-statured animal, broad and compact body; head characteristically heavy and face wrinkled; nose short, wide and black; jaws broad and square; body coat short, fine and smooth; whole coat colour acceptable and it may be various degree of red, brindle, fawn, fallow and white, and their piebald combinations; short tail thick at the root and tapering at the tip; males heavier than females; average height 35-40 cm and body weight 20-25 kg. (Fig. 9).
10. Bull Mastiff	Europe	A large-sized animal covered with short and hard body coat; coat colour may be pure and clear fawn, red or brindle; muzzle dark; ears V-shaped or turned back; average height of males 65-70 cm and of females 60-65 cm; body weight of adult 50-60 kg and adult female 40-50 kg; face broad and wrinkled, neck strongly muscular; tail thick at the root and tapering at the tip which is carried straight or curved.

11. Bull Terrier	England	Body compact and rounded with broad chest; back short and slightly convex; head long and strong; ears triangular, erect and short; body coat short, even and rough; tail coat white, white and black, or brindle and black; height of adult 50-55 cm and body weight 20-25 kg; tail short, low set and straight. (Fig. 10).
12. Cairn Terrier	Scotland	A small dog of pleasant disposition; body strong and compact, covered by double coat; outcoat long and rough, and undercoat short and soft like fur; coat red, sandy, blackish, brindled or grey; ears short, triangular and errect; tail short and straight; average height about 25 cm and body weight 6-7 kg; females normally lighter than males. (Fig. 11).
13. Chihuahua	Mexico	Perhaps smallest dog of the world, fine head, sharp muzzle, erect ears, short smooth coat of different colours; height 15-20 cm and body weight less than 1 to 2.5 kg; tail tapering. (Fig. 12).
14. Chow Chow	China	Active compact body covered with double coat; outer coat dense, coarse and long; undercoat soft and woolly; ears erect, well placed, small and slightly rounded at the tip; tail short, set high and carried over the back; coat black, red, fawn, blue, cream or white; height usually 45-50 cm and body weight 25-30 kg. (Fig. 13).
15. Collie	Scotland	A hairy medium-sized active dog; body coat dense, long and double; outer hair long and coarse, inner coat soft and woolly; coat and markings quite variable; ears small, moderately wide apart and slightly drooping at the tip; height 50-60 cm and adult body weight 20-30 kg; males heavier than females. (Fig. 14).
16. Dachshund	Germany	Low set, short-limbed animal with compact long body; there are 2 recognized strains of Dachshund, viz. Dachshund and Miniature Dachshund; each strain has 3 varieties, viz. (i) smooth haired, (ii) long haired and (iii) wire haired. Ears long and thick, large and drooping with rounded tip; height 20-25 cm and body weight 8-12 kg; height of Miniature Dachshund 12-20 cm and body weight 3-5 kg. (Fig. 15a, b, c)).
17. Dalmatian	Dalmatia (Austria)	Strong dog having muscular body; body coat short, dense, smooth and white colour with black spots or liver spots which may vary in size but never form patches, ears set high and gradually tapering to a round point and covered with spotted hair; height 50-60 cm and body weight 22-25 kg; tail short, fine and straight. (Fig. 16).
18. Dobermann-Pinscher	Germany	An alert dog has smooth, compact and muscular body; body coat smooth, short, thick and glossy; colour black, brown or blue; extremeties light in colour; ears small and erect, but slightly drooped forward; tail docked in early life leaving behind 2-3 cm long stump; height of adult male 65-70 cm and of adult female 60-65 cm; body weight 25-35 kg. (Fig. 17).
19. Dandie-Dinmont Terrier	England and Scotland	A low-set, short-limbed hairy long animal with short face and bulging head; coat soft, thick, woolly pendulous; ears covered by long fringes; colour yellowish; height 20-25 cm and body

		weight 8-10 kg; males heavier than females.
20. Fox Terrier	England	A light breed of medium height; body coat smooth or wired; in smooth variety coat hard, dense, straight and flat; in wired variety coat broken and twisted; ears small and V-shaped; height 35-40 cm and body weight 7-9 kg; tail curved. (Fig. 18).
21. French Bulldog	France	Active, small to medium size; coat smooth, close, short, fine and glossy; colour brindle, fawn, white-brindle or white; head heavy, broad and square; forehead somewhat convex; ears erect, long and rounded at the tip; average height about 30 cm and body weight 8-13 kg; tail short and straight. (Fig. 19).
22. Great Dane	Germany	Large-sized, muscular and strong animal of active disposition; coat short, dense, soft and glossy; colour whole black, fawn, pure white with black or blue patches; ears small and erect with falling tip; face long and narrow; average height usually more than 75 cm and body weight more than 55 kg; long and straight tail thick at the root and tapering to the termination below the hock joint. (Fig. 20a, b).
23. Greyhound	Egypt	Long-limbed, slender, thin animal; broad chest and narrow waist; face long and narrow with blunt pointed nose; coat fine, short and smooth; common colour red and fawn, specimen of black, brindle, white and other colours are also acceptable; height of adult male 70-75 cm and of female 65-70 cm; body weight 25-35 kg; tail is low set, long, tapering and strong. (Fig. 21).
24. Groenendael	Belgium	Medium-sized, sturdy body, broad head and long powerful muzzle; coat long and soft; colour black and glossy; ears pointed and erect; tail long haired; average height 55-60 cm and body weight 25-30 kg.
25. Husky or Eskimo Dog	Arctic/Tundra	Powerful working dog capable of tolerating rigours of harsh cold weather; coat double, outer being long and inner woolly; ears short, V-shaped and erect; tail bushy and curved; colour quite variable; height 55-70 cm and body weight 20-45 kg; coat colour of Siberian husky is black and white.
26. Irish Wolf-hound	Ireland	Heavy like Great Dane; head long, and frontal bone slightly raised; coat hard and rough on the body and long and wiry under the jaw; ears small, soft and folded; height 75-80 cm and body weight 45-65 kg; tail thick, long, covered with hair and slightly curved.
27. Italian Greyhound	Italy	Small-sized grey hound; body slender and graceful; coat thick, soft and glossy; ears soft and rose shaped; average height 25 cm and body weight 3-5 kg; tail long, fine and low. (Fig. 22).
28. Kerry Blue Terrier	Ireland	Small hairy dog; head and face thickly covered with long hair falling over eyes; a long and dense beard; body coat thick, soft and silky; colour preferably smoke blue and may have black points; height 45-50 cm and body weight 15-18 kg. (Fig. 23).

29. Lhasa Apso	Tibet	Small active house dog; body completely covered with long, straight, dense coat with golden, smoke, slaty, black, white, brown or particolour; ears drooping; eyes dark; average height 20-25 cm and body weight 6-7 kg. (Fig. 24).
30. Maltese	Malta	Toy breed covered with long, straight and silky coat of white colour; body weight less than 4.5 kg.
31. Mastiff	England	Heavy muscular, compact body and strong built; head broad and square; coat short, smooth and close, colour whole apricot, silver-fawn, dark fawn or brindle with black nose and muzzle; ears small, set apart and thin; height 70-80 cm and body weight 70-85 kg.; males heavier than females; tail set high, long and running down the hock, thicker at the root and tapering below. (Fig. 25).
32. Pekingese	China	Toy breed of China adopted in many countries; head wide with short muzzle and wrinkled face; coat long and straight with dense mane; outer coat coarse and under coat thick; colour red, fawn, black, cream or white; both whole colour and mixed colours with markings acceptable; height 15-20 cm and body weight 3-5 kg; tail curved and hairy. (Fig. 26).
33. Pembroke (Welsh Corgi)	Wales	Good house dog; body medium, low set and sturdy; dense body coat may be red, fawn, sable or black and tan with white markings; ears large, erect and rounded at the tip; height 25-30 cm and body weight 8-10 kg. (Fig. 27).
34. Pointer	Spain	Active dog, compact and muscular body with broad chest; coat short, fine, smooth and uniformly distributed; colour lemon, orange, lemon and white, liver and white, black and white and sometimes whole black; ears set fairly high, medium sized and lying close to the head; height 60-65 cm and body weight 25-30 kg; tail fairly long, smooth, tapering and carried straight in line with back. (Fig. 28).
35. Pomeranian	Poland	Toy breed, active; outer coat long, straight, coarse and thicker around the neck; undercoat soft and woolly; only whole colour free from any admixture is accepted; height 15-28 cm and body weight 1.5-13 kg; ears are small and erect; tail hairy and carried on the back. (Fig. 29a, b).
36. Poodle	Germany	A small animal of majestic look; various strains are standard poodle, miniature poodle, blue poddle and toy poodle; coat thick, curly and fluffy of different colours like whole white, black, brown, apricot, blue and silver; ears long, wide and drooping; height 25-40 cm and body weight 3-25 kg; toys are smallest followed by miniature and standard strains; tail docked and held high. (Fig. 30).
37. Pug	China	Small breed, short back and rounded ribs; coat short, soft, fine, smooth and glossy of black, silver or apricot fawn; ears are rose or button shaped; height 25-30 cm and body weight 6-8 kg; tail tightly curled and often double curled. (Fig. 31).

38. Pyreneam Mountain Dog	France	Large breed of heavy body; body coat double; outer coat long, thick, flat and straight or wavy, under coat is fine white; ears medium sized, V-shaped with rounded tip and carried close to head; height and body weight of adult male 70-80 cm and 45-55 kg, respectively, and of female 60-70 cm and 40-45 kg respectively; tail runs below the hock and curled high on back when alert.
39. Retrievers (a) Curly coated Retriever	England	Smart, strong and active dog; coat curled and free from the patches of straight hairs; colour black or liver; ears short lying close to head; height 55-65 cm and body weight 25-35 kg; tail long, straight and hairy. (Fig. 32 a).
(b) Labrador	New Foundland	Active dog of strong body; coat short, dense, smooth and glossy; colour black, chocolate or yellow and free from markings; ears large and hanging close to head; height 50-60 cm and body weight 25-35 kg; tail thick at the root and tapering towards the tip.
(c) Golden Retriever	Scotland	Active and powerful; coat flat or wavy and dense with water-resistant undercoat; colour any shade of gold and cream but not red or tan; ears moderate in size; height 50-60 cm and body weight 30-35 kg; tail long, straight and feathered. (Fig. 32 b).
(d) Flat coated	England	Active, medium-sized dog; coat fine, dense and flat; of black or liver colour without markings; ears small and close to the sides of head; height 50-60 cm and body weight 25-30 kg; tail small, straight and well set.
40. Saint Bernard	Switzerland	One of the heaviest dogs with a massive and broad forehead, straight back, deep chest and heavy legs; coat either short-haired or long-haired and tough; it is flat in short-haired; any wavy in long haired; thighs and tail well feathered in long-haired dogs; height 65-75 cm and body weight 75-90 kg; occasionally up to 100 kg in some specimens; tail set high, long and slightly curved, and always carried low. (Fig. 33).
41. Samoyed	Siberia	Active, strong and sturdy sledge dog; double body coat made of outer long, rough and fluffy hair free from curls, and inner thick, soft and woolly shining undercoat; colour mostly pure white but may be cream or white and biscuit; ears medium-sized well apart, erect, slightly rounded at tip and covered with fine hair. (Fig. 34).
42. Spaniels		There are several varieties of spaniels.
(a) Cocker Spaniel	England	Small sporting dog of compact body; head round with deep and broad muzzle; ears long, drooping and covered with fine hair; coat flat, close, silky, soft and wavy of black, black and tan, liver-red and roan colour; height 35-40 cm and body weight 11-13 kg; the tail docked in early life and remains in line with the back. (Fig. 35 a, b).
(b) Clumber Spaniel	England	Large-sized, active; head massive, furrowed forehead; large ears, fully covered with hair; coat close, silky and straight; limbs feathered; height 40-50 cm and body weight 20-30 kg;

		tail docked in early life, feathered and carried at the level of back.
(c) Irish Walter Spaniel	Ireland	Sporting dog, extensively used for hunting acquatic birds; coat dense, tight and corrugated of liver colour; ears long lobe-shaped, hanging and covered with long curly hair; height 50-60 cm and body weight 20-30 kg; tail low set, straight and above hock joint.
(d) English Springer Spaniel	England	Sporting dog of medium body, strong and muscular; coat flat or wavy, thick, medium in length, fine and glossy; common colours liver and white, black and white, liver, black or roan; ears lobular, hanging and set close to the head; height 25-30 cm and body weight 20-25 kg; tail docked in early life, well feathered and carried below the level of back.
(e) Sussex Spaniel	England	Medium-sized, well-developed body, deep chest and well-developed back and loin; coat flat and heavy with feathering limbs and tail; ears long, lobular covered with soft and wavy hair; height 35-40 cm and body weight 15-20 kg; tail docked in early life, set low and carried below the level of back.
43. Sydney Silky	Australia	Toy breed of compact body and small and flat face; ears small and erect or curved at tip; coat long, fine and silky blue, blue and tan or sandy colour; height less than 25 cm and body weight 3-5 kg; tail feathery and carried above the level of back.
44. Yorkshire Terrier	England	Very small toy breed of compact body; head small and flat; nose black; coat silky, heavy, parted straight down the back; colour dark steel blue or tan; height 20-25 cm and body weight 1.7-3.5 kg; tail half docked and hairy. (Fig. 36).

SOME INDIAN BREEDS OF DOG

A large variety of domesticated, semi-domesticated and feral dogs are found in different parts of India. Dogs are kept as pets in urban and rural areas but only sporadic attempts have been made for the identification, maintenance, breeding and utility of local dogs. Indeed in many parts of India one can see dogs having similar characteristics. A few well-bred, family-bred and locality-confined dogs of India are the Rampur hound, Gaddi, Bhutia, Banjara/Sanehta and hunting Rajapalayam dog of Madras region. (Fig. 37).

1 2	3	4
1. Gaddi	India	Heavy and muscular strong animal of active habits; considered to be developed from the wild dog of Yamuna riverine of Meerut region; probably evolved by a demon (asur) named "Mahidand"; body coat short, close and rough with long hair on thighs and terminal part of tail; body coat may grow longer in winter; coat colour usually dull white with lighter colour on the belly; height 50-70 cm and body weight 25-50 kg; males heavier than females; tail hairy, extends up to hock; ears small and curved. (Fig. 38).

PLATE-1

Fig. 1. Afghan Hound

Fig. 2. German Shepherd

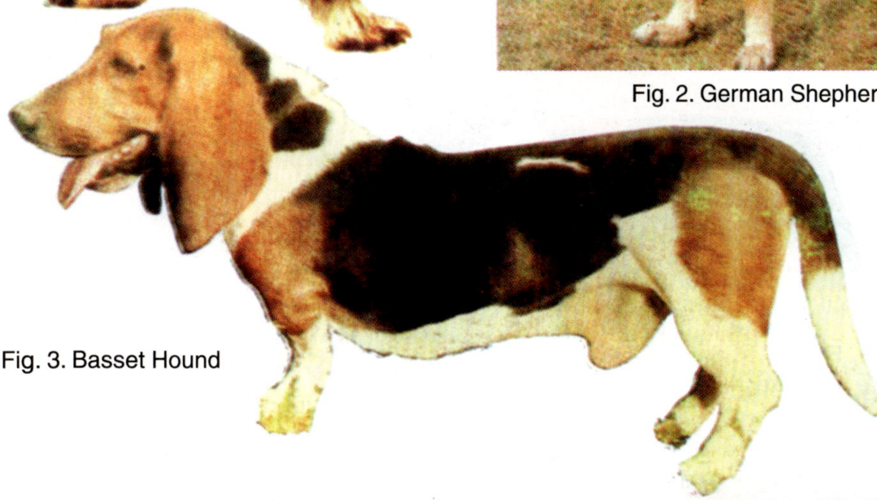

Fig. 3. Basset Hound

Fig. 4. Beagle

Fig. 5. Blood Hound

PLATE-12

Fig. 45. Akita Inu

Fig. 46.
Bernese Mountain Dog

Fig. 47. Bordeaux Mastiff

Fig. 48. Giant Schnauzer

PLATE-13

Fig. 49.
Great Pyreneese

Fig. 50.
Hamiltonstovara

Fig. 51. Hovawart

Fig. 52. Kuvasz

PLATE-16

Fig. 62. English Setter

Fig. 64. Irish Setter

Fig. 63.
Gordon Setter

Fig. 65.
German Shorthaired Pointer

PLATE-17

Fig. 66.
German Wirehaired Pointer

Fig. 69.
Airedale Terrier

Fig. 67.
Weimaraner

Fig. 70. Scottish Terrier

Fig. 68.
German Pinscher

Fig. 71. Irish Terrier

PLATE-18

Fig. 72. Kerry Blue Terrier

Fig. 75.
Miniature Pinscher

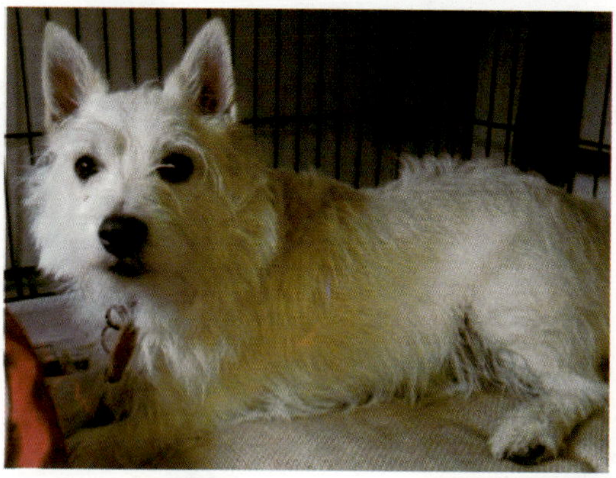

Fig. 73.
West Highland Terrier

Fig. 76.
Monkey Dog

Fig. 74.
Border Terrier

2. Banjara/Tazi/ Sanehta	India	Thin dog of slender body; coat small and close; colour preferably fawn, mixed orange and sometimes striped (zebra marked); ears small, curved and set apart; face long and narrow; height 40-60 cm and body weight 20-30 kg; tail long, straight and tapering. (Fig. 39).
3. Rampur Hound	India	Thin, slender dog of bony appearance; coat short, close and rough of fawn to brown colour; ears small and half curved; chest broad and waist narrow with raised croup; height 40-60 cm and body weight 25-40 kg; males being heavier than females; tail long, straight and tapering. (Fig. 40).
4. Bhutia	India	Normally 2 varieties; the small one is known as Bully. Active animal of Himalayan region and can thrive in tropical plains. Dogs strong and ferocious; body coat of small variety long while that of long variety short; coat colour black, black and white, brownish; dogs with black whole coat and brownish extremities and nose; ears medium and half curved; average height of small variety about 20 cm and body weight 3-10 kg; large variety 40-50 cm in height and 15-30 kg body weight; tail thick, hairy. (Fig. 41).
5. Rajapalayam	India	This breed is a native of Rajapalyam village of Kerala, which was developed in a hunting dog in Tamil Nadu and Karnataka. Dogs tall, long and slender with broad chest and narrow waist. Body coat short and dense; colour is usually dull white. The height at shoulder usually 40-50 cm. Males always heavier than females. (Fig. 42).
6. Himalayan Sheep Dog	India	A beautiful dog of majestic look. Face broad and body smooth and carried on strong limbs. Tail curled and ears small and drooping. Coat dense and smooth which grows long when dogs are taken to high altitude with sheep flock. Colour is usually creamy white but other colours also found. Height at shoulder is usually 40-70 cm and males heavier than females. (Fig. 43).
7. Desi (Mongrel)	India	Non-descript dog distributed throughout India, called *desi.* There is large variation in their shape, size, body weight, habits and behaviour. Body coat may be of different size and kind; colour may be red, tan, black, white and mixed. A few specimen have been very obedient and useful. (Fig. 44).

A few other recognised breeds of Indian dogs are Chippiparai (South Indiia), Combai (Madras), Mudhol (Karnataka and Maharashtra), Sindh Hound (West part of (Gujrat), Sikkimese Terrier (Sikkim), Alangu (Tanjore and Trichinapalli), Bisben (Himalayan region), Kaikadi (Kaharashtra), Kuchi (Tanjore), Patti (Tamil Nadu), Tripuri Lushai hills) and Vikhan (Chitral and Kinapur in Himachal Pradesh). However, most of these breeds need further investigations on their reproduction and performances under kennel conditions.

2

BREEDING AND REPRODUCTION

Breeding dogs is an important function of kennels since people are particular while selecting a dog as a pet. A large number of breeds and varieties of dogs have been evolved in the economically advanced countries of Europe, America and other continents.

The selection of potent male and female is the basis of any breeding programme. Dogs contain 39 pairs of chromosomes contributed by both parents in equal numbers. Wolves also contain 39 pairs of chromosomes. In dog breeding, selection is a difficult task because the tastes of different individuals have to be catered to. Indeed intelligent breeders select breeding animals to meet larger demands. Pedigree is helpful in estimating the genotype of brood dogs but phenotype expression depends on the heritability of traits.

Breeding male dog (sire) should be of very high grade, produced by selection through several generations for many desired characteristics.

SYSTEMS OF BREEDING

Inbreeding, line breeding and outbreeding or outcrossing are the three systems of breeding followed by the registered dog breeders and kennels.

Inbreeding

Breeding between very close relatives within the family is known as inbreeding. Interbreeding between sire and daughter, dam and her son, and brother and sister are the common systems of inbreeding. Since inbreeding increases homozygosity in the breed, it is considered a good breeding system for the accumulation of desired traits in the subsequent generations, but it is not possible to predict the transfer of actual genes. Several unwanted traits are carried in recessive genes. These traits mostly hidden in normal cases but may appear due to inbreeding and spoil the expected results. In spite of this serious drawback, inbreeding is practised in dogs, and pups detected for defects in early life are culled.

Line Breeding

Mating between the distant relatives of the same family is known as line breeding. The common examples of line breeding are the mating between grandfather and grand daughter, grandmother and grandson, two cousins or half-sister and half-brother and so on. Line breeding is relatively less risky than inbreeding although both systems involve mates of the same family. In line breeding it is important to breed stud dogs with only phenotypically good descendants and not with any member of the family.

Outbreeding or Outcrossing

Mating between the individuals of different families of the same breed is known as outcrossing or outbreeding. It is an easier method of dog breeding but its use is much less in the advanced studs.

Dog breeding programmes should not be planned only on the basis of the pedigree of the mates, but the actual animals to be mated should be checked phenotypically for the genotype claims.

MALE GENITAL SYSTEM

The male reproductive system of dog has a tubulo-muscular and a glandular structure extending from testis to glans penis. The various organs of the male reproductive tract are a scrotum, a pair of testes, ductus deferens and spermatic cords, a prostate gland, a penis, a male urethra and a prepuce (Fig. 77a, b).

Scrotum

The scrotum is a thin-skined membranous sac divided by a median septum into two compartments. Each compartment of the scrotum contains a testis, an epididymis and the distal part of the spermatic cord. The skin of scrotum is thin, highly pigmented and contains some fine hairs. It also contains well-developed sebaceous and tubular glands. Beneath the skin is dartos, formed of smooth muscle fibres mixed with collagenous and elastic fibres. Dartos extends to form scrotal septum and dorsally joins the abdominal fascia. In cold weather contraction of tunica dartos retracts scrotum and draws testes very close to the body.

At the time of descending, the testis is enveloped by a double-walled invagination of peritoneum known as the vaginal process (processus vaginalis peritonel). It is covered by the fascia of abdominal wall. Vaginal process along with internal and external spermatic fascia and internal abdominal fascia form the spermatic fascia covering the spermatic cord. The cremaster muscle of scrotum originates from the posterior free border of the internal abdominal oblique muscle (sometimes from the transverse abdominis muscle) and blends with the parietal vaginal tunic at the level of the testis. Cremaster muscle acts in conjunction with the dartos in contraction of the scrotum in cold weather.

The scrotum is capable of heat regulation due to thin skin, a few hair, lack of subcutaneous adipose tissue and contractile action of the dartos assisted by the cremaster muscle. It provides protection to testis and epididymis from the external injuries, climatic exposure and other factors. Blood supply comes from the external pudendal artery and femoral artery. Fine branches innervate the region from the third and fourth lumbar and the first three sacral nerves.

Testes

Testes are paired and are found in the scrotal sac. The testis is oval and thick dorsoventrally. Its size and weight vary in different breeds. In a dog weighing 10 kg the average length is 2.8-3.0 cm, breadth 2-2.2 cm, thickness 1.8-2 cm and weight 7.5-8 g.

The testis is covered by visceral tunica vaginalis and tunica albuginea. The testicular parenchyma or lobuli testis is formed of numerous seminiferous tubules and glandular cells (Leydig cells) which secrete testesterone (the male sex hormone).

Ductus Deferens (Vas deferens)

The epididymal duct extends to form the ductus deferens of each side for the passage of spermatozoa. It is 17-18 cm long and 1.6-3 cm in diameter in a 10 kg dog. The two ducts come close together about 2 cm prior to their entrance into the prostate gland. The ductus deferens is formed of *tunica adventitia, tunica muscularis* and *tunica mucosa.* The last one is formed of simple or pseudostratified columnar epithelium. Blood supply comes from the branches of prostatic artery, a visceral branch of the internal iliac artery. The pelvic part of ductus deferens is supplied by a branch of hypogastric nerves. Parasympathetic fibres generally supply to the epidydimis and muscle fibres of the vas deferens.

Spermatic Cords

Each spermatic cord is made up of a vas deferens, testicular blood vessels and nerves, and serous membrane coverings. The spermatic cord begins at the deep inguinal ring and leaves the abdominal cavity. The constituent organs of spermatic cord are combined together by the tunica vaginalis, formed of loose connective tissue and peritoneum.

Prostate Gland

This is a musculoglandular mass that encloses the proximal part of the urethra at the neck of the urinary bladder. It is the only gland in the male genital system and develops from several buds of the pelvic urethra. The average weight of the gland does not exceed 0.7 g/kg body weight under normal conditions. The dorsal boundary of the prostate gland is the rectum. Ventrally it is supported by the abdominal wall and symphysis pubis. It is semi-oval in transverse section with flattened dorsal surface. The gland is divided into right and left lobes by a prominent median septum. Numerous ducts from the prostate gland drain into the urethra. The gland is covered by a fibrous capsule containing smooth muscle fibres. The functions of the prostate are not yet fully known. Its secretion contains citrate, lactate, cholesterol and several enzymes. It provides a suitable medium for the survival and motility of sperms. The source of energy for the spermatozoa is not known because the semen does not contain reducing sugars as found in other species. Prostatic artery arises from the internal pudendal artery. The blood is drained away by the prostatic and urethral veins. The nerve supply is from the branches of hypogastric and pelvic nerves.

Penis

Penis, the organ of copulation is divided into root, body and glans penis. The glans penis is formed of a glandular bulb (bulbus glandis) and a pars longa glandis. It is lined by epithelium and remains retracted in the prepuce in non-erection condition. The length of the penis is 6-24 cm depending on the breed. The root and body of the penis are formed of corpora cavernosa penis, corpus spongiosum penis, penile urethra and enlarged proximal end of the penis bone (Os penis). The corpora cavernosa penis contains several large venous spaces. The corpus spongiosum is situated in a groove on the urethral aspect of the penis covering the penile urethra throughout its course. The bulbus glandis of penis is a bilobed expansion of the erectile body. Several valves are present in various connections between the bulbus glandis and corpus spongiosum, which control the return of blood flow. The glans penis of dog is a bipartite organ formed of a bulbus glandis and a pars longa glandis. The anterior half of the bulbus glandis is normally covered by the posterior third of the pars longa glandis. They are separated by a connective tissue septum which continues as a sheath for corpus spongiosum and os penis.

The os penis is a long tapering bone. Its broader proximal extremity is situated in the corpus penis just behind the bulbus glandis. The bone is thicker dorsoventrally, tapering distally and ending as a slightly curved fibrocartilaginous projection. The entire glans penis contains abundant vascular anastomoses beneath the epithelium. Blood supply comes from the branches of internal pudendal artery, external pudendal artery and perineal artery. The blood is drained by the branches of internal and external pudendal veins. Nerve branches are supplied from the pelvic and sacral plexuses.

Male Urethra

The tubular structure for the passage of urine from the bladder to the body and passage of semen from the seminiferous ducts to the distal end of the pars longa glandis is called urethra. It is 10 to 35 cm in length depending on the mature body size. The urethra is divided into prostatic, membranous and penile parts. The prostatic part extends from bladder to the posterior border of the prostate gland. The seminal hillock is an oval structure in the centre of the urethral crest and opens through a fine opening into a tiny tube known as uterus masculinus. Vas deferens opens on each side of the seminal hillock (Colliculus seminalis).

The membranous middle part of the urethra extends between the prostate gland and the point of entrance of urethra into the bulbus glandis. The penile or cavernous part of urethra is the distal part extending from the bulb of corpus spongiosum to open into the distal end of the pars longa glandis. Blood is supplied by the prostatic and urethral arteries and drained by the urethral branches of the pudendal vein. Smooth muscles of the urethra are connected by the fine branches of autonomous nerves arising from the pelvic plexus.

Prepuce

Prepuce a tubular structure of soft skin covers the non-erected penis, pars longa glandis and a part of bulbus glandis. It is a continuation of the skin of the ventral abdominal wall. The prepuce is formed on an outer layer of skin and inner layers of mucosa lined by a smooth and thin layer of stratified squamous epithelium.

SEMEN EVALUATION

Semen

Normal semen is a moderately milky viscous fluid. It contains 3 fractions. The first fraction is clear and oozes before the full erection of the penis. It does not contain any spermatozoa and acts as a lubricant. The second fraction is ejected during the active coitus and contains a large number of potent spermatozoa. The last fraction is a clear fluid and is ejaculated during the tie-up position.

Semen Characteristics

Normally 7 ml of semen is ejaculated by a stud dog used after normal rest of 3-7 days. Semen volume per ejaculate may range from as little as 0.3 ml to as high as 23 ml. The pH ranges between 5.9 and 7.2 and forward motility between 60 and 95 per cent. Fructose content is very low in the semen. The number of spermatozoa is 70 million to 1,700 million per ejaculate. However, it also depends how frequently the semen is collected. Spermatozoa can tolerate a pH range of 5 to 10. In good quality semen abnormal sperms are not more than 20 per cent.

Semen Collection

Electroejaculation is not advisable. In practice semen is collected in the presence of a teaser bitch. For semen collection a sterile barrel of a 20 ml glass syringe is used. Now-a-days small artificial vagina is also available

Plate-19

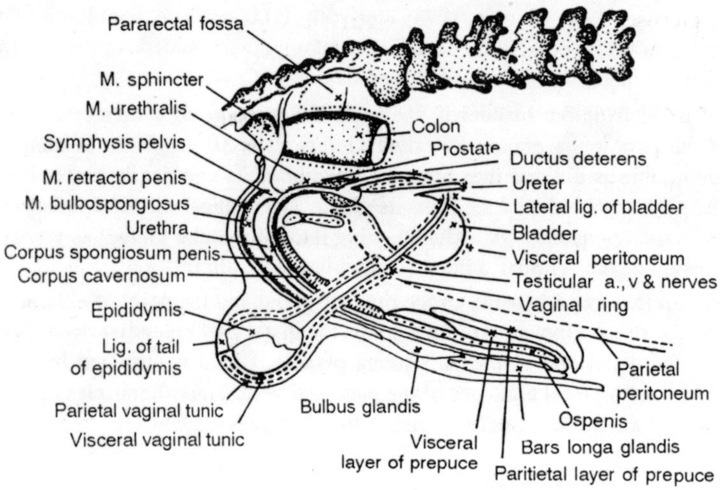

Fig. 77. (a) Relation of male genital organs with peritoneal cavity.

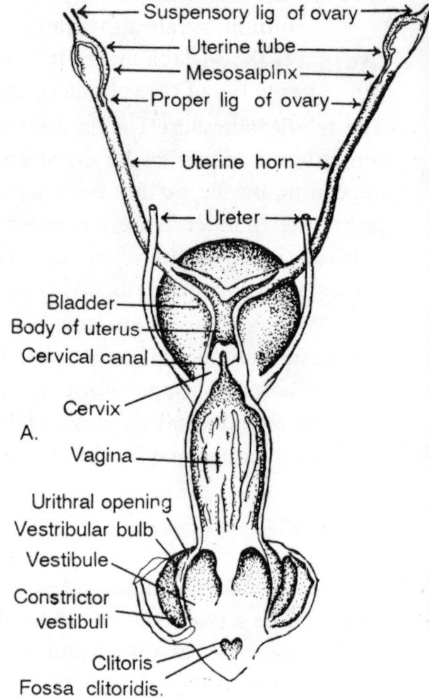

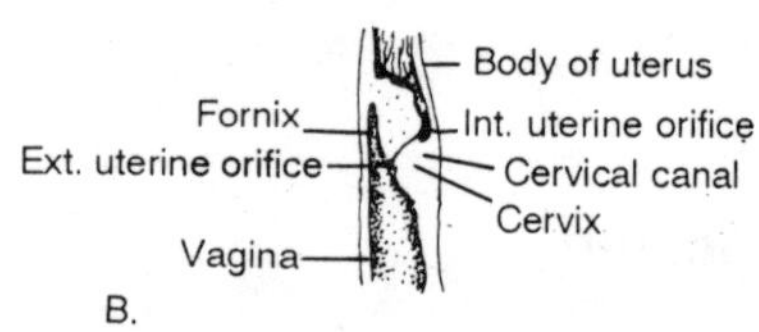

Sagittal Section

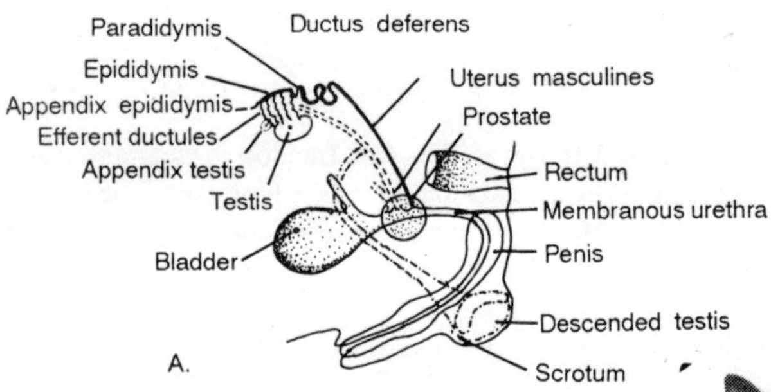

Fig. 77. (b) Genital organs of male (A) and female (B) dog.

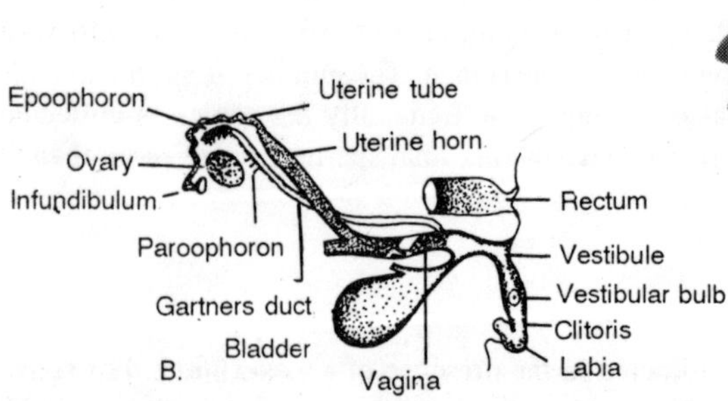

Fig. 78. The female genital tract (Dorsal view).

Fig. 79. Small breed of bitch showing litter size of 5 pups.

for this purpose. Semen may also be collected by digital manipulation. Collection of semen through artificial vagina is preferred for hygienic and aesthetic reasons.

The semen is diluted in 1 : 10 to 1 : 20 ratio with an extender of the following composition (in per cent):

Sodium citrate dihydrate, 1.16; glucose, 1.00; glycine, 0.75; egg-yolk, 20.00; sterile double-distilled water, 77.00. In each millilitre of extender 1,000 IU penicillin and 1 mg streptomycin are added for prolonging the storage life of the spermatozoa. Diluted semen may be preserved for 6 days at 4° C. Normal untreated semen will only remain viable for 15-20 hours. Dog semen may also be deep frozen.

CONTROL OF SEX VICES IN MALE DOGS

High libido is quite common in male dogs even from a very young age. Domestic pets get easily excited while playing. This habit may be controlled by scolding the dog or by following one of the following measures.

The dog should not be overfed; laxative diets should be fed frequently for cleaning the bowel; the dog should be exhausted by vigorous exercising; some mild tranquilizers may be administered orally; licking of prepuce should be checked by applying some non-irritant repellent; in a chronic case, vasectomy is most effective; stud dogs should not be put to frequent service; the prepuce and glans penis should be cleaned at regular intervals with a mild antiseptic lotion.

FEMALE REPRODUCTIVE SYSTEM

The female reproductive system of the dog is formed by a pair of ovaries and a tubulo-mascular structure consisting of a pair of fallopian tubes, horned uterus, vagina, vulva and urethra. The various reproductive organs are united by the broad litgaments (Fig. 78).

Broad Ligaments

The right and left broad ligaments are the paired double fold of peritoneum which unite reproductive organs and attach ovaries, oviducts and uterus with the dorsolateral wall of the abdominal and pelvic cavities. Blood vessels and nerves supply to various genital organs are found embedded in the broad ligament.

The broad ligament can be divided into the mesovarian, the mesosalpinx and the mesometrium attaching ovary, oviduct including horns and cranial part of vagina respectively.

Ovaries

The ovaries, one on each side, are located in the abdominal cavity near the posterior aspect of the kidney. It is oval, 1.5 cm in length, 0.7 cm in breath and 0.5 cm in thickness in a mature bitch weighing 10-12 kg. The average weight of each ovary is about 300 mg. The surface of the ovary is smooth in prepubertal stage, and becomes rough and nodular after breeding. In addition to the mesovarian portion of the broad ligament the ovary is attached by the suspensory and proper ligaments of the ovary.

The ovary is formed of a medulla and a cortex. The medulla carries all the supplies like blood vessels, lymphatics and nerves in a core of muscle fibres and connective tissue. The cortex is composed of a connective tissue stroma containing a large number of developing follicles. A follicle is formed of an oocyte surrounded by the granulosa cells in a basement membrane, which separates the follicle from the ovarian stroma. Ovulation occurs during the oestrous cycle normally 48-60 hours after the receptive phase. However, fertile mating may take place as early as 54 hours before to as late as 120 hours after the ovulation. High fertility normally occurs on breeding the bitch after 12-120 hours of ovulation. Implantation takes place between 20.5 and 21.5 days after the ovulation on fertile mating.

Corpus luteum develops from the wound left after the ovulation. In case of infertile breeding, the corpus luteum gradually regresses into a connective tissue scar, the corpus albicans. In case of fertilization it remains fully functional during the gestation period and regresses after the whelping.

Ovarian branches of uterine artery and vein are responsible for the blood circulation. The lymphatics of the ovaries drain into the lumbar lymph glands. Nerve supply arises from the renal and aortic nerve plexuses.

Oviduct

The oviduct or uterine tube is located one on either side. It takes active part in the transportation of the oocytes to the uterine cornua. The infundibulum of the oviduct is a funnel shaped ovarian end of the tube and contains several finger-like projections, the fimbriae. The oocytes are picked up by the active movements of fimbriae and carried to the uterine horns by the peristaltic movements. The place of fertilization is normally the infundibulum.

The uterine tube is formed of an outer layer of tunica serosa, followed by circular and variable proportion of longitudinal and oblique fibres of smooth muscle. The luminal layer of the tunica mucosa is formed of a partially ciliated simple columnar epithelium. The cilia moves towards the uterine cornua during ovulation. It is supplied by the branches of ovarian and uterine arteries and veins. The lymphatics drain into the lumbar lymphnode. Nerves are supplied from the renal and aortic plexuses.

Uterus

The cornuated muscular uterus can be divided into the cervix (cervix uteri), the body (corpus uteri) and a pair of horns (uterine cornua). The Y-shaped tubular organ continues into the oviducts anteriorly and vagina posteriorly. The size of uterus varies with the breed. Its volume increases with age, number of pregnancies and stage of pregnancy (in a pregnant bitch only).

The musculomembranous uterine cornuae are present in the abdomen. They are attached dorsolaterally to the abdominal wall with the help of the proper ligament of ovary and the broad ligament. Usually the right horn is slightly longer than the left one. The corpus uteri is situated partly in the abdominal cavity and partly in the pelvic cavity. In multiparous bitches body of uterus may shift towards the abdominal cavity. The cervix is the posterior continuation of uterus, which may protrude a little into the vagina. There are 3 openings in the body of uterus one from each horn the ostium uteri internum and one external orifice directed outwards into the vagina, the ostium uteri externum. In pregnant bitches cervical canal is as usual sealed by a mucous plug.

The uterus is held in position by the broad and round ligaments. The uterus is formed of external tunica serosa, middle tunica muscularis (myometrium) and tunica mucosa (endometrium) lined by a temporarily ciliated layer of low columnar epithelium. Tunica propria contains several branched and coiled uterine glands. Branching and coiling is much less in comparison to other fram animals. The uterine blood vessels arise from the ovarian uterine branches. The lymphatics drain into the hypogastric and lumbar lymph nodes. Nerve branches emerge from the hypogastric plexus and the pelvic nerves.

Vagina

The dilated muscular membranous tubular connection between the uterus and the vulva is known as vagina. The cranial end is joined by the fornix, an intravaginal protrusion of cervix. Posteriorly it extends up to the urethral opening. There is no defined hymen in bitches. Its wall is formed of tunica serosa, tunica muscularis and tunica muscosa. The luminal wall is lined by a non-glandular stratified squamous epithelium. The blood vessels are the vaginal branches of internal pudendal artery and vein. The lymphatics open into the internal iliac lymph nodes. Branches of pelvic plexus and pudendal nerve innervate the vagina.

Vulva

Vestibule, clitoris and labia form the vulva. The vestibule connects vagina with the vulva. The urethral opening (external urethral orifice) is situated on the urethral tubercle, a ridge-like projection on the ventral floor of the vestibule. The vestibule narrows down near the clitoris. The outer boundary of vulva is formed of the vulvar labia which join together at dorsal and ventral ends to form dorsal and ventral commissures respectively. The latter extends as a pointed projection hanging beneath the tail. The clitoris is situated at the terminal end of the vestibular bulb in the fossa clitoridis. It is formed of a paired root (crura clitoridis), a body (corpus clitoridis) and a glans (glans clitoridis). The corpus clitoridis is made up of adipose tissue (with a few erectile tissue) covered by a thick layer of tunica albuginea. Rarely an os clitoridis may develop in some bitches but it does not affect normal breeding.

The inner surface of the vulva is formed of stratified squamous epithelium. It contains variable number of lymph nodes. The muscular layer is made up of the usual smooth muscle continuation of the tunica muscularis of vagina and additional striated circular muscles, the constrictor vestibule muscle and the constrictor vulvae muscle. Ischiourethralis muscles arising from the posterior-medial surface of the tuber ischii set were inserted in the less developed central tendon of perineum. A small ischiocavernosus muscle arises from the posterior border of the ischium and gets inserted at the root of clitoris. The orifice of female urethra contains a strong mascular sphinctor.

The branches of vaginal, and external and internal pudendal arteries supply blood. The bilateral veins drain away blood into the internal pudendal vein. Lymphatics drain into the superficial inguinal lymphnodes. The nerve supply is from the pudendal, genital, hypogastric and pelvic nerves.

PUBERTY

The dog attains puberty at 6-12 months of age depending on the breed, plane of nutrition and management. In a few breeds it may be as long as 20-24 months for the appearance of the first oestrus. Puberty in free living stray animals sets in earlier than in pets and kennel dogs. Females mature earlier than the males of the same breed when reared under identical management.

OESTROUS CYCLE

The oestrous cycle in bitches can be divided into anoestrus, pro-oestrus, oestrus and metoestrus. The last phase includes both metoestrus and dioestrus.

Anoestrus: In this phase there is no sexual activity and mating is not allowed. Its length is about 125 days but varies from 3 to 38 weeks.

Pro-oestrus: Average duration is about 9 days (range 3-16 days). The vulvar lips are hypertrophied increasing significantly in volume. The vaginal discharge is sanguineous. Eligible male dogs are attracted from some distance due to the characteristic odour emitted by the bitch. Mating is not allowed. Graafian follicles up to 20, mature as a crop.

Oestrus: The average duration of oestrus is about 9 $\pm$ 1 days (range 4 to 12 days). Some reduction in vulvar hypertrophy starts. The vulva is relaxed and dependent. Mucous discharge from vagina is clear. Spontaneous ovulation occurs within 4 days of the oestrus phase and it may occur in a batch of 1, 2, 3 or more at a time. This is evident from the variety of colour of pups in the same litter of stray bitches. The bitches remain receptive and allow repeated mating with one or more dogs throughout the oestrus phase.

Metoestrus: This phase also includes dioestrus. Its duration ranges from 50 to 100 days. During metoestrus regression of oedema and swelling of vulvar lips occurs. The vaginal discharge becomes brownish, viscous and odourless. It gradually decreases and stops completely within 3-4 days.

Seasonality of oestrous cycle: In the Indian climate breeding occurs twice annually, i.e. once in August-September and then in February-March.

OVULATION

The follicles develop during the pro-oestrus phase. They require 9 days for complete development. Oestrogen is secreted by the actively developing follicles. It induces significant changes in the external genitalia. Ovulation normally occurs 48-60 hours after the acceptance of male; this is normally the start of oestrous phase. However, the ovulation may occur about 2 days earlier than the onset of oestrus and up to 7 days post-onset period. In more than 93 per cent bitches ovulation takes place by 96 hours after reaching the peak level of leutinising hormone (LH), and over 77 per cent follicles rupture by 24-72 hours after the LH peak.

The duration of luteal activity is similar in pregnant and non-pregnant bitches. LH peak is attained by 20 days after ovulation followed by gradual decline in 70-80 days for complete regression of corpus luteum.

PSEUDO OR FALSE PREGNANCY (FANTOM PREGNANCY)

The signs of pregnancy in a few non-mated bitches during the luteal phase of oestrous cycle is called pseudo-(false) pregnancy or pseudocyesis. The condition is attributed to hormonal imbalance. This is characterized by a gradual deposition of abdominal fat, development of mammary glands, mucoid brownish non-odorous discharge from vulva and sometimes maternal behaviour nearly 60 days after the ovulation. The incidence of pseudo-pregnancy in different breeds and conditions varies from 3 to 40 per cent.

SIGNS OF OESTRUS OR HEAT

The oestrus in bitches is often referred to as the signs of ovulation, although the latter occurs after 48-60 hours of the receptivity in majority of the cases. The signs of oestrus are quite apparent and can be easily detected. They are as follows:

(i) At the onset of oestrus, i.e. during the pro-oestrus period, the vulva is enlarged and tense. The vulval lips are red.

(ii) Males are sexually attracted to the bitch and it is quite common to see several males moving behind a stray bitch expected to come in heat.

(iii) Frequency of urination increases significantly a few days prior to the onset of oestrus.

(iv) After a few days vulva becomes purple, hard and swollen.

(v) This is followed by a dark red and thck vaginal discharge. This period is referred to as the time of showing colour for mating. After about 6-7 days the vulva becomes loose and softer.

(vi) The vaginal discharge turns lighter and becomes almost colourless by the end of 2 weeks. During this period bitches allow consort with males but do not allow mating.

(vii) At the end of this phase the bitch in oestrus becomes receptive. She curls her tail apart from the vulva and stands quietly for mating when approached by a male dog. The bitch often thrusts her rear part towards any male. This phase is the actual oestrus period and commonly known as standing heat.

MATING

The coitus or copulation in dogs and other canines is quite different from the other mammalian species. The male mounts and holds the female. The non-erect penis is locked inside the vagina after intromission, and becomes stiff after erection. The male dismounts during ejaculation and remains tail-to-tail in a tie-up position. This period may last for 20-40 minutes, after which the dogs separate.

In breeding kennels often assisted mating is practised. Assisted mating may be conveniently arranged single-handed in small breeds but may require a helper for large breeds. At some places forced or guided mating is performed in small breeds.

FERTILIZATION

The spermatozoa survive up to 10-12 days post-insemination on natural mating. The loss of live spermatozoa is very little up to 5-6 days post-breeding period. The ovum is released from the ovary at a premature stage as primary oocyte and requires another 2-3 days to prepare for fertilization.

PREGNANCY OR GESTATION

Pregnancy or gestation is the stage when the fertilized ova get implanted or attached to the uterine wall. However, the duration of pregnancy or gestation length is counted from date of first mating. The pregnancy period may be divided into three periods. Period 1 extends for 15-20 days post-mating. In the early part of period 2, implantation of fertilized ovum takes place. This period extends for the next 2 weeks or up to day 33 post-mating. Period 3 is approximately of 30 days and is the period of active foetal growth. During this period over 90 per cent foetal growth takes place. The terminal period requires special attention for the supply of balanced nutrients.

Gestation Period

The average gestation length in a bitch is 63 ± 2 days but it ranges from 55 to 75 days under different conditions.

Pregnancy Diagnosis

The clinical signs of pregnancy appear in a bitch at about 25-30 days post-mating. The common signs are loss of appetite, nausea and vomiting tendency and depraved appetite. After 5 weeks post-mating there is significant increase in the appetite of the bitch and she will eat more food. It is rather difficult to diagnose the pregnancy between 30 and 45 days of gestation period due to the amniotic fluid surrounding the foetuses. During the last two weeks of gestation foetuses can be easily palpated. Radiography can also be used in this period to know the number of developing foetuses in the uterine horns.

Ultrasonic scanning instruments are available for pregnancy diagnosis in bitches. They give good results during the latter half of the gestation period.

PARTURITION (WHELPING)

The physiological function of delivery or parturition is commonly termed as whelping in bitches. About 24-28 hours prior to whelping the bitches show anorexia, restlessness and emesis, look at the flanks and shiver due to fall in body temperature. During this period she is engaged actively in nesting by collecting dry grass, old clothes and newspapers in the corner of her house. Stray bitches prefer delivery at an isolated sheltered place protected from strangers. She does not like the presence of a stranger and may attack furiously. Some of the pet bitches want to be with their master during the whelping, while majority like seclusion.

Whelping is induced by the relaxation of pelvic ligament, dilatation of the genital passage and strong contractions of the uterine muscle at short intervals under the influence of hormones. This is followed by forceful contractions of uterine muscle with an attempt to expel the pups. The foetuses move towards the cervix and water-bag appears out of the vulva. Subsequently the head of a foetus is expelled out of vulva by the uterine contractions, which is finally delivered. The pup is quickly licked/cleaned by the bitch. The foetal membranes are expelled and cut by the bitch. Delivery of first pup takes much longer than the others and it may be 30-40 minutes for the first and 1-15 minutes for subsequent pups of a litter.

The delivery is completed in the following 4 stages under normal conditions without any external assistance:

Stage 1: The following changes in the behaviour and external genitalia of the expectant mother occur during stage 1:

(i) Anorexia, nausea and vomiting, restlessness and frequent glancing at flanks.
(ii) Increased pulse and respiration rates; shivering may be due to sudden drop in the body temperature (1°-2°F) before the onset of labour pains.
(iii) The uterine muscles are relaxed. Light uterine contractions occur but the bitch does not strain for the expulsion of foestus.
(iv) Dilatation of cervix and opening of the os cervix take place.

Stage 2: Stage 1, which normally lasts for 6 to 12 hours, is followed by the active manifestation of labour pain in an attempt to expel out foetuses.

(i) Forceful contraction of uterine muscles starts.
(ii) Bitch strains and applies pressure for the expulsion of foetuses.
(iii) Water-bag or chorioallantoic sac enveloping the foetus pushes out of the vulva through the dilated cervix.
(iv) Water-bag ruptures and lubricates the external genital passage.
(v) This is followed by strong contraction of uterine and abdominal muscles.
(vi) Expulsion of foetus through vulva takes place.
(vii) Expulsion of placenta occurs.

Stage 3: It is normally of a shorter period after the complete delivery of litter. Weak labour pain co-ordinated by mild straining helps in the expulsion of remaining foetal membranes in the uterus.\

Stage 4: This stage lasts for several days.

(i) There is copious discharge of lochia, a tanned mucoid fluid which diminishes gradually and stops after a few days.
(ii) Involution of uterus takes place for returning back nearer to the original size, shape and position for future breeding.

N.B. The assistance of qualified veterinary doctor/surgeon should be sought as early as possible if the whelping does not start even after 2 hours of vigorous labour pain unless the animal had previous history of such unusual delay in delivery.

Litter Size

The breed and parity significantly affect the litter size. It is 1-5 in small breeds (Fig. 79) and 8-12 in large breeds.

POSTPARTUM OESTRUS INTERVAL

Signs of first oestrus after parturition may normally appear after weaning. Wide variation in postpartum oestrus, ranging from 30 days to more than 90 days, has been observed in different types of bitches.

WHELPING-CONCEPTION (W-C) INTERVAL

Although bitches show oestrus signs at about 30-90 days post-partum, ovarian activity is resumed at a latter date. The interval between whelping and subsequent conception is known as whelping - conception interval or post-partum ovarian activity interval. Normally it ranges from 150 to 220 days. The whelping - conception interval is significantly affected by the following factors:

Effect of milk yield: The whelping - conception interval is normally higher in bitches producing more milk during the nourishing period. An average of 171, 182 and 204 days of whelping - conception interval has been recorded in Croation sheep dog females producing about 18, 26 and 32 kg milk per lactation.

Effect of body loss during lactation: The whelping - conception interval is directly related with the loss in body weight during the nourishing period. An average of 178, 184 and 217 days of whelping - conception interval has been observed in bitches losing about 2.7, 3.9 and 4.8 kg, respectively, during the lactation period.

Effect of litter size: Average whelping - conception interval is longer in bitches producing large sized litters. It is about 179, 183 and 195 days for the small (4), medium (7) and large (8 pups) litter sizes respectively.

Effect of lactation period: Weaning has significant effect on the whelping - conception interval, and it is shorter (176 days) for short lactation period of 6 weeks and longer (186 days) for long lactation period of 8 weeks in heavy breeds.

Effect of the season of pregnancy: The season of pregnancy has no significant effect on the whelping - conception interval, and it ranges between 180 and 183 days for different seasons.

MAMMARY GLANDS OF BITCH

Normally 3-5 pairs of teats are found in bitches. They vary with the breeds and individuals. The milking capacity is usually lowest in pectoral teats and highest in the groin teats. Supernumerary teat, if any, is generally non-functional and yields little milk when functional.

MISALLIANCE OR UNWANTED MATING OR PREVENTION OF PREGNANCY

An injection of oestrogen within 24 hours of unwanted mating may stop implantation of ova but the bitch can be bred again in the next season only. It is preferred to complete the pregnancy and discard the pups if not required or their disposal is difficult. Now-a-days most rational approach is intramuscular injection of repository diethyl-stilbesterol in a single injection @ 2 mg/kg body weight. It will prevent implantation of fertilized ovum. This should invariably be done within the following 12-18 days because this is the time needed for implantation of the fertilized ovum. Uterine douches may also be used to remove the sperms but it is not a practical approach as the sperm may reach the fallopian tube approximately in 20 seconds.

Other methods of preventing pregnancy are segregation of bitches from other dogs during heat period, use of contraceptive tablets, and use of specially prepared tablets containing hormones (megestrol acetate, delmadinone acetate).

SPAYING

Some owners do not like breeding their pet bitches but sexual desire is very strong during the oestrous cycle. The bitch may cross reasonable barriers and males are also attracted from a distance. To avoid this unwanted situation surgical assistance for spaying is the most effective method. Various methods of spaying include ligation of oviduct, removal of oviduct or complete ovariohysterectomy. The operation is normally performed in the post-pubertal life, otherwise the effect of hormonal imbalance would be more pronounced. When spaying is required after harvesting a few litters, it is better to perform around the date of whelping and on the day of whelping in case of caesarian section. (For details see surgery section).

CASTRATION OF MALES

Male dogs may be castrated at any age for the ligation or partial removal of the spermatic cords. The testicles are removed in the post-pubertal period (for details see surgery section).

ARTIFICIAL INSEMINATION (AI) IN BITCH

For AI, bitch should be in the correct stage of heat or oestrous cycle. This can be confirmed by testing either using a male or by examining the vaginal smear microscopically. Normally, ovulation occurs about 48 hours after the commencement of true oestrus. At this stage vaginal smear shows cornified epithelial cells. This phase is usually 10 to 14 days after the beginning of the pro-oestral bleeding. Blood cells will reappear in the vaginal fluid 24-36 hours after ovulation. For AI purpose plastic pipette should be inserted until the tip is in the region of the cervix. It is difficult to inseminate directly through the cervix os. For this purpose a speculum and suitable illumination may be used to faciliate passing of the pipette. The pipette should be connected with glass syringe and the semen injected slowly. The hind legs should be elevated at the time of insemination to avoid loss of semen. After removing the pipette if the bitch is still in the elevated position, a finger covered with glove should be inserted into its vagina for 4-6 minutes. By this action bitch will get the satisfaction of natural mating and initiate the tie up condition which enhances the chance of conception.

TABLE 1: BREEDING GUIDE TO BITCH

Sl. No	*Average Values of Breeding Behaviour*	*Bitch*
1.	Age of puberty	6-12 months
2.	Age at breeding	12-18 months
3.	Type of oestrous cycle	Monoestrus (but usually 2 oestrous cycles per year)
4.	Length of oestrous cycle	6 months
5.	Length of oestrus (heat)	6-13 days
6.	Gestation period	55-75 days (63 days)
7.	Time of ovulation	48-60 hours after the receptive phase
8.	Proper time of AI	2-3 days after onset of true oestrus

(Contd.)

Sl. No	*Average Values of Breeding Behaviour*	*Bitch*
9.	Breeding season	Biannual: August to September, February to March
10.	Return of heat after parturition	16-20 weeks
11.	Recurrence after non-conception	Twice yearly
12.	Age of weaning	4-6 weeks
13.	Time of fertilized ova entering uterus	5-6 days post-coitus
14.	Time of implantation begins	15 days post-coitus
15.	Type of placenta	Endotheliochorial
16.	Expulsion of placenta	Immediately after each foetus
17.	Average pup/kitchen born	4-8 pups
18.	Birth weight	65-500 g
19.	Breeding span	7-8 years
20.	Life span	10-15 years (Record is 32 years)

TABLE 2. CHARACTERISTICS OF SEMEN AND ARTIFICIAL INSEMINATION

Entities	*Values*
Volume	0.3-23 ml
pH	5.9-7.2
Average concentration of sperms	1,428 million/ejaculate
Collection of semen for AI purpose	2-3 times a week
Site for semen deposition in bitch for AI	Cervix
Volume of diluted semen required for AI	1.5 ml
Minimum number of sperms required for AI	15 million
Rate of semen dilution for AI purpose	1 : 10
Extenders used for dilution	Egg-yolk citrate or heat-treated milk
Life span of diluted semen	6 days at 4°C
Life span of fresh/neat semen	18 hours

3

NUTRITION AND FEEDING

Dog is basically a carnivorous animal and prefers meat and meat products (raw as well as cooked) to other foods. However, it is not difficult to maintain an exclusively vegetarian dog. A large variety of foods can be fed to dogs without much adaptation difficulties except in some exceptional cases, where animals are reared on highly restricted and selected foods for a long period. High fibre feed may not meet energy requirement of simple stomached dog (Fig. 80).

A diet of cooked cereal with meat, fish or milk is quite common for the dogs. The vegetarian owners prefer to rear their pets on milk-cereal diet. Feeding of fish is more popular in the coastal areas and in the north-east region. A high protein and high fat diet is quite common in the feeding of dogs. Even smaller intake of such diets meets the nutritional requirements of dogs. When low fibre diets are fed for a long time, dogs develop a craving for fibre. This leads to their eating of clothes, grass etc. Therefore, it is necessary to provide some (4-6 per cent) crude fibre through the feeding of bran-mixed bread, roots, fruits and vegetables, etc. In early life care must be taken to provide the dog with adequate and balanced supply of the minerals necessary for bone development and blood formations and vitamins. If the diet is deficient, it should be either supplemented or a mineral - vitamin preparation should be administered once weekly. The nutritional requirements and role of different nutrients in the maintenance of body functions are described in this chapter. The amount of different kinds of foods for different body weights has been also given as a ready reckoner for dog feeding.

NUTRIENTS AND NUTRITIONAL REQUIREMENTS

All dogs require established nutrients like carbohydrates, fats, proteins, minerals, vitamins and water. Their nutritional requirements are affected by the following factors:

Mature body weight: Maintenance requirement of dogs per unit body weight is somewhat less in large and medium-sized breeds than in the toy breeds.

Physiological stage of the body: Requirement of major nutrients like energy and protein per unit body size in actively growing puppies is almost double the maintenance requirement of mature animals. The nutritional requirement increases marginally in the terminal trimester of the gestation period but considerably during the nourishing (lactation) period. The increase in nutrient requirement of lactating bitches depends on the litter size and the amount of daily milk production.

Climatic conditions: Environmental temperature has considerable effect on the nutrient requirement of dogs. The energy requirement is very high when temperature falls below the freezing point, and animals are generally unable to meet the requirement even though there may be more than 50 per cent increase in energy intake.

Work and exercise: Nutritional requirement particularly that of energy is much higher for working and hunting dogs.

ENERGY REQUIREMENT

Mean daily metabolizable energy requirement for maintenance ranges from 132 Kcal/kg metabolic body size ($W^{0.75}$) daily in mature dogs to 188, 200, 274 and 470 Kcal/kg $W^{0.75}$ in pregnant (last trimester), half grown, actively growing and lactating dogs respectively. Energy requirement increases during extremely cold weather and while performing heavy work. Carbohydrates and fats are the main sources of energy. Carbohydrates may constitute 40-70 per cent of the diets depending on the age and energy requirement of the dog. Cooked starchy foods are better utilized than uncooked food. Lactose and sucrose are poorly digested and cause intestinal disturbances.

Dietary fat is a concentrated source of energy providing about 2.25 times more energy than the carbohydrates and proteins. As low as 2 per cent fat in dry matter can supply the required essential fatty acids, but 10-15 per cent fat in dry matter may be required to meet the energy requirement of active dogs. Unsaturated fats are better than saturated fats. Fat in dog foods should be stabilized with antioxidants to reduce spoilage due to rancidity. Rancidity destroys fat-soluble vitamins leading to vitamin deficiencies. Linoleic acid in fat should be about 1.4% of diet (on dry-matter basis) to keep the body smooth. Pancreatic disturbance reduces the digestion of dietary fat resulting in dermatitis and reduced lustre of body coat. Maize-oil is useful under such a condition because it is highly unsaturated. It should be mixed with pancreatic enzyme in the diets of dogs suffering from the pancreatic dysfunction.

PROTEIN REQUIREMENT

Dogs, because of their simple stomach, require good sources of protein to meet their amino acids requirement. Arginine, valine, histidine, isoleucine, leucine, lysine, methionine, phenylalanine, threonine and tryptophan (remembered as AV HILL MPTT) are the dietary essential amino acids. About 15 per cent good-quality protein on dry-matter basis (3.5-4.0 Mcal ME per kg dry matter) in the diet is adequate for adult dogs. Providing some excess protein protects dogs against different kinds of stresses.

Standard diet of growing dogs should contain about 18-20 Kcal ME/g of protein in the diet, which will be equivalent to 20-22 per cent of diets containing 3.5-4.0 Mcal ME/kg on dry matter basis. In actively growing puppies protein requirement is significantly high.

In terminal trimester of pregnancy protein requirement is marginally higher. This can be compensated by the increased food intake, viz. 20-25 per cent higher intake than the maintenance requirement. Lactating bitches require 50-100 per cent higher or even more protein than required for maintenance depending on the quantity of daily milk production.

Additional protein supplementation is not required in the diets of working dogs. It is compensated by the increased food intake. The proportion of protein in diets should be increased when high energy diet containing greater percentage of fat is required for feeding the dogs engaged in strenuous work.

MINERAL REQUIREMENT

Minerals are important dietary constituents for normal growth, reproduction and maintenance of health. The various minerals required in the dog's diet are calcium, phosphorus, magnesium, iron, copper, zinc, iodine, manganese, cobalt, potassium, sodium, chloride and selenium. Some of the relatively less important minerals are molybdenum, fluorine, tin, silicon, nickel, vanadium and chromium. High concentrations of copper, selenium, molybdenum and fluorine in the diet are hazardous to the dogs.

Calcium and phosphorus: These two minerals are required mainly for the normal growth of bones. Ca: P ratio of 1.2 to 1.5 : 1 in the diet is optimum for their proper assimilation. Adequate supply of magnesium, fluorine, manganese, choline and vitamin D is essential for the normal development of skeleton. The average maintenance requirement of calcium and phosphorus in adult dogs is 100 and 85 mg/kg body weight respectively. High calcium content often results in phosphorus deficiency and vice-versa. Requirement of these minerals is slightly higher in growing puppies and lactating bitches. Pregnant bitches require about 60 per cent more Ca and P in the third trimester of pregnancy and lactating bitch almost 3 times of maintenance requirement. Complete diets containing 1-1.2 per cent calcium and 0.8-1 per cent phosphorus may meet the requirement of different physiological functions in dogs. Deficiency of these minerals causes rickets in growing pups (Fig. 81).

Magnesium: Magnesium is required in a small quantity for the development and maintenance of a healthy skeleton. Its deficiency may lead to various bone deformities like relaxed carpal joints, flat feet and knuckled legs, and may cause unusual increase of calcium in the heart and blood vessels.

Iron and copper: These trace elements are essential for normal haemopoesis. Their deficiency causes anaemia.

Cobalt: A small amount of cobalt is a dietary essential for stimulating the production of haemoglobin. Cobalt is required for the microbial synthesis of cyanocobalamin (Vitamin B_{12}) in the intestine which ultimately meets the dietary requirements.

Sodium chloride: This salt, essential for the normal physiological functions, is supplied through food, water and added table salt. Fresh meat contains little salt but some other feeds may contain enough sodium and chloride. Normally 1 per cent common salt is added in the air-dried feeds of dogs. Deficiency may cause fatigue, exhaustion decreased water intake, disturbance in body water content, depressed growth, dryness of skin and sometimes loss of hair.

Potassium: Cereals and other foods used for feeding dogs contain enough potassium. A concentration of 132 mg potassium/kg diet is adequate to supply the maintenance requirement of mature dogs, while double the maintenance is required for normal growth. Deficiency symptoms may be poor growth, restlessness, tendency to dehydration and muscular paralysis.

Iodine: Iodine supplementation is essential in iodine-deficient areas when dogs are reared on local feeds. Iodine deficiency is expressed by goitre, cretinism, myxoedema and skeletal deformities. Hairless pups may be produced by bitches on iodine-deficient diets.

Zinc: Common feeds supply enough zinc but excessive calcium intake reduces its availability. Zinc deficiency is shown by hyper-keratinization, scaly skin, alopecia, anorexia, disturbed growth and significant loss of body condition.

VITAMIN REQUIREMENT

Vitamins A, D, E and various B vitamins are recognised as dietary essential for dogs. Dogs normally do not require exogenous supply of vitamins K and C except when there is disturbance of intestinal microflora.

Vitamin A: Dogs can convert carotenes into vitamin A activity efficiently or their requirement may be met by the supplementation of natural and synthetic sources of vitamin A. About 5,000 IU of vitamin A activity/kg dry matter of feed is adequate to meet the requirement of all types of dogs. Deficiency signs are loss of appetite, loss of weight, xerophthalmia, conjunctivitis, corneal opacity and ulceration, skin lesions and lesions of mucous membrane. In pups deficiency may cause faulty bone development, in addition to other symptoms.

Vitamin D: Although vitamin D is produced in the skin through the action of solar radiation on certain lipids, this may not be efficient in dogs due to dense and large body coat covering larger part of the body in many breeds. Vitamin D can be supplemented in the diets as D_3 and D_2 vitamins. Severe vitamin D deficiency interferes in the normal calcification of bones resulting in rickets, irregular teeth, bone deformities and osteoporosis.

Vitamin E: Normally optimal requirement is supplied by the diet containing at least 2 per cent fat in dry matter. Rancidity destroys vitamin E and its feeding should be avoided. Deficiency is rare and characterized by muscle and nerve degeneration.

Vitamin K: This vitamin is normally synthesized in the intestine of dogs. Deficiency is generally observed when antibiotics are administered in large doses to disturb or destroy the intestinal microflora. Vitamin K deficiency may delay blood clotting from cut wounds. However, clear signs of vitamin K deficiency are yet to be established in dogs.

Vitamin C: It is not a dietary requirement under normal conditions. Deficiency causes scurvy and should be supplemented in the feed or otherwise. In the case of suspected deficiency ascorbic acid preparations should be administered daily @ 25-50 mg in dogs below 20 kg body weight and 50-100 mg in heavier dogs. Dogs fed citrus fruit juice usually do not suffer from vitamin C deficiency.

Vitamins of B-complex group: Most of the B vitamins are dietary essentials and they should be fed daily. A brief account of important vitamins of B-complex group is given below.

Vitamin B_1 (Thiamine): Thiamine is mainly involved in the utilization of carbohydrates in the body and its requirement is higher on a high carbohydrate diet. It is a heat-labile vitamin and is destroyed on cooking. Therefore, it is important to offer some raw feeds rich in thiamine or propriatary vitamin B_1 in the dog's diet. Some fish, ferns, bacteria, yeast and fungi contain antithiamine factors (particularly thiaminases) which inhibit the availability of vitamin B_1 and produce deficiency symptoms.

The common signs of thiamine deficiency are anorexia, disturbance in gastric secretions, nausea, vomiting, growth depression, loss of body weight, incoordination and often convulsions in severe cases.

A daily supply of about 20-25 mg thiamine/kg body weight would be adequate for the mature dogs. Double the amount should be made available to growing pups and pregnant and nourishing bitches.

Riboflavin (Vitamin B_2): It is a constituent part of flavoproteins or yellow enzymes. These flavoprotein enzymes are important for the transportation of hydrogen in the animal body. The common sources of riboflavin are meat, liver, milk, fish, egg, cereal grains and brewer's yeast.

The deficiency symptoms are poor appetite, progressive weakness, lowered respiration, muscular weakness, dermatitis, anaemia and conjunctivitis, etc. In acute cases sudden collapse, coma and death may occur.

The requirement of adult dog is about 48 mg/kg body weight, and for growing, pregnant and lactating animals it is about 95-100 mg/kg body weight.

Niacin/Nicotinamide/Nicotinic acid: Nicotinamide is the physiologically active form of the vitamin in the body, and it is present in coenzymes I and II. The enzyme plays an active role in the oxidation - reduction system by accepting hydrogen atom from the substrates for transferring to other hydrogen acceptors. The requirement of niacin is affected by the level of dietary tryptophan, which is metabolized into niacin.

Pellagra or blue tongue is the most prominent sign of niacin deficiency in dogs, the others being inappetance, loss in weight, ulcerative inflammation of mucosa of mouth and pharynx associated with profuse salivation often ropy with blood-stained drooling and foul breath. Inflammation and ulceration of small and large intestines and bloody diarrhoea occur in severe deficiency.

Average daily dietary requirement of adult dogs for maintenance is about 250 μg/per kg body weight. In productive dogs it is about 500 μg/kg body weight.

Vitamin B_6 (Pyridoxine, Pyridoxal and Pyridoxamine): Vitamin B_6 is present in the body tissues in three biologically active forms known as pyridoxine, pyridoxal and pyridoxamine, which are primary alcohol, aldehyde and amine forms respectively. All are converted into pyridoxal phosphate, an active coenzyme of various enzyme systems.

Its deficiency is expressed by reduction in growth rate, anorexia, loss in body weight, anaemia, epileptic convulsions and death. Sometimes alopecia and dermatitis may be observed. Since linseed contains a heat-stable antagonist named linatine, its use in dog's diet should be avoided.

Vitamin B_6 is found in most of the common feeds. Maintenance requirement for adult dogs is about 22 µg/kg body weight, and is double in growing, pregnant and lactating animals.

Pantothetic acid: It is a component of coenzyme A and helps in the transfer of acyl radical. Pantothenic acid deficiency is characterized by irregular feeding behaviour, slow growth rate, enteritis, and often vomition and alopecia. Death may occur in severe cases.

Average daily requirement for maintenance is about 220 µg/kg body weight and for production 440 µg/kg body weight of the dogs.

Folic acid: Folic acid is formed of glutamic acid, para-amino benzoic acid (PABA) and a pteridine nucleus. It participates in metabolic enzyme systems controlling the transfer of single carbon units and helps in the formation of methyl group and purines.

Deficiency of folic acid in dogs causes erratic appetite, reduction in growth rate, watery lachrymation, glossitis, hypochromic anaemia and leukopenia.

Average daily requirement is about 4 µg/kg body weight for adult dogs and 8 µg/kg body weight for growing pups. Common feeds contain adequate folic acid and normally its supplementation is not required.

Biotin: It is a constituent of adenosine - diphosphate (ADP) — biotin enzyme required for carboxylation reactions. Its physiological functions are not yet well known. Biotin is widely present in common foods and it is not a dietary requirement.

Choline: It is a controversial vitamin and it can be replaced by other compounds.

Vitamin B_{12} (Cyanocobalamin): It is also known as animal protein factor. It is associated with the formation of methyl groups from the single carbon units derived from formate, glycine and serine. Vitamin B_{12} is also required in many enzyme systems. Inadequate supply of dietary cobalt produces deficiency symptoms. Deficiency causes anaemia of different types.

Requirements of dogs have not been studied. Adult dog may be provided 0.5 µg B_{12}/kg body weight for maintenance and 1.0 µg/kg body weight for production.

WATER REQUIREMENT

Water is the most important of the various nutrients. The body of a newborn pup contains about 80 per cent water. It gradually decreases to about 60 per cent in adults. Water is the medium for various biochemical functions in the living cells and dehydration below the threshold results in death. Food, drinking water and metabolic water are the main sources of supply. The requirement of drinking water varies widely depending on the body weight, type of food, exercise and weather.

DIGESTIBILITY OF FOOD AND NUTRIENTS

Highly digestible foods like meat, milk, fish, cereal grains and leguminous seeds should constitute the diets. Digestibility of mother's milk is 92-94 per cent. Digestibility decreases with the inclusion of cereals and other vegetables in the feed. Age, type of food, level of feeding, breed and level of fibre in the diet affect the digestibility of food and nutrients.

Effect of breed: Average digestibility of various nutrients from the same diet increases with the body size and breed of the animals.

Level of feeding: Restriction of diet beyond a certain level reduces the digestibility of various nutrients. The effect is more pronounced on the digestibility of dry matter and protein of canned dog food. Such differences have not been observed on the feeding of semimoist diet.

Effect of fibre content: A gradual fall in the digestibility coefficient of nutrients may occur with the corresponding rise in the fibre content of diets. However, the effect of fibre percentage is more on the digestibility of dry matter and carbohydrates and least on crude fat.

Mean Transit Time of Digesta

Passage of digesta is slow when high meat diets are fed. It increases with the increase of crude fibre concentration in the feed. Mean transit time is approximately 37, 41, 33 and 29 hours on the feeding of diets containing 0.6, 6.5, 11.2 and 14.7 per cent crude fibre on dry-matter basis. On the feeding of low fibre diet occassionally unusual longer transit time averaging about 46 hours may be due to gastric disturbances caused by an almost fibre-free diet.

Defaecation Behaviour of Dogs

Defaecation behaviour in domestic dogs is a somewhat controlled involuntary physiological function. Number of daily defaecation may be 2 to 5 and it is significantly affected by the level of fibre in the diet. Under normal feeding of a cereal-meat diet 2-3 times daily defaecation is observed in pet dogs, mostly early in the morning and late in the evening.

FEEDING OF DOGS

Dogs belong to Order Carnivora, but domesticated dogs have been well adopted to omnivorous feeding habits. Dogs in India are often reared on vegetarian foods without any health problem, provided milk and milk products are included in their diet. The common feedstuffs used for the computation of balanced and palatable diets may be classified as follows:

Feeds of Animal Origin

(i) **Meat:** Variety meats, bone scrappings, meat-cum-bone, edible glands (like liver, heart and kidneys), cleaned and chopped/minced gut, etc., meat-meal, meat-cum-bone meal.

(ii) **Milk, milk products and byproducts** (whole milk, skimmed milk, dried milk powder, casein, cheese-meal, paneer, dahi and matha).

(iii) Fish and fish-meal.

(iv) Poultry and poultry products/chicken processing byproducts (head, legs, gizard and gut, egg, etc.)

(v) Edible fatty tissue and fat.

Feeds of Plant Origin

(i) Wheat, barley, oat, corn, sorghum, rice, pearlmillet, small millets, etc.

(ii) **Cereal byproducts:** Wheat germ-meal, maize germ-meal, maize gluten, broken rice, wheat middlings, wheat bran, etc.

(iii) **Pulses and byproducts:** Gram, pea, cowpea, green-gram, black-gram, beans, soyabean, kidney-bean and their husk removed grits, etc.

(iv) **Fruits and vegetables:** Pomace of apple, tomato and sweet citrus fruits, carrot, bean pods, leafy vegetable, leaf meals, banana, mango, peaches etc.

Feed Supplements and Additives

Miscellaneous feed supplements are common salt, mineral mixture and vitamin supplements. Main feed additives are antioxidants, bacteriostats, colouring agents (permitted edible colours) and flavouring agents.

Characteristics of Standard Feeds

A good feed for domestic dogs should possess most of the following characteristics:

It should be cooked except in cases where other treatments like pasteurization, irradiation, etc. have been suggested. Green vegetables should be half boiled. The diet should be balanced for essential nutrients and should be formulated according to the requirement of dogs, viz. a low energy diet is required for idle adult dogs, high energy diets for working dogs and high energy high protein diet for growing pups.

Precautions in the Feeding of Dogs

The following points should be considered carefully for the selection and preparation of feeds:

Pup's diet should be liquid or semi-solid.

Raw meat, bone, fish and chicken may transmit many infections and should not be fed without cooking.

Raw eggs contain antivitamin enzyme avidin. Hence they should be fed after proper cooking except for treatments.

Pets should be fed at a particular place in a clean dish (Fig. 82). It is better to use separate bowls for feeding and watering.

Drinking water should be offered fresh and changed frequently. Cold drinking water should be offered during the summer season.

A definite feeding schedule should be followed and it may be divided as light breakfast, lunch and dinner.

Diet should be prepared from a variety of feeds but there should not be frequent change in the diets and feeding schedule.

In transit dogs should be fed restricted amount of low fibre diet to avoid frequent defaecation in the journey.

Dogs should be allowed 15-20 minutes time for eating and any left over should be removed and discarded.

Dogs should not be allowed to develop a liking for some particular food. Such habits may often be inconvenient and in the long run may cause malnutrition leading to either obesity or undesired leanness.

Long fresh bones with open extremities should be offered from healthy carcass to chew for half to one hour. It keeps teeth and jaw muscles healthy.

Small bones and splinters in meat and fish pieces should be avoided in the dog meals.

Spoiled foods and damaged grains should never be fed because they may be potential source of infections and toxicosis.

Meat obtained from hormone-implanted animals and chemically caponised birds should not be used for the feeding of dogs particularly in the diets of breeding and growing animals.

FOOD REQUIREMENT

A standard balanced dog food should contain 20-22 per cent crude protein, 4-5 per cent fat, 5-10 per cent crude fibre and 4-5 per cent ash on dry-matter basis. Average energy content should be 3.3-4.0 Mcal per kg of food on dry-matter basis and it should be also balanced for essential minerals and vitamins.

The dry-matter requirement of dogs for maintenance is given in Table 3. Significant increase in food intake (2 to 3 times higher) occurs during the winter.

TABLE 3. DAILY DRY-MATTER REQUIREMENT FOR MAINTENANCE (ON DRY-MATTER BASIS)

Body weight (kg)	*Dry-matter requirement (g/kg body weight)*		
	3.3 Kcal/g	*3.5 Kcal/g*	*4.0 Kcal/g*
2.5	33	31	27
5.0	28	26	23
7.5	25	23	21
10.0	23	22	19
15.0	21	20	17
20.0	18	17	15
25.0	18	17	15
30.0	17	16	14
40.0	17	16	14
50.0	15	14	13
60.0	15	14	13
70.0 and above	14	13	12

Calculated from the values of NRC (1974) for diet containing 3.3 Kcal ME/g dry-matter.

The requirements of production, e.g. growth, work, pregnancy and lactation, are higher than the maintenance requirement. Diets supplying 3.5 to 4.0 Kcal ME per g dry matter are normally fed for production. Young pups in early life may require even higher energy content in their diets for optimum growth and development. Average ME requirement of mature idle dog is 132 Kcal per kg $W^{0.75}$ ($W^{0.75}$ = metabolic body size), which increases to 188 and 470 Kcal/kg $W^{0.75}$ in terminal trimester of pregnancy and lactation period respectively. The average requirement of growing and adolescent puppies is 274 and 200 Kcal/kg $W^{0.75}$ respectively. The increased nutrient requirement is normally supplied by increased food intake.

FEEDING OF PUPS

Under normal conditions newborn pups are nursed by their mother through natural teat feeding and they learn to eat mother's food after opening eyes at about 2 weeks of age (Fig. 83). Lactation period may last for more than 8 weeks but most of the dog breeders practice weaning at about 4, 6 or 8 weeks of age. Weaned pups are gradually shifted to artificial feeding of milk-based semi-solid or liquid diets. In an emergency like mother's inability to nurse their pups due to agalactia or mastitis and for orphan pups artificial feeding is required from the very first day of life. Such pups are usually deprived of mother's colostrum and they are more susceptible to infection requiring more hygienic care during feeding and watering.

Plate-20

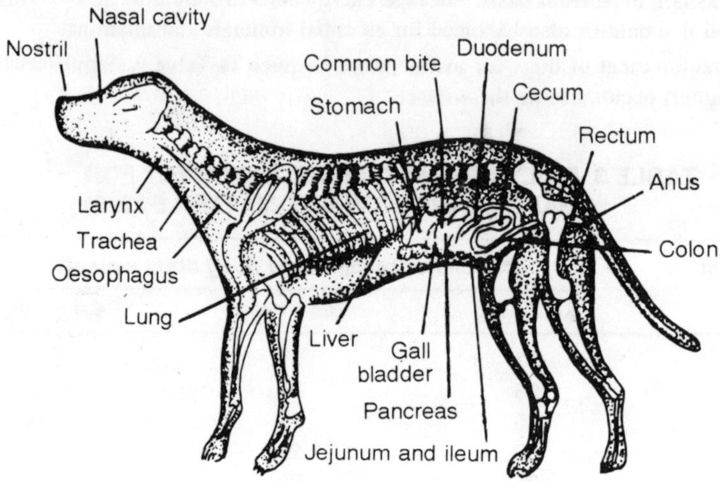

Fig. 80. Gastro intestinal tract of a dog.

Fig. 81. Pup suffering with rickets.

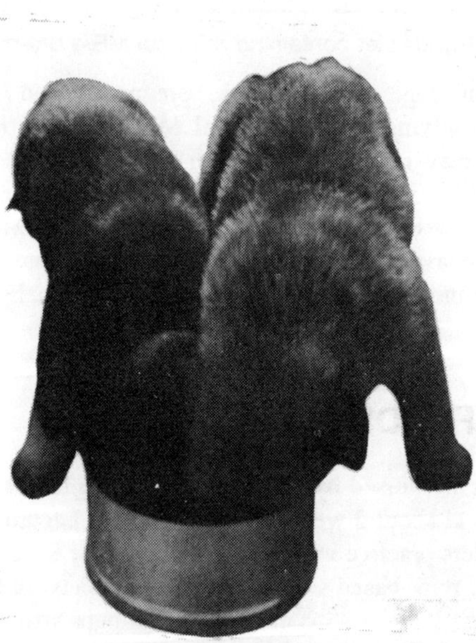

Fig. 82. Pups feeding in a clean bowl.

Fig. 83. Two week old pups showing opened eyes

Milk yield and composition: Milk yield in bitches is significantly influenced by the breed, age at first breeding, body condition, litter size and stage of lactation. Average daily milk in small-medium and large-sized breeds is about 2.4, 2.7 and 2.8 per cent of body weight in the beginning; about 3.4, 4.6 and 3.6 per cent of body weight at 4 weeks of lactation period; and then declines gradually to weaning at about 6-8 weeks of age. In a few bitches milk yield may be as high as 7.3 per cent of body weight.

Formula feeding of pups: Satisfactory commercial foods for pups are now available. In their absence baby milk food can be used. Good-quality starter pup diet can be easily prepared from milk and other foods at home (Table 4). It should contain about 30-35 per cent protein, and 30-35 per cent of edible fat and carbohydrates (starch, lactose and sugar). Adequate amount of minerals and vitamins may be fed in addition to starter diets. Antibiotics are normally added to provide protection against infections. The dry feed before being given to pups should be mixed with hot water in the ratio of 1 : 3 and then cooled near to body temperature before feeding.

TABLE 4. FEED FORMULAE FOR YOUNG PUPS

Ingredients (g)	*Diet 1*	*Diet 2*	*Diet 3*
Dried milk powder	200	-	-
Liquid whole milk			
Cow	-	700	-
Buffalo	-	-	800
Cream (30% fat)	200	200	100
Egg-yolk	-	50	50
Boiling water	400	-	-
Rice gruel/flour gruel (30% dry-matter)	200	50	50

NB: 1. For every 1 kg of liquid diet containing about 25-30% dry matter add about 2,000 IU vitamin, A, 500 IU vitamin D and 4 g citric acid.

2. Antibiotics preferably tetracycline @ 10 mg per kg feed should be mixed.

Method of feeding: Bottle feeding is almost necessary in the first 2 weeks when eyes are not open. It can be done with the help of a large teat dropper. It takes about 3-7 days to train the pup to feed from a dish.

Feeding schedule: The pups should be fed at 2-hourly intervals during the first week, 3-hourly intervals in day and 4-hourly intervals at night during the second week, 4-hourly intervals in day and once (6-hourly interval) at night during the next 2 weeks, and thrice daily feeding at 4-hourly intervals in day time only from the fifth week of life. A liquid feed containing about 25-30 per cent dry matter should be fed @ 14-16 per cent of body weight divided by the number of daily meals at each feeding.

FEEDING OF WEANED PUPS AND ADULT DOGS

The feeding of dogs after weaning at 6-8 weeks of age is much simpler and can be managed conveniently. The nutritional requirements for different physiological functions can be supplied by changing the amount of daily feed allowance. Standard diets of growing and adult dogs contain about 20-22 per cent protein and 3.5-4.0 Kcal ME per g of feed on dry-matter basis, and it should be balanced for minerals and vitamins.

Feeding of growing dogs: Growing dogs from weaning to maturity are fed diets composed of cereals, leguminous seeds, meat and/or other feeds of animal source, vegetables and fruits. The daily requirement varies according to body weight. It should be calculated to supply about 50-55 g dry matter per kg body weight during the active growth up to about 6 months of age. Afterwards quantity of diet should be reduced to 38-40 g per kg body weight up to maturity or 1 year of age. A few simple diet formulae are given for the feeding of growing dogs in Table 5.

TABLE 5: FEEDING SCHEDULE OF GROWING DOGS

Body weight	*Amount of various feeds (g/day)*			
(kg)	*Cereals*	*Meat*	*Milk*	*Fresh bone (Steamed)*
5	200	100	100	One metacarpal/metatarsal/ humour/femur of goat or sheep
10	400	200	100	
15	600	300	100	
20	800	400	100	
25	1000	400	100	

NB: About 50-100 g green leafy vegetable (half boiled) or fresh fruit and an egg should be fed daily in absence of meat/milk.

Feeding of adult dogs for maintenance: Adult idle and companion dogs taken out for walk or light exercise require about 32 Kcal ME per kg $W^{0.75}$. A feeding schedule of mature dogs is given in Table 6 for different mature body weights.

TABLE 6. FEEDING SCHEDULE OF MATURE DOGS

Body weight	*Daily food requirement (g)*			
(kg)	*Cereals*	*Meat*	*Green vegetables of legume pods*	*Milk*
5	100	50	50-60	100
10	150	50	60-80	100
15	200	100	80-100	100
20	300	100	100-150	-
25	400	100	100-150	-
30	450	150	100-150	-
40	500	150	150-200	-
50	600	200	200-300	-
60	700	200	200-300	-
70 and above	800	200	200-300	-

NB: 1-2 eggs should be fed daily if meat/milk is not given.

Feeding of pregnant bitch (in third trimester): Since active development of litter takes place in the terminal trimester of the gestation period, the pregnant bitches should be given about 20-30 per cent more food than the maintenance requirement after 6 weeks of gestation period. The ration schedule may be prepared from Table 7.

TABLE 7. FEEDING SCHEDULE OF PREGNANT BITCH

Body weight (kg)	*Daily food requirement (g)*				
	Cereals	*Meat*	*Milk*	*Green vegetable*	*Bone (Steamed)*
10	200	50	100	100	Fresh long bone of sheep, goat, cattle or buffalo
15	250	100	100	100	
20	350	100	100	100	
25	450	150	100	150	
30	550	150	100	200	
40	600	150	-	200	
50	700	200	-	250	
60 and above	800	200	-	250	

Feeding of working dogs: The energy requirement of working dogs engaged in strenuous work like pulling of sledge and running more than 100 km for hunting wild game may need as high as 3-4 times of the maintenance requirement (Table 8). The mean ME content of diet should be 4 Kcal per g on dry basis.

TABLE 8. FEEDING SCHEDULE OF WORKING DOGS

Body weight	*Daily food requirement (g)*			
(kg)	*Cereals*	*Meat*	*Vegetables*	*Bone (Steamed)*
30	1400	'500	300	One long bone of fresh carcass of cattle or buffalo
40	2000	500	300	
50	2500	600	300	
60	2800	600	400	
70	3000	600	400	

NB: The amount of cereals is partly replaced by adding edible fat @ 1 g for each 2.5 g cereals and percentage of protein is increased accordingly.

Feeding of stud male: Male dogs reared exclusively for breeding require more critical diets than the working animals. Stud males are fed according to the feeding schedule given for maintenance except the breeding season. Feed level should be increased by 25 per cent of the maintenance requirement about 3-4 weeks before the mating or semen collection. Dogs should also be given a boosting dose of vitamins A, E and B-complex either orally or in feed.

Feeding of fat (obese) dogs: To reduce the energy content the diet of obese dogs should be prepared from high fibre low energy feeds. A feeding schedule given in Table 9 may be used with minor modifications depending on the degree of fatness of the dog.

TABLE 9. FEEDING SCHEDULE FOR OBESE DOGS

Body weight	*Daily food requirement (g)*			
(kg)	*Lean meat*	*Skim milk*	*Green beans/vegetables*	*Bran-rich bread*
20	100	-	200	50
30	150	-	200	50
40	150	100	300	100
50	200	100	300	150
60	200	200	400	200
70	200	200	500	300

NB: Oral mineral vitamin supplement should be administered daily.

FEEDING OF SICK DOGS

Sick dogs should be fed as per the advice of a veterinary clinician or a veterinary dietician for the specific conditions. However, following precautions may be taken while selecting foods for dogs suffering from systemic and other diseases.

Diabetes mellitus: The proportion of starchy foods and sugars should be drastically reduced from the dog's diet. Quantity of skim-milk, green vegetables and bran-enriched chapati should be increased.

Cardiac insufficiency: The salt should be reduced drastically and as far as possible low sodium foods should be used. Lean meat, freshwater fish, egg-yolk and rice should be fed without salt. Milk, cream, butter, fish, nuts and eggs should be avoided.

Renal insufficiency: High protein diets should be restricted, and minimal amount of good-quality protein of high biological value should be fed along with high energy food.

Liver diseases: In case of stagnant liver easily metabolizable feeds like dextrose, rice and maize starch should constitute the source of energy, and protein of high biological value should be fed @ 3.5-4 g per kg body weight. Feeding of fish, fish-meal and glands should be avoided. A multivitamin preparation should be administered daily. In cases of chronic liver diseases and ascites feeding of high sodium feeds and common salt should be drastically reduced.

In hypoglycaemia: In acute hypoglycaemia glucose or sucrose should be fed @ 70 g per kg body weight. This may be given once or divided into 2 or 3 parts for feeding at 2-3 hours interval. The daily diet should be prepared from maize starch, rice, oat-meal, egg-yolk, meat-meal and mineral-vitamin supplement. Strenuous work should be avoided in working dogs and while working they should be fed frequently at intervals of 3-4 hours.

Urolithiasis: A suitable diet should be prepared on the basis of the composition of uroliths if detected in urine, otherwise low protein, low mineral food containing high percentage of common salt should be fed to increase water intake and urine volume. An increase in urination frequency and urine volume reduces the urinary concentration of involved materials.

Diarrhoea: The diet should contain low fibre cereals, low protein and easily digestible protein foods like paneer, cottage cheese, curd, eggs and liver. It should not contain more than 10-12 per cent fat on dry-matter basis. Proprietary diets containing flesh and high concentration of sugar, lactose and dried whey should be avoided. A high paneer or high egg diet should be supplemented for potassium deficiency. In acute case parenteral fluid feeding may be necessary to restore the body fluid volume and electrolytes. The following recipe may be useful in diarrhoea.

Food ingredients	*Quantity*	*Dry matter*
Cooked rice gruel or low fibre wheat flour gruel or sago gruel	500 ml	100 g
Sugar	60 g	60 g
Paneer or cottage cheese	200 g	50 g
Cream	100 g	30 g
Maize-oil or saflower-oil	15 g	15 g
Hard cooked egg	100 g	50 g
Dicalcium phosphate	10 g	10 g
Potassium chloride	15 g	15 g
Mineral vitamin supplement	as per dose on container	

NB: The above diet should be fed @ 100 ml per kg body weight daily in 5-6 split meals at equal interval.

Gastroenteritis: Irritant diets should not be fed when a dog is suffering from gastroenteritis. The diet may be prepared from chicken soup, egg white, milk, sago, vegetable soup, sugar and cream supplemented with dicalcium phosphate, trace minerals and vitamins.

Exposure (stress): Dogs exposed to hostile environment conditions like extreme cold or heat should be provided a high energy food at short intervals of 2-4 hours depending on the severity of exposure. A 50 per cent glucose solution @ 70 ml per kg body weight should be given orally in split meals at 3 hourly intervals and the animal should be offered fresh drinking water about 40-50 ml water per kg body weight during the first 24 hours. Table sugar solution can be administered in the absence of glucose or fructose. In case of sunstroke parental fluid therapy may be essential for which the help of a veterinary doctor should be taken as early as possible.

Pyrexia (fever): Energy requirement of dog increases in fever. It should be fed additional energy @ 7 Kcal per kg body weight daily for each degree rise above the normal body temperature. This can be accomplished by feeding cream, hard-cooked egg or maize oil in the diet. In case of anorexia, fluid diet should be administered with the help of a stomach tube.

Pica (depraved appetite): In case of mineral deficiency, particularly that of phosphorus, animals develop a habit of eating unusual substances like faeces, shoe, decaying bones, wooden piece, grass and other articles. The diet of such dogs should be balanced through mineral supplementation and they should be offered fresh long bone of healthy carcass. A hard rubber ball may be left for playing and chewing during the treatment but care should be taken to avoid habit formation.

Vomiting: Vomiting may be from the eating of spoiled foods or disease. Normally feeding should be avoided for the day. Dog should be offered fresh light diet as suggested for diarrhoea.

Ascites: Restriction of sodium intake or withdrawal of sodium from the diet, white eggs, solid high protein and fibre diet should be given; liquid diet should be reduced.

Grass Eating Habit in Dogs

It is a common belief that dogs eat grass for stimulating vomiting. However, a recent study in Federal Republic of Germany has shown that almost 90 per cent dogs eat grass at some time and it is not influenced by the age, sex, breed, type of food, method of feeding, health, weather or fibre content in the diet. Only a few animals vomit after eating grass. Dogs like to eat small quantity of tender leaves and soft grasses.

TYPES OF FOOD

Selection of food for dogs depends on several factors like the economic status of the owner, nutritional requirement of dogs for different physiological states of the body and the feeding value of different foods. A dog's diet may have one of the following 3 types of food or their various combinations.

Kitchen Residue

Usually all types of food normally eaten by man are also eaten by dogs. Kitchen residue contains a combination of all cooked food. It can meet the nutritional requirement of dogs provided it is not highly deficient in protein and minerals. Vegetarian diets in India are normally rich in carbohydrates and fat, but poor in good-quality protein foods. Such kitchen waste should be adequately supplemented through the feeding of milk and milk products, eggs, meat and fish. The chemical composition of kitchen residue is quite variable and often inadequate to meet the requirement of dog. Thus, it is difficult to maintain the level of nutrients concentration in the diet of dogs and it is important to balance by feeding additional foods of high nutritive value.

Home-Made Foods

Most of the home-made diets are unbalanced specially for protein and minerals due to the use of larger proportions of cereals and starchy tubers and corns in the human food. Some preliminary knowledge about the nutrients requirement of dogs and nutritional composition of common dog foods is essential for the preparation of balanced home-made diets. Freshly prepared home-made diets are generally more palatable than the proprietary foods. A balanced home-made diet should contain about 20-22 per cent protein (at least one-third from milk, meat or egg), 5-10 per cent fat, 5-10 per cent fibre and 3.5-4.0 Kcal ME/per gram of diet on dry-matter basis. In addition to this, adequate minerals and vitamins should be fed from the various proprietary products.

Preparation of home-made dog foods: Home-made dog foods are prepared by baking, roasting, boiling and cooking by different methods depending on the requirement. The various foods prepared are soup, broth, cooked meat and bone, boiled rice, chapati, brown bread, gruel, cooked semi-solid broken maize, oat, barley and wheat (dalia), boiled milk, corn-flakes, cooked meals of groundnut, sesame and linseed, boiled or fried eggs, half-cooked green vegetables or vegetables and fruit pieces dipped for 30-40 seconds in boiling water, fresh sweet (low acid) curd, steamed paneer, etc.

Proprietary Dog Foods

Dog owners usually prefer to feed their dogs a standard commercial diet which is balanced and prepared specially for the dogs. Generally, three types of commercial dog foods are marketed in the economically advanced countries.

Dry dog foods: All diets containing more than 90 per cent dry matter at the time of packing is known as dry food. Large-scale manufacture of good-quality balanced dog foods is economical and usually it is cheapest among all the three types of commercial diets. In addition to this packaging, transport, storage and feeding of dry foods is much more convenient than the soft moist food and canned foods.

Good-quality balanced and palatable diets are prepared by mixing several kinds of foods and supplements. For small-scale manufacturer it is processed by baking and for large-scale manufacturer extrusion is followed. Dry dog diets are supplied in the form of meal, kibble, flakes, wafer, biscuit and crackers. It is difficult to incorporate higher percentage of fat in the dry foods. Food is supplied in sealed cartons of 0.5, 1, 2, 5 or 10 kg. Open cartons should be kept protected from moisture, insects and house rodents.

Soft moist foods: It is also known as semi-moist or semi-solid dog food. Semi-moist dog foods contain 25-40 per cent water. These foods are normally marketed in small quantity to be finished in 1-2 days after opening. Spoilage of food is protected by adding antimicrobial edible and harmless substances like table sugar (sucrose), propylene, glycol and sorbitol. The foods are prepared from the common ingredients and cooked properly by direct heating, pressure cooking or autoclaving. Larger proportion of edible fat can be incorporated in the semi-solid foods (Table 10).

TABLE 10. SOME EXAMPLES OF SEMI-SOLID FOODS

Ingredients(%)	*Diet 1*	*Diet 2*	*Diet 3*	*Diet 4*
Cereal flour	10	5	10	10
Groundnut-cake	15	15	15	15
Meat-cum-bone-meal (50% protein)		15	15	15
Skim-milk (9% total solids)	45	-	-	-
Skim-milk powder (95% solids)	-	10	-	-
Eggs	-	-	-	40
Sucrose	20	15	20	20
Animal fat	5	5	2	2
Water	-	30	33	13
Propylene glycol	2	2	2	2
Sorbitol	2	2	2	2
Iodised salt	0.5	0.5	0.5	0.5
Mineral mixture + vitamins supplement	0.5	0.5	0.5	0.5

Canned dog foods: Canned diets of dogs contain about 70-75 per cent moisture and their shelf-life after opening the container is very short. Canned foods may be either complete balanced diet or meat preparation (protein supplement) to be mixed with cooked cereals at the time of feeding in the ratio given on the container.

4

MANAGEMENT

A standard management system is important for rearing an orderly, well-mannered and disciplined dog. A casual attitude in the daily routine of a dog can induce undesirable habits which may be difficult to rectify at later stage in the routine management.

The house pets in India are often indisciplined, easy-going show pieces probably due to improper training and casual attention of owners to their dogs. In domestic dogs, most of the problems arise because the owner fails to realize the importance of proper training. The aggression, attention seeking and elimination behaviour in dogs require psychological treatment.

The common problems are jumping on people, barking, begging, jumping on furniture, digging, chewing, fear of noise, over-protectiveness and repeated escape. Most of these problems are common in younger dogs of 6-12 months of age. Jumping on people tends to reduce gradually with the increase in age, whereas begging becomes more common. Neutered (castrated) dogs bite more often than the intact (entire) ones. These problems are normally not related with the age of the dog at the time of procurement and develop due to the prevailing circumstances in which the dogs are kept. (For common terms used in dog keeping, refer Appendix 6.)

BEHAVIOUR OF DOGS

A first-hand knowledge about the behavioural profile of dogs is a must for the selection of suitable breeds for different purposes. The behaviour profile is influenced by the following 4 factors and response to each factor is exhibited by several behavioural traits as follows:

Factors		*Behavioural traits*
Reactivity	(i)	Affection demand
	(ii)	Excitability
	(iii)	Excessive barking
	(iv)	Snapping at children
	(v)	General activity
Aggressiveness	(i)	Territorial defence
	(ii)	Watch dog barking
	(iii)	Aggression on other dogs
	(iv)	Dominance over owner
Trainability	(i)	Obedience training
	(ii)	House-breaking case
Other factors	(i)	Destructiveness
	(ii)	Playful nature

Aggressive Behaviour of Dogs

Various factors, inherent or acquired, responsible for the aggressiveness in pet dogs are given below:

Aggressiveness due to fear: This is shown by the postures of defensiveness, fear or submission. The ears are drawn back, tail is drawn down or tucked between the legs and the dog either approaches the other one in a surrendering posture with bent and almost staggering hind legs or withdraws from the scene.

Dominance aggression: It is a very complex and variable behavioural pattern. The dog occupies a stand over position and stares at the stranger with erect ear and tail. The posture becomes more rigid and it is accompanied by growling, baring the teeth, snapping and often biting.

Some of the dominant aggressive dogs do not exhibit apparent signs and posture of dominance but strongly resist when forced in submissive conditions.

Possessive aggression: It is displayed by growling, baring the teeth, snapping or biting when holding food, bone, toys, etc. and approached by some one.

Protective aggression: It includes aggression for protecting the home, yard or owner.

Predatory aggression: It is exhibited by intense visual scanning and attention to the area where they are anticipated. This is followed by stalking and chasing of a wide range of moving stimuli. The sequence of action is completed by barking, nipping and/or biting.

Punishment elicited aggressiveness: It is shown by growling, baring the teeth, snapping or biting. Experience of pain from punishment is not necessary for the aggressiveness.

Aggressiveness due to induced pain: It is shown by growling, baring the teeth, snapping or biting only on feeling pain, which may be caused during grooming, medication or injury.

Intra-species aggression: Normally it is inter-male or inter-female aggression. This is expressed by barking, growling, snapping and biting. The cause of aggression may be food, bone, toy or trespass.

Reaction Between Dogs of Different Localities

It is quite common to observe the territory of stray dogs living in a village or town. Normally dogs do not like trespassers and a fight on trespassing is quite common between the dogs of the same sex but very rare between the opposite sex and young pups. However, during the breeding season dogs of different areas cluster around the bitch in oestrus and continue to walk behind the bitch in a que almost in the order of physical strength. The bitch is normally possessed by the most aggressive dog of the group but in some rare cases specific liking for a particular dog may be observed in a few bitches. A bitch in oestrus may mate several times with a single dog or each time with a different dog under free living conditions.

HOUSING

A house for dogs is known as kennel. Normally special housing is not arranged for one or two pets. Pet dogs are provided a bed in a corner of the house. The owners of sporting breeds and guard dogs keep them at an isolated place in a clean and comfortable kennel, usually in the remote corner of a bungalow protected by boundary wall. Movable plastic pens are now available. These can be kept at a suitable place in the house and the pet trained to use it as his retiring room.

In indoor dog clinics and at breeding studs several dogs of different kinds may be required to be housed. For such conditions, kennels of variable size are constructed, depending on the type and number of bitches to be bred and the kind of dogs.

A kennel may be a permanent house constructed by bricks and concrete, or temporary of wood planks, plastic sheets, insulated asbestos sheet, etc.

Size and Furnishing of Pens

The size of pens varies with the breed, age and breeding of the dogs. Average size of pen for non-breeding pet dogs may be kept as follows:

1. ***Toy or small breeds:*** The pens may be 1 m long, 75 cm wide and 70 cm high, and covered with wiregauze. Front door should be well ventilated and sliding or dropping type.
2. ***Medium breeds:*** The pens may be 1.5 m long, 1 m wide and 1 m high.
3. ***Large breeds:*** It may be 2.5 m long, 2 m wide and 1.5 m high.

Each pen should be provided with a 15-cm-high wooden bench for resting, a bowl full of clean drinking water and a dish for feeding.

Pens should open in a fenced run for exercise. The height of fencing should be sufficient to prevent the escaping of dogs even during the breeding season when they are highly active and acrobatic. It should be more than 2.5 m for the large-sized sporting dogs.

The area for brood bitches should be at least double that for non-breeding bitches. The bench should be placed by the side of the wall and the open space should be blocked to prevent the entrance of pups beneath the bench. A cardboard box should be placed around whelping for the rest of newborn puppies. Each pen of a brood bitch should have an enclosed run for the exercise of pups. The floor should have a thick layer of ash, sand or soft grass. It should be kept clean, dry and free from sharp objects.

BEDDING

In tropical climate, dogs do not need any special bedding except a clean and dry wooden plank bench for rest and sleeping. A khadi duster or piece of bed-sheet may be comfortable bedding if at all it is necessary. Bitches should be provided with old clean clothes or newspaper for preparing bed (nesting behaviour) before whelping. Dry grass is used for winter bedding in rural areas. A piece of rug may be required in a frosty season. The dogs should be protected from the chill in cold season, from direct solar radiation in summer, and from dampness in the rainy season (Fig. 84 a, b).

Some owners dress their dogs in different types of jackets. This does not provide any significant comfort to the animal. However, newborn puppies need protection from the cold when separated from the mother at an early age. Suckling pups receive enough heat from the contact of mother.

HANDLING

Proper restraint of dogs is most important for handling during transportation and examination for purchase or clinical examination by a veterinary doctor. While handling a dog one should hear patiently the assurances of owners, but proceed according to the standard procedures. Otherwise it may not be unusual to experience one or two bites. It is advisable to involve the owner for restraining his pet.

The following methods are quite common:

Tape method: A 2 cm wide and about 1 m long cotton tape is used for the face restraint of dogs. Two half hitches are made in the middle of tape and slipped suddenly over the nose of the dog from behind when the dog is held by its ears by his owner. The tape is tied tightly and the ends are tied behind the ears. Minor adjustment is required with the short-nose breeds.

Muzzle application: Muzzles of different size should be kept in the clinic for different breeds with variable size of face. Muzzle is made of leather, smooth stainless wire and plastic strings. Muzzles are amply perforated because its application for longer duration may be required for preventing the licking of topical medicine applied on a wound, etc.

Remote control for the administration of drug: In case of restless and unruly dogs the chain connecting the strong neck or shoulder collar is pulled close to neck through a metallic ring fixed deep in the ground, platform or wall. One hind limb is lifted and the drug is injected intramuscularly in the hip or thigh and subcutaneously in the flank region. The procedure is normally adopted in follow-up treatments.

Ferocious and unruly dogs are kept tied with a chain during the day time or kept close in its pen when guests and visitors are expected in the house. A board warning visitors is displayed outside.

When the dog is taken for a walk, it is secured with a collar and chain or a stout leather string. It is always wise to secure even the most docile and disciplined dog while going out on the streets to avoid any unpleasant situation. Various types of collars and leads are used for control of dog.

CATCHING OF STRAY DOGS

Health departments frequently launch campaigns for eradication of stray dogs. The work is performed by a team of trained dog catchers. The following methods are used for catching of stray dogs:

Loop method: A sliding noose of strong rope on a long bamboo of 1.5-2 m is used for catching dogs. After capture dogs are collected in a caged van for destruction. Now-a-days iron instruments for dog catching are also available.

Tranquilizing gun method: The dogs are shot unnoticed with a pipe-gun located with a cartridge containing tranquilizer and fitted with a needle. The drug is injected by the pressure of a shot in the body and the dog becomes unconscious within 15-20 minutes.

HANDLING OF RABIED DOGS

The methods used for catching stray dogs may be used. However, operators must be immunized against rabies.

Euthanasia of Dogs

Destruction of dogs becomes necessary in rabies and incurable painful conditions. It is performed by several humane methods like a shot at the centre of the forehead, chemical destruction and electrical destruction. The job should be performed only by a trained person at an isolated place or in a dog clinic. Provision for electrical destruction is available in many big cities of India.

Common methods of euthanasia are:

Magnesium sulphate: Saturated solution should be injected rapidly by I/V or I/cardiac route. For small dog 10-20 ml. For large dog 20-40 ml.

Barbiturates: Pentabarbital sodium @ 60-70 mg/kg body weight I/V and 100 mg/kg body weight I/P or I/thoracic.

Chloral hydrate: 2.5 g/10 kg body weight I/V.

Shooting: The shot should be at the cross point of imaginary lines drawn from the base of the ears to the opposite eyes from a distance of 2-3 m. It causes profuse haemorrhage.

Other methods: Several compounds may be used for this purpose, viz. inhalent anaesthetics, carbon monoxide and hydrogen cyanide gas, which require a special chamber. Nuxvomica can be used, but produces severe convulsions in dogs.

CARE OF SKIN AND BODY COAT

The skin is a protective covering of the body. It is formed of an outer epidermis and an inner dermis. It protects the body from the physical, chemical and biological injuries. Almost entire skin except the areas, nose, foot-pads and some parts of the groin is covered with hair. Wide variation occurs in colour, length and texture of the body coat. These are characteristic of many breeds. Hair coat of the dog is classified as normal, short and long. The growth of hair is cyclic growing phase or anagenic phase, followed by a resting or telogenic phase. In the later stage of the second phase hair is shed, to be replaced by new hair. A healthy dog should have a good glossy coat.

The dog is regarded as a non-sweating animal. Its skin contains sebaceous glands. Functional sweat glands are present on the nose and foot-pads. Excess heat is normally eliminated by panting and excessive salivation. Body coat and air trapped between hair keep dogs warm in cold season. Hairs are raised in frosty cold weather and heat generated by shivering. The hair and skin of domestic dog should be kept clean by routine grooming.

A grooming kit of dog includes a chambered box or stand containing a clean and soft towel, dandy brush, long bristled brush, short bristled brush, common combs with fine and coarse teeth, the antiseptic lotion. Grooming should be a routine practice at a fixed place away from the living rooms and kitchen, preferably in the back varandah or garage. First large-sized extraneous objects should be hand-picked from the hair. The dust is removed by a dandy brush or coat brush. Hair is then combed to extract external parasites, if any. In the end, the body is wiped with a clean and soft towel gently starting from the face and ending at the feet-pads. The anus, vulva (in female) and prepuce (in male) should be cleaned with a piece of soft cloth soaked in a mild antiseptic lotion.

WASHING/BATHING

Washing of dogs is required to keep the skin and coat clean. The frequency of washing should be determined on the basis of breed, exposure of dogs to the outer environment and season. Daily washing and frequent bathing should be avoided. On an average bathing once a month or once a fortnight is quite satisfactory. The temperature of the water should be according to the environmental temperature. A toilet soap or human shampoo is good enough for the pets. One should not bother much if dog soap and shampoo are not available easily in the market. If the dog is infested with ectoparasites, it should be washed carefully with a shampoo containing an insecticide. The dog should be rinsed thoroughly with ample clean water and wiped dry with a clean towel. Precautions should be taken to protect the dog from chill during winter and warm water should be used for washing in an enclosed place. The dog should not be let loose when wet because most of the dogs roll on the ground after washing.

CARE OF FACE

Care of face involves daily cleaning of mouth, gum, teeth, nose, eyes and ears. For cleaning the face a set of 6 linen pieces of 15 cm × 20 cm and 2 small towels are required. These should be kept clean. Normally operation of face cleaning starts from the mouth. The lips, angle of mouth, gum, teeth and nose are gently cleaned with one wet piece of cloth. The second piece is used for the cleaning of eyelids and the inner and outer canthus of eyes. A mild boric acid lotion or other antiseptic eye-lotion may be used in case there is unusual thick mucoid deposit on the edges of eyelids. The third cloth piece is used for wiping the inner surface of the ear. At the end face is wiped with a moist towel, and the dog becomes fresh and active. This exercise also provides opportunity for the detection of a disorder, injury or other ailment on the face. A weekly mouth wash along with the cleaning of teeth with a pinch of finely powdered common salt may keep the gum and teeth healthy. Some tooth pastes are also available for the dogs but their use has little benefit when dogs are taken to clinic for annual check up and removal of excess tartar deposit on the teeth.

CARE OF CLAWS, DEW-CLAW AND FEET

Dew-claws are considered unnecessary and removed at a very young age of about a week. Nail cutting is normally not required in the working dogs put to adequate exercise but is usually required in toy breeds. Foot-pads and inter-toe grooves should be cleaned and checked thoroughly at the time of grooming for thorns, injuries and tick infestation.

HAIR DRESSING

Hair dressing is becoming popular among the long hair breeds. Lady owners often like hair cut and dressing of their dogs in different styles. In some advanced countries dog's hair dressing salloons have become quite popular. Minor hair dressing includes clipping or plucking of extraneous hair for making the coat smooth in appearance.

USE OF DEODORANTS

Since dogs live in the house as a part of the family, especially the companion dogs, it is desirable to reduce the characteristic dog odour through the use of common deodorants used by the human being.

DOCKING OF TAILS

Amputation of tail as per the breed requirement for registration in the kennel or due to clinical reason is known as docking of the tail. The operation is very simple and normally performed at a very young age with the help of a docking scissor under local anaesthesia. Antiseptic dressing is required for 5-7 days for complete healing of the uncomplicated operations performed before one week of age. (For details see chapter 13).

TRAINING OF DOGS

Pet dogs are kept for company, pleasure, guarding and guiding, etc. Untrained pet dogs may not understand the situation for action, which may annoy the master, his guests, neighbours and others. Therefore, it is important to impart necessary training to pets for proper behaviour and execution of instructions. Training of dog is a complex exercise and requires the trainer (master) to have immense patience.

Requirements of a Good Trainer

A good dog trainer should know dog's psychology, be firm, kind and serious but gentle. He should be wise with immense patience, be consistent but considerate, punctual and practical.

Requirements of Owner/Master

It is necessary for the owners to acquire some knowledge about the normal and abnormal behaviour of dogs, their temperament and psychology. Otherwise one may expect too much from his dog. The owner should develop patience and should try to develop most of the qualities of dog trainers.

Common Terminology of Dog Training

1. Training	The procedure of infusing obedience, cleanliness and reliability
2. Breaking	To make the dog perfect through regular and repeated practice for responding to instructions given orally, by signals and whistles or by eyes
3. Command of instruction	The known stimuli from owner expecting appropriate response
4. Collar	A leather or good plastic strap fastened round the neck. It contains a metallic ring for joining the lead (Fig. 85 a, b, c).
5. Lead	A strong cord of silk, plastic or leather or a metallic chain (Fig. 86).
6. Sit down	Instruction for sitting (Fig. 87)
7. Get up	Instruction for rising
8. Come on	Instruction for calling. The dog should be called by name, viz. come on Tony
9. Carry	Instruction for carrying an object holding with teeth. Food should be avoided
10. Fetch	Instruction for finding an object thrown away before the dog, e.g. to fetch a ball thrown in the lawn.

Short commands or instructions should preferably be used for dogs.

Training Schedule

The training syllabus of dog should start from organizing natural urges like hunger, urination, defaecation, rest and housing. This should be followed by training for obedience and then specialized training for guarding, house breaking, search and seizure, etc. The training should be divided into several lessons and different courses may be followed for the training of dogs for specialized purposes. In this chapter, essential obedience training for house dogs has been briefly described.

Practice to call name by natural urges: Natural urges include hunger, thirst, urination and defaecation.

(i) The dog should be given a single name on arrival in the house.

(ii) The place for feeding and watering should normally be fixed.

(iii) Fix places for urination and defaecation; the dog should not be allowed to urinate or defaecate at any other place in the house or yard. Dogs normally defaecate immediately after awaking and eating or drinking.

(iv) Practice to come back when called.

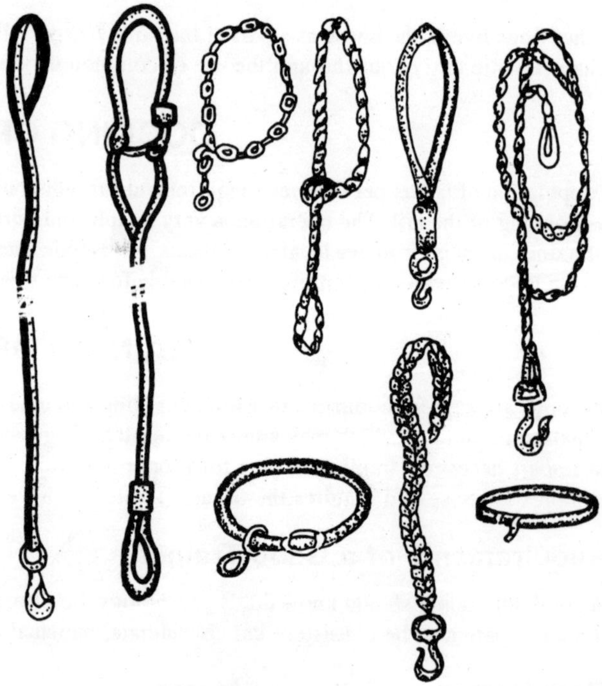

Fig. 85a Various types of collar and lead for dog

Training for obedience: The dog should be taught to understand the common instruction by practice like sitting down, lying down, getting up, go fetch, bark and lift fore-limbs (Figs 88, 89, 90).

PLATE-21

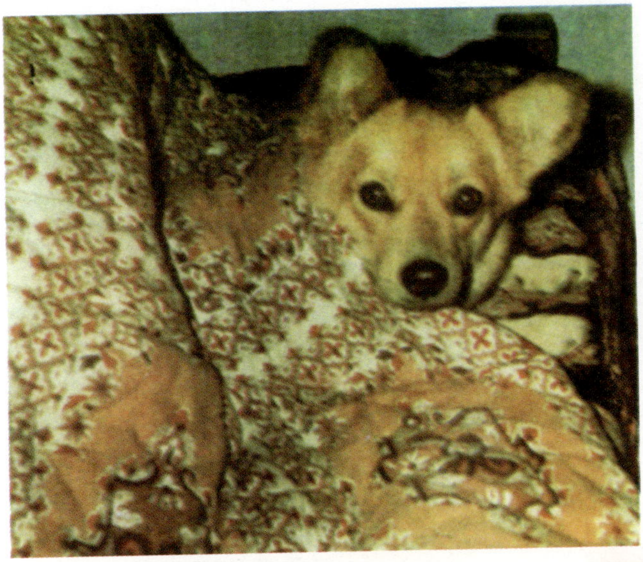

Fig. 84. (a) Bedding during cold

Fig. 86. (a) Showing lead

Fig. 86. (b) Showing lead

Fig. 84. (b) Bedding during summer

Fig. 85. (b) Showing metal collar

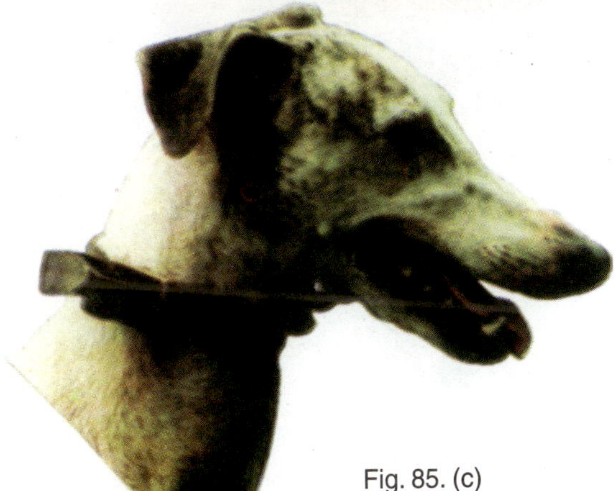

Fig. 85. (c)
Showing leather collar

PLATE-22

Fig. 87. Dog obeying order for sitting

Fig. 88. Dog obeying order for standing

Fig. 89. Dog responding order for barking

Fig. 90. Dog obeying order for lifting forelimbs

Training for collar and lead: A good-quality collar should be harnessed on the pet dog. A tag in the collar may bear the name of dog and address. A leather cord makes a good lead and does not inconvenience the owner when the dog is taken for a walk.

Training for guarding and barking: Dogs should be given ample practice for barking when strangers are likely to present at the door, or trespass.

Some Points to be Observed Carefully

(i) Good response should be appreciated.
(ii) Unruly behaviour should be punished appropriately and immediately.
(iii) Training should be gradual and too many instructions should not be given at a time.
(iv) The dog should not be allowed loose lead walking and it should walk parallel to or behind the master.
(v) Special care should be taken to avoid misbehaviour which is expected in the breeding season.

Detection of Hidden Objects

Certain breeds of dogs can detect hidden objects and are extremely useful in crime detection. The dogs are able to detect about 80% of the wooden objects, 67% of the metal objects and 60% of glass objects. In still air they can detect 84% of the objects, in still air but not enclosed 59% and in air in motion 51%.

REGISTRATION OF PETS

Each dog must be registered as per the rules and provisions of the Kennel Club of India. Dog lovers/owners should make it a point to get their dog registered with the municipalities/corporations, etc. and receive a licence from the registration body. Sometimes licence may be needed for medico-legal, dog show and other purposes. The licence should be renewed as per the rules of the registering body. It is also required for the identification of the dog during transportation and theft, etc.

TRANSPORTATION

Transportation of pet dogs may pose problems. The owners should know about the important aspects of the dog transport problems. Inland dog transportation is easier and does not pose serious problems. However, it is important to take the following precautions:

1. The dog should be protected against rabies.
2. It should be secured properly.
3. The dog should be muzzled while being carried in public transport like a bus and shared taxi.
4. The dog transported by train, ship and plane should be muzzled and mildly tranquilized if aggressive. It should be secured with a collar and chain and bear a number and address tag. The muzzle should be loose enough to allow drinking and feeding but protect from biting.
5. It is better to train the dog for housing in a wire-gauze cage for transportation in a similar cage.
6. The dog should be fed a light meal containing more meat and less fibre. This reduces the number of defaecation and thus soiling of the carriage for a reasonable period.

5

CLINICAL DIAGNOSIS

For the systematic treatment of any disease it is essential to diagnose the disease. Diagnosis is a complex of science and art, and in the case of pets special skill is required. Satisfaction of owner is equally important for proper treatment. The clinical examination of a dog should be carried in the clinic or on the examination table as far as possible in the presence of the owner. While examining the patient it is important to continue the queries with the owner regarding the occurrence of the disease and behavioural changes observed during sickness. For the proper diagnosis of a disease condition the clinician must be well versed with the behaviour and common ailments of dogs. This chapter provides a guideline in progressive order for the clinical examination and diagnosis of the disease, which includes general examination, signs of diseases, causes of diseases, clinical examination of the dog and recording of history by direct and indirect questions in a calm manner pacifying the owner. Detailed methods of laboratory diagnosis of faeces, blood, urine, skin scrapings and cerebrospinal fluid are also given for the biochemical and microscopic examination.

Health may be defined as the normal condition of the animal, viz., morphology, physiological functions and behaviour. A deviation from the normal morphological and physiological conditions of the animal is termed as diseased condition. A dog which is diseased is usually dull and depressed except in the case of an irritable disease. It prefers isolation and takes no interest in routine activities. Its nose is dry and the mucous membranes are pale and dry. The body and hair coat may be dull; often various degrees of inappetance and abnormal urination and defaecation may be noticed. The pulse, temperature, respiration and behaviour may be abnormal and the animal may exhibit pain. In most of the stress conditions, eyes appear drowsy.

The diseases in dogs may be hereditary, metabolic, or due to physical injuries, chemical and biological causes. The diseases due to biological causes are:

(i) viral,
(ii) bacterial,
(iii) rickettsial,
(iv) mycotic,
(v) protozoal,
(vi) ectoparasitic, and
(vii) endoparasitic:
  (a) roundworms,
  (b) flat worms, and
  (c) tapeworms.

The clinical examination of a sick dog involves the following sequence:

Registration of the patient and issue of the 'Treatments record card' to the owner. The card should contain the serial number of the patient register, date of entry, name of the owner and a brief description of the sick animal.

Interview with the owner for information regarding the history of the illness. The discussion should start in a pleasing manner and the veterinary doctor should try to pacify the worried owner of the sick dog before enquiring about the sickness. The enquiry generally includes questions to collect information about the time of commencement of the illness, signs of illness observed by the owner, behavioural changes observed by the owner, food and drinks offered during the last 24 hours, and any other aspect arising out of the discussions with the owner.

Clinical examination includes 4 steps, viz. general inspection, palpation, percussion and auscultation.

Laboratory examination of biological materials collected from the sick animal, viz. blood, serum and plasma, faeces, urine, nasal discharge, sputum, vaginal discharge, skin scrapings, cerebro-spinal fluid, and pus exudate.

Treatment: Symptomatic treatment is started as early as possible depending on the requirement of the sickness. Treatment after receiving the results of laboratory examinations includes cause-specific therapy. Supportive treatment involves fluid therapy, nutritional therapy, physical treatment, etc. It is important for the clinician to know the response to his treatment and also modifications in treatment schedule, if necessary.

CLINICAL EXAMINATION OF DOG

Normally, the dog should be examined in the presence of the owner as it enables easier handling of the dog. Interim enquiries, if any, may be made with the owner and some instructions regarding care and management may be given immediately.

As indicated earlier, the clinical examinations of dog are completed in the following sequence:

General inspection: General inspection reveals the deviation in physical appearance and behavioural changes in the dog, which may be useful in diagnosing some of the diseases. It is normally carried out from a distance of 1.5-2 m. It involves the following observations:

(a) General appearance
(b) Posture
(c) Gait
(d) Appearance of the body coat
(e) Behaviour
(f) Temperament (especially dullness or aggression)
(g) Colour of external mucous membranes
(h) Discharge from natural orifices like eyes, nose, ears and genital organs (particularly vaginal discharge in females)
(i) Responsiveness and
(j) Any other abnormalities.

Palpation: The animal should be secured properly and muzzle tape should be tied before the inspection of dog by palpation. The veterinarian is required to approach the dog gently and quietly. The suspected and adjoining parts should be inspected by light pressure for pain, swelling, oedema, haematoma and bone injuries. The affected part may be doughy as in the case of oedema, firm like liver, hard like bone, fluctuating or emphysematous. The organs can be inspected either,

(i) By direct palpation with the help of fingers, palm and fist, or

(ii) By indirect palpation using a probe.

Percussion: It involves the inspection of suspected parts by striking for the development of vibrations emitting characteristic or abnormal sounds. It may be;

(i) Immediate percussion by striking with fingers or wooden/metallic hammer,

(ii) Mediate percussion by putting the palm or fingers of one hand on the affected body part and striking by the fingers of another hand, and

(iii) Tactile percussion by combining palpation and percussion. Most clinicians find this a more informative and useful method.

Auscultation: Recording of sounds of visceral organs is called auscultation. It may be either;

(i) Direct by putting ear in the chest region for hearing the sounds of heart and lungs, or

(ii) Mediate auscultation with the help of stethoscope. The patient should not be disturbed and there should be no friction due to clothes between the body and chest piece of the stethoscope.

Area of percussion and auscultation of thoracic region: Percussion and auscultation are normally used for the examination of thoracic organs, i.e. heart and lungs. The area of thoracic region may be demarcated by the following 3 lines:

1. ***Dorsal (upper) line:*** An imaginary line extending from the posterior angle of scapula up to the tuber coxae parallel to the transverse process of vertebrae is the dorsal line.

2. ***Cranial (anterior) line:*** It extends from the caudal angle of scapula along with the caudal border of the triceps muscle to the olecranon process.

3. ***Ventral (basal) line:*** It runs from the olecranon process to intersect the dorsal line near the last few ribs. Normally it passes through the base of the 6th rib to the middle of the 8th rib, ending near the origin of the 11th rib in the dorsal line.

Area of heart percussion: It extends from the bottom of thorax to the 4th and 5th costo-chondral joints and a little lower in the 6th inter-costal space. The heart area is more prominent on the left side.

Area of liver percussion: Liver is normally situated in the upper third area of the thoracic region of percussion on the right side. It is situated in the abdominal cavity on the right aspect of the stomach. The area is also used for liver biopsy.

Area of lung percussion: Almost the entire thoracic area of percussion, extending on either side dorsal from the posterior angle of scapula to the angle of ilium, is used for the percussion of lungs.

Area of heart auscultation: The area for the auscultation of heart is more effective near the olecranon process. The aortic valve is generally present at the level of 4th intercostal space just below the shoulder. The pulmonary valve is present at the level of 3rd intercostal space on left side just above the sternum. The left auriculo-ventricular valve area is limited to the left 5th intercostal space at the level of the costo-chondral junction and the right one is in the 3rd or 4th right intercostal space between the olecranon process and costo-chondral junction.

Area of lung ausculation: The entire area of percussion on the thoracic region may be used for the auscultation of lungs which is an extensive observation covering the areas of both lungs.

Temperature, pulse rate and respiration rate: The normal temperature (rectal temperature) is 101°-102° F (38.3°-39° C), pulse rate 50-112 per minute and respiration rate 15-25 per minute. These values may be unusually low or high in some normal individuals and in some breeds, viz. normal pulse rate of Beagle dogs may be 45 to 220 (average 112) per minute. Pulse rate is recorded with the help of the thumb and fingers gently pressed on the femoral artery for 30 seconds or 1 minute as per the co-operation of the patient.

LABORATORY DIAGNOSIS

FAECAL EXAMINATION

Collection: The sample should invariably be collected directly from the animals. In small animals such as dog and cat, the faeces should be collected with the help of index finger from the rectum. If the faeces is not available, a simple lukewarm water enema may be given. This is not generally used because the dilution may affect proper interpretation. In case the sample is collected from the outside of the animal, it should be fresh, free from mud, dirt and other foreign materials. If the sample is to be collected from the soil, only a middle portion should be taken. Sample should be picked up with a wooden spatula and may be kept in discarded cups or any other suitable container not made of absorbant material.

Storage: Keep the faecal sample in a refrigerator if it is to be examined some time after collection. The material except where lungworms are suspected, can be preserved in 10% formalin.

Examination: Faecal samples can be examined by two methods.

Gross examination: It is done by naked eyes to obtain the following information:

(a) Colour of faeces,
(b) Consistency and form of the faeces like normal, hard and loose,
(c) Presence of blood,
(d) Adult parasite,
(e) Segments of parasite,
(f) Eggs (Fig. 91),
(g) Any other foreign material.

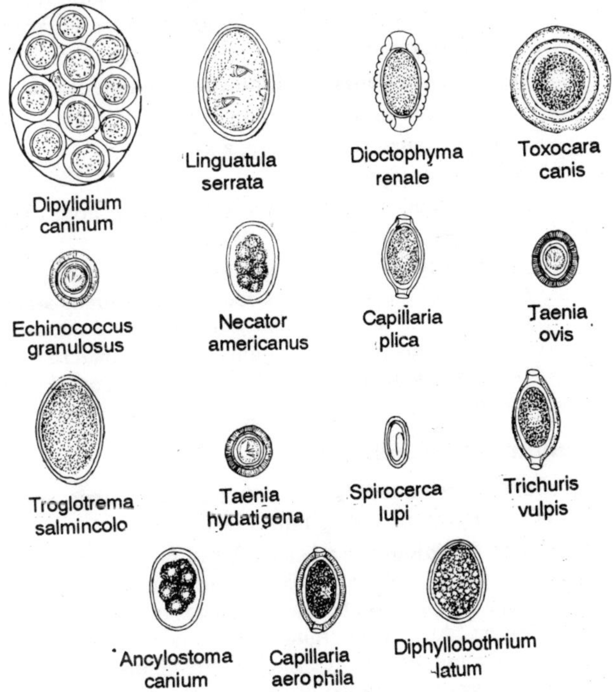

Fig. 91 Eggs of parasites of the dog

Microscopic examination: It can be done by the following methods:

Qualitative Examination

(a) ***Direct smear:*** A small quantity of faeces mixed with a drop of water, is placed on a slide, mixed uniformly with the help of either a smooth glass-rod, tooth-pick or match-stick and is covered with cover-slip. The slide is examined under a low-power microscope. The whole mass should be examined. At least 3 slides from different parts of the faecal sample should be examined. This method is suitable for very rapid examination, but usually fails to detect low-grade infection.

(b) ***Concentration method (Floatation method):*** This is done by Will's technique and is mainly based on the principle of floating the eggs or larvae of parasites due to gravity. The procedure is as follows:

(i) About 1 ml of mixed sample of faeces is taken.
(ii) This is diluted with 10-20 ml of concentrated salt solution in a suitable narrow cylinder filled to the top with the liquid.
(iii) A clean slide or cover-glass is put over the top of the cylinder so it can make contact with the liquid. There should be no air bubbles between the slide or cover-glass and the salt solution.

(iv) After 30-45 minutes the slide or cover-glass is removed and examined under a low-power microscope.

This method is not suitable for eggs of trematodes and most cestodes but is good for the majority of nematode eggs in a simple sugar solution instead of salt solution.

(c) ***Centrifugal floatation:*** This method saves time and is more accurate. The procedure is as follows:

(i) About 15-30 mg of stirred faeces is taken and mixed with about 500 ml water.
(ii) This is strained through a sieve of 1 mm or a set of sieves with mesh ranging from 3 mm to 0.25 mm.
(iii) The mixture is left to sediment for 10-15 minutes and the supernatant fluid poured off until the sediment is about to flow out. This is repeated until the supernatant is clear.
(iv) The sediment is shaken and sample poured into a centrifuge tube and mixed with an equal volume of glycerine.
(v) This is centrifuged at about 1,000 r.p.m. for 1-2 minutes. The eggs will be floating on top.
(vi) The eggs are removed by touching the surface with the end of a glass rod and transferred to a slide for examination.

Instead of glycerine the following solution can also be used:

(i) A concentrated solution of sugar (0.6 kg to 1 kg of water),
(ii) Saturated salt solution, and
(iii) Zinc sulphate.

This method may not show eggs of trematodes but this can be found useful if a heavy water-glass solution is used instead of glycerine.

(d) ***Simple floatation:*** A small amount of faecal sample is taken in a glass-beaker and mixed well with sugar solution with a glass-rod. The mixture is strained through a funnel fitted with a gauze piece into a test-tube to the brim. The solution should not spill over. The test-tube should be allowed to stand in a vertical position for 30 minutes. Some material is taken by putting the slide over it or by putting the plunger straight on the top and removing it quickly. The sample should be examined under a low-power microscope.

Quantitative Technique

Egg counting techniques help to obtain more accurate information on the severity of infection. The number of eggs per gram faeces is determined as follows:

Mc Master technique: In a beaker 2 g of faecal sample is taken and 28 ml of water is added and mixed. In a test-tube 1 ml of mixture is placed and 1 ml of saturated salt solution is added and mixed. After thorough shaking, the sample is withdrawn by means of a wide (8 mm) pipette and run into the counting chamber, filling all the spaces. After a few minutes eggs rise to the top, and are in focus against the upper slide. The cell is placed on the microscope and the eggs are counted within each ruled area. This is multiplied by 200 to get the number of eggs per g in the original sample.

Stoll's dilution method: In a test-tube 3 g of faeces is taken. This is dissolved in 45 ml of decinormal caustic soda solution and 10 to 20 glass-beads are added. The test-tube is shaken to give a homogenous suspension of the faecal material. As soon as possible after shaking, 0.15 ml of the well-mixed suspension is drawn off with a pipette graduated to show this amount and placed on a slide. This is covered with a coverslip. The eggs in all the fields are counted under low-power microscope. This is multiplied with 100 to get the total number of eggs per gram of faeces.

Examination for flukes: The eggs of flukes are heavy and do not float on top of the solution used in floatation techniques. The following method can be used for the examination of flukes.

Faeces is taken in a test-tube and mixed thoroughly with tap-water. The sediment is allowed to settle down and the supernatant discarded. The above steps are repeated at least twice and the supernatant discarded. A small amount of sediment is placed on a glass-slide. This is covered with a cover-slip and examined under a low-power microscope.

Examination of Blood in Faeces: In a test-tube, 5 ml of saturated solution of benzidine base (Merk) in glacial acetic acid is taken and 5 ml of hydrogen peroxide solution is added to it. In another test-tube 5 ml of the above-mixed solution is taken and 5-10 drops of the faecal suspension prepared in distilled water is added to it. If blue colour is developed, it indicates the presence of blood in the faecal material.

Culture of Faeces for Nematode Larvae

As specific diagnosis cannot always be made from eggs that hatch in free form, the stool should not be too wet or dry. If it is too wet, then sterilized and dried faeces of sheep may be added. If it is too dry, the faeces should be moistened with water. For proper culture of faeces the fresh faeces should be mixed thoroughly with an equal amount of charcoal and moistened if necessary, to form a damp but not wet, crumbly mixture. This is stored on filter-paper in a covered container (glass-jar) at room temperature (25°-30°C) for 5-8 days for growth of larvae to the desired stage; moisture content is maintained by adding water if necessary. The larvae are separated by a needle or soft brush for examination in a drop of water on a slide. It is advisable to kill the larvae by heating carefully over a low flame until movements cease and the worm lies fully extended.

Those larvae which do not migrate should be separated by means of Baermann technique.

Baermann technique: A glass funnel 20 cm in width at the top, and closed at the bottom end, attached with a clamped piece of rubber tubing, is taken and placed securely in a stand. A round piece of wire-gauze 9 cm in diameter of hardware cloth is put in the funnel. On the top of it a piece of linen, double the thickness of gauze and a size larger than the circular wire is placed. The incubated faeces is spread 2 cm deep on the linen, and lukewarm water (40° C) poured down the side of the funnel until the faeces is covered. The apparatus is left as such for some hours. When the larvae are noticed a few millilitres of water is drawn off from the bottom. By this method the larvae can be separated from the soil. It is very useful for this purpose too. If more magnification is needed, the larvae should be transferred to a glass-microscope slide, cover-slip applied and examined. If necessary, heat should be applied to inactivate them.

Separation of Free-living and Parasitic Nematode Larvae

While using the Baermann apparatus, nematode larvae should be collected from the contaminated samples. In dog, often faeces have free-living nematodes as well as parasitic ones. The parasitic forms may be separated from free-living nematodes by using a solution of 1 ml of concentrated hydrochloric acid added to 30 ml of water. The larvae should be transferred from the Baermann apparatus into this solution. All stages of the free-living nematodes will be destroyed almost instantly, but the parasitic forms will survive for a few minutes to as long as 24 hours.

Sporulation of Coccidian Oocysts

For identifying coccidia, sometimes it is necessary to retain them till they develop (sporulation to the infective stage). A fresh sample of faeces is taken and mixed with several volumes of 2.5% potassium dichromate solution. A thin layer of this mixture is transferred to petri-dishes or some other glass containers. Oxygen is a necessity for oocyst development. Potassium dichromate prevents the bacteria from finishing up the oxygen supply or the destruction of the oocysts. Thus, the layer of fluid must not be more than a few millimetres thick. If masses of oocysts are cultured in deep containers, an aquarium pump may be used to aerate the medium. Sporulation will occur in a few days to week's time, depending upon the conditions and the species. The oocysts for sporulation can be kept for an indefinite period in a closed container and properly refrigerated.

Preparation of Specimens from Faeces for Examination

Adult Helminths: Adult worms recovered from the faeces are washed in warm sodium chloride solution with prolonged shaking to promote relaxation, and are then examined fresh or are killed by fixing in solutions in toto or for sectioning. For large nematodes, 5 to 10 per cent formalin at 80°C with a small amount of glycerol makes a good fixative and preservative. Specimens may be left in the formalin or stored in 70 per cent alcohol after transfer through graded alcohols. Small nematodes may be fixed in warm 70 per cent alcohol and preserved in the same solution. Trematodes and the proglottids of cestodes may be examined by pressing them between slides or after relaxation of chilling in a refrigerator.

Proglottids may be cleared somewhat by mounting in 5 per cent acetic acid to dissolve the calcareous corpuscles or by gradually adding glycerine. They may also be cleared after a brief preservation in 70 per cent alcohol by immersion in carbolxylol (70 per cent carbolic acid, 25 per cent xylol), or dehydration in 95 per cent alcohol, 100 per cent alcohol, and immersion in oil of wintergreen. If the uterus of the proglottid is empty of eggs identification is different. A method for demonstrating the branches of the uterus is to inject India ink into the central uterine stem using a 1 to 2 ml hypodermic syringe with a 3/4 cm, 25-gauze needle. After injection, wash off excess ink on surface and press proglottid between slides. This is very satisfactory with fresh or relaxed proglottids. It may also be used on proglottids already fixed in alcohol.

Searching for the small scolices, scarcely larger than a pinhead, is a tedious but necessary task in checking the results of anthelmintic treatment of tapeworms. All post-treatment stools should be collected and washed through a 20-mesh screen.

Cysts and eggs in unconcentrated faeces: The examination for protozoan trophozoites and cysts, and helminth eggs and larvae may be made with fresh material or with fixed stained preparations. In fluid and semifluid faeces, bloody mucus or tiny specks of tissue should be selected, and in formalized faeces material should be scraped from the surface in several parts of the faecal mass.

Iodine and supravital staining: The treatment of fresh cover-glass mounts with iodine or supravital staining acids in differentiating protozoa. The iodine mount, which may be made on the same slide as the plain mount, is useful for the examination of cysts and eggs, but the trophozcites are killed. The chromatin material of amoebic cysts stands out in relief against the yellow-brown cytoplasm, the nuclear structures are differentiated, and the glycogen masses stain a mahogany brown. Iodine solutions of various strengths can be used. Equal quantities of 1 per cent isotonic eosin solution and 0.2 per cent brilliant cresyl blue added to a cover-glass preparation of faeces provide a satisfactory vital stain, the active trophozoites appearing as clear, translucent, shiny, pale-blue-green objects against a pink background.

Fixation and staining: The merthiolate-iodine-formaldehyde (MIF) fixative stain is a valuable asset in preserving specimens of faeces containing intestinal protozoa and helminth eggs intact for later laboratory examination. It is useful in preserving specimens in survey studies, in mailing faecal material to the laboratory, and in collecting large numbers for teaching purposes or for concentration procedures. The ordinary loss and deterioration of organisms in stools that are allowed to stand may be prevented by placing the faecal specimens in the fixative within 5 minutes after passage. The fixative stain consists of 2 solutions, which are combined just prior to the preservation of faeces. They are merthiolate-formaldehyde (MF) and Lugol's iodine.

Merthiolate-formaldehyde: Tincture of merthiolate (1 : 1,000), 200 ml; formaldehyde, U.S.P., 25 ml; glycerol, 5 ml; distilled water, 250 ml.

Lugol's iodine: Iodine, 5 g; potassium iodide, 10 g; distilled water, 100 ml.

For bulk faeces, the solutions are mixed in the proportion of 9.4 ml MF and 0.6 ml Lugol's for each gram of faeces, and in proportionate volumes for lesser amounts. The faecal material is added with an applicator and mixed thoroughly. The preserved material will keep for a year in tight-fitting bottles. Screw-top vials are convenient. The Lugol's solution should not be over 3 weeks old; if over 1 week, it should be increased by 25 per cent, and if over 2 weeks by 50 per cent. For examination, a drop of the surface layer of the sedimented faeces is removed to a glass-slide, the particles of faeces mixed, and a cover-glass applied. The staining reaction comprises an initial iodine-staining phase and a subsequent eosin stage that gradually replaces the iodine. Trophozoites stain immediately, but cysts respond more slowly. For floatation concentration, the supernatant fluid in the vial containing the bulk preparation is replaced with a brine solution and the usual procedure is followed. For fresh faecal specimens brought to the laboratory, a drop of distilled water is placed on a slide and an equal amount of MIF solution is added. A small fleck of faeces is thoroughly mixed, and the preparation is mounted with a cover-glass for examination.

Permanent and preserved mounts: Permanent mounts permit species differentiation through detailed study of structures and ensure material for demonstration or reference. This method requires fixation and staining. The method of choice is wet fixation, which causes less distortion of the parasites than dry fixation. The thin moist undried smear on a cover-glass or slide is immersed in the fixing solution. Material that contains no albuminous matter should be mixed with serum or smeared upon a slide coated with egg albumen to make it adhere. Schaudinn's sublimate solution and its various modifications are satisfactory fixatives. Canada balsam is also an excellent mounting medium which is commonly used for mounting purpose.

Polyvinyl alcohol fixation: Polyvinyl alcohol added to Schaudinn's solution is a good fixative, adhesive and preservative for protozoa in dysenteric faeces and other liquid material. The powdered polyvinyl alcohol should be added with continuous stirring to the solution at 75°C. It remains satisfactory for use for several months.

Polyvinyl alcohol fixing material is prepared by mixing Schaudinn's fluid (2 parts saturated aqueous solution of $HgCl_2$ to 1 part 95% ethyl alcohol) 93.5 ml; glycerol, 1.5 ml; glacial acetic acid, 5.0 ml; polyvinyl alcohol, powdered, 5.0 g.

One part of the faecal suspension may be mixed with 3 parts of the fixing solution in a vial. Smears may be prepared immediately or months later by spreading a drop or two of the mixture on a slide and then drying thoroughly at 37°C overnight. Relatively thin rectangular smears should be made to prevent wrinkling. The films may be stained by the long or rapid Heidenhaim iron-hematoxylin procedures. Before staining, the dried films should be placed in 70 per cent alcohol containing iodine to remove the mercuric chloride.

Permanent stains: There are many methods of staining faecal smears. Those that produce the best results are usually the longest and most complicated. The iron-hematoxylin method with its numerous modifications to increase the rapidity of the process is the classic method of staining protozoa in fixed preparations.

Permanent mount staining methods of Lawless provide a rapid method of staining trophozoites and cysts. The protozoa appear blue to purplish. The fixative stain remains stable for 6 months, if kept in tightly stoppered brown bottles. This stain is prepared by mixing saturated solution of mercuric chloride in water, 594 ml; alcohol (95%), 296 ml; glacial acetic acid, 50 ml; acetone, 50 ml; formaldehyde, USP, 10 ml; acid fuchsin, 1.25 g; fast green FCF, 0.50 g.

The staining solution is transferred with a pipette in sufficient quantity to cover the moist, faecal film. This is heated over a flame till steaming but should not be boiled. It is then washed gently in tap-water and drained. Then it is passed through 50 and 70% alcohols, 30 seconds each; and through 95 and 100% alcohol 15 seconds each; after which it is cleared in xylol for 1 minute and mounted in balsam or clarite.

Wheatley's modification of Gomori's trichrome stain gives a rapid method for staining of intestinal protozoa. The stain is prepared by mixing: chromotrope 2R, 0.6 g; light green SF, 0.3 g; phosphotungstic acid, 0.7 g; glacial acetic acid, 1 ml; distilled water, 100 ml.

The acetic acid is added to the dry ingredients, allowed to stand 15 to 30 minutes then distilled water is added. Good stain is purple.

Procedure: A thin, moist faecal smear is placed in Schaudinn's fixative for 10 minutes as follows:

Faeces is stained for 8-15 minutes and then rinsed in the following sequence: in 70% alcohol with iodine (amber colour) for 2 minutes; 50% of alcohol for 2 minutes; 70% alcohol for 2 minutes; 90% alcohol with 1% acetic acid for 10-20 seconds; and in 100% alcohol mixed twice. After this the slide is dipped in xylol for 1 minute or until clear. It is mounted with synthetic mounting medium — permount or harleco synthetic resin.

BLOOD EXAMINATION

Collection and Storage of Blood Sample

The blood can be collected conveniently from the cephalic and recurrent tarsal veins in small animals. A small amount may be drawn from ear-vein also. The anticoagulant may be put in the blood-collecting vials before hand.

Cephalic vein: In long-haired breeds hair should be clipped at the anterior surface of the forelimb over the cephalic vein. It is not needed in short-haired breeds. The area should be disinfected with spirit or 70% alcohol. The vein should be raised either with the help of an assistant or by applying tourniquet around the elbow. The skin over cephalic vein may be tensed with the help of the left hand and the thumb of the left hand put on the left side of the vein to fix the vein properly. Before inserting the needle, the vein should be felt with the help of finger and blood collected with the help of 20 or 22 gauge needle attached with a syringe. The needle should be inserted from the right side of the vein and stopped for a moment after penetrating skin and subcutaneous tissue. The needle should be inserted in the vein when a click-like noise is heard to collect the required amount of blood. After taking the blood, pressure on the vein should be released and some antiseptic should be applied. After removing the needle from the syringe, blood should be stored in a vial.

Recurrent tarsal vein: In this technique, blood is collected from the hind leg; pressure is applied on the stiffle joint and the needle inserted on the external side of the hock joint where the vein takes a round. The remaining procedure is the same as in the case of cephalic vein.

Ear-vein: Only a small amount of blood (1-2 ml) can be collected by this route. Ear-vein is situated on the dorsal aspect of the ear. First, the hair should be clipped with a pair of scissors and the area sterilized with spirit. The vein may be made prominent by applying pressure with the index finger and thumb. The vein must be felt with a finger before inserting the needle inside the vein. After blood collection, the vein should be pressed for 1 minute and then rubbed with a swab of spirit.

Storage of blood samples: The blood should be examined within 1-3 hours of collection. It should be properly mixed by rotating the vials to prevent clotting. If the sample cannot be examined immediately, it may be stored in the refrigerator up to 24 hours. The blood samples should be kept at room temperature at least for 30 minutes before doing the haematological examination and it must be properly mixed. Where refrigeration facilities are not available, the sample may be stored in an ice-box.

Anticoagulants: For haematological examination, un-coagulated blood is required. The following, anticoagulants can be used to prevent coagulation of blood.

(i) ***EDTA:*** EDTA (Sodium salt of Ethylene Di-aminetetra Acetic Acid) is one of the best anticoagulants suitable for haematological examination. It is used @ 1 mg/ml of blood. This anticoagulant is also marketed in the form of tablets. One tablet is sufficient per 5 ml of blood samples.

(ii) ***Sodium fluoride:*** It is best for blood chemistry, particularly for blood glucose estimation. It may be used @ 10 mg/ml of blood.

(iii) ***Ammonium and potassium oxalate (combined):*** This anticoagulant is commonly used for haemoglobin estimation, and R.B.C. and W.B.C. counts and haematocrit values. About 1 ml (6 g ammonium oxalate and 4 g potassium oxalate dissolved in 0.5 litre of distilled water) of anticoagulant solution is sufficient for 10 ml of blood. It is also available in the form of tablets. One tablet is required for 5 ml of blood.

(iv) ***Lithium oxalate:*** It is required when NPN (non-protein nitrogen) and BUN (blood urea nitrogen) estimations are to be done. The amount required is 1.5 mg/ml of blood.

(v) ***Heparin:*** Though costly, it is very useful for TLC, TEC, ESR and PCV, and also for the estimation of BUN and electrolytes. It is used in the form of 1 per cent solution @ 0.1 μl (1,000 μ)/100 ml of blood.

(vi) ***Sodium citrate:*** In addition to haematological examination, it can also be used during blood transfusion. It is prepared by adding 3.8 g of sodium citrate to 100 ml of distilled water. For 10 ml of blood 0.1 ml of solution is required.

Microscopic Examination of Blood

Microscopic examination of blood has great importance in the clinical diagnosis of the disease. In modern laboratories and clinics, regular haematological examination is conducted to arrive at a definite diagnosis before attempting treatment. Following parameters are taken for routine laboratory studies:

Differential Leucocytic Count (DLC): Examination of the blood smear required for presence of blood protozoa and microfilariae. Emphasis is given for diagnosis of diseases like babesiasis, trypanosomiasis, leishmaniasis and microfilariasis. Some of the septicaemic bacterial diseases like leptospirosis are also diagnosed by examination of the blood smear.

Determination of total erythrocyte (RBC).

Determination of total leukocyte (WBC).

Preparation of Blood Smear

Intact blood smear: The smear should always be prepared from fresh blood immediately after drawing the blood from the vein. Oxalated blood may also be used but it should be used within 20 minutes of blood collection. A small drop of the blood is taken on a clean non-greasy slide and a thin layer is made with the help of another smooth-edged slide and the smear dried by waving in the air.

Haemolysed blood smear: Distilled water (1-2 drops) should be added to 1 ml of blood before preparing the blood smear. This type of blood smear is very useful particularly in detecting the microfilariae in the blood.

Fixation of blood smear: The smear should be fixed with methyl alcohol (acetone free) for 4 minutes and dried in the air.

Staining: The following stains can be used.

Leishman stain: The fixed smear should be flooded with Leishman stain (BDH) for 2-3 minutes and then diluted with distilled water. This is allowed to act for 30-40 minutes. The smear should then be properly washed with distilled water, dried in air and examined.

Giemsa stain: The fixed blood smear should be flooded with diluted (1 : 15) Giemsa stain (BDH) and left for 25-30 minutes. The smear should then be washed with distilled water, dried and examined.

Wright's stain: Fixed or even unfixed blood smear can be stained by this method. A small amount of Wright's stain should be put on the blood smear for 2-3 minutes. A few drops of distilled water or a buffer solution having pH 6.4 to 6.8 should be placed on it and left for 10 minutes. After this, the slide should be properly washed, dried in the air and examined.

Examination of Blood Smear for Differential Leukocyte Count

The smear should be first set under a low-power microscope and a small drop of immersion oil put on it. The same smear should be set under oil immersion lens. Then different luekocytes should be counted by Battlement method, i.e. 4 fields should be counted horizontally, then 4 fields to the inside of the slide, then again 4 fields horizontally, and 4 fields to the inside of the slide, and so on. At least 200 or 300 cells and DLC is expressed in per cent. The following types of cells (Fig. 91) may be counted: neutrophils (stab and segmented), lymphocytes, eosinophils, monocytes and basophils.

To examine the blood protozoan parasites and microfilariae the smear is prepared and stained just like differential leukocyte count, but the smear should be thin. The smear is placed under oil-immersion lens of the microscope and examined for babesia, anaplasma, trypanosoma, leishmania, microfilariae and septicaemic bacterial organisms.

Determination of Total Erythrocytes (RBC)

Diluting fluid for erythrocyte count:

(i) Normal saline (0.85 g sodium chloride in 100 cc of distilled water).

(ii) Gower's solution (RBC): Crystalline sodium sulphate, 0.25 g; sodium chloride, 0.5 g; sodium sulphate, 2.5 g; distilled water, 100 ml.

Procedure: The improved Neubaur chamber of the haemocytometer is cleaned and the ruled area is covered with cover-glass. Blood is drawn exactly to the 0.5 mark (fresh or properly mixed oxalated blood) of the red cell diluting pipette marked 101, by sucking (red bead should be freely moved before sucking the blood).

If extra blood is sucked beyond mark 0.5, it should be removed with the finger tip. The diluting fluid should be immediately drawn up to the mark 101, and mixed well by rotating the pipette between the palm. The diluting fluid should be clear and filtered, if necessary, to be free of sediment. If the pipette is to be carried for a long distance to the laboratory, strech and block rubber band over the ends or a special closing device can be used.

A finger should be placed on the tip of the diluting pipette before the rubber tubing is removed. Before charging the fluid in Neubaur chamber, 3-4 drops of fluid should be discarded from the pipette. The cover-glass should be put over the ruled area so that it covers both the chambers. A drop should be placed at the end of the polished surface bearing the ruling, allowing the drop to flow under the cover-glass. It should be confirmed that space between ruled area and the cover-glass is filled up. There should be neither overflowing nor any air-bubble under the cover-glass. If it is there, the cover-glass should be discarded and the chamber filled again. It should be left aside for 3 minutes to settle the cells. The counting chamber should be placed under high-power microscope. Touching the cover-slip with the lens should be avoided. This may lead to an error in counting. Cells should be counted in the 5 medium squares of the central large square covering all the 80 small squares. Those erythrocytes touching the bottom and right hand lines should not be counted, but all cells touching the top and left hand lines should be included. Total number of cells obtained from the 80 small squares should be multiplied with 10,000 to get the cells per cubic mm of the blood sample (Fig. 92).

Determination of Total Leukocyte Count (WBC)

For determining the white cell count the following diluting fluids are used.

Thomas fluid: Glacial acetic acid, 1 ml; gentian violet 1 in 60 solution, 1 ml; distilled water, 100 ml.

A solution of 3 ml acetic acid + 97 ml distilled water is made.

In 100 ml distilled water 2.1 ml acetic acid is taken to which 1 ml of 1.1 aqueous solution of gentian violet should be added.

Procedure: Fresh blood or properly mixed oxalated blood should be sucked in the WBC diluting pipette (with white bead) up to mark 0.5. If excess blood is sucked, it should be removed. The diluting fluid should be drawn up in the diluting pipette up to mark 11 to make the dilution 1 : 20. The diluting pipette should be rotated thoroughly for

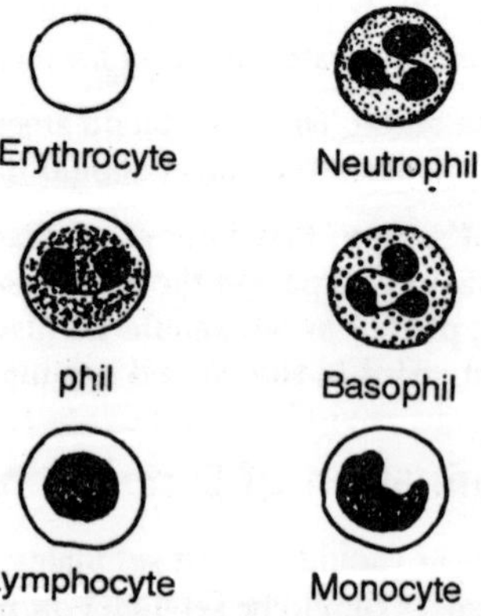

Fig. 92 Normal morphological picture of RBC & WBC of a dog

several minutes after removing the tube. Several drops should be removed from the mixed fluid before charging the chamber. The counting chamber should be charged as in the case of RBC counting, left as such for 2-3 minutes to settle the cells, and placed under a low-power microscope. The WBC should be counted in the 4 large corner squares by the method similar to red cell counting. The total cell count should be made in 4 corner squares and multiplied by 50. The result is expressed in thousands per cubic mm.

Determination of Coagulation Time of Blood

This may be determined by slide method, glass-bead method and capillary tube method.

Slide method: On a clean slide, 2 drops of fresh blood should be placed with a pointed object or a pin, the presence of strands of fibrin should be checked after every 30 seconds. This should be ensured by placing the pin on the second drop if no strand of fibrin is seen, then it should be recorded from the second drop of blood.

Glass-bead method: In a watch-glass with glass-bead 3 to 5 drops of blood should be placed. The stop-watch should be started at the same time. The glass-bead should be moved in blood and the movement observed. Whenever, the bead stops or does not show the movement freely, the stop watch should be stopped and the time recorded, which is coagulation time.

Capillary tube method: A small capillary (diameter of tube should be 0.5-1 mm and length 10 cm) tube is taken. With the help of a needle the tip of the ears should be pricked to allow bleeding. One end of the capillary tube should be placed on the drop of blood. The tube should be filled by capillary action and broken from the slide after every half a minute and the time recorded. When strands of fibrin have been formed, the time should be recorded indicating the coagulation time of blood.

Estimation of Haemoglobin

Three methods are used for estimating haemoglobin, viz.

(i) Hellige Sahli method,

(ii) Spencer Haemoglobin method, and

(iii) Haden Hausser method.

Of these Sahli method is easy and commonly used in most clinics and laboratories.

Sahli method: Material: Haemoglobinometer (Hellige Sahli), pipette, dropper, N/10 Hydrochloric acid and distilled water.

About 5 drops of decinormal (N/10) solution of hydrochloric acid should be placed in the measuring tube. Well-mixed oxalated or fresh blood (0.02 ml) should be taken to the mark 20. The unwanted blood should be removed from the sides of the tip of the pipette with the help of the finger. The blood from the pipette should be transferred into the measuring tube. One tip of the pipette should be under the surface of HCl. The last trace of blood should be removed by drawing the solution up in the pipette and expelling at least 2-3 times. The tube should be shaken to mix thoroughly, and allowed to stand for 8-10 minutes for the formation of acid hematinin. The mixture is diluted by adding drop by drop of distilled water with the help of a dropper and mixed by stirring. Reading should be taken every time. Repeated matching of the colour of the tube with the standard tube should be made until both tubes are of the same colour. Reading should be made at the scale of the measuring tube. The percentage figure on the tube at the lower edge of the miniscus should be read. The result is expressed in gram per cent.

Determination of ESR (Erythrocyte Sedimentation Rate)

It is done with the help of Westergreen sedimentation tube (calibrated from 0 to 200) as follows:

Westergreen tube should be chemically cleaned and dried. Oxalated blood should be sucked up to '0' mark, on the measuring tube. If air bubble is present, the tube should be filled again. The measuring tube should be fixed in vertical position in the Westergreen stand in between the spraying pad (on top) and rubber cork. After 1 hour, upper level of the sedimentation point of erythrocytes from the calibrations of the tube should be recorded. The result is expressed as mm fall/hour.

Wintrobe tubes (calibrated from 0 to 100) may also be used for ESR determination.

Determination of PCV (Packed Cell Volume)

Microhaematocrit method: Small disposable tube (size: diameter, 1.2 mm; and length, 75 mm) is taken. Before using, it should be treated with heparin. Heparinized tube should be filled by the blood obtained by capillary attraction from a sample of blood. One end of the tube should be closed by sealing it with a plastic cap. The tube should be centrifuged in micro-centrifuge apparatus for 5 minutes. The tube should be placed in a dam's microhaematocrit reader and percentage of packed cell volume noted.

Macrohaematocrit method: This is done with the help of Wintrobe haematocrit tube. Anticoagulant-mixed blood is needed for this method.

Wintrobe haematocrit is a flat-bottomed narrow glass tube having 2.5 to 3 mm diameter and 11 cm length. A cm scale commencing at the level of the inside bottom is attached on the glass. For this test, oxalated blood is needed.

Oxalated blood (5 ml) should be taken in a test-tube and mixed properly. The haematocrit tube should be filled exactly to the mark 100 with the help of a pipette or syringe and needle. Formation of air bubbles should be avoided. These tubes should be centrifuged at 3,000 rpm for 30 minutes. This method results in the upper layer being plasma, middle layer being buffy coat which contains leukocytes, and thrombocytes and bottom layer being the packed cell volume (mass of R.B.C.).

Determination of Mean Corpuscular Volume (MCV)

The packed cell volume should be first converted into per 1,000 ml of blood and divided by total erythrocyte count to determine mean corpuscular volume and expressed in cubic micron.

$$\text{MCV} = \frac{\text{PCV as percentage} \times 10}{\text{RBC count in million/mm}^3}$$

Determination of Mean Corpuscular Haemoglobin (MCH)

Haemoglobin expressed in micrograms should be divided by total erythrocyte count and converted to the number per 1,000 cc of blood. This gives mean corpuscular haemoglobin value which is expressed in micrograms.

$$\text{MCH} = \frac{\text{Hb in grams/1,000 c.c.}}{\text{RBC count in million/mm}^3}$$

Determination of Mean Corpuscular Haemoglobin Concentration (MCHC)

Haemoglobin in grams per 100 cc of blood is multiplied by 100 and divided by percentage packed cell volume to get mean corpuscular haemoglobin concentration. This is expressed as volume per cent.

$$\text{MCHC} = \frac{\text{Hb in grams/100 cc} \times 100}{\text{PCV as percentage}}$$

Examination of Blood for Microfilariae

Wet blood film method: A fresh drop of blood should be placed on a glass-slide and covered with 22 mm × 22 mm cover-slip. The entire area should be examined under the microscope at 10 (low-power) and 43 magnification (high-power). Such 10-12 slides may be prepared and screened before declaring the case as negative.

Direct blood smear examination: Just like DLC 4-5 slides should be prepared and examined under low-power and high-power lenses of microscope. This is not an efficient method.

Examination of plasma: Examination of the plasma just above buffy coat after centrifugation in the Wintrobe tubes or from the Westergreen tubes after making record of ESR gives good results.

Haemolysed blood smear test: In 1 ml of blood 1 or 2 drops of distilled water should be poured and 4-5 smears prepared to obtain the microfilariae on the slide. Leishman or Giemsa stain should be used.

Modified Knott techniques: This technique is used for killing and fixing the microfilariae. Freshly drawn blood (1 ml) should be added to 10 ml of 2% formalin and centrifuged at 1,500 rpm for 5 minutes. The supernatant fluid should be decanted and 2 drops of methylene blue (1 : 1,000) added. After mixing, 0.1 ml sample should be placed each on 2 glass-slides and the entire area under 22 mm × 22 mm cover-slip examined for microfilariae at 10 and 42 magnifications.

URINE EXAMINATION

Collection and Storage of Urine

The urine sample should be collected in a clean sample jar or a beaker free from any chemical and foreign substance. The container should be sterilized. The urine sample can be collected whenever the animal urinates or by applying external manual compression to the urinary bladder.

Urine Collection by Catheter

Male: The dog should be laid down in lateral recumbency, and the prepuce and penis cleaned with cotton or gauze. The glans penis should be exposed by retracting the prepuce posteriorly and cleaned with sterilized cotton or gauze. Gum elastic catheter should be passed gently without applying any force. Urine may be collected by pressing the abdomen and by connecting the catheter with needdle and syringe. After collection the catheter should be removed gently.

Female: The external genital organs of bitch should be cleaned with soap and water. Vagina should be dilated with sterilized vaginal speculum. Metal catheter should be inserted at right angle to avoid its insertion in the suburethral opening which is located just below the clitoris and is nearly 6-8 cm inside the lower vulvar commissure. The catheter should be pushed gently inside the urethra but much force should not be applied even if there is some obstruction. Slight pressure should be applied on the abdomen when the catheter has been inserted.

Urine can also be collected directly from the urinary bladder with the help of syringe and needle but strict aspectic measure should be taken. Urine can also be collected by giving a diuretic, but it will change the chemical content of urine.

Storage of urine: Urine sample can be stored by several methods.

By mixing with toluene: In this method a thin layer is formed on the top of urine. This method of preservation is mostly used in chemical analysis of urine.

By keeping the urine sample in freezer.

By adding 1 g crystal of thymol in 1 litre of urine. This may give false reaction for protein.

By adding 3-5 drops of 40% formalin to 1 litre of urine. This may give false positive reaction for glucose.

By adding a few drops of phenol in urine sample. This may give false positive reaction for glucose.

Physical Examination of Urine

Physical examination of urine is performed by the help of urinometer.

Colour: Colour should be seen immediately after the collection. The colour varies from colourless to amber from species to species.

Smell: Under normal conditions, the smell of urine is uraemic but under diseased condition it may change. Sometimes it may contain ammonia, acetone or it may also be foetid.

Transparency: It varies from animal to animal.

Specific gravity: It is measured by urinometer.

Microscopic examination: Microscopic examination of urine helps in diagnosing many diseases. For this, urine should be examined as early as possible after collection. The urine should be centrifuged to collect the sediment for further test. About 10 ml of urine should be taken in a centrifuge tube, put in centrifuge and the balance is made by adding equal amount of water. It should be centrifuged for about 8 minutes at 1,000-1,500 rpm and the supernatant discarded. One drop of sediment should be taken on a glass slide and covered with a cover-slip. If the sediment is too thick, smear should be made and stained with Giemsa or Wright's stain and examined under low-power microscope. If required, high-power could also be used. Following results may be obtained.

(i) ***Erythrocyte (RBC in urine):*** These cells are normally not present in urine. When urine is collected by catheterization, a few cells may be seen in a normal case also, but in case of haemorrhage and urinary tract infection, there are a large number of cells. The cells may appear rounded, crenated and swollen.

(ii) ***Epithelial cells:*** These cells are always present in normal animals but are few in number. In an animal suffering from inflammatory condition, the number of cells in the urine increases. The epithelial cell may be large, transitional (from fundus of the bladder), cuboidal (from renal tubules) and large squamous (from kidney).

(iii) ***Leukocytes:*** In a normal animal, the number of leukocytes is very little. Their presence in large number indicates inflammatory condition of urinary tract. Sometimes these cells may be confused with RBC, but the cells are granular.

(iv) ***Crystals:*** Size and shape of crystals vary according to the reaction of urine. In alkaline urine, amorphous phosphate, calcium carbonate, triple phosphate are present and in acidic urine the crystals are calcium oxalate, uric acid, amorphous urates.

(v) ***Bacteria:*** In an animal suffering with urinary tract infection bacteria may be seen in urine but the best way for bacterial confirmation is culture examination of urine.

(vi) ***Cast:*** Presence of cast in urine indicates tubular disturbances of kidney. These casts may be waxy, erythrocytic, hyaline, bloody, mucoid, epithelial etc.

Chemical Examination of Urine

pH of urine: In field cases the pH is mostly tested by dipping of red or blue strip of litmus paper. Changes of red strip to blue suggests alkaline pH and from blue to red acidic pH. Normally in carnivorous animals urine is acidic.

Sugar (Glucose): Benedict's reagent method (qualitative): In a test-tube 1 ml of urine sample should be taken, and to this 10 ml of Benedict's reagent added and thoroughly mixed. The mixture should be placed in a boiling water-bath for 5 minutes or heated over a flame. The tube should be kept in the test-tube stand for a few minutes. Results will be as follows:

Clear blue: Blue to green with heavy yellow sediment, +; yellow with heavy sediment, ++; yellow with heavy reddish sediment, +++; orange with heavy sediment, ++++.

Presence of albumin: Robert's reagent method: On 5 ml of Robert's reagent in a test-tube, 5 ml of urine sample should be stratified. Appearance of a white ring suggests that urine is positive for albumin.

Quantity of albumin can be shown as follows: No white ring, - ; a definite narrow ring, +; a definite wide ring, ++; heavy ring, +++; very heavy ring, ++++.

Nitric acid method: Take 0.5 ml concentrate nitric acid and put a layer of urine on the acid. White ring at the junction indicates the presence of albumin.

Sulpho salicylic acid method: In 2 tubes 2-3 ml of urine should be placed, and 5 to 10 drops of sulpho salicylic acid reagent added and shaken. The other tube should be treated as a control. The degree of turbidity should be recorded as -, +, ++, +++ and ++++.

Presence of bile in urine: Methylene blue test: This test is used as a liver function test for bile in urine. Five ml of fresh urine should be placed in a beaker, and 20 ml of distilled water added. The 0.2% aqueous methylene blue solution should be added drop by drop, the solution being shaken after adding each drop. The solution changes to blue. If more than 5 drops are required to change it to blue, it indicates liver disturbances.

Chloroform test: To 2-3 ml urine in a test-tube, 2-3 drops of chloroform should be added. In positive samples the chloroform becomes turbid and yellowish.

Gmelin's test (for bilirubin and biliverdin): In a test-tube 5 ml of yellow nitric acid should be taken. Urine (5 ml) should be added. The colour will be green and violet for bile pigments, blue for indican and red for urobilin.

Hay's test for bile acids: About 10 ml of urine should be taken in a test-tube and a small amount of flour of sulphur put on the surface of the sample. If the flowers sink the sample is positive, if not negative.

Foam test: About 10 ml of urine sample should be taken in a test-tube and shaken vigorously. An abundant foam of yellow colour indicates the presence of bile.

Blood in Urine: In glacial acetic acid 2 ml of prepared saturated solution of benzidine base should be taken and an equal amount (2 ml) of hydrogen peroxide solution added. The tube containing the reagent and 2 ml of urine should be mixed well. Blue colour indicates positive for blood.

Presence of acetone in urine: Rothera's test: In a test-tube with 3 ml of urine, 2 ml of concentrated ammonium hydroxide is added. Dark purple colour indicates the presence of acetone in the sample.

Nitroprusside test: In a test-tube, 0.5 g of the nitroprusside reagent (1 : 100 of sodium nitroprusside and ammonium sulphate) should be taken, and 3 ml of urine added to it. A layer of concentrated ammonium hydroxide is added.

The presence of a purple to dark purple ring at the junction indicates positive test for acetone in urine.

Test for differentiation between haemoglobinuria and myoglobinuria: In a test-tube 10 ml of urine should be taken, and 5.6 g of ammonium sulphate added and shaken properly. The solution should be left to settle. Clear supernatant indicates haemoglobin and if the original colour of urine returns it is positive for myoglobin.

Presence of calcium in urine: In a test-tube, 2.5 ml urine should be taken and the same amount of Sulkowitch reagent added. In another test-tube, 2.5 ml of urine should be taken and same amount of distilled water added to it for control. The test-tube should be kept in stand and read at intervals of 2 and 10 minutes. Results are as follows:

No visible precipitate, - ; mild precipitate, +; light cloudy precipitate, ++; light to moderate milk white precipitate, +++; heavy chalky precipitate which settles down rapidly, ++++.

EXAMINATION OF SKIN SCRAPINGS

For Mange Mites

Samples from the periphery of active lesions should be taken as they have a high concentration of parasites. The affected area should be moistened with 10 per cent (KOH or NaOH)/mineral oil. The lesion should be pressed in between the thumb and fingers and the skin scraped deeply, but the cut should not reach the skin, as blood ooze out. Collected sample may be preserved in 10 per cent KOH or NaOH.

(i) ***Direct smear method:*** After treating the sample for 1 hour with 10 per cent KOH or NaOH at room temperature, one drop of the treated material should be placed on the glass-slide and covered with a cover-slip. It should be microscopically examined under low-power lens.

(ii) ***Sedimentation method:*** The sample on collection should be kept in 10 per cent KOH/10 per cent NaOH at least for 45 minutes, so that debris is digested. It could be slightly heated. The sample should be centrifuged at 1,500-2,000 rpm for 5 to 10 minutes. The collected sediment should be smeared on a slide and covered with a cover-slip.

(iii) ***Sugar floatation method:*** The sample should be first treated as in sedimentation method and the supernatant discarded. Half the centrifuge tube should be filled with sediment and distilled water, and the rest by adding an equal quantity of saturated sugar solution. It is again centrifuged on 1,500-2,000 rpm for 5-10 minutes. The parasites come to the top by gravity. A drop of the sample should be taken on a glass-slide from the top and covered with a cover-slip.

For Fungal Infection

Before collecting the skin sample, lesion should be cleaned with spirit or absolute alcohol to remove any other infection of saprophytic fungi. The deep skin along with hair should be collected by a mineral-oil-treated scalpel. The sample should be collected in 10 per cent KOH or NaOH and kept at least 30 minutes before examination.

Lactophenol cotton blue mounting fluid: This is used for preparing mounts for the study of fungus cultures. It is prepared by dissolving 20.0 g (melt in water-bath, then weigh) of phenol crystals, 20 g of lactic acid, 20 g of glycerine and 0.05 g of cotton blue (Poirrier's blue) in 20 ml of distilled water.

India ink: Undiluted ink is used to demonstrate the capsules of *Cryptococcus neoformans* in sputum, spinal fluid, urine, other body fluids, or from the growth in culture. A loopful of the specimen is mixed in a drop of India ink on a clean slide, and a cover-slip is added. This wet mount is examined under the microscope. If the preparation is too dark, it may be diluted with a small drop of water.

Staining methods: The following staining methods are commonly used.

Periodic acid-Schiff stain: This is an excellent stain for differentiation of fungi in scrapings and tissue sections.

Staining methods for skin scrapings are as follows:

Thin scrapings should be spread on a slide coated with Mayer's albumen. The scrapings may be collected directly with the fixative placed on the lesion. The scales on the surface should be scraped off and immediately pressed on the surface of a clean slide. It should then be heated gently and checked to see if skin scrapings are fast on slide. Immerse the fixed scrapings as follows:

The slide should be immersed for 1 minute in 95 per cent alcohol, in 5 per cent periodic acid for 5 minutes, and in a solution (consisting of 0.1 g basic fuchsin, 5.0 ml of 95 per cent alcohol and 95.0 ml of water) for 2 minutes. The slide should be rinsed under tap-water, again immersed for 10 minutes in a solution containing 1.0 g zinc (or sodium) hydrosulphite, 0.5 g tartaric acid and 100 ml water. The slide should again be rinsed in tap-water and counterstained with one of the following:

Saturated aqueous solution of picric acid (1.0 g light green, 0.10 ml glacial acetic acid and 10 ml of 80% alcohol) for 2 minutes, or light green for 5 seconds. The slide should be rinsed again for a short time in tap-water and dehydrated for about 10 seconds in 95 per cent alcohol and 1 minute in 100 per cent alcohol, and then the slide should be finally rinsed twice in xylol for about 1 minute each and mounted in permount or other mounting media.

The fungi stain a bright red or purplish-red after periodic-acid hydrolysis to release aldehydes which can combine with Schiff reagent. The carbohydrates in the cell-wall will take the red stain as a result of the reaction.

For tissue sections: Tissue should be fixed, dehydrated, embedded in paraffin, and sectioned by the routine method: They should be placed in xylol to deparaffinize, then rinsed in 100 per cent alcohol. After washing in distilled water, they should be immersed in 1% periodic acid for 10 minutes, and rinsed in tap-water for 5-10 minutes. They should then be immersed in a solution containing 0.1 g basic fuchsin, 5.0 ml a 95 per cent alcohol, and 95.0 ml water for 2 minutes. The slide should be rinsed in tap-water for 30 seconds and again immersed for 30 minutes (or possibly up to 2-3 hours for some material) in the solution containing 1.0 g zinc (or sodium) hydrosulphite, 0.5 g tartaric acid and 100 ml water.

After rinsing in tap-water for 3-5 minutes, they should be immersed in light green (light green, 1.0 g; 0.25 ml glacial acetic acid; 100 ml of 80 per cent alcohol) for 2 minutes, rinsed for a short time under tap-water and dehydrated for about 10 seconds in 95 per cent alcohol, 1 minute in 100 per cent alcohol, rinsed twice in xylol for about 1 minute each and mounted in permount or other mounting media.

Examination Methods

Gross examination: In Dermatophytosis this test should be performed on the animal itself. Chloroform should be applied on the affected area of the skin. Change in colour of hair to white after the evaporation of chloroform would indicate that the animal is suffering from ringworm infection.

Wood's ultraviolet lamp method: It should be also performed directly on the animal in a dark place (also on collected scraping). Ultraviolet rays should be given to sample result as follows:

No fluorescence - *Tricophyton* sp.

Greenish-yellow fluorescence - *Microsporum* sp.

Microscopic examination: One or two drops of treated skin scrapings (10% NaOH or KOH) are taken on a glass-slide and covered with a cover-slip. If the skin scraping is placed directly on the glass-slide then 1-2 drops of 10 per cent KOH or NaOH are added and then covered with a cover-slip. Vaseline is applied around the cover-slip and the slide gently heated from the bottom for about 30 seconds. The slide should be examined under the microscope for spore as well as hyaline chains.

Culture examination: For culture examination skin should be properly cleaned with 70 per cent alcohol and the collected material should be cultured on Sabouraud's agar medium. A small amount of sample should be placed on the slant and kept at room temperature for a few days. After growing the colonies, it may be examined by naked eyes as well as by microscope. Following media may be used.

Sabouraud dextrose agar (SDA): This is used for primary isolation of most fungi pathogenic to man and animals. It consists of 40 g of dextrose, 40 g of peptone, 20 g of agar and 1,000 ml of distilled water. The pH should be adjusted to obtain final pH of 5.6.

If the dehydrated product is used, then sufficient extra agar should be added to bring agar content to 2 per cent. This ensures a firm, dry-surfaced medium. It is important not to overheat this medium during sterilization. For tubed media, 10 minutes at 120° C is adequate for sterilization.

Sabouraud-cycloheximide-chloramphenicol medium (SCCM): This medium consists of Sabouraud dextrose agar (2% agar contents), 0.5 mg/ml Cycloeximide and 0.05 mg/ml Chloramphenicol. The SCCM is prepared as follows:

Dehydrated SDA (65 g), to which 5.0 g of agar has been added to bring it to 2% content, is suspended in 1,000 ml distilled water and heated to boiling point. Chloramphenicol (50 mg suspended in 10 ml 95% alcohol) is added to boiling medium, removed quickly from heat and mixed. Cycloheximide solution (500 mg in 10 ml acetone) was added, mixed well and distributed into tubes. It was autoclaved at 118° C for 10 minutes, then slanted and the media allowed to harden. This composition is needed for 1 litre media.

Brain-heart-infusion-cycloheximide-chloramphenicol medium: This medium is used for the isolation of nutritionally fastidious fungi, such as *Histoplasma capsulatum* and *Blastomyces dermatitidis,* at 25° C or room temperature.

It consists of 37 g of brain heart infusion, 0.5 mg/ml of cycloheximide, 0.05 mg/ml of chloramphenicol, 20 g of agar and 100 ml of distilled water.

EXAMINATION OF EXUDATES AND TRANSUDATES

During the collection of a sample all aseptic measures should be followed. All equipments and materials should be properly sterilized. About 25 ml of the samples should be collected in a test-tube. Small amount of fluid should also be collected with anti-coagulant (sodium citrate or lithium oxalate). Local anaesthesia may be given to avoid pain during collection.

The samples are examined both physically and chemically.

Physical Examination

(i) Colour mainly depends upon disease/type of bacterial infection and of cells present in the exudate and transudate.

(ii) Specific gravity is measured by urinometer. Exudate-specific gravity is 1.017, and transudate-specific gravity is 1.006 to 1.017.

Microscopic Examination

(i) ***Total cell count:*** The leukocyte counting pipette should be filled to the mark 0.5 by diluting fluid (0.85% NaCl), then with exudate/transudate fluid to mark 11; it should be mixed properly and the first 2 drops discarded. The haemocytometer chamber should be charged as in blood cell counting. The cells are counted after 2 minutes in all ruled areas on both the sides of counting chambers (16 in 1 mm square) and multiplied by 0.06 to get the total number of cells per mm^3.

(ii) ***Differential cell count (DLC):*** The fluid should be centrifuged and the supernatant discarded. A smear should be made with sediment and stained for DLC and the result recorded like DLC in per cent.

Chemical Examination: Chemical examination for proteins is conducted as follows:

Distilled water (100 ml) should be taken and, 0.1 ml of glacial acetic acid and one drop of the fluid added. In the exudate, a distinct bluish-white cloud appeared but not in transudate.

Bacteriological examination: This can be done by one of the following methods:

(i) Smear and staining method,

(ii) Cultural examination; culture may be grown on several media to examine different types of bacteria, and

(iii) Laboratory animal inoculation test; this is for rat, rabbit and pig.

EXAMINATION OF CEREBROSPINAL FLUID (CSF)

Collection: In dogs and cats cisternal puncture is used for collecting CSF. It is located at mid-line depression directly cranial to the arch of the atlas and is easily palpated. The neck of the pet should be supported to maintain the cervical vertebrae in the horizontal plane to ensure the mid-line puncture. CSF should be collected under general anaesthesia.

Examination of sample: The sample should be examined for colour, pH, coagulation and turbidity. The colour of normal CSF is clear and colourless, just like distilled water. Its pH is normally alkaline. Normal CSF does not coagulate and is not turbid. Coagulation may be seen if there is an increase of proteins due to some pathological condition. The fluid is plain transparent but turbidity may occur whenever the number of cells increases.

Diluting fluid for total cell count: For this purpose 10 ml of glacial acetic acid + 90 ml of distilled water + 0.1 g of crystal violet should be used. This diluting fluid should be filtered prior to use. The procedure of examination is the same as TCC method of exudate and transudates.

Differential cell count: CSF should be centrifuged and supernatant discarded. A smear should be made from the sediment and stained with Giemsa, Wright's or Leishman stain. It should be examined under the microscope. As in DLC of blood, 100 cells should be counted.

Protein examination: In normal CSF, the amount of protein is very small, i.e. 12 to 40 mg/100 ml.

Qualitative Examination

(i) ***Pandy's method:*** Pandy's reagent (1 ml) consisting of 10 g of carbolic acid crystals in 100 ml of distilled water is taken in a test-tube. A few drops of CSF are added, mixed properly and shaken. If, by shaking turbidity develops, globulins are present. Normal CSF produces slight turbidity, whereas during disease, the globulins increase resulting in definite white turbidity. This may be scored as -ve, 1 to 4 + according to the degree of turbidity. Increased globulins indicate inflammation of brain or spinal cord.

(ii) ***None Apelt test:*** Saturated ammonium sulphate (1 ml) solution should be taken in a test-tube, and 1 ml of CSF carefully over-laid. Tubes should be allowed to stand for a few minutes. In normal condition, no ring is formed at the junction of spinal fluid and reagent, but the formation of white to greyish ring at the zone of contact indicates the presence of globulins.

Quantitative examination: Proteins may be examined by Greenberg method, same as that used for estimation of protein in serum.

Examination for chloride: Procedure for determination of glucose in CSF is the same as that utilized for estimation of glucose in blood.

TABLE 11. AVERAGE NORMAL HAEMATOLOGICAL VALUES OF DOG

Blood entities	*Values*
Haemoglobin (g/dl)	13.00
Packed cell volume (%)	42.00
Erythrocyte count ($X10^6/\mu l$)	6.25
Leucocyte count ($X10^3/\mu l$)	8-11
Neutrophils (%)	62-80
Lymphocytes (%)	18-28
Eosinophils (%)	2-14
Monocytes (%)	3-9
Basophils (%)	0-2
Platelet count ($X10^3/\mu l$)	15.5
Mean corpuscular volume (fl)	66.0
Mean corpuscular haemoglobin (Pg)	23.50
Mean corpuscular haemoglobin concentration (g/dl)	34.50
Mean corpuscular diameter (μ)	4.15
pH of blood	7.30-7.70
Specific gravity of whole blood	1.054-1.062
Relative viscosity of whole blood	4.0
Erythrocyte's fragility (% NaCl Conc.)	0.45-0.36
Erythrocyte sedimentation rate (mm/hr)	5-13
Myeloid/erythroid ratio (M/E)	0.75-2.4/1
Bleeding time, clotting time (min)	1-5
Capillary tube (min)	1-5
Lee white (min)	3-13
Activated clotting (sec) time (ACT)	60-100
Proximal thromboplastin time (sec) PPT or APTT	18-25
Prothrombin time (sec)	8-13
Thrombin time (sec)	7-12
Fibrinogen degradation products (FDP mg/ml)	up to 64
Blood pressure	45/100
Blood volume	8 to 9% of B.W.
Icterus index	2-6 units

TABLE 12: NORMAL HAEMATOLOGICAL VALUE OF SOME IMPORTANT DOG BREEDS

Haemato-logical values	*Alsatian*	*Bhutia*	*Cocker Spaniel*	*Cross-bred*	*Labrador*	*Mongrel*	*Pekingese*
TEC	4.65±0.90	6.59±039	5.41±0.84	6.75±1.15	6.55±1.26	5.16±0.45	5.88±0.44
(million/mm³)	(3.25-5.85)	(5.85-8.55)	(4.57-6.25)	(5.75-7.50)	(4.25-8.60)	(3.25-6.25)	(5.25-6.75)
TLC	9.96±1.53	8.99±0.71	10.05±1.52	10.22±0.96	11.45±0.75	11.76±1.40	7.56±1.30
(thousands/ mm³)	(7.250-14.400)	(7.58-11.10)	(10.53-13.58)	(8.53-12.75)	(9.40-14.95)	(8.11-13.26)	(6.23-12.50)
Hb (g%)	12.64±1.21	13.50±0.50	15.85±0.65	14.50±1.00	14.00±1.44	12.70±1.05	15.66±0.40
	(11.00-14.00)	(12.00-14.00)	(13.20-17.50)	(13.0-15.5)	(13.80-15.00)	(10.00-16.50)	(12.50-17.75)
ESR (mm/hr)	20.00±11.43	12.50±5.87	5.00±1.00	2.75±1.03	10.00±0.10	0.83±0.62	13.00±1.00
	(0-35)	(2-25)	(4-6)	(0-5)	(8-11)	(0-3)	(2-5)
DLC (%)							
N	64.00±5.97	66.50±8.50	70.50±2.50	55.50±5.69	58.33±6.33	62.25±8.52	65.66±3.18
	(46-79)	(46-80)	(48-80)	(45-70)	(46-67)	(41-80)	(50-71)
L	29.57±6.56	24.50±10.09	22.00±8.50	35.50±2.96	28.66±8.7	33.50±8.80	30.00±2.89
	(18-49)	(19-52)	(11-33)	(30-42)	(15-45)	(16-57)	(23-35)
M	1.57±0.57	3.0±0.57	2.60±1.00	4.25±0.85	3.33±2.03	1.25±0.95	3.00±1.50
	(0-4)	(0-2)	(1-3)	(0-8)	(0-7)	(0-13)	(0-2)
E	4.85±0.69	6.00±2.72	3.50±1.50	4.00±0.85	9.66±5.28	3.00±0.41	3.00±1.50
	(0-10)	(3-15)	(2-8)	(0-6)	(0-16)	(2-7)	(2-6)
B	0.00	0.00	2.00+1.00	0.75+0.20	0.00	0.00	0.00
			(0-2)	(0-4)			
PCV (%)	40.50±2.63	44.50±3.46	39.00±1.00	42.50±2.50	40.00±2.00	40.50±3.60	36.00±2.00
	(36-48)	(38-50)	(38-40)	(40-45)	(38-44)	(32-50)	(34-38)
MCV	76.64±8.07	69.32±4.36	70.82±12.34	66.47±2.77	64.42±15.56	70.31±9.70	60.92±2.17
(cu μ)	(68.57-84.71)	(64.96-73.68)	(58.48-83.15)	(63.70-69.23)	(48.80-86.00)	(60.61-80.00)	(64.75-69.09)
MCH	23.50±4.75	21.12±0.31	20.77±0.77	21.94±1.14	26.40±4.18	29.26±4.07	21.83±0.39
(m mg)	(18.75-28.24)	(18.75-21.43)	(20.00-23.54)	(20.00-22.75)	(22.22-30.57)	(25.19-33.33)	(21.0-23.22)
MCHC (%)	32.74±1.63	31.10±3.10	30.97±1.52	32.91±0.41	34.96±0.75	37.31±3.33	29.97±2.36
	(31.11-34.37)	(28.00-31.21)	(29.47-32.50)	(32.50-33.33)	(34.21-35.71)	(34.00-40.62)	(27.63-32.35)

N, neutrophil; L, lymphocyte; M, monocyte, E, eosinophil; B, basophil.

TABLE 13: NORMAL BLOOD BIOCHEMICAL VALUES OF DOG

Entities	*Values*
Proteins	
Total protein	5-7.5 g/100 ml serum 5.3-7.5 g/100 ml plasma
Albumin	3.3-4.8 g/100 ml serum or plasma
Globulin	1.3-3.2 g 100 ml serum or plasma
Albumin - globulin ratio (A/G ratio)	1.5-2.3
Fibrinogen	0.3-0.5 g/100 ml plasma
Serum Proteins by Electrophoretic Fractionation	
Albumin	53.50 per cent
Alpha globulin	13.80 per cent
Beta globulin	20.40 per cent
Gama globulin	12.30 per cent
Non-protein Nitrogenous Constituents (NPN)	
Non-protein nitrogen (NPN)	20-35 ml/100 ml blood
Urea nitrogen	10-20 mg/100 ml blood
Creatinine	1-2 mg/100 ml blood
Uric acid	0.0-1.0 mg/100 ml blood (values over 1.0 mg in Dalmation)
Allantoin	0.8-1.34 mg/100 ml plasma 0.57-0.64 mg/100 ml plasma (Dalmation)
Amino acids	7-8 mg/100 ml blood
Lipids	
Total cholesterol	140-210 mg/100 ml serum
Cholesterol esters	84-168 mg/100 ml serum
Free cholesterol	28-84 mg/100 ml serum
Serum total lipids	47-725 mg/100 ml plasma
Lecithin	220-470 mg/100 ml plasma
Cephalin	18-22 mg/100 ml plasma

(Contd.)

Entities	*Values*
Sphingomyelin	50-55 mg/100 ml serum
Phospholipids	75-200 mg/100 ml serum
Neutral fat	
Total fatty acid	
Carbohydrates	
Glucose	60-100 mg/100 ml blood
Enzymes	
Alkaline phosphalase	3-6 units/100 ml serum (Bodansky) 7.5-15 units/100 ml serum (King Armstrong) 2.4-48 units/100 ml serum (Kaplan and Narahara) 2.20-10.50 units/100 ml serum (Kind and King)
Acid phosphatase	1-4 units/100 ml serum (Gutman and Gutman)
Amylase	12.5 mg maltase/ml plasma (Lugarlaf) 423-462 Somoggi units/100 ml serum
Lipase	0.1-1.15 ml of N/20 NaOH
Serum glutamic oxaloacitic-transaminase (SGOT or AST)	12-48 units/100 ml serum (Reitman and Frankel) 13-27 units/100 ml serum (Sigma-Frankel) 6-13 I.U./litre
Serum glutamic pyruvictransaminase (SGPT and ALT)	10-60 units/100 ml serum (Reitman and Frankel) 10-50 units/100 ml serum (Sigma-Frankel) 5.24 I.U./litre
Lactic dehydrogenase (LDH)	100 mu/ml
Sorbitol dehydrogenase (SDH)	1-7 vol. activity units/litre
Creatine phosphokinase (CPK)	8-69 mμ/ml
Glutamate dehydrogenase (G.D.)	4-14 units/litre
Isocitric dehydrogenase (ICH)	2-10 units/litre
Ornithine carbamylase transferase (OCT)	3-15 vol. activity units/litre
Inorganic Substances	
Calcium	9-11.5 mg/100 ml serum 4.6-6.1 m Eq/litre serum

(Contd.)

Entities	*Values*
Sodium	135-160 m Eq/litre plasma 134-149 m Eq/litre serum
Potassium	3.7-5.8 m Eq/litre plasma
Magnesium	1.4-2.4 m Eq/litre plasma 1.3-2.0 m Eq/litre plasma
Chlorides	420-570 mg/100 ml blood as NaCl 70-97 m Eq/litre blood as chloride 570-644 mg/100 ml plasma, as NaCl 98-100 m Eq/litre plasma as chloride
Sulphates	2.0 m Eq/litre plasma
Inorganic phosphorus	2.6-5.0 mg/100 ml serum
Carbon dioxide	45-70 vol/ml plasma
Copper	70.50-150.00 μgm/100 ml serum
Iron	228.50-409.00 μgm/100 ml serum
Zinc	170.00-350 μgm/100 ml serum
Manganese	3.00-15.00 mgm/100 ml serum
Bile Pigments	
Bilirubin	0.1-1.0 mg/100 ml serum
Icterus index	2-5 units
Hormones	
17-hydroxycorticosteroids	3-10 μg/100 ml serum
Protein-bound Iodine	0.0-2.4 mg/100 ml serum
Other Tests	
pH, serum/plasma	7.31-7.42
Thyroid uptake of radio-iodine	11-40 per cent after 72 hours per injection
Bromosulphophthalein Liver test (BSP)	less than 5 per cent dye remaining at 30 minutes
Rose Bengal liver test	50 per cent or less dye remaining at 8 minutes
Phenolsulpopthalein (PSP) kidney test	25% excretion (30 mts)
Partial pressure of O_2	85-95 mm Hg
Partial pressure of CO_2 (PCO_2)	29-42 mm Hg
Osmolality	280-305 mosm/kg

TABLE 14. NORMAL BIOCHEMICAL VALUES OF SOME IMPORTANT BREEDS OF DOG

Biochemical values	***Alsatian***	***Bhutia***	***Cocker Spaniel***	***Crossbred***	***Labrador***	***Mongrel***	***Pekingese***
Blood glucose (mg/100 ml)	80.75±4.36 (58.00-92.00)	80.25±9.04 (70.00-96.00)	80.00±6.00 (74.00-86.00)	114.00±7.07 (62.00-152.00)	107.00±3.61 (102.00-114)	98.66±14.56 (0062.00-146.00)	78.00±20.00 (58.00-98.00)
Serum bilirubin (mg/100 ml)	0.60±0.20 (0.04-0.90)	0.66±0.17 (0.05-0.75)	0.70±0.10 (0.60-0.80)	0.75±0.26 (0.20-1.20)	0.41±0.04 (0.35-0.50)	0.40±0.37 (0.10-1.10)	0.45±0.02 (0.40-0.50)
Total protein (g%)	8.06±0.92 (6.20-9.50)	7.82±0.84 (6.25-9.30)	8.75±1.35 (6.50-9.30)	8.97±1.28 (7.70-9.25)	8.00±0.85 (7.00-9.00)	8.38±0.57 (6.50-9.70)	8.75±1.50 (7.25-9.25)
Albumin (g%)	3.90±0.46 (3.20-4.75)	4.62±0.62 (3.20-5.00)	4.75±0.54 (4.00-6.25)	4.22±1.02 (4.20-6.25)	4.50±0.60 (4.90-5.50)	4.88±0.47 (4.5-5.0)	5.13±0.14 (5.00-5.25)
Globulin (g%)	4.16±0.58 (3.60-4.75)	3.20±0.33 (2.25-3.75)	3.00±0.25 (2-3.75)	3.75±0.24 (3.50-4.00)	3.50±0.45 (3-4.50)	3.20±0.33 (2.00-4.10)	3.62±1.37 (2.25-5.00)
A:G Ratio	0.94	1.44	1.92	1.39	1.29	1.62	1.42
Sodium (meq/litre)	135.71±6.55 (102-158)	134.22±11.50 (110-165)	126±8.50 (116-140)	125.00±6.76 (11-142)	148.66±7.69 (134-160)	140.33±10.89 (113-160)	145.00±5.00 (140-150)
Chloride (meq/litre)	70±6.09 (50-90)	72.0±10.74 (50-100)	74.00±22.00 (50-96)	67.75±9.38 (52-95)	80.00±4.00 (72-84)	73.33±12.49 (33-110)	66.00±6.00 (62-72)
Potassium (meq/litre)	5.21±0.69 (2.40-6.90)	3.40±0.82 (1.30-5.70)	2.58±0.22 (2.36-2.80)	4.56±0.61 (2.60-5.20)	4.91±0.99 (2.85-6.10)	5.82±0.44 (4.20-7.00)	3.65±0.14 (3.50-3.80)
Calcium (mg/100 ml)	10.75±0.59 (9.00-12.80)	8.81±0.44 (7.75-9.25)	7.75±0.50 (7.25-8.25)	8.68±1.10 (5.50-10.50)	10.90±0.97 (10.00-11.50)	10.40±1.45 (5.10-12.70)	10.37±0.39 (10.25-10.50)
Phosphorus (mg/100 ml)	4.88±0.63 (2.60-7.30)	3.25±0.37 (2.75-3.80)	3.40±0.20 (1.20-4.60)	3.63±1.03 (2.00-6.58)	5.48±2.71 (2.40-8.30)	4.27±0.87 (1.10-7.15)	3.25±0.10 (3.25-3.32)
Cholesterol (mg/100 ml)	130.16±6.31 (100-180)	168.00±16.32 (140-195)	172.00±13.09 (160-185)	136.12±7.91 (150-185)	144.66±22.93 (116-190)	121.73±33.86 (111-197)	161.00±1.00 (160-162)
Phospholipids (mg/100 ml)	122.00±15.75 (65-183)	81.25±9.25 (73.75-95.00)	80.00±15.60 (50-115)	90.25±25.75 (50-162.00)	137.00±67.25 (60.257.50)	106.75±21.75 (47.50-178.75)	81.25±2.50 (79.50-83.00)
C:P Ratio	1.07	2.07	2.15	1.50	1.06	1.14	1.98

PROFORMA USED IN CLINICAL DIAGNOSIS

Proforma for Prescription Writing

Name of Institute/Hospital/Clinics ______________________________

____

____

Clinic No______________ Species ______________

Owner ______________ Breed ______________

Clinician Dr ______________ Age and Sex ______________

Diagnosis ______________

____

Rx

PROFORMA FOR HAEMATOLOGICAL EXAMINATION

Name of Institute/Vety. Hospital/Clinics ______________________

____

____

BLOOD EXAMINATION REQUEST/REPORT

Clinic No ______________ Species ______________

Date ______________ Breed ______________

Owner ______________ Age and Sex ______________

Referred by Dr. ______________

History:

____

CHECK TEST(S) DESIRED

Haemogram

1. Haemoglobin ______________ g/dl
2. E.S.R. ______________ mm/hr
3. P.C.V. ______________ %
4. R.B.C. Count ______________ $X10^6/\mu l$
5. Reticulocyte Count ______________ %
6. W.B.C. Count ______________ $X10^3/\mu l$
7. Differencial Count
8. Blood Parasites:
   Protozoa ______________
   Microfilariae ______________
9. Bacteria ______________
10. Blood Picture:
    Neutrophils:

    Myelo ______________ %
    Juv ______________ %
    Stab ______________ %
    Seg ______________ %
    Lymphocytes ______________ %
    Monocytes ______________ %
    Eosinophils ______________ %
    Basophils ______________ %

Anaemic changes ______________

Leukaemic changes ______________

Haemostasis Tests

1. Platelet count ______________ $X10^3/\mu l$
2. Bleeding time ______________ /minute
3. Coagulation time ______________ /minute
4. Prothrombin time ______________ /second

Officer-in-Charge

PROFORMA FOR BLOOD CHEMISTRY EXAMINATION

Name of Institute/Hospital/Clinics ____________________

____

____

BLOOD CHEMISTRY REQUEST/REPORT

Clinic No ____________________ Species ____________________

Date ____________________ Breed ____________________

Owner ____________________ Age and Sex ____________________

Referred by Dr. ____________________

History:

CHECK TEST(S) DESIRED

Blood Sugar

(use sodium fluoride as anticoagulent) ____________ mg%

Serum cholesterol ____________ mg%

SGOT ____________ units

SGPT ____________ units

Bilirubin ____________ mg%

BSP (Clearance test) ____________ % Ret./45 minutes

B.U.N. ____________ mg%

Miscellaneous test	Check test(s) desired
Cerebrospinal fluid	Total cell count
Synovial fluid	Pandy's protein
	Coagulation
	Differential count
	Bacteria

Any other examination required

Officer-in-Charge

PROFORMA FOR FAECAL EXAMINATION

Name of Institute/Hospital/Clinics ______________________________

____

____

FAECAL EXAMINATION REQUEST/REPORT

Clinic No ______________________ Species ______________________

Date ______________________ Breed ______________________

Owner ______________________ Age and Sex ______________________

Referred by Dr. ______________________

____

History:

____

CHECK TEST(S) DESIRED

Faecal examination result

Eggs ______________________

Ciliates ______________________

Protozoans ______________________

E.P.G. ______________________

Nasal washing

Eggs ______________________

Spores ______________________

Officer-in-Charge

PROFORMA FOR URINE EXAMINATION

Name of Institute/Hospital/Clinics ______________________________

____

____

____

URINE EXAMINATION REQUEST/REPORT

Clinic No. ______________ Species ______________

Date ______________ Breed ______________

Owner ______________ Age and Sex ______________

Referred by Dr. ______________

Histor: ______________________________

____

CHECK TEST(S) DESIRED

Colour ______________ Bile salts ______________

Sp. gravity ______________ Bile pigments ______________

Consistency ______________ Occult blood ______________

Reaction ______________ Urobilinogen ______________

Protein ______________ Calcium ______________

Sugar ______________ Others ______________

Ketone bodies ______________

Microscopic Examination

R.B.C. ______________ Epithelial cells ______________

W.B.C. ______________ Crystals ______________

Casts ______________

Cultural Examination

Officer-in-Charge

PROFORMA FOR SKINS SCRAPING EXAMINATION

Name of Institute/Vety. Hospital/Clinics ______________________

____

____

____

SKIN SCRAPING EXAMINATION REQUEST/REPORT

Clinic No. ______________ Species ______________

Date ______________ Breed ______________

Owner ______________ Age and Sex ______________

Referred by Dr. ______________

____

History

____

CHECK TEST(S) DESIRED

Skin scraping examination result

Ectoparasites ______________

Mites ______________

Fungus ______________

Bacteria ______________

Officer-in-Charge

PROFORMA FOR INDOOR-OUTDOOR PATIENT-RECORD

Name of Institute/Vety. Hospital/Clinics ____________________

CASE SHEET

Case No. ____________________ In/Out Patient ____________

Date of Admission ____________________ Date of Discharge ____________

Clinician Dr. ____________________ Student ____________

History and Duration of Illness

Description of the Patient and Condition on Admission

Colour	Breed	Sex	Age
General condition	Temp.	Heart	Lungs
Skin	Limbs	Abdomen	

Tentative Diagnosis ____________________

Final Diagnosis ____________________

Secondary complications if any after final diagnosis

Results C D Dd I NI R DC A

Note: C-cured; Dd-Died; NI-not improved; DC-Discontinued; D-Discharged; I-Improved; R-Relieved; A-Advised.

INVESTIGATION

Blood Urine Faeces Skin scraping X-ray Electrocardiogram

Explanation in detail of abnormality of system(s).

Treatment:

Rx

Surgical Details

Pre-operative diagnosis	Assistant (s)	Date of operation	
Post-operative diagnosis	1	Type of Procedure	
Surgeon	2		
Anaesthesia	3	Minor	Major

Findings

Procedure

Details in (special sheet)

Treatment:

Rx

DISCHARGE SUMMARY

Admitted on ____________________ Discharged on ____________________

1. Presenting symptoms	4. Investigations	7. Final diagnosis
2. Physical findings	5. Operative findings	8. Condition at discharge
3. Clinical impression	6. Treatment	9. Recommendation

Signature of Doctor-in-Charge

PROFORMA FOR ELCTROCARDIOGRAM

Name of Institute/Vety. Hospital/Clinics ____________________

____

Clinic No ____________________ Sp. ____________________

Date ____________________ Breed ____________________

Owner ____________________ Age and Sex ____________________

Referred by Dr. ____________________

____

History

____

Results/Interpretation

Treatment:

Rx

(i)	aVR
(ii)	**aVL**
(iii)	**aVF**

V1

V4

V2

V5

V3

V6

Name and Signature of the Vety. Surgeon

PROFORMA FOR RADIOLOGICAL EXAMINATION

Name of Institute/Vety. Hospital/Clinics ______________________

____

Film No. ______________

Clinical No. ______________ Owner ______________ Date of X-ray______________

Animal No. ______________ Species ______________ Breed ______________ Sex ______________

Age______________

Part to be radiographed ______________

Position ______________

Special procedure required ______________ Referred by Dr. ______________

History and Experimental Procedure in Brief:

Radiographic Factors:

Part Radiographed	kVp	mAs	F.F.D.	With or without Grid	Any other detail

Radiographic details:

Radiographic interpretations:

(Radiographer) Signature of Radiologist with Seal

PROFORMA FOR REPRODUCTIVE PERFORMANCE

Name of Institute/Veterinary Hospital/Clinics etc. ____________________

Name of the place ____________________ Date __________ Name of the Veterinary Surgeon ____________________

Species and breed,	General condition Excellent A Very good B Good C Fair D Poor E	Identity	Owner's name and address	Age/ date of birth Y/M/D	No. of pregnancy/ whelping (indicate abortion, stillbirth)	Date of last whelp-ing	No. of heats after whelp-ing	Date of iast mating	Investigation of sexual organs: ovaries uterus cervix vagina and vulva	Remarks

Name and Signature of the Vet. Doctor with Seal

6

INFECTIOUS DISEASES AND THEIR CONTROL

VIRAL DISEASES

The viruses are minute living organisms of nucleoproteins capable of replicating. Since there is no source of energy for reproduction, the viruses live in living cells and utilize the cellular nutrients and energy for their multiplication. Most of the viruses are disease producing. The common viral diseases of the dogs are rabies, canine distemper and infectious canine hepatitis. The other less prevalent viral diseases are pseudorabies or Aujeszky's disease, canine herpes and parvo-virus infection.

1. Canine Distemper (CD)

It is a highly fatal disease next to rabies in dogs. The disease occurs in acute or subacute form and it is highly contagious. Since wild and stray carnivores harbor the canine distemper virus, it is not possible to eradicate the disease but can be prevented through vaccination.

Aetiology: A paramyxovirus of 120-300 nm particle size.

Epizootiology: All canines like dog, jackal, wolf, fox, dingo and other animals like mink, otter, panda and ferret.

Clinical signs: It is normally a contagious disease which affects animals 3-12 months of age. It is characterized by high fever, loss of appetite, bronchitis, gastroenteritis and dehydration, mostly terminating fatally in colostrum-deprived pups. The following clinical signs may be observed in pups over 3 months of age. Fever for 1-2 days, recurring again after a gap of several days of initial exposure; second temperature rise may be associated with conjunctivitis, rhinitis, bronchitis and gastroenteritis; vomiting, coughing, watery nasal discharge, lacrymation, bloody diarrhoea and often dehydration; presence of pustules on the abdominal surface usually in the groin region; and nervous symptoms such as depression, epileptic convulsions, inco-ordination and circling; in more severe cases there may be ataxia, paresis and chorea.

Diagnosis:

(i) Clinical signs.

(ii) Presence of cytoplasmic and intranuclear inclusion bodies in the epithelial cells of respiratory tract.
(iii) Fluroescent antibody test.
(iv) Virus isolation in susceptible ferrets.
(v) Serological test.

Prevention: For prevention animals should be vaccinated at 4, 8, 12 and 16 weeks of age. Annual vaccination is recommended.

Treatment:
(i) Broad spectrum antibiotic for preventing secondary bacterial infection.
(ii) Application of antiseptic lotion/cream on pustules.
(iii) Symptomatic treatments for systemic disorders.

2. Infectious Canine Hepatitis (ICH)

Infectious canine hepatitis is a contagious disease of dogs. It is characterized by slight rise in body temperature, congestion of mucosa of natural orifices, severe leucopenia and prolonged bleeding time.

Aetiology: Canine adenovirus type 1 (CAV-1).

Epizootiology: All canines, viz. dog, wolf, jackal and fox.

Clinical signs: Fever up to 40.5°C which falls after 24 to 48 hours but normally relapses after 24 to 48 hours, anorexia, increased thirst and congestion of mucous membranes; congestion of buccal mucosa is often haemorrhagic. Tonsilitis, extensive subcutaneous oedema spreading from the head to the inguinal region, enlargement of the liver due to acute hepatitis. In acute cases conjunctivitis, photophobia and sometimes serous discharge from the eyes occurs. It is also known as blue eye hepatitis.

Diagnosis:
(i) Symptomatic elimination of canine distemper, leptospirosis and certain poisoning.
(ii) Prolonged clotting time in case of haemorrhage.
(iii) Presence of characteristic intranuclear inclusion bodies in liver cells.
(iv) Fluorescent antibody test.

Prevention: First vaccination at about 9 weeks of age and second after 3-5 weeks of first vaccination. Annual vaccination is recommended.

Treatment:
(i) Antibiotic coverage to prevent secondary infection.
(ii) Febrifuge.
(iii) Liquid diet feeding.
(iv) Symptomatic treatments for systemic disorders.

3. Rabies

It is the most dangerous of all the viral diseases. It is communicable to human beings. Almost all warm-blooded animals are susceptible to this infection. The incubation period is normally 15 to 50 days. In exceptional cases it may be more than a year. The viral infection causes acute encephalomyelitis. This results in unusual change in the behaviour of the dog like mad aggressiveness, excessive salivation, progressive paralysis and death. The disease is transmitted by contamination of wound with the saliva or bite by the infected animal.

Aetiology: An organism of rhabdovirus group of approximately 60 mm × 175 nm size; and contains ribonucleic acid.

Epizootiology: Almost all warm-blooded animals including man are susceptible to this fatal contagious disease.

Clinical signs: Two types of clinical signs are commonly observed in dogs.

(i) *Furious or aggressive form:* The dog becomes mad and develops a tendency to attack and bite without provocation. It becomes restless and nervous. There is excessive salivation, inco-ordination of gait and the voice is hoarse.

(ii) *Dumb form:* Protrusion of tongue, drooling of saliva, severe depression, inability to swallow and aimless walking.

The disease terminates fatally and death occurs in 1-3 weeks.

Diagnosis:

(i) Clinical signs and history.

(ii) On post-mortem disease is confirmed by the presence of Negri bodies or lyssa bodies in the cytoplasm of hippocampus of dog's brain.

Prevention: Vaccination with an available vaccine according to prescribed schedule.

Post-infection treatment:

(i) Wash the fresh bite wound with soap and water and apply 70% ethyl alcohol or tincture of iodine.

(ii) Infiltration of anti-rabies serum around the wound.

(iii) Daily subcutaneous vaccination of a killed rabies vaccine for 14 days.

4. Pseudorabies or Aujeszky's Disease

It is also known as mad itch. The disease occurs sporadically and is characterized by severe pruritus causing self-mutilation due to continuous chewing of the infected parts. The disease is fatal. The animal mostly dies in 2 to 3 days.

Aetiology: A DNA virus of herpes virus group ranging from 100 mμ - 150 mμ in size.

Clinical signs: Severe pruritus, refusal of food and water, intense pain, loss of response to owner, convulsions, paresis, inco-ordination, coma and death are the usual sequence of clinical signs.

Diagnosis: Clinical signs and death within 24 to 72 hours of the initial sign.

Prevention: Commercial vaccine is perhaps not available.

5. Canine Herpes

This infection is more serious in young pups. In older dogs it is quite mild.

Aetiology: A herpes virus affecting young pups.

Epizootiology: Normally young pups below 1 week of age suffer from the fatal illness. *In utero* infection in pups may occur during whelping in a bitch recently infected by the virus.

Clinical signs: Disease symptoms usually appear between 5 and 18 days post-whelping. The common signs are a soft yellow-green faeces without offensive smell, difficult breathing, inappetance, abdominal pain and vomiting. The disease terminates fatally in young pups. In aged dogs the clinical signs are mild and the animal may suffer from rhinitis and pharyngitis.

Diagnosis:

(i) Characteristic lesions and

(ii) Isolation of herpes virus.

Prevention: Vaccine is not yet developed.

6. Parvovirus Infection

The disease is characterized by gastrointestinal disorders like vomiting, diarrhoea and enteritis and other symptoms like jaundice in young pups. The disease was recognized some time in 1978.

Aetiology: A DNA virus known as Parvovirus.

Clinical signs: Vomiting, diarrhoea, gastroenteritis, myocarditis and hepatitis associated with jaundice and death in young pups. Normally very mild clinical signs are observed in adult dogs which disappear unnoticed during the process of symptomatic treatments.

Prevention: Vaccination with a parvovirus vaccine in young age as per the instructions of the manufacturers.

The other viral diseases which occurs less commonly in dogs are canine adenovirus, canine corona virus, canine parainfluenza virus, reovirus infection, lymphocytic choriomeningitis and mass cell sarcoma.

BACTERIAL DISEASES

The various bacterial diseases encountered in dogs are brucellosis, tuberculosis, listeriosis, tetanus and leptospirosis. Secondary wound infection with staphylococi is also observed sometimes which leads to chronic pruritis and often does not respond to treatment. In most of such infections animals are euthanized due to failure of treatments.

1. Brucellosis

The failure to conceive after successful breeding and frequent abortions are suspected for uterine infectious diseases. Although *Brucella canis* infection is more common but abortions and breeding failure have also been observed due to the infection of other species like *Br. abortus, Br. suis* and *Br. melitensis.* Thus, the disease has significant zoonotic importance and a laxity in the care of infected pet may be hazardous for the owners too.

Aetiology: *Brucella canis, Br. abortus, Br. suis* and *Br. melitensis* are responsible for brucellosis in dogs.

Epizootiology: Dog and other carnivores. *Br. canis* may be transmitted to cat and man.

Clinical signs: Clinical signs do not appear for a long time. Lymphglands are enlarged in non-pregnant females and abortion between 7 and 9 weeks of gestation period usually occurs in the pregnant ones. The vaginal discharge is either mucoid, serous or greenish-grey and may continue for 5-6 weeks after abortion. There may be infertility in infected bitches.

Infected male dogs suffer from the inflammation of genitalia and atrophy of one or both testicles may be there. There may be low fertility or complete sterility.

Diagnosis: Serological tests.

Prevention: No vaccine is in use.

Treatment: Antibiotics may suppress the infection. Elimination is the only known control measure.

2. Tuberculosis

The infection of mycobacterium produces diffuse or localized lesions in the internal organs over an extended period. The infection of internal organs depends primarily on the route of infection. Ingestion of infected materials causes pathogenesis in the gastrointestinal tract, while inhalation produces lesions in the respiratory tract. The dogs are more resistant to tuberculosis and infected dogs may not exhibit clinical signs for a long period. This is a very dangerous situation and an infected pet may spread disease for a long period.

Aetiology: *Mycobacterium tuberculosis* is the main causative agent followed by *M. bovis.* Sporadic infection of *M. avium* may also be observed.

Epizootiology: Widespread disease. It is inter-communicable between the species and other animals.

Clinical signs: Normally it is a chronic disease and dogs remain carrier for quite a long period. The common signs of this disease are continuous loss in weight, tachypnea, dyspnoea and chronic cough. In abdominal infection there may be painful ascites and generalized peritonitis. In cutaneous form, non-healing ulcers are present on the face and neck in association with subcutaneous abscesses.

Diagnosis: Tuberculin test may be used along with radiography, history, clinical signs and sputum examination for presence of acid-fast bacteria.

Treatment:

(i) Isoniazid is given a 5-10 mg/kg B.W. for 24 hours. Usually 50-100 mg is given twice daily, orally.

(ii) Streptomycin 0.5 to 0.75 g daily, I/M.

(iii) PAS (Para-aminosalicylic acid) 3-6 g twice daily, orally. Treatment is always better with a combination of 2 or 3 of the above-mentioned drugs.

(iv) Rifampicin is given @ 10-20 mg/kg B.W. (max. 500 mg). Other drugs like ethambutol and cycloserine @ 15-25 mg/kg B.W. and viomycin @ 40 mg/kg B.W. I/M may also be used. Treatment is always recommended for 6 months - 2 years.

3. Listeriosis

The disease is rare but dangerous. It is produced by the infection of *Listeria monocytogenes* which causes primary encephalitis in the dogs. The disease may be confused with other diseases like cerebral form rabies and distemper but listeriosis has a short course of a few hours to 3-4 days.

Aetiology: *Listeria monocytogenes* may cause primary encephalitis.

Epizootiology: Infection occurs in almost all domestic animals all over the world.

Clinical signs: Initial signs may be confused with those of canine distemper and rabies. Common clinical signs are anorexia, depression, pneumonia, irritability, eye discharge and dilated pupils, chewing the gum, unnecessary barking, lameness, convulsions and stupors.

Diagnosis:

(i) Differential diagnosis of clinical signs.

(ii) Isolation of organism from the cerebrospinal fluid.

Prevention and treatment: There is no effective vaccine or treatment.

4. Tetanus

Tetanus is produced by an exotoxin produced by the infection of *Clostridium tetani* through the open wounds and lacerations. The exotoxin is carried by peripheral nerves and circulation to central nervous system. The signs of the disease appears in about 5 to 8 days of infection and it is characterized by generalized muscular spasms. There is prolapse of the third eyelids and lockjaw. Most of the cases terminate fatal in 4-5 days and a few recovering may prolong more than 2 weeks.

Aetiology: An exotoxin produced by *Clostridium tetani* introduced normally through the open wounds.

Epizootiology: Cosmopolitan distribution.

Clinical signs: Incubation period is usually 5-8 days but may be longer (up to 21 days) in a few cases. Common symptoms are generalized muscular spasms usually initiating from the temporal muscles causing convulsion of the third eyelids, stretched upper lids, retracted lips and ears followed by lockjaw syndrome. The animal becomes stiff assuming a seahorse posture and lastly opisthotonus. Termination is mostly fatal.

Diagnosis: Characteristic clinical signs appearing in mostly wounded dogs.

Prevention: Immunization with antitoxin and toxoid sera.

Treatment:

(i) Parenteral administration and topical application of penicillin preparation.
(ii) Parenteral administration of antitoxin in a higher dose.
(iii) Supportive therapy includes administration of fluid, electrolytes and nutrients.

5. Leptospirosis

This disease has more zoonotic significance than the disease in the dog itself. The dogs are mostly reservoirs for the infection of *Leptospira icterohaemorrhagiae* and *L. canicola.* Initially the disease may occur in acute febrile form responding effectively to antibiotic treatment. However subclinical infection is more dangerous and causes interstitial nephritis and in some cases jaundice also.

Aetiology: Common organisms are the *Leptospira canicola* and *L. icterohaemorrhagiae.* The disease is communicable to man.

Epizootiology: Infects man, dog, domestic and wild animals.

Clinical signs: The disease may be subclinical, subacute, acute, peracute or chronic. Common signs are rise in body temperature, anorexia, vomiting and diarrhoea. Dehydration and depression in prolonged cases may be associated with jaundice.

Diagnosis: Isolation of organism from the urine or blood of the suspected cases.

Treatment: Common antibiotics like penicillin, streptomycin and tetracycline are effective. However, streptopenicillin is most effective for controlling the disease.

Other Bacterial Infections

The other bacterial infections encountered mostly in stray dogs are anthrax *(Bacillus anthracis),* infertility and keratitis produced by the infection of *Pseudomonas aeruginosa,* purulent eye infection, tonsillitis and enteritis caused by the infections of *Clostridium, Proteus* spp., *Streptococcus* spp., *Escherichia coli* and *Pasteurella septica.*

C. CANINE VACCINES

Since dogs are the most common pets and are also responsible for many communicable and zoonotic diseases, it is important to take utmost care for the protection of pets against the important infections. A brief description of various vaccines, their availability and uses have been given for all the important infectious diseases in this chapter.

Rabies Vaccine

Vaccine incorporates 33% chick embryo tissue infected with flury (LEP) strain of rabies virus in a suitable medium and freeze dried.

Use: Used for 4-month-old healthy dogs against rabies.

Reconstitution: Contents are reconstituted with 3 ml of chilled sterile distilled water.

Dose: Administered I/M, 3 ml deep into thigh muscle of dogs at 4 months of age and revaccinated at 1 year.

Immunity: For 3 years.

Precautions: The vaccine should be used immediately after reconstitution and puppies below 4 months are not vaccinated as it is a prophylactic vaccine and not a curative one.

Manufacturer: Indian Veterinary Research Institute, Izatnagar, Uttar Pradesh - 243122.

Rabies Vaccine

Vaccine incorporates flury strain in a freeze-dried vaccine.

Use: Used as prophylactic against rabies.

Dose and reconstruction: Dried vaccine is reconstituted in 2 ml distilled water. Injected deep I/M into hip muscle.

Immunity: For 1 year.

Storage: At 4°-10°C; it keeps well for 1 year.

Precautions: Anaphylactic reaction may occur. Epinephrine hydrochloride should be used to control it. Syringe and needles should be sterilized in boiling water for 10 minutes.

Manufacturer: (Bio-Med); C-96 site No. 1 Bul. Industrial area Ghaziabad - 201001.

Rabisin

The vaccine is produced on cell culture consisting of fixed rabies virus inactivated by beta propiolectone and heat absorbed on aluminium hydroxide.

Use: Used against rabies for immunization in dogs.

Dose: Primary immunization with 1 ml (S/C or I/M) vaccine can be carried out from the age of 4 weeks in pups. If a vaccinated bitch has delivered, it can be done in the 11th week. In larger animals 8 weeks and above. Revaccination after 3 years.

Post-bite vaccination: For all ages, breeds and sizes of dogs 1 ml S/C. The first injection should be given on the day of the bite, second injection on day 3, third injection on day 7, fourth injection on day 14, 1st booster on day 30, 2nd booster on day 90.

Storage: At 2°-8°C in the dark.

Manufacturer: Serum Institute of India, Veterinary Division, 212/2, Hadapsar, Behind Akashwani, Pune - 411208.

Dura-Rab 1 and Dura-Rab 3

Dura-rab is an activated rabies virus vaccine.

Use: Used against rabies for immunization in dogs.

Dose: Inject 1 ml I/M at 4-6 months of age, repeat after 6 months (booster). Repeat annually with dura-rab 1, every 3 years with dura-rab 3.

Manufacturer: Tech America (Marketed by Vestas, New Delhi).

Antirabic Vaccine

The vaccine consists of 5% suspension of sheep brain infected with fixed virus of rabies and inactivated by beta propiolactone to a final concentration of 5%.

Use: Either for immunization or treatment.

Dose: It is given S/C in loose tissue.

Dogs weighing up to 15 kg are given 2 ml daily for 14 days if they are receiving it for the first time, and for 7 days if they have received it previously.

Dogs weighing 15-100 kg are given 5 ml daily for 14 days if receiving for the first time and 5 ml daily for 7 days if received earlier.

Storage: At 2°-5°C; keeps well for 6 months.

Precautions: Not used for pups below 2 months of age.

Manufacturer: Indian Veterinary Research Institute, Izatnagar, Uttar Pradesh - 243122.

Penta Dog (A Pentavalent Vaccine)

Pentadog consists of 2 vaccines which have to be mixed while using. It is used against rabies, distemper, hepatitis and leptopirosis.

Use: It provides immunity against the above diseases in dogs only.

Dose: First injection (2 ml S/C or I/M) is given at the age of 7 weeks and above in pups, second injection 3-4 weeks after the first injection and booster 1 year after the 2nd injection.

Packing: Box of 1 vial DH + 1 syringe LR for single dose only.

Immunity: The vaccine confers immunity for 3 years for rabies component and 1 year immunity for DHL. In case of rabid or suspected rabid animal bite a booster injection is indicated.

Storage: To be stored at 4°-8°C in the dark; should not be freezed.

Packing: Box of 10 doses. Plastic pack of single dose.

Manufacturer: Serum Institute of India, Pune - 411028.

Canine Distemper Vaccine

It is a live freeze dried vaccine.

Use: For primary immunization of dogs at 4 weeks of age or older against canine distemper. Dogs vaccinated before 9 weeks of age should be revaccinated at 12 weeks of age and booster at 16 weeks of age. Annual vaccination is recommended.

Dose: Reconstitute the vaccine (1 ampoule) with 2 ml sterile diluent (distilled water) and give entire content I/M or S/C.

Storage: At 2°-7°C..

Caution: In case of anaphylactic reactions administer epinephrine immediately.

Manufacturer: Indian Veterinary Research Institute, Izatnagar - 243122.

Canine Distemper Vaccine with Canine Hepatitis Vaccine

Use: Live freeze-dried vaccine used at the age of 10-12 weeks. When used under the age of 10-12 weeks, repeat after 3 weeks. Repeat every year.

Dose: Reconstitute the vaccine in 2 ml of distilled water and give I/M deep in thigh muscle.

Immunity: Full development of immunity takes about 3 weeks and remains up to 1 year.

Precautions:

(i) It may cause anaphylactic reaction in a few cases, then epinephrine hydrochloride (1 : 1,000) or an equivalent drug should be used.

(ii) Syringe sterilized in spirit or alcohol should not be used. Syringe boiled in water or autoclaved should be used.

Storage: In refrigerator, at 4°-10°C in the dark. Vaccine retains activity for 1 year.

Manufacturer: (Biomed), C-96, site No. 1, Bul. Rd. Industrial Area, Ghaziabad.

Candur DHD Vaccine

Use: Active immunization against canine distemper and hepatitis.

Dose: S/C or I/M - 2 ml; 1st injection 7-9 weeks of age; 2nd injection 12-14 weeks of age; booster - after 1 year.

Immunity: 1-2 years.

Precaution: Dogs in poor condition, especially those infested with parasites should not be vaccinated.

Storage: At 2°-6°C; should be used before expiry date.

Manufacturer: Hoechst Pharmaceuticals, Hoechst House, Nariman Point, 193, Bombay - 400021.

Caniffa Vaccine

Use: Used in dogs 7-10 weeks of age as a prophylactic measure against distemper, hepatitis and leptospirosis.

Dose: Route - S/C /I/M 1 ml. 1st injection 7-10 weeks of age; booster injection 1 year after the 1st injection and booster injections given annually during the life span.

Storage: At 0°-6°C in the dark; should not be freezed.

Precaution: Should be done under perfectly healthy conditions.

Manufacturer (IFFA Product): Department of Veterinary de Institute, Merieux - 17 Cadex, 1 France.

Canilep DHL

Use: Vaccine against distemper, hepatitis and leptospirosis.

Dose: S/C. 1st injection 7-9 weeks of age 2 ml, 2nd injection not less than 12-14 weeks of age 2 ml.

Manufacturer: Glaxo International Laboratories, Dr. Annie Besant Road, Worli, Bombay - 400025.

Canine Parvo Virus Vaccine

Use: Against canine Parvo virus disease.

Dose: Puppies less than 3 months of age 2 injections; 1st injection at 6-8 weeks of age; 2nd injection after 12 weeks of age; dogs more than 3 months old: 1 injection.

Booster: Yearly vaccination particularly in infected kennels; 1 ml I/M, I/V or S/C.

Storage: At 2°-8°C in the dark. Do not freeze.

Manufacturer: Serum Institute of India, Veterinary Division, 21212 Hadapsar, Behind Akashwani, Pune - 411028.

Parvocine Vaccine

Parvocine is a stable parvo virus vaccine produced in a perma cell line.

Use: Against canine parvo virus disease.

Dose: 1 ml S/C or I/M - puppies less than 3 months of age 2 injections. Ist injection at 6-8 weeks of age; 2nd injection at 10-12 weeks of age; dog more than 3 months old 1 injection. Booster injection should be given every year.

Manufacturer: Tech America and marketed by Vestas Pharmaceuticals and Biologicals, A-21, Rajouri Garden, New Delhi-110027.

Nobi-Vac - DHL

Use: Live attenuated strain of canine distemper virus, infectious hepatitis and inactivated leptospirosis bivalent vaccine used against canine distemper, infectious hepatitis and leptospirosis in dogs.

Dose: The 1st vaccination is given at 7-9 weeks of age 2 ml S/C; 2nd vaccination: 12-14 weeks of age 2 ml S/C; revaccinated at 1-2 years intervals.

Packing: Vials (with a vial of solvent).

Manufacturer: Inter Vet. Pharmaceuticals, Pragati Bhawan, Mezzanine Floor, Jai Singh Road, New Delhi.

Adenomune-7 (Multivalent Vaccine)

Adenomune-7 consists of 7 vaccines (Canine Distemper, Adenovirus type 2, Hepatitis, Parainfluenza, Parvovirus, *Leptospira canicola* and *Leptospira icterohaemorrhagiae,* modified live and killed virus).

Use: It is multivalent, highly antigenic immunogen; for the protection of puppies and adult dogs against above diseases. The live viruses have been so attenuated as to assure safety upon administration without destroying their antigenecity. All virus fractions represented are modified live antigens with the exception of the Parvo virus and the Adeno virus type 2 which are inactivated to assure complete safety while retaining a high level of immunogenicity.

Dose: The desicated vaccine is aseptically rehydrated with the accompanying fluid. Reconstituted vaccine is injected @ 1 ml S/C or I/M. First vaccine should be administered at 9-12 weeks of age and it should be repeated at 14-16 weeks of age. It should be repeated annually.

Manufacturer: Tech America and marketed by Vestas Pharmaceuticals and Biologicals, A 21, Rajouri Garden, New Delhi-110027.

Tetanus Antitoxin

Use: Prophylactic and therapeutic use against tetanus.

Packing: Tetanus antitoxin 1,500 I.U. 1 ml × 25 ampoules. Vial containing 10,000 IU, 3.4 ml ampoules and Vial containing 20,000 IU, 5 ml ampoules.

Dose: Phrophylactic: 250 units S/C; therapeutic: 10,000 - 20,000 units I/V.

Manufacturer: Haffkine Institute, Bombay.

Tetanus Toxoid I.P.

Use: For prophylaxis against tetanus.

Packing: 1 ml × 10 ampoules; 10 ml vials.

Manufacturer: Haffkine Institute, Bombay (Maharashtra).

Tetanus Vaccine

Packing: Tetanus vaccine absorbed 0.5 ml × 10 ampoules and 5 ml vials.

Manufacturer (Haffkine): Biopharmaceuticals Corporation Ltd., Acharya Donde Marg, Worli, Bombay 400 012.

Tet - Vac

Each 0.5 ml contains Tetanus toxoid absorbed on 2.5 mg of aluminium phosphate.

Use: Active immunization against tetanus by I/M injection.

Packing: 0.5 ml × 10 ampoules.

Manufacturer: Glaxo International Laboratories, Dr. Annie Besant Road, Worli, Bombay - 400025.

Lyophilised Polyvalent Anti-Snake Venom Serum

Contains enzyme refined equivalent to 10 ml of purified globulins.

Use: Snake bite in animals and man; 1 ml of reconstituted serum neutralises; 0.6 mg of dried cobra venom, 0.45 mg of dried common krait venom, 0.6 mg of dried Russel's viper venom and 0.45 mg of dried Saw scale viper venom.

Dose: Reconstitute the content of 1 ampoules in 10 ml pyrogen-free water. This antivenom serum should be injected as soon as possible, after the bite. As a first dose at least 20 ml of the reconstituted serum should be injected intravenously very slowly (not over 1 ml per minute). The second dose should be repeated after 2 hours of first dose or even earlier. If symptoms persist further dose should be given at every 6 hours until the symptoms completely disappear. In case of a viper bite some serum should also be injected around the site of the bite to prevent gangrene of the tissue.

Prevention of serum reaction: If anaphylactic reaction develops the following medicines may be given or these medicines should be given 15-30 minutes before injecting the serum:

(i) Adrenaline 1 ml (1 : 1000) I/M.

(ii) Antihistamine.

(iii) Corticosteroids and analgesic drugs should also be given.

Packing: Ampoule with 10 ml pyrogen-free water.

Manufacturer: Serum Institute of India (P) Ltd., 212/2, Hadapsar, Pune - 411028, India. It is also manufactured by Haffkine Institute, Bombay (Maharashtra).

7

PARASITIC DISEASES

The parasitic diseases have been described separately for endoparasites and ectoparasites. The parasites are more prevalent in the stray dogs but domestic pets also frequently suffer from different kinds of parasitism. Parasites are of two types, viz. endoparasites and ectoparasites.

1. Endoparasitic Diseases

Endoparasites of gastro-intestinal tract are more prevalent than those of heart and respiratory tract. The common signs of the presence of gastro-intestinal parasites are diarrhoea and/or dysentery followed by dehydration, vomiting, anorexia and weakness. The condition is easily diagnosed by the microscopic examination of faeces. The infection of haemoprotozoan and filarial worms causes lack of growth, loss of conditions, anaemia, weakness, alopecia, dermatitis and ulcerative crust formation, thickening of the skin and often pot bellied. The conditions are diagnosed by the microscopic examinations of blood smears.

There are many other signs which may be suspected for parasitism in dogs, they include cutaneous ulceration, lacrimation, photophobia, coughing, sneezing, nasal discharge, loss of body weight, anorexia, dehydration, haematuria, subcutaneous oedema and allergy.

The history is very helpful in the diagnosis of parasites which are further confirmed by the signs, lesions and microscopic examination. Recently some serological tests are also available for a few parasitic diseases.

2. Ectoparasitic Diseases

Any laxity in the grooming and management of dogs often leads to serious ectoparasitic infection by the infestation of mites, ticks and lice. The dermatitis caused by ectoparasites is further contaminated by bacterial and fungal infections if left uncared and under unhygienic conditions. Mange is the most serious of all ectoparasites.

Ectoparasitism is manifested by various degrees of alopecia, pruritus, dermatitis and even ulceration in severe cases. The common parasitic dermatitis of dogs are pediculosis, flea bite, mange caused by *Demodex canis, Sarcoptes scabiei* and *Cheylatiella* spp. A mite, *Otodectes cynotis* is mainly responsible for the pathogenesis of otitis externa. Infestation of ticks causes pruritus, erythematous nodules formation, itching and alopecia. The diagnosis of parasitic skin infestation is simple and effective treatments have been given for the specific ectoparasite.

The details regarding the various parasites and their treatment are given in the following tables.

(I) ENDOPARASITIC DISEASES AND THEIR TREATMENT

Organwise Parasitic Diseases and its Aetiology	*Main Clinical Symptoms*	*Diagnosis on the Basis of*	*Line of Treatment*
1	*2*	*3*	*4*
Small intestine			
Ancylostoma caninum (Canine hookworm disease).	Pneumonia, blood loss, anaemia, black tarry faeces with diarrhoea, anorexia.	History, clinical signs, presence of elliptical, thin-shelled eggs (65 μ x 40 μ) in the faeces	1. Tetramisole compounds (a) Ascaris tab (Mercury), orally Pup: 50 mg tab, Adult: 150 mg tab. (b) Decaris tab (Ethnor), orally Pup: 50 mg tab, Adult: 150 mg tab. 2. Levamisole compounds (a) Vermisole tab (Khandelwal), orally. Pup: 50 mg tab, Adult: 150 mg tab (b) Helmonil tab (Alved), orally, 150 mg tab/10 kg B.W. (c) Helmonil injection (Alved): @ 1 ml/5 kg B.W., S/C. (d) Vizole cap. (M.M. Lab), orally. 150 mg cap 3. Disophenol compounds (a) Ancylol injection: 4.5% (Cyanamid) @ 1 ml/4.5 kg B.W., S/C. 4. Pyrantel pamoate compounds (a) Pyrantel suspension (Dolphin), orally. 50 mg/ml @ 10 mg/kg B.W. for 3 days. (b) Pyromoate tab (Franco-Indian). 250 mg tab @ 10 mg/kg B.W. for 3 days 5. Bephenuim hydroxynapthoate: (a) Alcopar (B.W.) orally Pup: 2-3 g, Adult: 3-5 g

(Contd.)

Organwise Parasitic Diseases and its Aetiology	Main Clinical Symptoms	Diagnosis on the Basis of	Line of Treatment
1	2	3	4
			(b) Hoopar (Cadila) orally. Pup: 2-3 g, Adult: 3-5 g. 6. Mebendazole Compounds (a) Wormin (Cadila), orally @ 0.5 mg/kg B.W. (b) Endazole (Biddle Sawyer), orally. 100 mg tab. 1 tab BID for 3 days. (c) Mebex (Cipla), orally. 100 mg tab. 1 tab BID for 3 days. (d) Zodex powder (Concept), orally. Pup: 1/2 T.S.F. Adult: 1 T.S.F. (e) Zodex bolus 500 mg (Concept), orally. Pup: 1/2 bolus, Adult: 1 bolus. (f) Humla (ACI), orally, 5 mg/kg B.W. (g) Robendole (TTK), orally. 100 mg tab., 1 tab BID or TID.
Small intestine			
Toxocara canis, Toxocara leonina (Ascarid worm infection/Ascaridiasis).	Lack of growth and loss of condition, pot bellied, rough hair coat, respiratory distress, diarrhoea, vomiting, pneumonia, intestinal obstruction, unthriftiness	History (the infection may be transmitted from mother to foetus); clinical signs; presence of oval, thick-shelled, pitted eggs (75 μ x 85 μ) in the faeces	1. Piperazine adepate, hydrate and citrate compounds: (a) Piperex (Sarabhai), orally. @ 100 mg/kg B.W. (b) Vermex liquid, orally (Pfizer). @ 2.5 ml/10 kg B.W. (c) Antepar liquid (B.W.) orally @ 2.5 ml/10 kg B.W. (d) Piperazine liquid (Ethicare), orally. @ 2.5 ml/10 kg B.W. (e) Piperazine adepate (ICI), orally. @ 100 mg/kg B.W. (f) Helmacid (4.5%) (Glaxo), orally. @ 0.2 ml/kg B.W.

(Contd.)

Organwise Parasitic Diseases and its Aetiology	Main Clinical Symptoms	Diagnosis on the Basis of	Line of Treatment
1	2	3	4
			(g) Verban liquid (Cyanamid), orally. @ 0.2 ml/kg B.W. 2. Pipirocid (Arex), orally. 2.5 ml/10 kg B.W. 3. Mebedanzole and levamisole compounds may be used as in Ancylostoma infestation. 4. Caricide (Cyanamid), orally. 50-70 mg/kg B.W. for 10-20 days. 5. Tetramisole compounds as in hookworm disease.
Small intestine			
Strongyloides stercoralis (thread worm infestation or Strongyloidiasis).	Blood streaked mucoid diarrhoea, emaciation, loss of body weight, shallow rapid breathing and little pyrexia, verminous pneumonia, consolidation of lung, enteritis with haemorrhage and mucus.	History, clinical signs; presence of small thin-walled & rounded eggs or larvae in faeces.	Compound containing mebendazole may be used in similar doses and route as indicated *vide supra.*
Large intestine			
Trichuris vulpis (whip worm infection or Trichuriasis)	Loss of body weight, diarrhoea, presence of fresh blood in faeces, pot-bellied; mild form of disease may not show the symptoms.	History, clinical signs, eggs (30 μ x 40 μ) yellowish, lemon-shaped and plug at pole.	Compound containing levamisole and mebendazole as mentioned earlier should be used in a similar manner.
Oesophagus/stomach/arteries			
Spirocerca lupi (Oesophageal worm infestation,	Vomiting, haemorrhage, emaciation, watery or bloody faeces with putrid odour, difficulty in swallowing	History, clinical signs; presence of thick-shelled, parallel eggs with blunt side ends (30μ x 15μ) in the faeces	I. Compound containing Diethyl carbamazine citrate. 1. Caricide (Cyanamid), orally. 15 mg/kg B.W. for 7 days. 2. Banocide (B.W.) orally. 50 mg tab. @ 1 tab TID for 10 days.

(Contd.)

Organwise Parasitic Diseases and its Aetiology	*Main Clinical Symptoms*	*Diagnosis on the Basis of*	*Line of Treatment*
1	*2*	*3*	*4*
			3. Hetrazan (Lederle), orally. 50 mg tab @ 1 tab TID for 10 days. 4. Unicarbamezan (Unichem), orally. 50 mg T.I.D. for 10 days. 5. Carbamyl syrup (Kopran) orally. @ 5 mg/kg B.W. for 7-10 days. II. Disophenol preparation 1. Ancylol 4.5% (Cyanamide) @ 1 ml/4.5 kg B.W. S/C.
Right ventricle and adjacent vessels like anterior vena cava, posterior vena cava, pulmonary artery and hepatic vein. *Dirofilaria immitis, D. repens, Dipetalonema reconditum, Dip. dracunculoides* (Heart worm disease, filariasis or microfilariasis) (Fig. 93)	Chronic dyspnoea, cough, rough body coat, or dermatitis, lack of stamina, easily tired, lack of interest in exercise, anaemia, ascites, hydrothorax, enlarged liver, haemoglobinuria, some blunt cut lesions on tongue.	History, clinical signs; presence of microfilaria in blood (may be seen hanging blood drop, stained blood smear or by modified Knott technique); microfilaria may also be recovered from urine and skin scrapings.	Preparation containing Diethyl carbamazine citrate. 1. Caricide (Cyanamide). orally. 25-40 mg/kg B.W. for 30 to 60 days. 2. Banocide (B.W.) orally. 50 mg tab @ 1 tab TID for 1 month. 3. Hetrazan (Lederle) orally 50 mg tab @ 1 tab TID for 1 month. 4. Unicarbazan (Unichem) orally. 50 mg tab @ 1 tab TID for 1 month. 5. Carbamyl syrup (Kopran), orally. @ 5 mg/kg B.W. for 1 month. Antimony preparations like Fouadin (Trivalent antimony compound) given I/V as 6.3% aqueous solution 2.5 ml daily for 12 days. 1. Anthiomaline (M and B) @ 0.5 ml in small breeds;

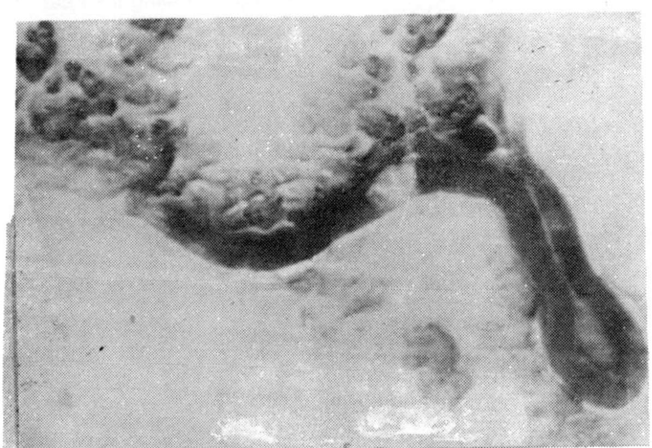

Fig. 93. Blood smear showing the microfilarial or *Dirofilaria sp.* (1000 X)

(Contd.)

Organwise Parasitic Diseases and its Aetiology	*Main Clinical Symptoms*	*Diagnosis on the Basis of*	*Line of Treatment*
1	*2*	*3*	*4*
			@ 1 ml in large breed; I/M for 5 days. 2. Antimosan (Bayer) @ 0.5 ml in small breeds; @ 1 ml in large breeds; I/M on alternate days, 4-5 injections. **Others** 1. Caparolate sodium diacetate @ 2 ml/kg B.W., I/V. 2. Dithiazine Iodide, orally @ 50 mg/kg B.W./day. 3. Capasotate, orally @ 500 mg/kg B.W. for 1 week or more. 4. Ivermectin, orally @ 0.5 mg/kg B.W., single dose. 5. Ivermectin (Dynamic Pharmacals) @ 0.5 mg/kg B.W. S/C. 6. Arsenamide @ 1 mg/kg B.W. daily for 15 days. 7. Dithianzine iodide, orally. 200 mg/kg B.W. in food, for 10-20 days. 8. Levamisole, orally. 11 mg/kg B.W. for 6-12 days. Supportive therapy should be given during the treatment period such as vitamin B complex, antihistaminic drugs, skin tonics, etc.
Kidney			
Dictophyma renale (Giant kidney worm infestation).	Marked loss of body weight, anaemia, haematuria, frequent urination, severe abdominal lumbar pain, pet may cry, stretch, display nervousness and trembling.	History, clinical signs, presence of parasitic eggs in urine, eggs are ellipetical, brownish, thick-shelled, pits on all parts except poles (80μx50μ). Radiographic examination.	No effective treatment. Only surgical removal of worm is useful.
Nasal and respiratory passage			
Linguatula serrata (Tongue worm infestation).	Severe irritation, sneezing, coughing, fits and difficult breathing, uneasiness, rest-	Eggs are (90μ x 70 μ) oval, thick-shelled, yellowish; eggs may be found in the nasal	Injection or inhalations are not very effective. Trephining of the nasal pas-

(Contd.)

Organwise Parasitic Diseases and its Aetiology	Main Clinical Symptoms	Diagnosis on the Basis of	Line of Treatment
1	2	3	4
	lessness, dog rubs its nose with forefeet and snores while sleeping; blood-stained mucous discharge from nostrils.	discharge or in the faeces.	sage and removal of parasites followed by irrigation with antiparasitic or antiseptic drugs is useful.
Duodenal and Jejunal mucosa			
Trichenella spiralis (Trichenella infestation or Trichinosis).	**Initial stages** (About 24 hours after taking infected meat), gastroenteritis, diarrhoea, nausea, vomition, slight fever and mild abdominal pain. **Muscle invasion stage** (after 1 week). Emaciation, dyspnoea, oedema, muscular pain, anorexia, slight, fever.	History, clinical signs; adult worms may occasionally be found in the faeces; larvae may be demonstrated in muscle biopsy, the sample being examined, either pressed between two pieces of glass or after digestion in an acid pepsin (1 : 1) solution. Haematological examination indicating high percentage of eosinophils (about 25%). Number of immunodiagnostic tests such as complement fixation, haemagglutination, etc. are used.	1. Thiabendazole compounds are effective against both adult intestinal and larval muscle phases. (i) Thiabendazole premix (Arex), orally. 50 mg/kg B.W., repeat after 3 weeks. (ii) Thiabendole bolus (MSD), orally. 50 mg/kg B.W. repeat after 3 weeks. 2. Methyridine is also effective against the muscle stage of the infection. Methyridine product 20 ml S/C.
Eyes			
Thelazia coliforniensis (Eye worm infestation).	Corneal opacity, lacrymation, photophobia, severe conjunctivitis.	Larvae and adult worms in tear ducts and under the eyelids.	Manual removal of parasite by fine forceps in local anaesthetics and antibiotic or sulpha eye drops; piperazine salt 0.5% with sterile normal saline solution for irrigation of eyes. Methyridine product 20 ml S/C, local application of 3% boric acid, 0.05% mercuric chloride, 0.05% iodine, 0.5% lysol or 0.5% diethyl carbamazine give good results.
Bronchi, trachea			
Cremosoma vulpis (Lung worm infection).	Bronchitis, pneumonia, coughing, necrotic lesions in lung or liver.	History, clinical signs; presense of eggs in faeces or in the nasal discharge.	Fouadin and anthiomaline is effective.
Lung			
Filaroides osleri (F.mildki;	Harsh persistant coughing,	Eggs ($80\mu \times 50\mu$) thin-shelled,	Preparations containing

(Contd.)

Organwise Parasitic Diseases and its Aetiology	*Main Clinical Symptoms*	*Diagnosis on the Basis of*	*Line of Treatment*
1	*2*	*3*	*4*
Tracheal worm infestation (Filaroidiasis).	loss of body weight, anorexia breathing with the mouth, ataxia.	colourless, larvated.	tetramisole and levamisole as mentioned earlier should be used in a similar manner.
Subcutaneous tissue of limbs			
Dracunculus insignis (Dracunculosis).	Non-healing ulcer and swelling of subcutaneous tissue.	History, clinical signs, presence of adult parasites under the skin of the limb; larvae may be detected from faeces.	1. Removal of worms through incision. 2. Diethyl carbamazine in high doses.
Bladder			
Capillaria plica (Bladder worm infestation).	Cystitis, cloudy urine, sometimes irritation while urinating	Eggs in urine nearly colourless, slightly long, wormed, 65μ x 25μ in size.	There is no effective treatment. Surgical removal of worm may be done.
Skin			
Pelodera strongyloides (Pelodera dermititis).	Pustular and erythematous lesions on thorax, abdomen, auxillary, inguinal region, upper part of limbs and presence of scabs.	History, clinical signs, and by finding nematodes in skin scraping from the affected area.	Organophosphophate local application of antibiotic ointments; provide clean and dry shedding.
Blood vessel			
Angiostrongylus vasorum (Angiostrongylus infection).	Loss of body weight/and condition, easily tired, lesions found in the right ventricle of the heart and pulmonary arteries, blood coagulation time is increased.	History, clinical signs, presence of eggs or larvae in the stool.	Preparation containing tetramisole and levamisole as mentioned above should be used in a similar manner.
Lung			
Paragonimus spp. (Fluke infestation).	Anaemia, jaundice, wasting oedema, cough, dysponea.	History, clinical signs, presence of operculated eggs with yellowish colour in the faeces.	1. Trodax (M&B) 0.2 ml/5 kg B.W. S/C. Repeated after 1 month. 2. Flukaphene (Ethicare) orally. 0.5-0.75 g/10 kg B.W. 3. Flukin (Arex), orally 100 mg tab. 1 tab single dose.
Liver			
Fasciola hepatica (U.K. and Europe)	Diarrhoea, anaemia, jaundice, weakness, emaciation and loss of appetite.	-do-	-do-

(Contd.)

Organwise Parasitic Diseases and its Aetiology	*Main Clinical Symptoms*	*Diagnosis on the Basis of*	*Line of Treatment*
1	*2*	*3*	*4*
F. gigantica (Asia, Africa & other Tropical countries) (Fasciolíasis).			
Small Intestine			
Diphylobothrium latum, Echinococus granulosus; Spirometra species, *Taenia pisiformis, T. taeniaeformis, T.hydatigena, Dipylidium caninum* (Tape worm infection or Taeniasis).	Unthriftiness, capracious appetite, intermittent diarrhoea and constipation, anaemia, stunted growth, pot bellied, rubbing anus on the ground and attempt to bite the anal region due to irritation in advanced cases; nervous signs, sometimes tape worm segments pass in faeces; skin coat harsh and dry; dehydration.	History, clinical signs; presence of segments of tape worm in faeces; presence of tape worm egg in faeces.	I. Preparation containing niclosamide may be used orally. (i) Niclex (Alved) 1g tab/7.5 kg B.W. (ii) Niclosan (Biddle Sawyer) 500 mg tab; 3-4 tab. 2. Preparations containing mebendazole may be given in double doses. 3. Preparations like Panacur (Hoechst), containing Fenbendadozle may be given @ 50-100 mg/kg B.W. for 3 days. **Others** 1. Cestophene (Pearl Chemical), orally 0.2 g/kg B.W. 2. Niltape (Ethicare) orally 2-4 g. 3. Bunamidine orally @ 25 mg/kg B.W. 4. Bithional orally @ 50 mg/kg B.W. **Herbal preparations** 1. Helmex PW. (Vetmed), orally 4-10 g. 2. Pulp arecanut, orally 3-5 g. 3. Taenil pw, orally 2-5 g. 4. Krimos orally 20-30 g.
Muscle Fibre			
Cysticercus cellulosae (cysticercosis).	Dogs with cysts in brain may show symptoms resembling those of rabies.	History, clinical signs, presence of cysts in muscle fibres. Eggs are present in faeces.	As above, but specific treatment is not available.

(Contd.)

Organwise Parasitic Diseases and its Aetiology	*Main Clinical Symptoms*	*Diagnosis on the Basis of*	*Line of Treatment*
1	*2*	*3*	*4*
Small Intestine			
Nanophyetus salmincola, Alaria spp., flukes).	Haemorrhagic enteritis, dull, depressed and loss in body condition.	History, clinical symptoms with presence of eggs in faeces.	1. Carbon tetrachloride, Tetrachloro ethylene is used in the fluke infestation. Simultaneously Tetracycline is also used for rickettsial infection.
Small intestine			
Giardia canis (Giardiasis)	Blood and mucus pass with stool, excessive straining during defaecation, irregular appetite and diarrhoea.	History, clinical signs,presence of cyst in stool.	Preparation containing metronidazole are very useful; duration and treatment depends upon severity of the disease. 1. Flagyl (M&B) orally. 1 tab TID for 7-14 days. 2. Unimezol (Unichem), orally. 1 tab TID for 7-14 days. 3. Unimezol suspension (Unichem), orally. 5 ml TID for 7-14 days. 4. Metron (Alkem), orally. 1 tab TID for 7-14 days. 5. Metrogyl (Unique), orally. 1 tab TID for 7-14 days.
Large intestine			
Entamoeba histolytica (Amoebiasis)	Chronic diarrhoea with, or sometimes without blood or mucus, mild to severe haemorrhagic enteritis and ulcer in intestinal mucosa. Pain in abdominal region.	History, clinical signs, presence of amoeba cysts in stool.	Same as in Giardiasis.
Intestine			
Eimeria canis, Isospora canis, I. bigemina and *I. revolta* (Coccidiosis)	Dysentry, loss of appetite weakness, anaemia, dehydration; stool may also be passed with blood and mucus; loss of body weight.	History, clinical signs; presence of oocyst in the faeces.	Preparations containing sulphonamides are choice of drugs. 1. Sulpha bolus (Sarabhai), orally. @ 1 g/5 kg B.W. followed by 0.5 g/5 kg B.W. daily for 5 days. 2. Sulphadimidine (Arex), orally. 150 mg/kg B.W. followed by half dose for 5 days.

(Contd.)

Organwise Parasitic Diseases and its Aetiology	Main Clinical Symptoms	Diagnosis on the Basis of	Line of Treatment
1	2	3	4
			3. Diadin (Pfizer), orally. 1/2 Tab/10 kg followed by 1/4 Tab/10 kg B.W. for 5 days. 4. Coccil liquid (Akelvi), orally. 150 mg/kg B.W. on first day; followed by 75 mg/kg B.W. for 5 days. 5. Hamidin (HAL) orally. 200 mg/kg followed by half dose for 5 days. 6. Oriprim tab (Cadila), orally. 1 tab first day followed by half tab for 5 days. 7. Robatran Vet granules (TTK), orally. 15 g on first day followed by 7.5 g for 5 days. II. Preparations containing nitrofurazone. 1. Neftin (SKF). 1 tab TID for 4-5 days. 2. Enterovioform (Ciba), orally. 1 tab TID 3. Entobax, orally 1 tab TID.
Whole Body			
Toxoplasma gondi (Toxoplasmosis).	Coughing, pneumonia, dyspnoea, discharge from nose and eyes, haemorrhagic enteritis, anaemia, enlargement of lymphnodes, increased body temperature, nervous signs like convulsions, paralysis and chorea	History, clinical signs, presence of bradyzoides and Tadryzoides in faeces, by serological test, viz. haemagglutination test.	Preparations containing triple sulpha should be used. 1. Pyremethamine (Daraprim), orally. @ 2.2 mg/kg B.W. followed by half the dose daily for 2-3 weeks. 2. Trinamide (M&B) orally. @ 1 g/7 kg B.W.followed by 0.5 g/7 kg B.W. daily for 2 weeks. 3. Equal parts of sulphadimidine, sulphadiazine and sulphapyridine may be mixed and given in same manner as above preparations.
Skin			
Leishmania tropica, L. donovoni (Leishmaniasis)	**Cutaneous form:** Dry or wet ulcer covered with thick brown scabs; boundary of lesions is	History, clinical signs, presence of the parasites in blood or lymphnode smear,	There is no specific treatment. Preparations containing antimony compound

(Contd.)

Organwise Parasitic Diseases and its Aetiology	Main Clinical Symptoms	Diagnosis on the Basis of	Line of Treatment
1	2	3	4
	red and hairless, itching **Visceral form:** Anaemia, emaciation, debility, kerato-conjunctivitis, enlarged spleen and liver, epistasis, lameness and diarrhoea.	serological test.	may be used.
Blood *Haemobartenella canis* (Haemobartenellosis)	High temperature, anaemia, dull, depressed, pale mucous membrane, urine dark brown & contains bilirubin; enlarged spleen and lymphnodes; paracentral necrosis.	History, clinical signs, presence of coccoid, oval, ring or rod-shaped organisms in enlarged spleen followed by anaemia.	Broad spectrum antibiotics like oxytetracycline, tetracyclin, Chlorotetracyclin and Chloramphenicol @ 5 mg/kg B.W. I/M may be used. Five injections should be given. Berenil (Hoechst). @ 0.1 g/10 kg B.W., I/M or S/C.
Blood *Trypanosoma evansi, T.cruzi T. brucei T. rangeli* (Trypanosomiasis)	Enlarged lymphnode, intermittent fever, anaemia, subcutaneous oedema, keratoconjunctivitis, weakness and convulsions	History, clinical signs, presence of trypanosoma in blood smear, serological tests.	1. Berenil (Hoechst); similar dose as in babesiosis. 2. Babesan (ICI); doses similar as for babesiosis. 3. Corridan (HAL). 1 g PW should be mixed in 5 ml water. @ 0.025 to 0.040 ml/kg B.W. S/C, single injection.
Blood *Babesia canis, B. gibsoni, B. vogeli* (Babesiosis)	High temperature, increased pulse and respiration, haemoglobinuria, anaemia, jaundice; acute form is mostly fatal.	History, clinical signs, presence of babesia organism in blood smear, serological tests.	Preparations containing 4, 4-diaminodiazo amino benzene diaceturate is the best drug for babesiosis. Berenil (Hoechst), @ 0.8-1.6 g/100 kg B.W. S/C or I/M. Babesan (Quinuronium sulphate B-Vet.C) (ICI) @ 0.2 ml of 0.5% solution 4.5 kg B.W. S/C injection. Trypan blue B. Vet. C. (Ethicare), orally. 20-150 mg according to size and severity of disease, slow I/V, injection.

(II) ECTOPARASITIC DISEASES AND THEIR TREATMENT

Ectoparasitic Disease(s) and its aetiology	*Clinical Signs*	*Diagnosis*	*Treatment*
1	*2*	*3*	*4*
Ear mange/Otitis/Cancer			
Otodectes sp. (Fig. 94)	Dog shakes its head, stretches the ears, brown to blackish waxy powdery deposit in ear.	History, clinical signs; by removing parasite from waxy powdery deposit of the infected ear.	1. Use insecticide spray in the ear to kill the mite. 2. If there is more wax then clean by putting lukewarm water containing a pinch of washing soda. If there is any sign of pus, blood or a foul smell, consult a veterinarian.
Cheletiella mite infection			
Cheletiella sp.	Itching of the body, mostly involves neck and back.	History, clinical signs, presence of reddish colour mite in the skin scraping.	Insecticide spray.
Scabies			
Sarcoptes scabiei (Fig. 95)	Highly contagious skin disease; thickening of skin, intense irritation, alopecia, bare patches on the skin, hyperkeratitis thickened and folded appearance of skin. (Fig. 96, 97)	History, clinical signs, presence of mite in the skin scraping examination; 10% NaOH or 10% KOH should be mixed in skin scraping to separate the mites.	Remove the hair, insecticide spray may be used: 1% solution sevin, kilex carbaryl, 1:500 solution of asuntol 16% liquid. Ascabiol - (M & B), Scabitex (Ballotun) Gamma BHC. Scrab (Aristo), Emscap (MM Lab), Lorexane (ICI). GAB (Guffic), Ethnoscab (Ethnor). DDT, Benzyl Benzoate preparations. Scabinidon (Indopharma). Herbal preparations Karanj oil - 50 ml. Garlic extract - 15 ml. Turmeric powder - 10 g. Lemon extract - 4 ml. Camphor - 1g. Onion extract - 20 ml. Mix and apply BID for 5-10 days. Other herbal drugs are Himax, Pestoban (Indian herbs), Sorin (Vet. Med.).

(Contd.)

Plate-23

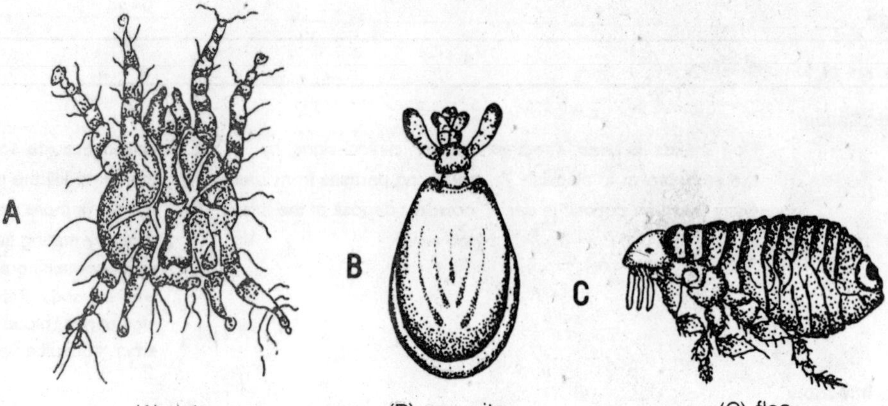

(A) tick, (B) ear mite, (C) flea

Fig. 94. The morphology

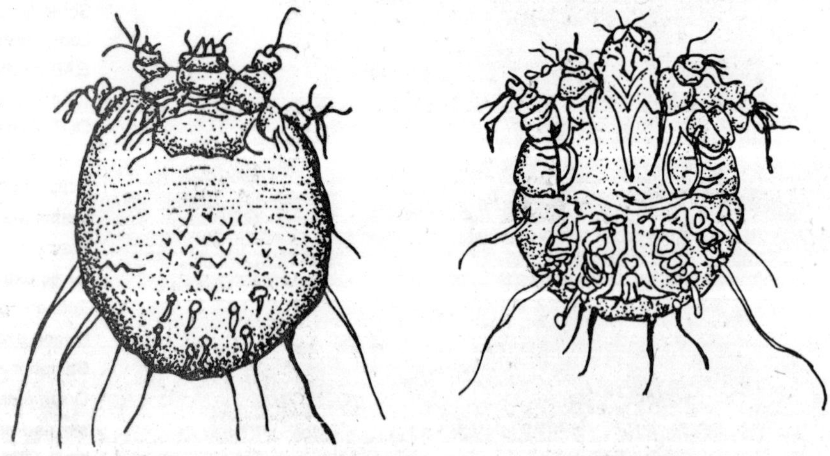

a - Male, b - Female

Fig. 95. The diagram of *sarcoptes scabiei.*

Ectoparasitic Disease(s) and its aetiology	*Clinical Signs*	*Diagnosis*	*Treatment*
1	*2*	*3*	*4*
Demodectic mange or follicular mange			
Demodex canis *(D. folliculorum)* (Fig. 98)	These mites live in hair follicles and sebaceous glands. Loss of hair, thickening of the skin is found (Fig. 99). **Squamous form:** Scaly wrinkled often resembling ringworm infection, sebarrhoea. **Pustules type** Formation of pustules, hyper- and secondary bacterial infection may develop.	History, clinical signs, presence of cigar-shaped mites in the skin scraping.	Clip the hair, bathe with antiseptic solution like Savlon, Dettol or Piripol. Give broad spectrum antibiotic treatment to check bacterial infection and antihistaminic drugs like Avil, Phenargan. Above-mentioned insecticides, acaricides, and Ben zyl benzoate and gamma BHC preparation may be given. Supportive therapy with vitamin B complex and fluid therapy advanced cases euthanasia is the only course.
Pediculosis (louse infection/lousiness)			
Linognathus setosus, Trichodectes canis, Heterodoxux spinigir (Fig. 100).	Blood-sucking or biting lice causing pruritis, dermal irritation; dog scratches, rubs or bites infected area; rough, dry hair coat and small wounds are seen.	History, clinical signs and lice seen on hair and body coat.	1. Clip the hair. Insecticide spray as in scabies or by spraying rotenone in 1% or malathion in 2% dilution or in talcum powder, lorexane lotion or cream (ICI). Ethnoscab cream (Tthnor) Pestoban (Indian Herbs). Same spray advocated for ticks may be used.
Tick infestation (Acariasis)			
Hyalomma sp., *Dermacentor andersoni, Rhipicephalus sanguineus* (Fig. 94)	Local inflammation, worry of the host, dermatitis, irritation, occasionally paralysis may develop due to tick toxins, anaemia, scratching of the body.	By seeing the ticks on the body including inner part of the ear. Ticks may also be seen near bedding or kennel.	Spray of sevin-0.5-1% Malathion-0.5-1% Lindane-0.03% Toxaphene-0.50% Sumithion-1% Asuntol-0.5% Chlordane-0.1% Ectozide dusting powder. (Balloun). Herbotick powder (Herbolab). Pestoban (Indian

(Contd.)

Ecto-Parasitic Disease(s) and its aetiology	*Clinical Signs*	*Diagnosis*	*Treatment*
1	*2*	*3*	*4*
			Herbs). Anti-tick vaccine may also be given if available.
Flea infestation			
Ctenocephalides canis (Fig. 94)	Dirty skin due to heavy infestation; dog becomes puzzled, itching, hypersensitization corrugated appearance looking like skin of rhinoceros, allergic dermatitis due to hypersensitivity to the flea, loss of condition.	Presence of flea; allergic sensitivity test with flea antigen.	Same spray as used for tick infestation. Flea repellant may be tied on the collar or around the neck, care being taken to ensure that the dog does not eat the flea repellant. For allergic reaction, antihistaminic drugs should be given.
Flies infestation (Myiasis)			
Common house fly.	Irritation by biting, larval stage of fly may produce maggot worms which may become septic, sometimes causing very deep wounds in the skin.	Presence of larva in the wound.	Use fly repellant, like turpentine oil, eucalyptus oil, lorexane cream; maggot wound may be cured by putting turpentine oil or Sevin powder in the wound along with topical and parenteral antibiotic therapy to check secondary bacterial infection. For control of flies, dog house or kennel should be cleaned properly and sprayed with insecticides like DDT, gamma BHC. Sevin 50% wp @ 0.5 to 1% spray once in 2 months.
Mosquito infestation			
Common mosquitoes like anopheles, culex etc.	Irritation by biting, causing restlessness.	Presence of mosquitoes in the dog house or nearby places.	Mosquitoes may be controlled by providing mosquito net fencing (wire) or doors, windows, by insecticides spray as in fly control and by avoiding dampness and humidity near the kennel.

PLATE-24

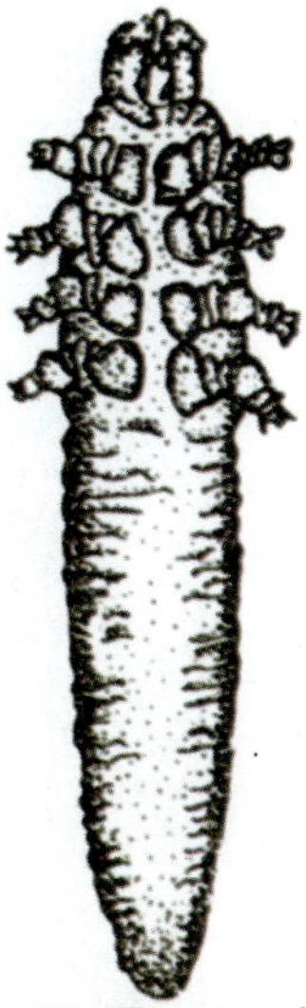

Fig. 98. The morphology of *Demodex canis*

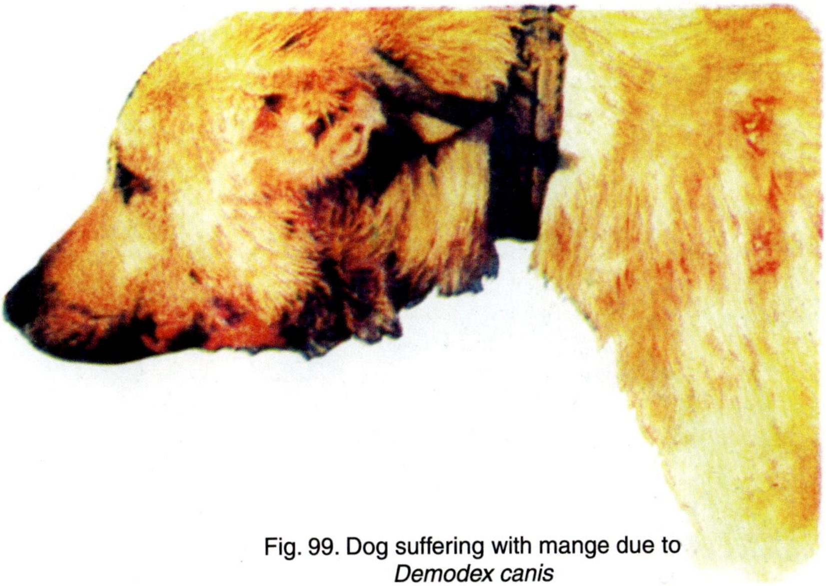

Fig. 99. Dog suffering with mange due to *Demodex canis*

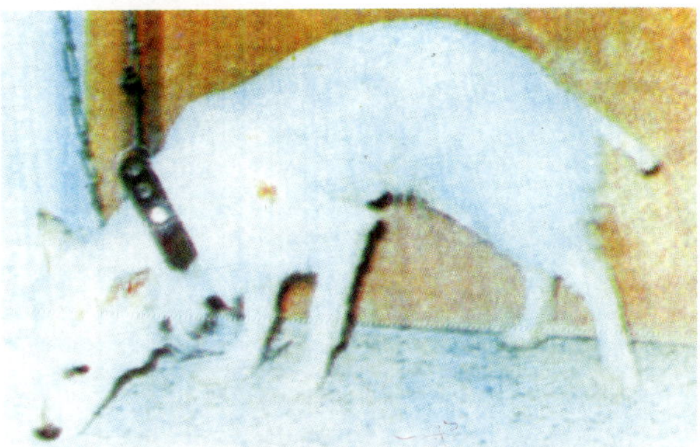

Fig. 96. Dog suffering with mange due to *Sarcoptes scabiei*

Trichodectes canis *Heterodoxus* spp. *Linognathus* spp.

Fig. 100. Different types of lice in dog

Fig. 97. Dog suffering with mange due to *Sarcoptes scabiei*

PLATE-25

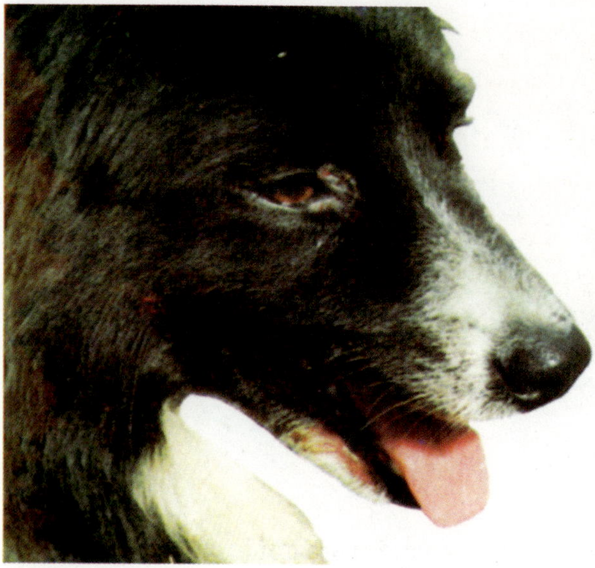

Fig. 101. Ringworm lesion on the face

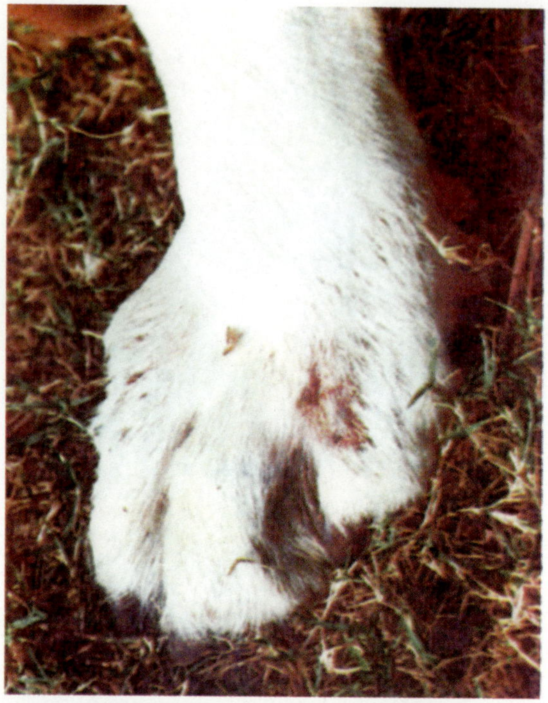

Fig. 102. Ringworm lesion on the toe

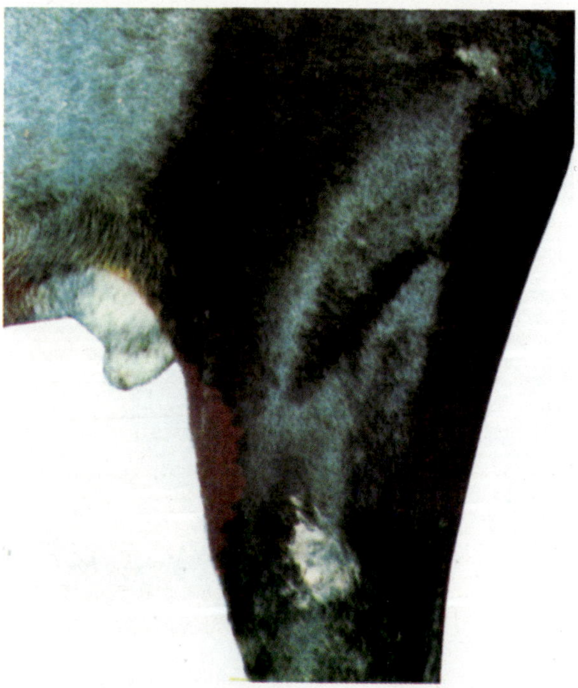

Fig. 103. Ringworm lesion on the thigh

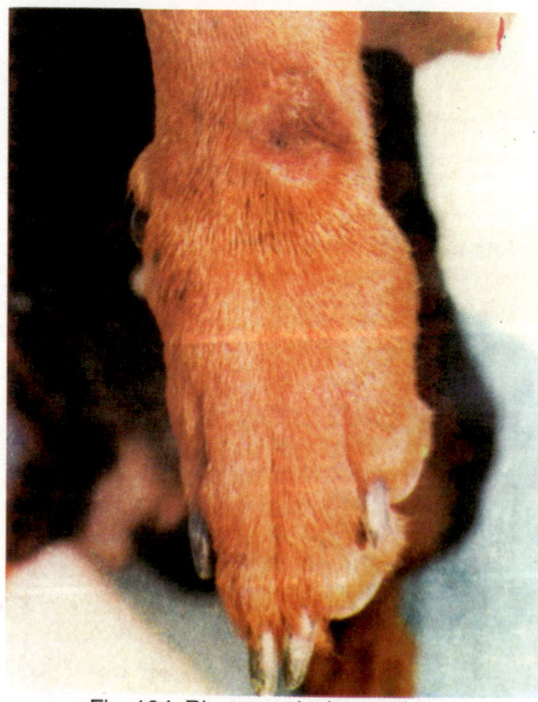

Fig. 104. Ringworm lesion on the arm

8

MYCOTIC DISEASES AND THEIR TREATMENT

Several fungi are responsible for internal and external disease conditions. The causes of pathogenecity are mostly the toxins produced by the fungi. Mycoses may be described as dermatomycoses responsible for skin lesion. Deep mycoses are responsible for systemic diseases.

The term dermatomycosis denotes the fungal infestation and lesions limited to the cornified layer of the skin. Dermatophytes prevalent in the dermatophytosis of dogs are *Microsporum canis, M. gypseum* and *Trichophyton mentagrophytes, T. rubrum* and other species of these fungi. The lesions are ring-like, development of alopecia and pruritis giving the common name ringworm. The disease is diagnosed by the presence of hyphae and spores in the skin scrapings.

The subcutaneous mycoses are more severe conditions produced by the penetration of the fungi, which include different species of *Sporothrix, Zygomycetes, Actinomyces, Nocardia, Streptomyces, Curvularia* and *Aspergillus.* The subcutaneous mycoses are mostly characterized by the swelling and ulceration of superficial lymph nodes, raised and granulomatous lesions often associated with fistulous tracts and a thick exudate. In aspergillosis in addition to subcutaneous tissues, respiratory tract and gastrointestinal tracts are involved. It produces pneumonia and enteritis respectively.

The systemic mycoses are caused by the infection of *Blastomyces dermatitis, Histoplasma capsulatum, Cryptococcus neoformans* and *Coccidioides immitis.* These fungi mostly produce pathogenesis in the respiratory tract, which is manifested by pyrexia, anorexia, dyspnoea, coughing and unthriftiness. Sometimes central nervous system, nasal sinuses and facial sinuses are also involved. The defects of various mycotic conditions are given in the form of a table.

Fungal Diseases and aetiology	*Clinical Signs*	*Diagnosis*	*Treatment*
1	*2*	*3*	*4*
Dermatomycosis			
(Ringworm)			
Microsporum canis	Scattered lesions on the	History, clinical signs; direct	Griseofulvin - 25-50 mg/kg
M. andovinii	body; loss of hair and discrete	examination of skin in 10%	'B.W.; generally treatment is

Fungal Diseases and aetiology	*Clinical Signs*	*Diagnosis*	*Treatment*
1	*2*	*3*	*4*
M. distortum *M. vanbre seghenii* *M. cookie* *M. gypseum* *Trichophyton mentagrophytes* *T. verrucosum* *T. schoenleinii* *T. rubrum* *T. equirum* *T. gallinae*	circular areas of hair loss with scaling and sometimes inflamed borders are common; crust may also develop; in severe cases heavy crusted areas of widespread hair loss or hair scaling and erythema, itching and irritation; lesions always spread from centre to periphery indicating recovery from centre showing ring-like lesions. (Fig. 101-104)	KOH mount showing mycelium and chains of arthrospores; examination of hair in 10% KOH showing sheath of small spores (2.8 μ) in mosaic, completely surrounding the hair at the base; easily separated from hair in preparation; mycelium running within the hair, parallel to its length; Wood's light examination may give bright yellow, green fluorescence in infected hair in some cases.	given for 1 month but depending on the severity of the disease, it may be reduced or increased. Preparations of Griseofulvin; Fulvi (Indica), 125 mg tab; Grisovin - FP (Glaxo), 125 mg tab; Idifulvin (IPPL), 125 mg tab; Mycoral (Plazma), 125 mg tab; Walavin-FP (Carter-Wallace) 125 mg tab. Preparations for local application. Captan (1:200 sol), 2-5% boric acid, potassium permanganate (1:5,000), benzoic acid 6%, Sulphur, salicylic acid, resoscinol 10%, phenol 0.5-1%, Iodine 2.5%. (Tincture or ointment) of 1% Sevin 50% wp, 1% chlorophos, 0.2% thimerosal solution, 1% kilex carbaryl 50% w.p. Tinaderm (Ful Ford). Apply twice daily. Jadit ointment or Jadit solution or Jadit H (Hoechst). Apply twice daily. Mycostatin ointment (Sarabhai); apply twice daily. Kanaderm ointment (Sarabhai): apply 2-3 times daily. Himax (Indian Herbs): apply 2-3 times daily. Quadriderm (Ful Ford): apply twice daily. Pentaderm (Mercury Laboratories), apply twice daily.
Histoplasmosis			
Histoplasma capsulatum (Fungus invades the reticulo-endothelial system in various tissues or organs).	Chronic cough, persistant diarrhoea, fluid faeces darker than normal, enlarged mesentric lymphnodes, often palpable, loss of weight, dehydration, photophobia, iris swollen and pupil constricted, anaemia, temperature fluctuating	History, clinical signs; demonstration of organism in tissue or by culture examination includes buffy coat; peripheral blood; biopsy specimens from enlarged lymph node; secretion and exudate from respiratory tract and	Amphotericin B-50 mg. Mix with 10 ml sterile water added to 5% dextrose in water to make final volume of 230 ml. Give this solution @ 1-1.25 ml/kg.B.W. I/V. After a day's rest, give second dose of 1.5-2 ml/kg. B.W. followed by another day's rest; third and sub-

(Contd.)

Fungal Diseases and aetiology	*Clinical Signs*	*Diagnosis*	*Treatment*
1	*2*	*3*	*4*
	from 102.5° F to 105.5° F	mouth ulcer	sequent doses are continued on alternate days until 12 I/V, injections are completed. Supportive therapy includes sodium bicarbonate for keeping urine alkaline. Avoid vitamin B and analgesics and corticosteroids.
Blastomycosis			
Blastomyces dermatidis (May infect organs like lung, eyes, skin, muscle).	**Pulmonary form:** Persistant non-productive cough, bronchial rales; loss of weight, fever, nasal exudate, neutrophilia. **Ocular form:** Aqueous humour becomes cloudy, iris swollen, pupil constricted and photophobia. **Cutaneous form:** Small papules, scaly ulcerated lesions, small abcesses, bone lesions involve long bone, mostly soft tissue over bone lesions are swollen and very sensitive to touch.	History, clinical signs, serological test like CFT, exudate from S/C abscesses should be mounted in a drop of 10% NaOH for 15 minutes and examined under microscope for round, thick-walled usually single budding yeast (size 8-20 μ). Sabourod's agar media.	Do
Cryptococcosis			
Cryptococcus neoformans (organs involved are skin, lungs, CNS oro-nasal and foot).	Irritability, lameness, blindness, ulcerated soft tissue, swelling with clear and brown exudate from skin lesions; focal granulations in lung, thickened gelatinous meninges.	History, clinical signs; by seeding the fungus in tissues or in culture; by serological tests.	Same as in histoplasmosis by Amphotericin B.
Coccidilodomycosis			
Coccidia immitis	Dyspnoea, cough, exudate from nose, poor appetite, intermittant diarrhoea, loss of weight, enlarged joints, temperature 102°-104° F. Nasal and ocular discharge.	History, clinical signs; presence of fungus in nose discharges, serological tests.	Same as in histoplasmosis by Amphotericin-B.
Nocardiosis			
Nocordia asteroides	Dyspnoea, coughing, anorexia nasal and ocular discharge, diarrhoea, temperature 102°-104° F.	History, clinical signs, direct microscopic examination, by culture examination.	Sulphonamides orally are the drugs of choice in canine; dose rate is 1-2 g daily (4-6 weeks). Penicillin alone or in combination with sulphonamide is also used.

(Contd.)

Fungal Diseases and aetiology	*Clinical Signs*	*Diagnosis*	*Treatment*
1	*2*	*3*	*4*
Actinomycosis			
Actinomyces bandeti	More common in older and hunting dogs, cutaneous actinomycosis is more prevalent in dogs. Chronic granulomatous pruritus, subcutaneous lesions like abscess, fistulous tracts.	History, clinical signs and definite diagnosis can be made by identification of organism from culture.	Potassium or sodium iodide 0.5 g daily until signs of iodism appear or the visible lesions are markedly reduced in size. Penicillin in effective.
Candidiasis			
Candida albicans	General debility, favour the development of diabetes mellitus, diarrhoea, anorexia dehydration.	History, clinical signs and definite diagnosis can be made by identification of organism from culture.	Amphotericin-B.
Aspergillosis			
Aspergillus fumigatus *A. glaucus* *A. niger* *A. nidulans*	Formation of yellowish caseous nodules in most of the organs of the body, Pneumonia, elevated temperature, mucopurulent discharge, conjunctivitis and coughing.	-do-	No effective treatment exists.

9

ZOONOTIC DISEASES AND THEIR PREVENTION

The term zoonosis means inter-communicable diseases from animals to man and vice versa. Since dog is the most popular pet which usually lives within the house in close contact with human beings, it is essential to have an adequate knowledge about the zoonotic diseases. This will be helpful in adopting preventive measures and precautions in the routine management and handling of the pets. The zoonosis has been classified into the following four categories:

Direct (Ortho)

Zoonosis: From vertebrate host to man by direct contact or by a mechanical vector (no development in vector) e.g. Rabies, Trichomoniasis and Brucellosis.

Cyclozoonosis: More than one vertebrate host (but not invertebrate host) is required to complete life-cycle, e.g. Taeniasis and Echinococcosis.

Metazoonosis: Transmitted by invertebrate vectors, e.g. Plague, Arbovirus infection and Schistosomiasis.

Saprozoonosis: Have both vertebrate and a non-animal developmental site (like organic matter, soil and plants) e.g. Larva migrans and Mycotic infection.

The term *anthropozoonosis* has been widely used for the diseases transmissible from animal to man or *vice versa.* In W.H.O. reports the term zoonosis not only includes the infectious diseases transmitted from animals to man but also the diseases produced by non-infective agents like toxins and poisons.

More than 100 infections or diseases of domestic and wild animals are potential threats to human health through contact with diseased animals or animal products, consumption of tissues or products of diseased animals, and consumption of animal products contaminated during processing, storage or delivery.

The zoonotic diseases of bacterial, viral, rickettsial, mycotic and parasitic nature have been tabulated.

COMMON ZOONOTIC DISEASES

Name of Disease	*Causative agent*	*Host*	*Mode of infection to man*
1	*2*	*3*	*4*
1. **Bacterial Diseases**			
Brucellosis (common)	*Brucella canis*	Dog	Contact, ingestion of infected secretions.
Tuberculosis (common)	*Mycobacterium tuberculosis* var. *hominis*	Dog	Contaminated secretions, water and aerosole.
Salmonellosis (common)	*Salmonella typhimurium*	Dog	Infected meat, contaminated food and water etc.
Hemolytic			
(i) Scarlet fever	*Streptococcus pyogenes*	Dog	Through contact
(ii) Sore throat	*Streptococcus epidermidis*	Dog	Through contact
Leptospirosis (rare)	*Leptospira pomona* *Leptospira canicola*	Dog	Contact and exposure
Anthrax (rare)	*Bacillus anthracis*	Dog	Contact with hair and contamination of food.
Diphtheria (rare)	*Corynebacterium diphtheriae*	Dog	Contact
Pasteurellosis	*Pasturella multocida*	Dog	Bite, contact, contamination etc.
2. **Viral Diseases**			
Rabies (common)	Neurotrophic virus	Dog, Cat, Wild animals	Animal bite, abrasion
Aujeszky's disease/ Pseudorabies (rare)	Virus	Dog	Contaminated secretions
Lymphocytic-chorio-meningitis	Virus	Dog	Ingestion
Reovirus infection	Virus	Dog	By contact with a carrier dog
Mumps	Virus	Dog	Contact
3. **Parasitic Zoonosis**			
(a) **Protozoan Diseases**			
Toxoplasmosis	*Toxoplasma gondii*	Dog	Ingestion and contact
Chagas disease (not in India)	*Trypanosoma cruzei*	Dog	Faecal material of bug
Leishmaniasis, visceral (Kala-azar)	*Leishmania donovani*	Dog	Sand fly bite
Balantidiasis	*Balantidium coli*	Dog	Food and water contamination

(Contd.)

Name of Disease	Causative agent	Host	Mode of infection to man
1	2	3	4
Amoebic dysentry	*Entamoeba histolytica*	Dog	Contaminated food and water
Giardiasis	*Giardia* spp.	Dog	Contaminated food and water
B. Helminthic Infections			
Ascariasis	*Toxocara canis*	Dog	Contaminated food and water
Hydatid disease	*Echinococcus granulosus*	Dog	Swallowing parasitic eggs through contamination with dog faeces
Dracunculosis	*Dracunculus medinensis*	Dog	Drinking infected pond water
Filariasis	*Dirofilaria immitis*	Dog	Mosquito
Trichuriasis	*Trichuris vulpis*	Dog	Infection of larvae
Schistosomiasis	*Schistosoma japonicum*	Dog	Mosquito (through skin)
Fasciolopsiasis	*Fasciolopsis buski*	Dog	Eating infected snails
Echinostomiasis	*Echinostoma ilicanum*	Dog	Raw aquatic plants
Hook worms and related infections	*Ancylostoma ceytanicum*	Dog	Through broken skin
Strongyloidiosis	*Strongyloides stercolaris*	Dog	Through skin
Larva immigrans	*Bunostomum* spp., *Ancylostomum* spp. and *Toxocara canis*	Dog	Through broken skin
Diphilobothriasis	*Diphilobothrium latum* *Dipylidium caninum*	Dog	Eating raw fish
Gnathostomiasis	*Gnathostomum* spp.	Dog	Eating infected flies
C. Mites			
Scabies (mange)	*Sarcoptic scabiei*	Dog	Contact
Follicular mange	*Demodex canis*	Dog	Contact
Cheleticlar scabies	*Cheyletiella yusguri*	Dog	Contact
Flea allergy and dermatitis	*Ctenocephalides canis*	Dog	Flea bite
4. **Fungal and Rickettsial Zoonosis**			
Mycotic Diseases			
Ringworm	*Trichophyton* spp.	Dog	Contact
Coccidioidomycosis	*Coccidioides immitis*	Dog	Inhalation and through wounds
Histoplasmosis	*Histoplasma capsulatum*	Dog	Inhalation of dust and ingestion.
Cutaneous streptothricosis	*Dermatophilus congolensis*	Dog	Contact
Nocardiosis	*Nocardia asteroides*	Dog	Contact
Candidiasis	*Candida albicans*	Dog	Endogenous in nature usually
Blastomycosis	*Blastomyces* spp.	Dog	Injury, trauma, wound and inhalation
Sporotrichosis	*Sporotricum* spp.	Dog	Injury

PRECAUTIONS TO AVOID ZOONOTIC DISEASES

1. Diseased dog should be kept away from healthy dogs and human beings, especially children.
2. Kissing a pet should be avoided because it can potentiate danger of worm infection and rabies if the dog is suffering from these conditions.
3. Dogs should not be permitted to lick your face, hands, legs and other body parts as this may transmit some disease.
4. Regular and periodical deworming and vaccination of pet is absolutely necessary to prevent the transmission of zoonotic diseases.
5. Regular spraying of insecticide to check ectoparasitic infestation.
6. Proper bathing using suitable soap should be done at regular intervals.
7. Hair should be clipped and groomed regularly. This is necessary for the cleanliness of dog.
8. Use protective gloves, spectacles, dangri, gumboots while handling a rabid dog.
9. Shoes and clothes used for handling a dog, suffering with zoonotic diseases should be properly washed and kept separately.
10. After handling a dog hands and feet should be washed properly with soap or antiseptic solution.
11. Children must not be allowed to play with a sick dog or pup.
12. Utensils for a dog should be kept separately and cleaned properly with soap or detergent.
13. Children should not be allowed to play with the utensils of dogs.
14. A pregnant lady should take precautions while gardening or working near the dog house as the soil may be contaminated with dog faeces which may have *Toxoplasma gondii* oocyst. It is a very dangerous disease and may be transmitted to foetus while in the womb.
15. Regular and proper cleaning of dog house or kennel and premises must be done with disinfectant but avoid the use of carbolic-containing compound.
16. Place of defecation and urination should be away from the public places. In case dog defecates or urinates in the house, excreta should be disposed properly.
17. Pup or dog should not be allowed to share the bed/bedding with children/adult.
18. Dogs should not be allowed to mix with stray dogs and wild animals.
19. Raw meat or meat from diseased animals and offal should not be given to the dogs.
20. Notification of infectious and communicable diseases should be recorded immediately. Information must be relayed throughout the country through media such as radio, television, and newspaper.
21. Quarantine - New arrivals: pet(s) at the house or dog kennel specially from other states and countries where some diseases are zoonotic should be kept in isolation ward to observe the signs of any infectious diseases as per the quarantine rules.
22. Sick pets especially when suffering with zoonotic disease must be kept isolated from healthy pets and human beings.
23. All hygienic measures such as cleaning of pet, house, utensils and other belongings of pet should be maintained to minimize the infections.
24. Wild animals like fox, dog and jackals are mainly responsible for spreading the infectious diseases like rabies in human population. Therefore, destruction of the wild animals and stray dogs is important to

control diseases like rabies.

25. The carcass of animals which have died of rabies, brucellosis and other such diseases should not be kept open, but immediately disposed off by burning or burial. Burial should be at least 1.8 metres deep with layers of lime sprinkled over the carcass.
26. Disinfection is the important preventive measure for control of infectious diseases. This can be achieved by using U.V.-rays, heat, chemicals like sodabicarbonate, mercuric chloride, bleaching powder, copper sulphate, sodium carbonate, lime and gases like HCN, sulphur dioxide and formaldehyde.
27. During breeding season the pet should not be allowed to mate with stray dogs where it can pick up some infection.
28. If any person is suspected for zoonotic illness he should contact a doctor immediately and the pet should be taken to a veterinary doctor.

10

COMMON POISONS AND THEIR TREATMENT

It is difficult to define precisely a poison. Misuse of most of the things may be poisonous. In day-to-day life pets are exposed to small amounts of different harmful substances but body detoxifies and eliminates them regularly. The toxic effect depends upon the quantity of the poison induced in the body, the nature of the compound, and age and body condition of the dog. Young pups and aged dogs are more susceptible.

Almost all toxic substances are chemicals but they may be natural chemicals, synthetic chemicals or biochemicals synthesized in plant and animal tissues and organs. The hazardous toxic substances are insecticides, pesticides, rodenticides, fertilizers, petroleum products, plant toxins, and poisonous animals like snake, scorpion, bee, wasp and lizard.

Over-dosing of some drugs, minerals and vitamins may also be toxic. The non-judicious use of chloroform, atropine, barbiturates, aspirin, formaldehyde, phenol, morphine, digitalis and some antibiotics may cause serious illness and often result in death. The brief information about the source and signs of poisoning and its diagnosis and treatment are given in the tabular form for easy understanding.

Type of poison	*Source of poison*	*Main symptoms*	*Line of treatment*
1	*2*	*3*	*4*
Acid (Sulphuric acid, nitric acid and hydrochloric acid).	Contaminated feed by accident; due to change of gastric pH (indigestion or infection etc.); mistakenly in therapeutic preparation.	Vomiting, abdominal pain, diarrhoea, convulsion, staggering gait, restlessness dyspnoea, tympany, corrosion of the mucus membrane of the upper digestive tract.	1. Chalk or kaolin 15-30 g orally. 2. Sodium bicarbonate 5-20 g orally. 3. Sodium bicarbonate, lime water followed by sedative and stimulants. In case of burn, first flood with water, then with dilute alkali. 4. Other weak alkalies, milk and water.

(Contd.)

Type of poison	*Source of poison*	*Main symptoms*	*Line of treatment*
1	*2*	*3*	*4*
			5. Magnesium carbonate or magnesium oxide 1-5 g orally. 6. Magnesium hydroxide (milk of mg) 1-15 ml orally.
Alkalies (Caustic soda, caustic potash and other weak alkalies like ammo-- nium carbonate).	Contaminated feed by accident; due to change of gastric pH (indigestion or infection etc.); mistakenly in therapeutic preparation.	More or less same as in acid poisons.	1. 5% acetic acid/citric acid/glacial acetic acid. Give according to body weight and severity of poison (normally 50-300 ml orally). 2. Weak acids like acetic acid, citric acid, glacial acetic acid, hydrochloric acid 1-5 ml in 1 litre of water, orally. 3. Vinegar, 20-50 ml orally. 4. Sour wine 10-30 ml diluted in water, orally. 5. Milk, demulcents and oil. 6. Tannic acid 200-500 mg in 30-60 ml of water, orally.
Ammonia (Ammonium phosphate and ammonium carbonate)	Contaminated feed, excessive dose in therapy.	Dyspnoea, convulsions, restlessness, pulmonary oedema results in forced rapid breathing, severe colic, staggering, marked thumping pulse, violent struggle and death.	As stated in alkali poisoning. When air passage is affected, inhalation of diluted acetic or citric acid and hot water vapour inhalation should be given.
Arsenic	Feed contaminated with arsenic spray, accidental use of arsenical preparation, concentrated arsenic dipper, spraying at animal to control the ectoparasites, use of arsenic preparations as weed killer, insect poison and wood preservative.	Intense abdominal pain, staggering gait, paralysis, excessive salivation along with thirst and vomition. In sub-acute case anorexia, paralysis of hind quarters, trembling, and convulsions, coldness at extremeties, diarrhoea, collapse and death.	1. Gastric lavage with lukewarm water or oil or saline purgation. 2. Prompt emetic. 3. Precipitated iron oxide in emergency. Add a solution of ferric chloride and washing soda. Filter through muslin or thin cloth. Wash precipitate. Administer in large quantity as lukewarm water at 5-10 minutes intervals or mix 3 parts of solution per chloride of iron with 17 parts of water, add calcinated magnesia (1 : 17) in water, dose 1-5 ml every 5-10 minutes. 4. Sodium thiosulphate 0.5-1 g as 15% solution I/V, 5 g orally

(Contd.)

Type of poison	*Source of poison*	*Main symptoms*	*Line of treatment*
1	*2*	*3*	*4*
			in 0.5 litre of water in a day. 5. Dimercaprol-(BAL) 3-5 mg/kg B.W., I/M. Repeat every 4 hrs for first 2 days, 4 times on 3rd day and twice daily up to 10 days.
Antimony (Tartar emetic)	Contaminated feed, miscellaneous use in therapy.	Same as in arsenic poisoning.	1. Gastric lavage and purgative 2. Strong tea, tannic acid, milk demulcents, small dose of washing soda and diluted acids. 3. Patient should be warmed and treated with some stimulants. 4. Dimercaprol (BAL) same as in arsenic poisoning. 5. Milk of magnesia and lime water of calcium hydroxide.
Carbon monoxide	Coal gas due to fume from stone.	Asphyxia and dyspnoea, intermittent heart beat, coma and death. Visible mucous membrane showing pink colour, blood becomes cherry red.	1. Treat with pure oxygen containing 5% carbon dioxide 2. In severe cases or in coma give respiratory analeptic such as nikethamide or leptazole.
Cyanide	By enemity/cyanogenic fodder feeding.	Excessive salivation, jerky movement of the eye ball, convulsions, paralysis, stoppage of respiration even before that of heart beat, bright red colour of blood. Death within few seconds.	Sodium nitrite (1%), 16 mg/kg B.W. I.V.; sodium thiosulphate (20%), 30-40 mg/kg B.W. I/V.
Copper	By feed contaminated with copper sulphate, due to rich copper-containing soil which causes chronic poisoning, due to heavy dose of copper sulphate used for snail control, treatment of foot-and-mouth disease, and foot-rot and parasitic infestation and while being used as a spray or dip.	**Acute cases:** Excessive salivation, nausea, vomition and purgation, abdominal pain, convulsions, paralysis of body parts and death.	1. In acute poisoning animal should be handled as in irritant poison such as by using purgative, emetics and gastric lavage. BAL may also be used. 2. Chronic cases may be treated with 15-70 mg of ammonium molybdate and 50-60 mg sodium sulphate daily for 20 days by adding the molybdate in diet.

(Contd.)

Type of poison	Source of poison	Main symptoms	Line of treatment
1	2	3	4
			3. Lavage with egg and milk, sodium bicarbonate, morphine, saline purgatives are also useful. 4. Ferrocyanide (sodium salt) 0.3-0.5 g oral.
Carbolic acid (Phenols and cresols)	By heavy use as disinfectant, by contaminated feed, by accidental use, used as wood preservative, by licking of wood.	Nausea, vomiting, convulsions, staggering gait, restlessness, weakness, jaundice and anaemia	1. Emetics, enema, epsom or glauber's salt, white of eggs, milk and stimulants. In case of dermatitis treat with soap and water or alcohol. 2. For emetics, use strong salt solution or large crystal of washing soda or mustard and water. 3. **In small animals:** Apomorphine hydrochloride, 0.9 mg/kg B.W. S/C or I/M. Sodium bicarbonate, kaolin, bismuth orally and glycerine over the affected skin is very useful.
Iodine	Prolonged use of iodine preparations as a therapeutic agent, accidental use.	Lachrymation, nasal catarrah, scurfiness, skin rashes of variable character, anorexia, heavy and prolonged treatment of iodine may cause atrophy of testicles, blindness, paralysis, palpitation of heart and sweating.	1. Stop use of iodine. Give milk and starch mucilase as demulcents. Nikethamide or leptazol may also be given. Sodium bicarbonate is orally given.
Fluorine	Excessive fluorine in water. Intake of large amount of soluble fluorine compounds. Feeding of fluorine contaminated feed. Presence of fluorine in excessive quantity in plants in some areas.	**Acute:** Gastroenteritis, diarrhoea, vomiting, abdominal pain, muscular weakness and death **Chronic:** Lameness, bone abnormalities, presence of dental lesions with dark pigment deposit in defective enamal and pitted teeth.	Aluminium sulphate or chloride 0.25-1 g daily, orally. Calcium borogluconate, 60-150 ml I/V.
Lead	By licking of lead paints, lead pipes. By taking the contaminated feed, water with lead spray, Spray on fruit. Used as in therapy (lead	**Acute poisoning:** Staggering gait, muscles of head and neck showing tremor, rolling eye and frothing mouth, muscular	1. Wash the stomach and give saline purgative and emetics. 2. Give sedative such as siquil or largactil. Milk,

(Contd.)

Type of poison	*Source of poison*	*Main symptoms*	*Line of treatment*
1	*2*	*3*	*4*
	acetate white lotion).	spasm and tetany, during convulsions animal may become blind, and sometimes try to climb a wall or a tree. In severe poisoning, abdominal pain and intermittent circling in different directions, constipation followed by diarrhoea. **Chronic poisoning:** No tremor and excitement, animal lying in recumbent form.	white portion of eggs, or tannic acid should be given. Sodium sulphate or magnesium sulphate or both. Sodium calcium EDTA is the drug of choice, dose 30-50 mg/kg B.W. daily for 5 days I/V as 100% solution. 3. Calcium salt and vitamins or BAL may also be given.
Mercury	By contaminated feed. By accidental use. While as fungicide on grains.	Severe gastroenteritis, diarrhoea, stomatitis, patient shows sign of acute nephritis. Difficulty in breathing, coughing, nasal discharge, colic and subnormal temperature.	Remove all the material from stomach. Give white raw egg followed by purgative. BAL same as in arsenic poisoning. Sodium thiosulfate, 2-10 ml 20% solution, I/V.
Urea	Accidental use of urea.	Acute pain, shivering, staggering gait, rapid breathing, jugular pulse and death.	1. Give 50-200 ml of 5% acetic acid. 2. Inject adrenergic blocking agent. 3. Give calborol 50 ml orally.
Strychnine (Nux Vomica).	By accidental ingestion; by enemity, poisoning may also be caused due to ingestion of rat or mice which died due to Nux Vomica poisoning.	Nervousness, restlessness, twitching of skeletal muscle, stiffness of the neck, and spinal cord, convulsion is developed by slightest external stimulus such as touching, talking or sudden noise. Pupil is dilated and death occurs due to asphyxiation or respiratory paralysis.	1. Check disturbance and external stimuli. 2. Emetics such as morphine or apomorphine may be given instead of stomach tube to empty the stomach when convulsions have already appeared. Apomorphine HCl may be given 3-6 mg S/C or by dropping a prepared tablet into the conjunctival sac. 3. (a) Pentobarbital-Na is good for controlling convulsion. The dose is half of an anaesthetic dose (10-15 mg/kg B.W.) I/V. (b) Gardenal (Phenobarbitone tab), 30-300 mg according to B.W. Thiopentone sodium, 15 mg/kg B.W. I/.V.

(Contd.)

Type of poison	*Source of poison*	*Main symptoms*	*Line of treatment*
1	*2*	*3*	*4*
			4. Gastric lavage using warm hypertonic saline solution or $KMnO_4$ 1 : 1,000 or strong tea or 2% tannic acid solution can be attempted. High enema with warm saline may be advantageous.
Datura Stramonium (contains alkaloids atropine, hyoscyamine and hyoscine).	By enemity	Nausea, vertigo, thirst, Dilated pupil and quick death	1. Gastric lavage, kaolin or tannic acid per os. 2. Respiratory stimulants should be given. 3. Cardiac stimulants. (i) Aminophylline, 5-7 mg/kg B.W. TID (ii) Calcium gluconate 20% sol. 10-15 ml/kg B.W. I/V until the heart rate is normal. (iii) Digoxin tablets; the total digitalization dose for the dog is 0.075 mg/kg B.W. orally for equal dose over 2 days. (iv) Epinephrine sol. 1:1,000, 0.1 to 1.0 ml S/C or 0.01 ml I/V.
Mycotoxicosis, aflatoxicosis (aflatoxins).	By ingestion of infected food due to *Aspergillus flavum* fungi	In all animals the first sign is an outbreak, reduced growth, loss of condition and inappetance. After 7-14 days or before death icterus and haemorrhagic enteritis may be seen.	Any food containing fungus or even suspected for fungal infection and spoiled food should not be given to the pet.
Mouldy corn toxicosis	Due to consumption of diet containing mouldy field corn (maize).	Gross icterus and tissue haemorrhage. In acute case, massive haemorrhages are observed in most of the tissues. In chronic cases extensive icterus and cachexia are prominent gross findings. Other findings include depression and anorexia.	No treatment, only prevention by avoiding mouldy corn.
Aspergillosis toxicosis	*Aspergillus spp.* through dog meal.	Hepatitis, diagnosis can be made on the basis of history and clinical symptoms.	Food contaminated with fungus should not be used. Antifungal drugs and symptomatic treatment.

(Contd.)

Type of poison	*Source of poison*	*Main symptoms*	*Line of treatment*
1	*2*	*3*	*4*
Snake Bite: Venomous snake can be divided into two classes. 1. Elpine snakes includes corba, mamba, and coral snakes. 2. Viperine snake (i) True vipers puttadder Russelis, viper. (ii) Pit viper, e.g. Rattle snakes, cotton mouth moccasin, Fex delane etc. Elpine snake has short fangs and chew their victim. Their venom is neurotoxic and kill by paralysing the respiratory centre. Viperine have long-hinged fangs. They strike once and withdraw and venom is mainly haemotoxic. However, all snake venoms contains both neurotoxic and haemotoxic factors.	Dogs are frequently bitten on their legs but the most common site is probably the shoulder and thigh next in order. The presence of hair may hide the typical fang marks, though a close examination should reveal the point of entry of the venom.	Venoms from viperine snakes may produce prolonged intense pain, impaired vision, muscular weakness, nausea, paralysis, oedema, shock, cyanolysis, oedema, shock, cyanosis, haemolytic anaemia, necrosis of the tissue and the bleeding tendencies. The venom of rattle snake causes an almost immediate reaction in the form of extensive swelling around the wound. When dog is bitten on face or head their lips, face and submaxillary region becomes grossly swollen, causing dyspnoea, sloughing of the skin in the region of the wound. Shock is severe in snake bite. If a dog has been exercising violently as is frequently the case and if the venom is deposited in a highly vascular area death occurs commonly in 5-10 mins.	1. First aid should be given immediately. Animal should be placed at rest and hair should be clipped from the wound. If bite is on limb, a wide tourniquet should be placed 5 cm above the bite. It should not be so tight as to arrest arterial circulation 2. In case of a bite from a dangerous snake such as rattle snake, the fang wound should be enlarged with linear incision. Rubber tube or any other such material should be applied to remove the venom by sucking it out as early as possible. 3. Polyvalent antivenom should be given as early as possible; the initial dose per day may be as high as 100 ml; 1-5 ampoule (10 ml) should be administered. All antivenom should be given I/V. A little antivenom may also be injected at the site of bite. Anti-snake venom polyvalent (10 ml; Haffkine) is available. 4. Corticosteroids prolong the survival time. 5. Broad spectrum antibiotic should be administered. 6. Blood transfusion or infusion of isotonic saline or dextrose solution is beneficial. 7. Incision wound should be kept open and draining should be

(Contd.)

Type of poison	Source of poison	Main symptoms	Line of treatment
1	2	3	4
			continued until the animal shows improvement. 8. Tetanus antitoxoid should be given in the prophylactic doses. 9. If antivenom is not available and if the animal is seen by the veterinarian within an hour and if the bite is located in the area where tourniquet cannot be applied, then excision of an area of skin 5-6 cm in diameter, including the associated S/C tissue may be life saving in the course of a bite by a viper or pit viper. 10. Excessive heat or cold is contraindicated. 11. Some cobras are capable of spitting their venom at the eyes of their victim from a distance of several feet, causing severe pain and temporary blindness. For this the eyes should be washed with water or diluted serum.
Bee sting and wasp.	By biting of bee and wasp.	Bee and wasp stings produce severe local swelling in the form of urticarial weals on the skin, pain, iritation due to deposition of the formic acid on the skin by stings which is responsible for irritation, restlessness and excitement. In case of attack on head dyspnoea and difficulty in feeding. Severe bites may sometimes result in death.	1. Remove stings as early as possible. 2. Affected area of the body should be washed with washing soda (30 gm in one litre of water). 3. Antihistaminic preparations (Avil, 0.5-1 ml I/M; Phenargan, 0.5-1 ml I/M should be given. 4. Pet should not be disturbed and proper management and feeding help in recovery.
Tick paralysis (Neurotoxin)	Caused by *Dermacentor variabilis* (wood tick).	Varying degree of paralysis, tick paralysis occurs commonly in U.S. Animal becomes weak	Either spray insecticide over the dog or dip it into the solution, or remove manually.

(Contd.)

Type of poison	Source of poison	Main symptoms	Line of treatment
1	2	3	4
		and then suffers a complete ascending flaccid paralysis.	Recovery usually takes place in 1 to 3 days.
Lizard poisoning.	Mexican beaded lizard *(Heloderma horridum)* and the Gila monster *(Heloderma suspectum)* are poisonous, mostly found in USA Accidental ingestion of lizard such as in milk also causes poisoning.	Venom transmitted through bite wounds inflicted by the lizard's upper teeth; animal starts vomiting; shock and death.	Immediately give purgative, antihistaminic drug, and supportive therapy for wound. Apply some antiseptic and antibiotic therapy.
Insecticides (a) Organophosphorus insecticides like thimet, TEPP, VP, Parathion, malathion, ciordin, diazinon, cythion carbopheno-theion, dichlorvos, dimethoate, trichlorophon, disulphoton, arinphosmethyl, nuvan etc.	Ingestion by accident. By spray on animals and crops.	**Acute poisoning:** Lachrymation, weakness of voluntary muscles and musIcuar twitching. Excessive salivation, difficulty in breathing, constriction of pupil, abdominal pain, along with protrusion of tongue; animal shows watery discharge from nose and diarrhoea, a bronchial secretion and spasm, irregular violent contractions.	In case of oral poisoning give saline purgative, 5% dextrose I/V. Phenobarbitol 30-300 mg according to B.W. Inject acetyl cholinesterase reactivator (Prolidoxime, 5 mg/kg B.W.) atropine sulphate 4 mg/kg Later B.W. 1/3, 1/V. remainder S/C or I/V. The dosage may be repeated. **2PAM:** Hydroxyiminomethyl-N-methyl pyridinium is of practical value-20 mg/kg B.W. S/C. TMB-4 is also considered very good.
		Chronic poisoning: Hypermotility of the gastrointestinal tract and excessive secretion. Twitching of the muscular part of the body and later on death due to respiratory failure.	Artificial respiration and administration of oxygen is advantageous. Tranquilizer should be avoided at least for one week.
(b) Organochlorine, insecticides like chlorinated hydrocarbon. BHC, DDT, aldrin, methoxychlor, heptachlor, telodrin, chlordane, toxophene, strobane, endosulfan, dieldrin.	Taken by accident. By spray on animals.	**Acute poisoning:** Animal shows symptoms within 24 hours. Hypersensitivity and hyperexcitability, spasms of facial and cervical fore quarter and hind quarter muscles. Concurrently there may be increased salivation with chewing movement of the jaw	1. Give only saline, not oil purgatives to remove the poison in oral intake. 2. Phenobarbitone sodium. 3. Calcum borogluconate, 15-75 ml I/V. 4. If due to spraying, wash the body and remove poison. 5. In oral as well as in

(Contd.)

Type of poison	*Source of poison*	*Main symptoms*	*Line of treatment*
1	*2*	*3*	*4*
		which adhere to the lips. Later on inco-ordination, staggering, jumping on imaginary objects and movement in a circle. Abdominal posture, fever, grinding teeth, coma death **Chronic poisoning:** Usually similar as in acute poisoning but tremors in muscles of neck and head are observed which extend to other muscles of body convulsions, depression, respiratory failure and death.	spray, give atropine sulphate 0.5 mg/kg B.W., I/V. 6. Anticonvulsant drug, i.e. methadone is effective in all animals except toxophene toxicity in dogs. 7. Riboflavin in DDT poisoning. 8. Dioxyanthraquinone @ 0.1 mg/kg in the form of aqueous suspension in 2 daily doses and glucose therapy.
Rodenticides Warfarin 3-(d-acetonylbenzyl hydroxy coumarin)	1. Warfarin can be added as a act of maliciousness to meat or other bait palatable to dogs and cats. 2. Poisoning in dog and cat by ingestion of rat or mice that died from warfarin poisoning.	Haemorrhage is a prominent symptom. The haemorrhage may be internal but is usually manifested by loss of blood externally as in vomitus or finally fatal haemorrhage from the body opening. Other symptoms are pale or cyanosed mucous membrane, rapid and weak pulse, shock, sub-normal temperature, prostration and collapse leading to death.	The emulsion of Vitamin K should be injected I/V for prompt therapeutic effect. If blood is not available immediately then glucose and saline solution may be substituted.
Alfanapthyl Thiourea (ANTU)	(i) By accidental ingestion. (ii) By enemity (iii) Poisoning may also be caused due to ingestion of rat or mice which died due to ANTU poisoning	Dyspnoea, pulmonary oedema, vomition, foaming in the airways	Stomach is promptly emptied. Silicone aerosal (10%) is administered to prevent the fatal foaming in the airways associated with pulmonary oedema.
Zinc phosphate (Zn3 P2)	By eating large number of rats which died due to zinc phosphide poisoning which is commonly used for killing rats. By enemity. By accidental ingestion.	Repeated administration of smalll quantities of zinc phosphide results in death which may occur immediately after ingestion; chronic poisoning of high quantity so the symptoms are frequently not observed. The symptoms are	Stomach is promptly emptied. In chronic cases symptomatic treatment may be beneficial but in acute poisoning treatment is not so effective. Gastric lavage with a 5% solution of sodium carbonate; zinc phosphide should be given to clear

(Contd.)

Type of poison	*Source of poison*	*Main symptoms*	*Line of treatment*
1	*2*	*3*	*4*
		not diagnostic. Anorexia and lethargy are followed by rapid deep breathing that often becomes wheezy or stertorous, vomiting with presence of dark blood in vomitus, weakness; finally animal gasps for breath. Hyperaesthesia or convulsion may occur. Lesions, acute congestion and liver necrosis, dark colour blood, enlargement of heart, odour of carbide (acetylene) in the stomach contents. It is due to liberation of phosphane from zinc phosphide.	the entire gastrointestinal tract; calcium gluconate 1/6 M sodium lactate may help in counteracting the acidosis. Sodium thiosulphate (10% sol.) hepatonic agent and dextrose may check the liver damage.

SOME IMPORTANT DRUG POISONING DUE TO OVERDOSE OR GIVEN BY MISTAKE/ACCIDENT

Drugs	*Antidotes*
1. Alcohol or methylated spirit	Sodium bicarbonate or sodium citrate (1%); use as gastric lavage or give 100 mg/kg B.W./day orally.
2. Aerocholine	Atropine sulphate @ 0.2-0.5 mg/kg B.W. I/V, S/C or I/M.
3. Aspirin	Alkalinization of urine above pH 8 by giving sodium bicarbonate, emetics, respiratory stimulants like coramine.
4. Barbiturate	Amphetamine sulphate @ 0.5-1.0 mg/kg B.W. S/C, I/V, I/P, Doxapram @ 3-5 mg/kg B.W. I/V. Leptazol, glucose is also useful.
6. Barium	Magnesium sulphate.
7. Belladona	Tannic acid 200-500 mg in 20-60 ml water orally.
8. Benzoic acid	Sedative like siquil, largectil and also use dextrose.
9. Benzyl benzoate	Washing with soap or detergent, tranquilizer, dextrose.
10. Bromide	Chlorides (sodium or ammonium salts) @ 0.5-1 g/day orally.
11. Camphor	Sedative like siquil, largectil and saline diuretics.
12. Castor oil	Gastric lavage, atropine sulphate, tranquilizers.
13. Ephedrine	Gastric lavage, emetics.
14. Chloroform	Oxygen, coramine, calcium borogluconate-I/V.
15. Formaldehyde	Gastric lavage with sodium and ammonium carbonate (1%) solution.

(Contd.)

Drugs	*Antidotes*
16. Morphine	Nalorphine 5-10 mg I/V.
17. Digitalis	Propranolol 0.5 mg/kg B.W. gastric lavage, I/M. Sodium sulphate or magnesium sulphate.
18. Coumarine anti-coagulants	Vitamin-K or Menadione @ 1 mg/kg. B.W. I/V, I/M, orally.
19. Analeptic	Pentylene tetrazol (10% solution) @ 10-20 mg/kg. B.W. I/V.
20. Narcctic analgesic	Demerol @ 15 mg/kg B.W. S/C.
21. Iron toxicosis	Deferoxamine @ 20 mg/kg B.W.
22. Inorganic phosphorus	Copper sulphate 0.2-0.4% solution 20-100 ml orally.

11

COMMON SYSTEMIC DISEASES

On the arrival of a patient in the clinic the clinician record the history of the ailments. This is followed by the physical examination of the patient. The various systemic diseases encountered in dogs have been described in brief giving important informations about the causes, clinical signs and line of treatment. This is followed by emergency cases commonly found in dogs and are listed along with the measures of first aid. Treatment of non-specific disease manifestations like fever, pain and eczema has also been given. In routine treatment of patients, the manifestations of diseases first draw the attention of a veterinarian for their immediate management. This is followed by detailed checkup of the patient and laboratory examination of the biological materials for the diagnosis of the disease for deciding the line of treatment.

1. Halitosis (Foul breath)

Halitosis or foul breath in dogs is due to lack of maintenance of mouth hygiene.

Causes: Primary halitosis is caused mainly due to teeth and gum infection. Other conditions like bronchiectasis, rhinitis, hepatic disorder, chronic indigestion and chronic cold; cough and pharyngytis may also lead to this condition.

Treatment

(i) For therapy, one should first search for the specific cause of this ailment and treat accordingly.
(ii) Antibiotics or sulpha drugs may be used to check the infection.
(iii) Hydrogen peroxide (3%) with equal part of water may be used 2-3 times a day.
(iv) Antiseptic solution like potassium permanganate (1 : 1,000) solution in water may also be used to clean the oral cavity.
(v) Liver tonics may be given to correct the liver disorder.

2. Stomatitis

Generalized inflammation of the mouth cavity including the inflammation of gums (gingivitis), lips (cheilitis), tongue (glossitis), cheeks and pharynx may be referred to as stomatitis.

Causes: Traumatic injuries, malformation of teeth, excessive deposit of dental tartar, bacterial, viral and mycotic infections, chemicals and indigestion.

Clinical signs: Excessive salivation, loss of appetite, difficulty in the ingestion of food, foul smell from the mouth, enlarged lymphnodes and loss of hair in the case of cheilitis due to rubbing of the mouth and muzzle.

Treatment: Symptomatic treatment is taken up along with specific treatments in infectious conditions. The line of treatment includes:

(i) Topical application of anaesthetic ointments on lips and muzzle for reducing the irritation.
(ii) Cleaning of mouth, gum and teeth with mild antiseptic and detergent lotions.
(iii) Surgical repair of injuries.
(iv) Cauterization of ulcers with silver nitrate solution.
(v) Feeding of liquid and non-irritant laxative diet.
(vi) Administration of vitamin B-complex.

3. Pharyngitis

The inflammation of pharynx is called pharyngitis.

Causes: Mechanical, chemical or thermal injuries due to food and drug administration, microbial infections, tonsilitis, enlarged soft palate and any growth on the pharynx.

Clinical signs: Difficulty in intake of food and water. Coughing, expulsion of foamy phlegm, loss of appetite, foetid mouth odour, and thick deposit on the tongue.

Treatment: Symptomatic, supportive and specific treatments include:

(i) Application of boroglycerol thrice a day.
(ii) Feeding of liquid non-irritant diet at body temperature.
(iii) Removal of foreign body, if any.
(iv) Surgical correction of excessive growth or cyst, if any. Parenteral administration of antibiotics in infections.
(vi) Mouth wash with mild antiseptic lotions.

4. Gastritis

The inflammation of stomach is known as gastritis.

Causes: Overfeeding, eating of spoiled and fermented feeds, irregular feeding, eating of garbage, foreign articles, bones, plastic and grass, etc. Accidental ingestion of caustic and irritant chemicals and drugs and parasitic infections.

Clinical signs: Abdominal pain, various degree of anorexia, nausea, vomiting, acidity followed by dehydration and exhaustion. In chronic cases there may be anaemia and loss of condition due to less food intake and indigestion.

Treatment:

(i) Removal of cause; antiemetic drugs for control of nausea and vomiting.
(ii) Feeding of non-irritant liquid diet.
(iii) Administration of antacids in small and frequent oral doses.
(iv) Gastric lavage with ice-cold water.
(v) Administration of vitamin B-complex.

5. Constipation

Difficult defaecation or inability to defaecate in spite of excessive straining.

Causes: Common causes are faulty feeding, depraved appetite, lack of exercise, overfeeding of solid foods, feeding of low fibre diets, gastro-intestinal atony, and due to other diseases and injuries.

Clinical signs: Very hard faeces, difficult and irregular defaecation, excessive straining for defaecation, various degree of anorexia, general weakness, dehydration and loss of condition.

Treatment:

(i) Feeding of bran gruel and other high fibre feeds in mild constipation.
(ii) Administration of laxative or oily purgative.
(iii) Enema in severe cases.
(iv) Fluid therapy to restore body fluid volume.
(v) Deworming in parasitism.
(vi) Parenteral or oral administration of vitamin B complex and liver extract.

6. Vomiting

The process of oral expulsion of gastric ingesta is known as vomiting or emesis. It is an abnormal behaviour of the digestive tract usually associated with gastric disorders. Vomiting is a complex disorder of motor nerves. While vomiting, pylorus is closed, stomach contracts, cardia opens and gastric ingesta is propelled through oesophagus into the mouth and out of the mouth.

Causes: Various gastric disorders, indigestion, ingestion of spoiled food and foreign body, oesophageal dilatation, pyloric stenosis, gastritis, gastric ulcers, neoplasms in stomach, over-eating, eating of grass and irritant chemicals, oral administration of irritant drugs, hepatitis, nephritis, uraemia, pyometra, otitis, diabetes mellitus, encephalitis, poisoning and worm infestation.

Clinical signs: Nausea, retching, oral expulsion of undigested food mixed with gastric contents, saliva and sometimes bile, foetid smell, depression, dehydration.

Treatment: The line of treatment depends on the causes of vomiting and includes:

(i) Administration of gastric sedatives.
(ii) Removal of the cause.
(iii) Administration of antiemetic drugs.
(iv) Fluid and electrolyte therapy.

7. Gastro-enteritis and Enteritis (Diarrhoea)

The inflammation of stomach and intestines is known as gastro-enteritis and that of latter as enteritis. It may be infectious or non-infectious and characterized by diarrhoea, dysentery and dehydration.

Causes: Spoiled foods, over-eating, acidity, irritant chemicals and drugs, bacteria, virus, protozoa and helminths, etc.

Clinical signs: Abdominal pain, anorexia, constipation followed by diarrhoea and/or dysentery, dehydration and dullness.

Treatment: The treatment depends on the severity of the condition and cause of the disease.

(i) Food should not be given for 12-24 hours.
(ii) Dextrose saline and electrolytes are administered to check excessive dehydration caused by the loss of body fluid in diarrhoea.
(iii) Administration of antibiotics and/or sulphonamides in bacterial infection.
(iv) Treatment of protozoal and worm infestations.

(v) Oral administration of gastric astringents.

(vi) Administration of enzymes, yeast, liver extract and vitamin B complex.

(vii) Feeding of liquid diet.

8. Hepatitis

The inflammation of liver cells is known as hepatitis.

Causes: Ingestion of toxic chemicals and drugs, nutritional deficiencies, excess feeding of fat and infectious diseases caused by bacteria, virus and parasites.

Clinical signs: Common clinical signs are various degrees of anorexia, constipation followed by diarrhoea; pale mucus membranes and jaundice. Dullness and depression; hyperexcitability and convulsions in severe cases; frequent vomiting, ascites; hyperthermia in infectious hepatitis.

Treatments:

(i) Feeding of low fat, protein diets of high energy from digestible carbohydrates.

(ii) Parenteral administration of glucose.

(iii) Administration of liver tonics, liver extract and vitamin B-complex.

(iv) Antibiotics treatment in infectious diseases.

(v) Complete rest.

(vi) Administration of parasiticidal drugs in parasitic infestations.

9. Ascites

Ascites may be defined as accumulation of fluid in peritoneal cavity manifested clinically by increased circumference of the abdomen (Fig. 105).

Causes: Ascites is a relatively common later stage development in canines with progressive hepatic diseases. It is also developed secondary to varying degrees of hypoalbuminemia, renal salt and water retention. Ascites may also be caused due to various parasitic and infectious diseases.

Treatment:

(i) Low sodium diets should be given. In severe cases complete salt restriction is necessary.

(ii) Diuretics should be given if low sodium diets are ineffective in controlling the ascites. Excessive use of diuretic can cause dehydration. When ascites is controlled, diuretics should be stopped.

Mechanical removal of fluid may be done by various means.

(i) Paracentesis aspiration of fluid should be done slowly when patient is feeling dyspnoea and discomfort and ascites has not responded to the medical therapy. Avoid acute dilation of vessels and subsequent peripheral circulatory failure which may be precipitated by aspiration.

(ii) Two surgical procedures for long-term control may be considered in medically non-responsive ascites.

(a) A one way, pressure-activated valve, the La Veen shunt may be used in chronic ascites. The valve is inserted into the peritoneal cavity and connected by SQ tubing to the jugular vein. This valve allows continuous reinfusion of ascites fluid back into the systemic circulation.

(b) Surgically created portal systemic venous shunts are also useful.

The treatment of ascites should be aimed to remove primary diseases.

As supportive therapy, liver tonic drug may be given.

10. Jaundice

Jaundice or icterus is a clinical manifestation in which the visible mucous membranes along with all the secretions and excretions of the body turns yellowish due to the presence of excess of either haemobilirubin or cholebilirubin or both in the blood stream. This yellow discoloration is markedly visible in sclera. Jaundice is commonly classified as:

(i) Pre-hepatic (Haemolytic),
(ii) Intra-hepatic (Toxic), and
(iii) Post-hepatic (Obstruction).

Causes: The common causes of jaundice are protozoa, helminths, viruses, bacteria, chemicals, animal and plant poisons, incompatible blood transfusion, etc.

Clinical signs: Digestive disturbances, poor appetite, vomition, loss of body weight, constipation followed by diarrhoea and yellowish visible mucous membrane alteration, bigger size of liver and abdominal pain are the common signs.

Clinical and Differential Diagnosis:

Clinical status	*Haemolytic*	*Toxic*	*Obstructive*
1	*2*	*3*	*4*
Colour of faeces	Increased pigmented	Normal colour	Hypopigmented (clay coloured)
Consistency of faeces	Normal	Normal	Greasy (fatty)
Colour of urine	Light yellow	Intense yellow	Intense yellow
Icterus index	Low to moderate	Moderate	High
Vanden Bergh reaction	Indirect	Biphasic	Direct
Total serum cholesterol	Normal	Decreased	Increased
Blood prothrombin time	Normal	Prolonged	Prolonged
Colour of the mucous membrane	Slight to moderate yellow	Slight to moderate yellow	Intensive yellow
Colour of serum and plasma	Slight to moderate yellow	Slight to moderate yellow	Intensive yellow

Treatment:

(i) Complete rest, fat and salt-free diet is recommended.
(ii) In haemolytic jaundice haemolysis should be prevented by suitable measures.
(iii) If it is due to any kind of parasites, specific treatment against respective parasite should be done or if it is due to bacteria, specific bactericidal drug should be given.
(iv) In obstructive jaundice, cause of obstruction should be removed first.
(v) In toxic jaundice, vitamin-B complex preparation can be given orally, daily.
(vi) Liver extract preparation also can be given.
(vii) Administration of cortisone has also importance in management of jaundice.
(viii) Adequate calcium intake should be ensured by oral or parenteral administration of calcium salt for the

guanidine intoxication.

(ix) Dextrose therapy is also important in jaundice.

11. Pneumonia

Inflammation of lungs is known as pneumonia and when bronchioles are involved, it is called bronchopneumonia.

Causes: Inhalation of irritants like dust, pollens, gases, exposure to cold, bad hygiene and dirty housing and various infectious conditions caused by bacteria, virus, fungi and parasites are the common causes of pneumonia.

Clinical signs: Rise in temperature, coughing, nasal discharge, increased respiration rate, dyspnoea in severe condition.

Treatments:

(i) Housing at a dry, clean and airy place.
(ii) Administration of antibiotics.
(iii) Oral administration of expectorants.
(iv) Administration of antispasmodics.
(v) Feeding of liquid diet.
(vi) Administration of vitamin C.

12. Epistaxis

Nose bleeding is called epistaxis.

Causes: The common causes are trauma, sudden change in weather, hereditary, high blood pressure and nutritional deficiency.

Clinical signs: Sudden bleeding from nose is the only sign.

Treatments:

(i) Surgical repair in case of injury.
(ii) Application of ice-cold pack on the nasal and frontal bones.
(iii) Administration of vitamin K.
(iv) Removal of the cause.

13. Common Cold

It is known as nasal catarrah.

Cause: A number of irritants like foreign bodies, dust, pollen grains, gases, fumes, smokes, exposure to cold, inadequate ventilation and dampness. Other causative agents are virus, bacteria, fungus and parasites.

Clinical signs: In dogs it is characterized by watery to mucus discharge, high fever, sneezing, muscular pain, pharyngitis, dysphagia, dyspnoea, restlessness and loss of appetite.

Treatment: Therapy should be given according to aetiological agent:

(i) In parasitic nasal catarrah, first patient should be free of worms.
(ii) In case of bacterial as well as viral infections, patient should be treated with antibiotic or sulpha drugs.

(iii) Antifungal drugs must be used in fungal infection.

(iv) Along with this symptomatic treatment may be given.

(v) To remove viscid secretion inhalation of Tincture Benzoin may be given.

(vi) Analgesic, antipyretics, antiallergic, vitamins, nasal decongestants should also be given.

14. Uraemia

Uraemia occurs as a result of high nitrogenous waste products in the circulatory blood, plasma or serum, caused by generalized renal failure and other catalytic process. The products of catabolism, associated with the uraemia are urea, reacting phenolic compounds and guanidine. The uraemia may be classified as pre-renal, renal and post-renal azotaemia (uraemia).

Causes: Three factors are mainly responsible:

(i) ***Pre-renal causes*:** Dehydration due to blood loss of any origin, reduced cardiac output, decreased osmotic pressure, shock and hypoadrenocorticism. Besides this septicaemia may also cause this condition.

(ii) ***Renal causes:*** Nephritis, nephrosis and jaundice, sulphonamide and NaCl-toxicity may act as a predisposing factor.

(iii) ***Post-renal cause:*** Urethral obstruction, bladder obstruction, ruptured bladder, bilateral ureteral obstruction.

Clinical signs: Tremor, abdominal gripping pain, lethargy, dullness, comatic, pruritus, pallor, petechiae, and pigmentations are the manifestations related to the dermatological disorder. Gastro-intestinal disorders are anorexia, dry vomition, dry mouth and haemorrhagic diarrhoea. There will be respiratory distress, bradycardia, polyuria, oligouria and anuria. Ammonia/urea smell from mouth. Conjunctivitis, keratitis and anaemia may also be seen.

Diagnosis: Simultaneous consecutive measurement of urine pH, specific gravity (SG) with blood urea nitrogen (BUN) and serum creatinine (SC) is necessary for the diagnosis of disease. Qualitative test for albumin, glucose, bile etc. may be supportive diagnostic aids.

Treatments:

(i) Remove the primary cause of the disease.

(ii) Treatment should be aimed at restoring the renal function, removal of toxic substance to ease the strain on the kidney and normalization of pH value and electrolyte concentration.

(iii) To eliminate the toxin laxative fluid therapy is indicated.

(iv) To control acidosis, alkaline mixture is to be provided.

(v) Catheterization is advised in severe case.

(vi) In comatose condition respiratory stimulant is indicated.

(vii) Carbohydrates are to be supplemented and protein intake should be restricted in case of oligouria and fluid therapy restricted.

(viii) Haemodialysis may be initiated in acute dehydration.

15. Cystitis

It may be defined as the inflammation of urinary bladder and characterized by dysuria, painful micturition, frequent micturition and low fever.

Causes: Cystitis is usually the result of an infection of ascending nature from the lower urinary tract and also from kidney. Rarely disseminated or local bacterial infections spread to the bladder via the hematogenous route. Infection in the upper urinary tract may serve as a contributing factor of recurrent infection. *E. coli, Proteus* spp., *Staphylococcus* spp., *Streptococcus* spp., and *Klebsiella* spp., are the most common causes. Predisposing factors are urinary stasis due to trauma, abnormal urine composition, calculi, neurological dysfunction and metabolic disorders.

Clinical signs: It may be acute or chronic in nature. Frequent painful micturition, straining, occasional haematuria, pain on abdominal palpation, stiffness in hind quarters and vomition are observed. Last part of urine may be dark cloudy or red.

Diganosis: It is also based on clinical findings, qualitative urine examination. Cystocentesis should be done to collect urine for microscopic and cultural examination for isolation of organism.

Treatments:

(i) Removal of primary cause.
(ii) Correction of urine pH should be done.
(iii) Combined treatment with urinary antiseptic and alkalisers is useful in mild and chronic infection.
(iv) Anti-bacterial therapy after isolation of organism with A.S.T.
(v) Antispasmodic therapy may be necessary to control pain and adequate fluid intake is important.

16. Haematuria and Haemoglobinuria

Blood (RBC) in urine, and later on whole blood may be voided in urine. This gives red or deep red colour to the urine. It is seen in a number of diseases.

Causes: The causes could be prerenal, renal and post-renal.

Pre-renal causes are toxaemia, septicenia, trauma etc.

Renal causes are pyelonephritis, renal infarction, acutė glomerulonephritis, embolism of renal artery, tubular damage caused by calculi or tumours in kidney and trauma. Parasites like *Capillaria plica, Dictophyma renale, Dirofilaria immitis* and bacteria such as *Leptospira* spp. also cause haematuria.

Post-renal causes are cystitis, urolithiasis, injury in urethra or urinary bladder, faulty catheterization and tumor. Tumor especially venereal granuloma is very common.

Clinical signs: Urine in haematuria is deep red or brown because of red blood cells in it. On centrifugation of urine sample RBC will be found packed at the bottom of the test-tube. In haemoglobinuria red blood cells are haemolysed and urine is coffee coloured. Occult blood test should be carried in urine when the colour is not indicative. In case of haematuria, blue colour reaction is seen.

Treatments:

(i) Specific treatment should be given according to cause of the disease.
(ii) Symptomatic treatment should be given as per the signs of various diseases. Haemostatics, alkalizer, urinary antiseptic, etc. are the common drugs for this condition.

17. Nephritis

Inflammation of kidney is called nephritis.

Causes: The various causes are ingestion of toxic elements and chemicals and infections caused by bacteria, viruses and parasites.

Clinical signs: The common clinical signs are pain and tenderness in loin region, increased thirst, depression, loss of appetite, renal pain, frequent urination, increased respiration rate, vomiting, oedema and arched back.

Treatments:

(i) Removal of causes.
(ii) Complete rest.
(iii) Feeding of low protein and high energy diets.
(iv) Control of dehydration by parenteral administration of dextrose solution.
(v) Administration of diuretics.
(vi) Antibiotic treatment for infections.
(vii) Administration of parasiticidal drugs in parasitic infestations.
(viii) Surgical management of renal stones.

18. Anaemia

Abnormal decrease in red blood cells and haemoglobin concentration is known as anaemia.

Causes: The common causes are chronic wasting diseases, malnutrition, infectious diseases, parasitic infection, ingestion of toxic chemicals and drugs.

Clinical signs: Gradual loss of body condition, general weakness and depression, pale mucous membranes, anorexia, haematuria, haemoglobinuria, dyspnoea, jaundice, oedema.

Treatments:

(i) Removal of causes.
(ii) Antibiotic treatment of infections.
(iii) Administration of haematinics, liver extract and vitamin B-complex.
(iv) Feeding of nutritious diets.

19. Heart Failure

Due to some intrinsic defects of cardiac muscle heart fails to maintain the circulatory equilibrium at rest and is defined as heart failure. It is characterized by congestion of venous side accompanied by dilatation of blood vessels, oedema of lung, enlargement of heart and increased heart rate. Heart failure may be acute or congestive heart failure. Heavy and overweight dogs are more prone to heart failure. Anatomy of heart is shown in Fig.106.

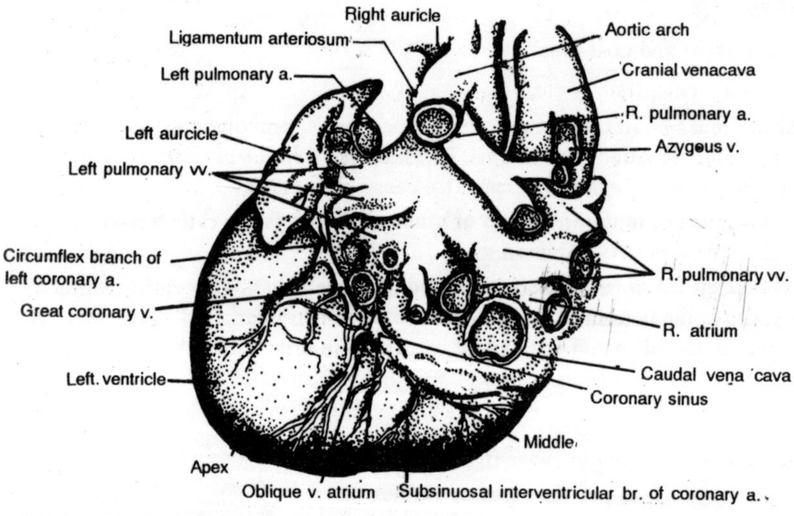

Fig. 106 The heart (dorsal view) of dog

Acute Heart Failure

This is manifested by the sudden loss of consciousness, falling with or without convulsions. There will be severe pallor of mucous membrane followed by either recovery or death.

Causes: Myocardial infarction, massive pulmonary embolism. Paroxysmal tachycardia, myocarditis, calcium therapy and rapid I/V injection, severe trauma and anaphylactic reaction.

In this case death occurs due to shock. Shock is generally due to either peripheral circulatory failure or cardiac failure.

Peripheral circulatory failure happens due to haemorrhage, trauma, burns, neurogenic involvement, anaphylaxis and also due to liberation of histamine, septic shock and injections.

Cardiogenic shock is characterized by cardiac oedema, tachycardia, ventricular fibrillation and muscular dystrophy and deficiency in the myocardial ability to pump.

Treatment: Treatment may not be possible in most cases.

Antishock and oxygen therapy are indicated to save the animal.

Congestive Heart Failure

Causes: Pericardial, endocardial or myocardial disorders may be responsible for this condition.

Pericardial disorders are caused by cardiac tamponade, pericarditis, haemopericardium and hydropericardium. Congestive cardiac failure may be left sided or/and right sided.

Left-sided cardiac failure is manifested by respiratory trouble, respiration at the base of the lung, coughing, pulmonary oedema, alteration of pulse and enlargement of heart.

Right-sided cardiac failure is manifested by oedema, hydrothorax, pneumothorax, ascites, albuminuria, jugular pulse and cyanosis.

Endocardial disorders are produced by endocarditis and congenital valvular defects.

Myocardial disorders are caused by myocarditis, myocardial dystrophy, neoplasm, cyst in the heart and acute drug toxicity.

Treatments:

(i) Complete rest should be given and exercise avoided.
(ii) Excitement of any type should be avoided.
(iii) Salt-free diet should be offered.
(iv) Diuretic tablets may be given orally which contain potassium sparing diuretic.
(v) In respiratory trouble, respiratory stimulant should be provided.
(vi) Digitalization may be necessary.

Methods of digitalization are intensive, rapid and slow.

For diet see chapter 3.

20. Conjunctivitis

The inflammation of conjunctiva is called conjunctivitis.

Causes: Many irritants cause conjunctivitis, e.g. irritant gases, dust, infections from viruses, bacteria, fungi and parasites, corrosive chemicals and traumatic injuries.

Clinical signs: Profuse lacrymation, redness of conjunctiva, mucopurulent discharge, irritation, rise in temperature in infectious cases, severe pain in eyes.

Treatments:

(i) Removal of causes.
(ii) Irrigation with cold normal saline.
(iii) Application of antiseptic and astringent eye lotions.
(iv) Application of antibiotic eye ointments.

21. Keratitis

It may be defined as inflammation of cornea. Keratitis is often found in dogs. Keratitis may be associated with conjunctivitis leading to keratoconjunctivitis (Fig. 107).

Keratitis is classified according to etiology (viral, bacterial, mycotic, parasitic, traumatic and chemical keratitis) or lesions (vesicular, pigmentary, superficial, deep spotted, suppurative and parenchymatous keratitis).

Clinical signs: Lacrymation, photophobia, congestion in the cornea. Impairment of vision is common in chronic cases. In more prolonged cases there will be corneal opacity.

Treatments:

(i) Eye should be washed with antiseptic lotion.

(ii) Topical antibiotics and steroid preparations are recommended.

(iii) Subconjunctival injection with corticosteroid is also helpful.

22. Coma

Coma may be defined as the terminal stage of unconsciousness. It is the manifestation of the depression of the cerebrocortical function.

Causes: Encephalomyelitis, any disease which causes increase in intracranial pressure, cerebral anoxia, hypoglycaemia, uraemia, heat stroke, most of the poisonings or infections which affect the brain, electrolyte imbalance and drug toxicity.

Treatments:

(i) Removal of the cause of the disease.

(ii) Fluid therapy.

(iii) Cardiac and respiratory stimulant should be given.

23. Ataxia (Inco-ordination of Gait)

Ataxia may be called as an inco-ordination of muscular action or gait that results from abnormal cerebellar function. In general terms there are defects in the rate, range, force and direction of movement.

Ataxia is frequently seen in dogs due to primary disease of nervous system or due to lesions in the bone. Pain in joints, muscles, skin and abdominal organ may cause abnormal and painful movement. Besides this pain in uterus or testes may also cause abnormal and painful movement.

Abnormal gait due to neurological disorders are due to lesions in cerebellum, upper motor neuron hemiplegia, spastic paraplegia, chorea as a sequel to distemper, common in young dogs.

Clinical signs: The affected animal stands with legs wide apart, sways and falls in any direction. The head oscillates and the limbs do not move in unison. The movements are grossly exaggerated, muscular strength is usually preserved and feet are not properly placed.

Treatments:

(i) Treatment depends on the nature of aetiology.

(ii) Tranquilizer can be given.

(iii) Fluid therapy and vitamin B-complex preparation may restore the condition.

24. Epilepsy

It may be defined as a condition characterized by tonoclonic convulsion accompanied by loss of consciousness. Epileptic seizures are the clinical manifestation of an active, cerebral, bizzare neuronal irritative process involving billions of cortical neurons (Fig. 108).

Components of an epileptic attack: Each epileptic event has 5 components:

1. ***Prodrome or aura:*** This constitutes signs that precede an epileptic event.

2. ***Ictus:*** The actual seizure, which lasts from a few seconds to several minutes and may be generalized, partial or non-motor.
3. ***Post-ictus (post-ictal or post-seizure phase):*** The period of confusion, depression, coma, blindness, and moving in circles that follows the seizure.
4. ***Interictal phase:*** This is the period between seizures lasting from a few seconds to months. The behaviour during this period ranges from normal to mild or severely abnormal.
5. ***Status epilepticus:*** These are the seizures that run together and do not have a period of normalcy in between.

Classification: Epilepsy can be classified by several methods including nature of seizure, neuroanatomic location of the origin of the seizure and the aetiology of the seizure.

1. ***Classification based on aetiology:*** They are of 2 types, viz. Idiopathic epilepsy (Unknown aetiology)/ caused by
   - (i) Grandmal - (Major),
   - (ii) Petitmal - (Minor);
   - (iii) Status epilepticus - (Continuous)

     Symptomatic epilepsy may be caused by:
     - (i) Space occupying lesion.
     - (ii) Inflammatory process of C.N.S.
     - (iii) Distemper and cryptococcus.
     - (iv) Congenital defect in cranial region.
     - (v) Uraemia and hypocalcaemia.
2. ***Classification of epilepsy based on the clinical form of seizure:***
   - (a) ***Major motor seizure:*** Tono-clonic are the most common and easiest to recognize.
   - (b) ***Minor motor seizure:*** This is a partial, non-generalized seizure which originates in one part of the brain and is reflected by movement of only the affected part of the body.
   - (c) ***Behavioural seizure:*** This is non-motor seizure, characterized by periodic, paroxymal events of personality or behaviour. This seizure is characterized by a wide variety of clinical manifestations including staring, growling, vomiting, retching, fly snapping and viciousness.
   - (d) ***Sensory seizure:*** This is a hysterical, running seizure. The pet runs aimlessly.

Treatments:

- (i) Symptomatic epilepsy should be treated by giving specific therapy after confirming the aetiological factor involved in it.
- (ii) Vitamin B-complex and vitamin A preparation may be helpful in relieving the problem.
- (iii) For treatment of grandmal epilepsy and epilepticus, any central nervous system depressants should be administered.
- (iv) Appropriate fluid and electrolyte should be administered.
- (v) Body temperature should be maintained at normal range by warming or cooling as per requirement.
- (vi) For prevention of self-inflicted injury care should be taken.
- (vii) Castration in male and ovariohysterectomy in female are considered to have a beneficial effect over this long-lasting problem.

25. Paralysis

Paralysis may be defined as a condition where nervous control over any bodily function has failed completely or incompletely. This loss of nervous control may be either sensory or motor type or both. Paralysis is characterized by an inability to make purposeful movements. But in paresis contracting power of muscle becomes weaker than the normal.

Paralysis can be classified as central or peripheral according to the anatomical position of the lesion. Central paralysis can be again subclassified into spinal and cerebral paralysis.

Causes:

(a) ***Spinal paralysis:*** Injury to the spinal cord due to trauma, vertebral column fracture, abscess in the cord, hernia of the intervertebral disc, ancylosis of the vertebrae, meningitis, myelitis, and concussion of the spinal cord.

(b) ***Cerebral paralysis:*** Encephalitis, tumor, cyst, abscess, fracture of the cranium and compression of brain.

(c) ***Peripheral paralysis:*** Injury to the nerve trunk, rheumatic condition of muscles and nerves, and deficiency of vitamins B_1, B_6 and B_{12}.

Classification of paralysis can also be done based on the part of motor neurons affected and also the nature of paralysis.

(a) ***Spastic paralysis:*** It is due to the lesion of upper motor neuron characterized by loss of voluntary movement, increased tone of limb muscles and increased tendon jerks.

(b) ***Flacid paralysis:*** It results due to the lesion of lower motor neuron and is characterized by loss of voluntary movement and decreased tone of limb muscles, absence of tendon jerks and wasting of the affected muscle.

Clinical classification of paralysis:

(a) ***Monoplegia:*** It indicates the paralysis of the region supplied by one or a few nerves, e.g., paralysis, tibial paralysis.

(b) ***Hemiplegia:*** It indicates paralysis of one side of body only, e.g. left or right side of the body.

(c) ***Diplegia:*** It is a condition where both the sides of the body are involved.

(d) ***Quadriplegia:*** This term is used to indicate a condition where all the four legs are affected.

(e) ***Paraplegia:*** It is the condition when hind quarter paralysis occurs.

Position classification of paralysis:

(a) Nuclear paralysis.

(b) Infra-nuclear paralysis.

(c) Supra-nuclear paralysis.

Diagnosis: By history, clinical signs and neurological examination.

The paralysis may simulate mineral deficiencies, hip dysplasia, poisoning of various origins, myopathy, tumor of spinal cord, canine distemper.

Treatments:

(i) For the restoration of paralytic condition nursing is of prime importance.

(ii) Easily digestible, soft, palatable food and comfortable bedding should be provided.

(iii) Animal should be turned from one side to another.

(iv) For counteracting the severe pain, analgesic should be administered. Vitamin B-complex preparation containing B_1, B_6 and B_{12} should be administered.

(v) Physiotherapy is helpful in some cases.

(vi) Liniments are also indicated in paralysis.

(vii) Anabolic steroid and stimulant are beneficial in paralytic patients.

26. Polyneuritis

Polyneuritis may cause disturbances in either sensory or motor functions; it is also known as peripheral neuritis.

Causes: Vitamin B_1, B_6 and B_{12} deficiency are the main causative factors. Besides metabolic disorders like diabetes mellitus, infections like pyemia, septicaemia, meningitis and myelitis may damage the nerve leading to polyneuritis. Rheumatoid disease and neurotoxic drugs, e.g. streptomycin, nitrofurantoil, antimony, arsenic and copper, may also cause polyneuritis.

Treatments:

(i) Attempt should be made to identify the specific causes and then specific therapy given.

(ii) For vitamin-B deficiencies, drugs having B_1, B_6 and B_{12} either in the form of tablet or injection should be given.

(iii) To control the diabetes, oral hypoglycaemic drugs may be used.

(iv) For control of infection antibiotic therapy is recommended.

(v) Physiotherapy may be helpful in some cases.

27. Eczymatous Dermatitis/Eczema

It is also known as allergic dermatitis and allergic reactions may occur as a result of various allergens. Eczema may be defined as a superficial skin inflammation which may be produced by various external or internal substances against which cells are sensitized, but it always involves a special local or general predisposition.

Causes: Eczema occurs when the sensitized skin cells are brought into contact with allergens.

Endogenous allergens:

(a) Food allergen, viz. vegetables, meat, eggs, lettuce, milk, rice, salmon, spinach, tomato, wheat and may be due to other foods also.

(b) Protozoan allergen, viz. leishmaniasis.

(c) Bacterial allergen, viz. tuberculosis and leptospirosis.

(d) Viral allergen, viz. exanthematous form of distemper.

(e) Fungal allergen, viz. trichophytosis.

(f) Helminthic allergen, viz. ascaris, hookworm, tapeworm and whipworm.

(g) Allergic skin condition caused by sera, vaccines and other protein substances.

Besides the above allergens there are a few drugs, viz. potassium iodide and bromide, and phenothiazine, that may also cause allergic response.

Exogenous allergens:

(a) External parasites like fleas and lice.

(b) Antiseptic and disinfectant washes.

(c) Miscellaneous — painted floors, bedding materials, rubber balls, dyes, synthetic fibres, pollen grain, etc. Sometimes it may be due to mixed allergens or uncertain aetiology.

Predisposing causes: Inherited susceptibility, hepatic disorders, hormonal imbalance, heat, cold, light etc. repeated wetting or dampness.

Pathogenesis: Antigen and antibody reaction produce a antigen - antibody complex which causes degranulation of cells responsible for releasing pharmacologically active amines like 5-HT, histamine, bradykinin, prostaglandin etc. These active amines cause sensitization reaction in the affected cells leading to the allergic manifestations in the skin, viz., erythema, pruritus and oedema.

Clinical signs: Though eczema presents complex and varied clinical pictures but it always takes the form of a superficial skin change. Initially there will be appearance of a small reddish spot. Sometimes papulae or inflammatory vesicles of varying sizes are present. At the same time there will be swellings either diffuse oedema or localized urticarial oedema of the superficial layer of the skin. According to the duration of the disease it may be acute or chronic and according to the nature of the eczema it may be dry or moist. In moist cases there may be exudation of serum and pus, and in chronic cases lesions may become dry, thickened and hyperkeratotic along with constant pruritus (Figs 109, 110).

Diagnosis: It is difficult to make a definite diagnosis of eczema because differentiation between it and dermatitis makes problem. In eczema lesions are superficial and recur when the skin is exposed to the same or other sensitizing substances.

Treatments:

(i) The first step in treating an eczema is removal of the causative agent or agents.

(ii) Bearing in mind the dual origin of eczema it is necessary to provide both internal and external treatment.

(iii) The diet must be readily digestible and should have all the vitamins and minerals in adequate level.

(iv) Meat and egg-restricted diet helps in early recovery.

(v) Milk/vegetable soup or liquid diet is more favourable for patient.

(vi) For the suppression of action of histamines, antihistamines should be given.

(vii) Steroids are also helpful in symptomatic relief of the allergic dermatoses.

(viii) Antibiotic should be used to prevent secondary bacterial infection.

(ix) Local treatment that varies with stage of development of disease is also beneficial in allergic dermatoses.

(x) Recently some enzyme and antiproteinase are considered to be valuable in management of this disease.

28. Emergency Cases

A pet can meet with an accident any time and care should be taken not to panic and to tackle the situation calmly. One should be careful while handling an injured pet to minimize the risk of aggravating the injury.

A series of emergency conditions which need immediate attention are epistaxis, shock, fracture, cardiac failure, fits and other changes in normal behaviour, haematuria and haemoglobinuria, dystokia, prolapse of rectum/vagina, poisoning (accidental or deliberate), bites by snakes, wasp, bees, etc., heat stroke, burns and scalds, severe vomiting and diarrhoea leading to dehydration, colic/abdominal pain and coma.

Shock

Symptoms: In a state of shock, the pet generally collapses. The gums are pale, pupils are dilated, breathing is shallow and rapid, and temperature is subnormal. Sometimes the temperature of extremities is low even though the internal body temperature is increased. The pulse becomes weak and even thready compared to normal.

Treatment: Under these conditions the following measures should be adapted.

(i) The pet should have access tc fresh air and artificial respiration should be given if required.

(ii) Corticosteroids should be given in large doses either intramuscularly or intravenously.

(iii) The animal should be kept warm by wrapping in blankets.

(iv) Broad spectrum antibiotics should be given.

(v) Transfusion of blood is recommended if haematocrit (PCV) is less than 20%. However, its use should be avoided in endotoxic shock.

(vi) The animal should be kept calm.

Fracture

In case of a fractured or a broken leg, the leg swings and cannot bear the weight. A limp rear end and rigid extension of the front legs is noticed in fracture of the back. In pelvic fracture, a dog cannot use hind legs, drooping tail and pain on the back portion of the body.

The fracture should be repaired immediately after consulting a veterinarian. However, care should be taken that the dog gets no jolts or jerks during transportation.

Internal Haemorrhages

In this case, paleness of visible mucous membrane such as of gums is noticed and the pet is in a very weak condition. Blood in urine, stool, rectum and cough is noticed depending upon the organ involved.

The internal haemorrages can always be fatal as the symptoms are not noticed immediately after injury. However, similar measures as in shock should be taken.

Profuse Bleeding

Profuse bleeding can occur due to injury.

Treatment:

(i) It can be checked by applying pressure compress with a clean handkerchief or cloth on the wound and wrapping a bandage or tape around it.

(ii) If the leg is involved a tourniquet midway between the body and the wound should be applied to check the bleeding.

Burns

The burns are considered according to the depth of tissue injury and categorized as first, second and third degree burns. In first degree burn only the superficial layers of skin are involved. Such burns are painful but healing is rapid. In second degree blistering is observed and deep tissue of skin is involved leading to the loss of fluid. In third degree burn there is complete destruction of skin and inner layers are involved. The wound does not heal unless the dead tissue is removed.

Treatment: A burn of simple nature is easily treated with repeated dressing with antiseptics. In second and third stage burns the extent of tissue damage is to be taken into consideration and treatment done accordingly which includes:

(i) The burn should be cleaned and dressed.

(ii) Sedatives, tranquilizers and intravenous fluid therapy should be given.

(iii) Antibiotics should be given parenterally.

(iv) Antihistaminics, corticosteroids and antitetanus injections may be given.

(v) If shock is expected, plasma extenders should be given. Liniment of lime (lime water 100 ml and linseed oil 100 ml) may be applied.

ACCIDENTS OR INJURIES

Accident can occur due to various kinds of vehicles or due to any other object.

Treatment: Mainly depends on the degree of accident. Following drugs may also be given as per requirement, i.e. administration of dextrose saline, immediate application of ice-cold water preferably cold normal saline for blunt injuries, topical application of soothing ointments containing antibiotics and topical application of local anaesthetics.

Heat Stroke

Hyperthermia caused by exposure to sun is called heat stroke.

Cause: Sudden and excessive exposure to hot sun, dehydration, lack of water supply, excessive exercise in dry hot climate, hot humid climate, obesity and lack of heat tolerance.

Clinical signs: The animal is exhausted, dull, depressed and lies prostrate with high fever.

Treatments:

(i) Administration of Coramine.
(ii) Frequent cold bath.
(iii) Application of cold pack on body.
(iv) Fluid therapy.
(v) Administration of febrifuse.
(vi) Use of tranquilizers, if necessary.
(vii) Feeding of cold milk.

Pyrexia (Fever)

An increase in body temperature may be caused by viral/bacterial/parasitic infections, immune-mediated reactions, neoplastic granulomatous conditions, dehydration, high environmental temperature, toxicoses and drugs. Temperature lower than 105°F is seldom harmful to the patient and is in fact useful in inhibiting the proliferation of pathogens. The mode of onset and severity of temperature may be a useful clue to diagnosis and guide in assessing efficacy of specific drug therapy. When temperature is more than 106°F, it may lead to brain damage, cardiac arhythmias, dehydration etc. In such condition emergency measures must be taken to reduce the body temperature quickly to the safe level.

Treatments:

(i) Cool baths or cold ice pack, or cold enema should be given to reduce the temperature.
(ii) Antipyretic drugs should also be used to reduce the temperature by getting the hypothalamic temperature regulating centre with subsequent increase in heat loss.
(iii) Salicylates like sodium salicylates or aspirin may be given @ 10 mg per kg b.i.d., paracetamol (acetaminophen) and phyenylbutazone may also be used to reduce the temperature.
(iv) Only after reducing the temperature specific treatment like antibiotic or sulpha may be followed.

Pain

Analysis of pain is difficult in dumb creatures. To judge the intensity, degree and nature of pain, a veterinarian has to depend upon the unusual postures, vocalization, defensive reactions to palpation, autonomic responses and muscular splinting of the affected area of body of the dog. The degree of response to the painful stimuli will vary with the severity, nature of problem, its chronicity, aetiology and setting, and also on the temperament of the individual animal. It is very difficult to judge the nature of pain and where it hurts because of the many variables. Therefore, it is suggested to provide analgesic drugs in such a case.

Treatments:

(i) For treatment of specific disease, relieving of pain is of utmost necessity.
(ii) Cases of superficial or deep somatic pain of mild to moderate intensity (as in case of incision of body wall, arthritis, muscular injuries, cystitis, dental injury, gastro-eneritis) may be treated with non-steroidal anti-inflammatory analgesics, i.e. non-narcotic analgesics (aspirin, acetaminophen and phen-acetin).
(iii) Whereas relief from severe somatic or visceral pain requires administration of central acting narcotic, analgesics like morphine sulphate or hydrochloride may be given @ 0.25 mg/kg body weight I/M, I/V or S/C. Other drugs like codeine phosphate, methadone, meperidine etc. may also be used.

PLATE-26

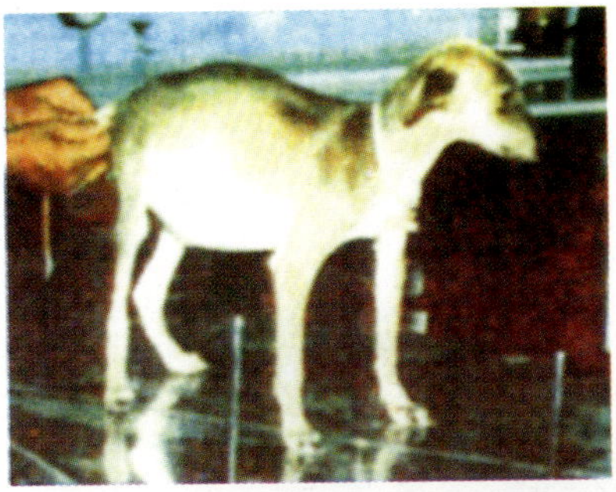

Fig. 105. Dog showing ascites

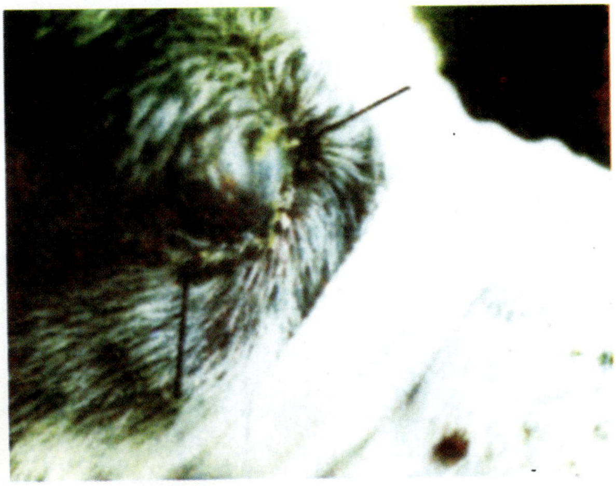

Fig. 107. Dog suffering with keratitis

Fig. 108. Dog exhibiting signs of epilepsy

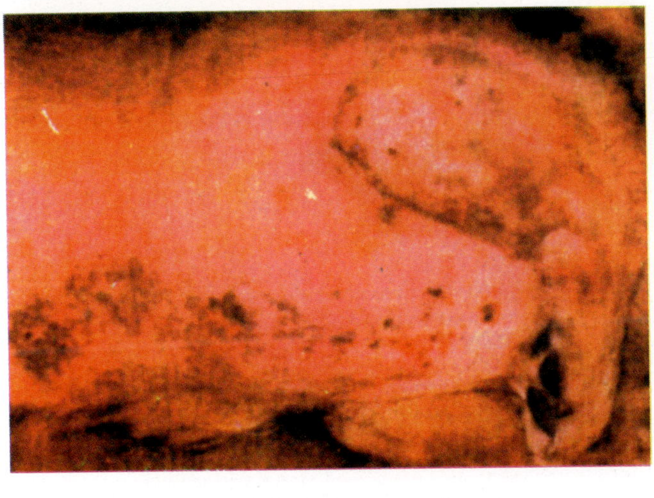

Fig. 109. Whole body eczema in a dog

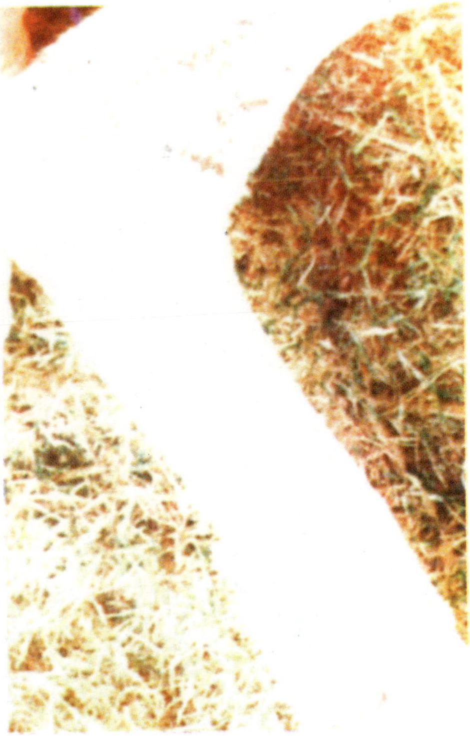

Fig. 110. Eczematous dermatitis of leg

PLATE-27

Fig. 112. Dog showing haematoma of ears

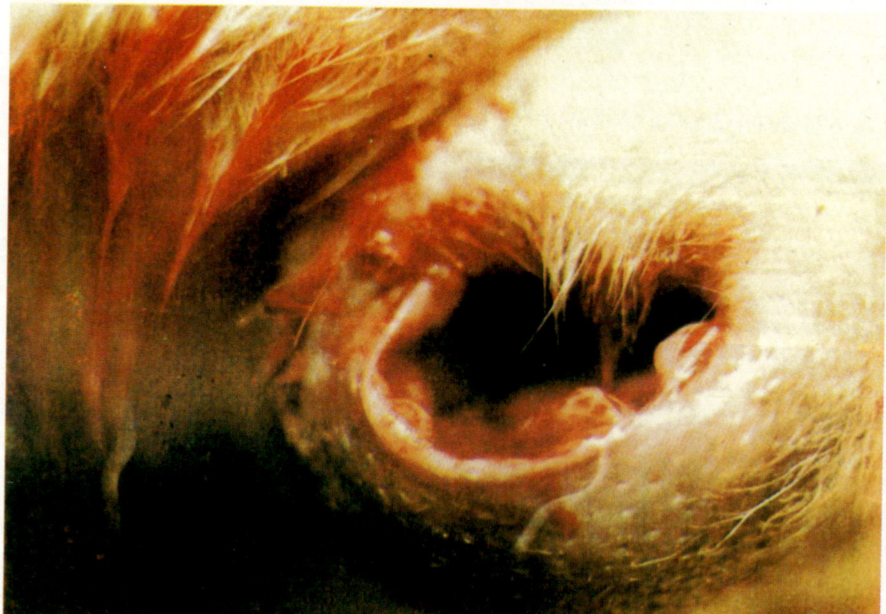

Fig. 113. Female dog suffering from vaginal tumor

EMERGENCY KIT

A clinician must always be ready to meet the requirements of emergency case and must handle them boldly. For this purpose a readily available kit is necessary. The necessary medicines and equipments required in a kit are:

Medicines:

(i) Antibiotics	Tetracycline, Pencillin, etc.
(ii) Analgesics	Baralgan, Novalgin, Pethidin
(iii) Antispasmodics	Atropine sulphate
(iv) Antihistaminics	Avil, Phenargan
(v) Tranquilizers	Largactil, Siquil
(vi) Antiseptics	Antibiotic or sulpha ointment for skin, eye and ear
(vii) Intravenous infusion	Dextrose saline 5%, Dextrose - 10%, Ringer lactate, Calcium gluconate etc.

Besides these medicines Tincture of iodine, Tincture of benzoin, Potassium permanganate, Dettol, Spirit, Liquid paraffin, Adrenaline, Coramine, Corticosteroids, Stemetil, Avomine, Paracetamol etc. are also essential.

Instruments: Clinical thermometer, stethoscope, syringes, needles, gauze, cotton and dressing material, bandage, catgut, suturing needles, stomach tube, catheter, pair of scissors, scalpel, blades, forceps, artery forceps, gloves etc. are of prime importance.

MANAGEMENT OF EMERGENCY CASES IN GENERAL

1. A veterinarian should be consulted immediately.
2. The jaws of the dog should be tied with bandage or string.
3. First aid should be given at once.
4. The dog should be wrapped in a blanket to give warmth and sedatives can be given if needed.
5. The dog should be gently lifted and jolt or jerk to it avoided.
6. Attention should be paid towards heart rate, respiration, temperature and blood circulation.
7. Foreign bodies, if any, should be removed and bleeding should be checked.
8. Surgical intervention be made, if necessary.
9. Fluid therapy is advisable, if shock is expected due to severe injury.
10. Specific and non-specific antidotes should be given in case of known and suspected poisoning respectively.

Suggestions for Indoor Patients

1. Orders should be written in chart clearly explicit to avoid misinterpretation and should be signed by the attending veterinarian. They should be revised as and when needed.
2. Previous orders should be cancelled before new orders are written in the chart.
3. General observation should be written regularly in the chart, viz. pulse, temperature, frequency, respiration (TPR) and central venous pressure. Also general care instruction should be given, e.g. diet, exercise, fluids and bowel care. Symptomatic treatment of fever, pains, etc. should be written. Specific therapy for patient should also be written. Methods for prevention of complication should also be mentioned.

Suggestions to the Owner

The veterinarian should write his suggestions for treatment and care of the patient at home in simple and clear language.

These suggestions/orders should be signed and dated by the attending veterinary doctor.

12

GENERAL SURGERY

PREPARATION FOR SURGER Y

Surgery is an art of application of knowledge of Veterinary Science for the management of surgical and pathological conditions. Surgery should be performed in an aseptic environment without causing pain to the patient. The requirements for this purpose are surgical pack, sterilization of the surgical instruments, preparation of the site of operation, preparation of the surgeon and supporting staff required at the operation table, anaesthesia, tranquilizers, arrangements for blood transfusion and fluid therapy.

The use of anaesthesia in dogs is important for painless surgery, easiness of handling, control of the animal for avoiding sudden and jerky movement which may damage the organs during the operation. General anaesthesia must be used by an experienced person and for minor surgery use of local anaesthesia is adequate.

The suturing material should be strong and sterilized. The wound should be dressed aseptically under antibiotic umbrella to prevent infection and pyogenesis at the site of operation. The various aspects have been described, in detail, step-wise in the following pages for the convenience of the surgeon.

SURGICAL PACK

For routine surgical operations, the following instruments and materials are required:

Scissors 4: Straight - 2 (1 small, and 1 big);
Curved with blunt points - 2 (1 small, and 1 big);
B.P. handle No. 3 and 4 (2 each);
Assorted blades for above handles;
Artery forceps - 8 (4 curved and 4 straight, 15 cm);
Grooved director - 1;
Dissecting forceps (Allis type) - 2, 15 cm;
Towel clips - 4;
Tissue forceps (Allis type) -4;
Needle holders - 2;
Suture needles - 4; Semicircular 5 to 8 cm with non-cutting edge,

Semicircular 10 or 12 cm with cutting edge;
Semicircular 7 or 8 cm with cutting edge;
Semicircular 4 or 5 cm with cutting edge;
Suturing thread: Linen No. 20, 60, chromic cat-gut No. 00, 000;
Surgical gloves - 2 pairs as per size of surgeon and assistant surgeon;
Gloves case with powder;
Surgical gown - 2;
Face Mask - 2;
Caps - 2;
Surgical swabs (gauze) - 1 to 2 dozens;
Surgical drapes - 4;
Shrouds - 2 (with or without slits, 1 m × 1 m);
Surgical towels - 2 (20 cm × 30 cm);
Surgical instrument drum - 1;
Surgical pack wrapper - 1;
Wooden splints - 4 to 6;
Metallic bone pins;
Plaster of paris;
Medicated adhesive tapes, and
Medicine cup (for sterile saline solution).
Other special instruments may be needed for a particular operation.

STERILIZATION

The surgical instruments should be cleaned and washed properly with soap or detergent solution, rinsed and dried. Prior to sterilization they should be free from dust, spots of blood, pus, grease, hair, drug etc.

General surgical pack should be sterilized in autoclave at 6.75 kg pressure at 121°C for 15 minutes.

Dry heat method of sterilization may also be used for surgical pack. Ethyl alcohol (70%) can be used for 30 minutes for instruments only. The surgical dressings can be sterilized by saturated steam under pressure, for which an ordinary pressure cooker may be used.

The usual method of sterilization is using boiling water (100°C) for 30 minutes; this is not effective. For enhancing the efficacy of this method 2% sodium carbonate or 0.1% NaOH may be added to the water to reduce the boiling time from 30 to 15 minutes. The instruments should be properly covered in the water.

Of all the methods, the best method of sterilization for surgical pack is autoclaving.

PREPARATION OF SURGEON

The finger nails of the surgeon should be cut short and there should not be any injury or wound on the hand. The surgeon should wash his hands thoroughly with soap, for at least 7-10 minutes and all the lather removed by washing in running water. Hands should be dried in air by keeping fingers in upward directionand then dipped in 70% ethyl alcohol.

PREPARATION OF THE OPERA TIVE FIELD

(i) The operation site should be shaved properly.

(ii) After shaving, the site should be cleaned properly with soap and water to remove all dirt.

(iii) The operation site should be scrubbed with a piece of gauze dipped in 70% ethyl alcohol and allowed to dry.

(iv) The operative wound should be checked for contamination. This is very important. The scalpel used for skin incision should be discarded and a new one used.

(v) All cut edges of the skin should be kept covered during the operation.

(vi) At the end of the operation and just before closing the upper layer of the skin, the draper used during the operation should be removed and replaced by new sterile drapes.

(vii) It is always better to use sterilized rubber gloves to minimise the contamination.

(viii) The surgeon should always wear surgical gown, face mask, and cap during the operation.

(xi) Local and parenteral antibiotics should be given to minimize the chances of infection.

ANAESTHESIA

Anaesthesia may be defined as the loss of sensation of part of the the body or whole body. It is induced by various drugs which depress the activity of the nervous system. These drugs may produce local, general or regional anaesthesia.

The general view regarding the action of anaesthetic drugs is that they act by reducing oxygen intake of the body tissues. Since the oxygen requirement of nervous tissues is higher as compared to the requirement of other body tissues, they are the first to be affected by anaesthesia. The resulting changes, viz. unconsciousness, reduced reflex actions, muscular atony and respiratory paralysis, are due to the depression of cerebral cortices, mid-brain, spinal cord and medulla caused by anaesthetic drugs. These drugs also have depressant and paralytic effect on the Central Nervous System which produces unconsciousness and loss of voluntary motor function.

PREANAESTHETIC DRUGS/AGENTS

Drugs are used before the anaesthetic agent to prepare the patient for anaesthesia. The most important functions of these drugs are to reduce the excitability of the patient, secretions like saliva and mucus so that there will be no problems in respiration, gastrointestinal motility and vomition, quantity of anaesthetic drugs and discomfort of the patient during recovery. The following preanaesthetics are commonly used in veterinary practice.

Tranquilizers: Tranquilizers reduce anxiety and make the patient feel released. These work as preanaesthetic agents and are used as an antiemetic in dog suffering from transport sickness. They are also used before anthelmintics if the animal has a tendency to vomit. There use inhibits the pet from licking its injury, chewing bandages and helps to secure excited and hypersensitive pets during clinical examination.

Phenothiazine derivatives: In this group of tranquilizers phenothiazine is the parent compound.

(i) Triflupromazine HCl (Siquil) - 1-2 mg/kg B.W. I/V.

(ii) Promazine HCl - 0.5 mg/kg B.W. I/V or 1.0 mg/kg B.W. I/M.

(iii) Chlormazine HCl - 5 mg/kg B.W. oral; 2.5 mg/kg B.W. I/M or 1.2 mg/kg B.W. I/V.

(iv) Ethyl isobutrazine (Diguel) - 2-4 mg/kg B.W. I/V or 4-10 mg/kg B.W. I/M.

(v) Perphenazine (Trilafon) - 10 mg/kg B.W. I/V or I/M.

(vi) Xylazine (Rompun) 10% solution - 1-2 mg/kg B.W. I/V.
(vii) Pecazine - 2 mg/kg B.W., I/M.
(viii) Trimeprazine - 2-4 mg/kg B.W., orally; 1-2 mg/kg B.W., I/V or I/M.
(ix) Acetylpromazine - 0.5-1.0 mg/kg B.W. I/M.
(x) Propiomazine HCl (Tran Vet) - 0.5-2.0 mg/kg B.W., I/M or I/V.
(xi) Mepazine - 5 mg/kg B.W., I/V.

Reserpine alkaloid derivatives:

(i) Reserpine (Serpasil) - 0.025 mg/kg B.W. orally, or 0.05 mg/kg B.W. I/V.

Propanediol derivatives:

(i) Hydrozyzine pamitate and Dihydrochloride - 1 mg/kg B.W. I/M.
(ii) Meprobamate - 100-400 mg total dose, T.I.D., orally.
(iii) Diazepam (Valium) - 0.5-1 mg/kg B.W. I/M.

Anticholinergics: These drugs also work as pre-anaesthetic agents.

(i) Atropine sulphate - 0.04 mg/kg B.W., and total dose 0.5-1.5 mg I/V, I/M or S/C.

Morphine derivatives: These drugs also act as preanaesthetic agent although morphine derivatives act in various forms in the body.

(i) Morphine sulphate - 0.5-1 mg/kg B.W. S/C or I/M.
(ii) Meperidine HCl (Pethidine) - 10 mg/kg B.W.
(iii) Methadone HCl - 1 mg/kg B.W. I/V or S/C.
(iv) Anileridine (leritine) - 1-3 mg/kg B.W. I/M or S/C.
(v) Dihydromorphinone HCl 5-10 mg/kg B.W. orally.
(vi) Papaveratem - 10-20 mg I/M.
(vii) Thiambutene HCl (Themalon) - 5 mg/kg B.W. I/V or 20 mg/kg S/C.
(viii) Oxymorphone HCl - 0.75 mg/kg B.W. I/M or S/C.

Tranquilizer and narcotic combination: Combination of both the above drugs may also act as preanaesthetic agent.

(i) Methadone - Acetyl promazine combination - 1 + 1 mg/kg, B.W. I/M or S/C.
(ii) Meperidine - Acetyl promazine - Below 17 kg 1/2 ml mixture; above 17 kg 1 ml mixture.

LOCAL ANAESTHETIC DRUGS

These drugs produce loss of sensation of a limited body part or organ (recommended concentration of some important local anaesthetics).

Drugs	***Infiltration***	***Topical***	***Local and regional***
Cocaine	Not used	4.1%	Not used
Chloroprocaine (Nesscaine)	0.5-1%	Not used	2-3%
Dibucaine (Nupercaine)	0.5%	2%	2%
Hexyclaine (Cyclaine)	0.5%	2.5-5%	1-1.5%
Lidocaine (Xylocaine)	2%	2-4%	1-2%

(Contd.)

Drugs	*Infiltration*	*Topical*	*Local and regional*
Piperocaine (Methycaine)	0.5-1%	2-4%	1-3%
Procaine (Novocaine)	4-5%	Not used	1-2.5%
Tetracaine (Pontocaine)	0-1%	2%	0.2%
Prilocaine (Citanest)	0-5%	2%	1-2%
Dyclonine (Dyclone)	0.5%	0.5%	0.5%
Butacaine (Butyne)	1%	2%	1%
Tutocaine	2%	-	2%
Cinchocain	0.5%	-	1-2%
Decicaine	1-2%	2%	2%
Bupivacaine	0.5%	-	0.5%
Propoxycaine	0.5%	-	0.5%

REGIONAL ANAESTHESIA

Loss of sensation in a larger area of the body is referred to as regional anaesthesia. Regional anaesthesia may be obtained by injecting local anaesthetic agent into the spinal cord. In epidural anaesthesia, the anaesthetic solution should be deposited within the canal outside the duramater. When it is injected into cerebrospinal fluid it is called subarachanoid anaesthesia.

According to the site of injection, epidural anaesthesia may be classified as:

(i) Caudal,

(ii) Lumbosacral, and

(iii) Lumbar or anterior (high) and posterior (low).

In canines, lumbosacral epidural anaesthesia is usually preferred. It can be used for ovariohysterectomy, castration, mammectomy, fracture and management of wounds of hind limbs, caesarean section and caudectomy. The site of lumbosacral epidural anaesthesia is lumbosacral space (between the last lumbar vertebra and sacrum). Some of the regional anaesthetic agents are 2% procaine @ 1 ml/2 kg B.W., and 2% lidocaine @ 2-10 ml/2 kg B.W. Preanaesthetics should be used to restrain the animal during injection.

GENERAL ANAESTHETICS

It is known as complete loss of consciousness on the administration of anaesthetic drugs.

Anaesthetic Gases:

(i) Nitrous oxide - 50-70% nitrous oxide with 30-50% oxygen.

(ii) Ethylene - 85% ethylene with 15% oxygen.

(iii) Cyclopropane - 20-50% cycloprane with oxygen.

Intravenous Anaesthetic Agents:

(i) Chloralose - 50-60 mg/kg B.W., 1% aqueous solution.

(ii) Katamine HCl - 4-8 mg/kg B.W.

(iii) Chloral hydrate - 0.22-0.33 g/kg B.W.

(iv) Thialbarbitone sodium - 45 mg/kg B.W., 4-5% solution.

(v) Thiamylal sodium - 17-20 mg/kg B.W.
(vi) Thiopentone sodium - 22-25 mg/kg B.W.
(vii) Barbital sodium - oral sedative dose 150-1,000 mg.
(viii) Phenobarbital sodium - 25-30 mg B.W.

Inhalation anaesthetics:

(i) Chloroform - 1.35% for light anaesthesia; 1.65% for deep anaesthesia.
(ii) Trichloroethane - 0.5-0.75%.
(iii) Ethyl chloride - 3.0%-4.5%.
(iv) Methoxy flurene (Penthrane) - 0.4-1% for maintenance and anaesthesia.
(v) Halothane - 2-4% produces plane anaesthesia.
(vi) Ether (Ethyl ether, diethyl ether) - 3.5-4.5% concentrate by volume.
(vii) Vinyl ether (Divinyl ether) - 4% concentrate in inspired air.
(viii) Fluroxene (Trifluroethyl vinyl ether) - 2.4% concentrate produces stage 3 plane anaesthesia; 6-8% concentrate produces plane 3 anaesthesia.

Some terms commonly used in relation to depression of nervous system are as follows:

(i) ***Surgical anaesthesia:*** Unconsciousness accompanied by muscular relaxation to such a level that operation may be performed painlessly without struggle.
(ii) ***Basal anaesthesia:*** mild general anaesthesia, mostly produced by preanaesthetic agents. It helps in deeper anaesthesia.
(iii) ***Analgesia:*** defined as state of relief from pain.
(iv) ***Sedation state of low level:*** control, depression in which pet is conscious but calm and unaggressive.
(v) ***Narcosis:*** State of deep sleep along with analgesia.
(vi) ***Hypnosis:*** State of artificially induced sleep by moderate depression of central nervous system.

BLOOD TRANSFUSION AND FLUID THERAPY

Blood Transfusion

It is an attempt to replace blood or its components when life is endangered. It is often a life saving measure, but it also has the potential of doing much harm and should be applied with extreme care.

The homologous blood from one animal (the donor) is transferred to the blood stream of another (the recipient). The transferred erythrocytes, like the recipient's own red cells, serve for oxygen transport.

The objectives of transfusion are to sustain life when threatened by reduction in the red blood cells; and to maintain the level of circulating haemoglobin that ameliorate most clinical signs in sick dogs with chronic non-regenerative anaemic condition. Blood transfusion is required to be done under poisoning and emergency conditions. The indications in general are as follows:

(i) In acute and chronic losses of whole blood during an accident.
(ii) In cases where certain constituents of the blood are lacking.
(iii) As a prophylactic measure in surgical operations in which considerable loss of blood is expected.
(iv) In cases of blood poisoning (chemical and microbial).

(v) To provide substances which are specifically lacking such as proteins, clotting factors, platelets, red blood cells.

(vi) To provide specific and non-specific antibodies in auto-immune haemolytic diseases.

Replacement of red blood cells is advised when the PCV of the dog is 15% or less (Hb 5 g%). In acute blood loss, the PCV may remain unchanged for several hours and is unreliable in determining the need for blood transfusion. In less acute losses a PCV of less than 25% indicates the need for blood transfusion. In chronic cases of anaemic patients blood needs transfusion only when PCV level goes below 15%.

BLOOD GROUPS AND INCOMPATIBILITY

Dogs are classified into 8 blood group systems based on canine erythrocyte antigens. The 8 canine erythrocyte antigens (CEA) are identified using monospecific sera produced by deliberate isoimmunization. Erythrocyte antigens CEA-1 and CEA-2 are the most reactive. Nearly 60% of the rare canine population is positive for the strongly haemagglutinating CEA-1 antigen and the remaining 40% is negative. Severe haemolytic reactions are reliably produced when CEA-1 or CEA-2 erythrocytes are transfused to dogs normally without these antigens but previously sensitized by transfusion. Because of prior sensitization, recipient dogs will have produced anti-CEA-1 or anti-CEA-1, 2 isoantibodies. Naturally occurring anti-CEA-1 and CEA-1, 2 isoantibodies have not been detected. Another canine red cell antigen Tr (CEA-7) should also be considered when transfusing blood since it exists in half the rare dog population. The most ideal canine blood donor should be negative for CEA-1, CEA-2 and CEA-7. The remaining canine erythrocyte antigens are usually slightly reactive in previously sensitized dogs.

Naturally occurring antibodies do exist against some of these erythrocyte antigens. Canine blood typing does not ensure compatibility. Accordingly, cross-matching by standard technique should be done whenever required. Other ways to avoid mismatched transfusions include typing the recipients to determine their specific needs and alternatively using red blood cells only when absolutely necessary (PCV 15%).

Cross-matching methods: This method is of limited use as it only detects incompatibility if the recipient has been previously sensitized by transfusion of incompatible blood. It is essential if repeated transfusions using untyped donors are undertaken. Sensitized dogs destroy transfused red blood cells immediately (7-10 days) and the pups of bitches so sensitized may develop haemolytic diseases if they are CEA-1 positive and are allowed to suck colostrum.

Different types of cross-matching tests are helpful. These are:

1. ***Direct method:*** On a clean glass slide 3 separate drops of sodium citrate solution are taken. Donor's blood is added to drop 1, recipient's blood to drop 2, and 1 drop each of donor's and recipient's blood to drop 3. Agglutination reaction in drop 3 indicates incompatibility. Drops 1 and 2 act as controls.
2. ***Indirect or cross-reaction:*** Blood is collected from both the donor and the recipient, and allowed to clot. The red cell suspension (5%) of each animal is prepared following washing with normal saline and the test-tubes are arranged in the following order:
   (i) Donor red blood cells (2 drops) are mixed with recipient serum (2 drops) (major match).
   (ii) Recipient red blood cells (2 drops) are mixed with donor serum (2 drops) (minor match).
   (iii) Donor red blood cells (2 drops) are mixed with 2 drops of normal saline (control).

   After incubation at 37°-38°C for up to an hour the tubes are centrifuged and examined for the evidence of haemolysis. The cells are then re-suspended and examined for evidence of agglutination reaction on haemolysis on a warm slide. All the reagents must be kept at 38°C.
3. ***Oehlecker's biological screening test:*** In the recipient animal 10-20 ml of donor's blood is injected intravenously and the animal is observed for about 10 minutes. Mild incompatibility is evidenced by

defaecation, and acceleration of pulse and respiratory rates. In severe cases, there is dyspnoea, shivering, sweating, restlessness, defaecation and urination. In more severe cases pulse becomes weak, haemoglobinaemic, collapse and death results.

Blood collection and storage methods: Donor's blood may be obtained and used in the following 2 ways. In the first case live donor animals are kept with the owner and bled when needed for transfusion.

The advantages are that the blood is always fresh, platelets and white blood cells are functional, and blood has a longer post-transfusion life; health status of donor animal and haematology may be checked regularly; veterinarian is the legal owner; dogs with good temperament may be selected; dog's blood may be typed and only CEA-1 negative dogs can be retained.

The disadvantages are that since a large dog is required, its maintenance and feed is expensive; delay in blood collection may be critical in an emergency.

The second method is to have live donors with regular blood collection and storage.

The advantage of this method is that blood is always readily available at an emergency.

The disadvantages are that the blood may become outdated before it is used for transfusion and the clotting factor and platelets have no value.

Site of blood collection: Blood is collected from jugular vein, femoral artery or carotid artery. Local anaesthetic is advised at the site of venipuncture in conscious donors and a large-bore needle should be used. Anticoagulants used during the collection of donor blood which has to be stored are described below:

(i) ***Acid Citrate Dextrose (ACD):*** Each 100 ml contains 2.2 g sodium citrate (anticoagulant), 0.73 citric acid anhydrous (preservative), 2.45 g dextrose (nutrition to red cells), and water for injection, Q.S.

Storage: 1° to 6°C (32°-46°F).

A minimum of 25 ml ACD solution is used for 100 ml of blood.

(ii) ***Citrate Phosphate Dextrose (CPD):*** If blood is not to be stored then the anticoagulants used are Heparin (20-30 mg/500 ml) and Ethylene diamine tetra acetic acid (400 mg/30 ml blood).

Canine whole blood collected in these specific solutions should be maintained at room temperature between 32°C and 45°C. If properly collected and stored, blood can be used within 21 days. After 21 days of storage at least 70% of transfused canine red cells survive for 24 hours after administration. The biochemical changes in stored blood are called storage lesions. They are: Decrease in pH, PO_2, glucose, bicarbonate and increase in PCO_2 and lactate levels; intracellular and extracellular potassium and sodium tend to equilibrate so that present potassium levels tend to rise slightly; and red blood cells swell and become more liable to haemolysis.

DOSAGE AND ADMINISTRATION PROCEDURE

The dose of blood is calculated on the percentage of haemoglobin available and the percentage to which it should be increased (at least 75% of the normal level). Since an animal contains 40 ml blood per kg of body weight the formula used is

$$\frac{40 \times \text{body weight (in kg)}}{100} = \text{ml of blood required to raise Hb to 1\%}$$

Administration: For blood transfusion cephalic, recurrent tarsal and jugular veins are mostly used in dog at the rate of less than 10 ml/kg/hour. The first portion of the transfusion is usually administered slowly and stopped if urticaria develops. The dose of 10-20 ml/kg/24 hours. should not be exceeded unless there is continuing haemorrhage. Drip infusion is invariably undertaken at the rate of one drop/second.

The administration of cold blood which is also more viscous, lowers body temperature and may cause vasoconstriction and cardiac arrythmias. Excessive warming (45°C) will cause haemolysis. The blood should be warmed to 37°-40° C by passing the giving set through a warm-water bath at that temperature and not by warming the bottle or bag itself. It is also desirable to resuspend the cells evenly by repeated inversions of the bottle or bag before the administration is performed.

Fluid Therapy

It is a supportive and often life-saving therapy in critically ill patient. Fluid therapy is given during water imbalance (dehydration), combined water electrolyte imbalance, and acid-base disturbance. It may take precedence over other forms of treatment and efforts for diagnosis.

Its aim is to rapidly restore and to maintain an adequate circulating blood volume; replace and obtain rapid systemic distribution of water, electrolytes and nutrients and provide nutrients. The fluid therapy is given in common conditions like shock, diarrhoea, vomition, burns, renal insufficiency, dehydration, kidney diseases and post-operative conditions.

Body fluid consists of water and among other things electrolytes (ions). The primary electrolytes of importance in evaluating fluid balance/therapy are sodium, potassium, chloride and bicarbonate. Under normal circumstances, first 3 electrolytes are supplied by food, and bicarbonate is formed in the body from carbon dioxide. In sick animals increased loss of water, decreased intake of water or both may lead to dehydration. Increased loss of water is caused by diarrhoea, vomition and polyuria. Decreased intake of water caused by anorexia.

After prolonged state of dehydration (e.g. in conditions like diarrhoea and persistent vomition) both water and electrolytes are lost.

Disorders of acid-base balances may be respiratory or metabolic.

Dehydration may also be classified as follows:

(i) ***Isotonic dehydration:*** In this water and electrolytes are lost in equal proportions, e.g. through diarrhoea and vomition. Rectifying this condition requires restoration of extracellular space with a solution that approximates the composition of that fluid. Colloidal solutions are ideal to fill up the deficit in the extracellular space.

(ii) ***Hypertonic dehydration:*** In this there is excessive loss of water as compared to electrolytes. This condition may be caused by heat exhaustion, excessive sweating, or inability to swallow.

(iii) ***Hypotonic dehydration:*** In this there is loss of electrolytes in excess of water, e.g. renal insufficiency.

Clinical evaluation: Correct assessment of the patient is essential to provide the most beneficial therapy. In sick animals administration of wrong fluids may worsen the condition and similarly there will be no improvement by infusion of inadequate quantities of fluids. The following procedure may help to evaluate the nature and intensity of the condition of the animal.

1. ***History:*** It is a very important source. Accurate history can provide valuable information. Many a times it is the only criterion to assess the nature of imbalance furnishing qualitative information. It includes the duration of illness, nature, frequency and volume of vomitus and faeces passed, amount of food and water intake and other factors which may be relevant to calculate the fluid loss or deficiency in intake during illness.
2. ***Clinical examination:*** In this the degree of dehydration is estimated (expressed as per cent of body weight). Dehydration with 5% loss of weight is the minimum detectable sign with dry inelastic skin. At 7% loss, the skin becomes more dry and inelastic, and the eyeballs are sunken. At 10-12% dehydration, these symptoms are more pronounced, shock ensues and involuntary muscle twitching is noticed. Oral mucosa becomes dry. At 12-15% dehydration shock is marked and death is imminent. Low body temperature signifies less body fluids and peripheral circulatory failure. Signs attributable to water and

sodium deficiency include thirst, dry mucous membrane, loss of skin elasticity, loss of weight, generalized weakness and lassitude. Red and dry conjunctivae indicate water depletion.

In sodium depletion, animal will be extremely dull and unable to stand due to orthrostatic discomfort due to reduction in extracellular fluid volume. Tachycardia is the early sign of impending circulatory failure. Oliguria is the early sign of water or sodium depletion in isotonic fluid.

Potassium deficiency is characterized by generalized muscle weakness and abdominal distension due to reduced intestinal tone and motility and leakage of rectal contents due to relaxed anal sphinctor. Rapid and deep respiration in metabolic acidosis and hyperactive reflexes in metabolic alkalosis are some of the signs detected during clinical examination.

3. ***Laboratory aids:*** These are more diagnostic. Their value is more in confirming the nature of fluid imbalance.
   (i) ***Packed cell volume (haematocrit, PCV):*** In isotonic fluid depletion, PCV will be high and may be used to give an estimate of fluid requirements. Approximately 10 ml of fluid/kg body weight is required for each 1% rise in PCV over 45%. (Table 14).
   (ii) ***Haemoglobin (Hb):*** The Hb values changes in cases of anaemia. This needs to be taken into consideration.
   (iii) ***Total serum protein:*** It helps in accurate diagnosis of the fluid disorders (Table 14).
   (iv) ***Blood urea and creatinine levels:*** Their value may also rise during dehydration. Renal disease may also induce a rise.

COMMON DISEASES WITH FLUID IMBALANCE

1. ***Diarrhoea:*** Water, bicarbonate, sodium, potassium and chloride are lost through the diarrhoeic faeces resulting in dehydration and acidosis. Lactated Ringer's solution with 5% dextrose is preferred for fluid therapy (Table 15).
2. ***Vomiting:*** Water, chloride and H^+ion are lost, resulting in metabolic alkalosis. Normal saline or Lactated Ringer's solution is preferred (Table 15).
3. ***Anorexia:*** Severe dehydration with no loss of electrolytes except in prolonged cases of some chronic diseases. Dextrose solution 5% is preferred.

In general, existing fluid deficit should be replaced with a similar fluid. The animal's response is the only criterion to judge the efficacy of the treatment.

INJECTABLE FLUIDS

The following are some of the injectable fluids used during various diseases (Table 15).

Dextrose solution 5%: Isotonic, provides intravenous hydration supply through immediately available water and carbohydrate.

Dextrose solution 10%: Useful for venous hydration.

Dextrose saline 5%: Isotonic; supplies calories (energy), water, sodium and chloride. Useful in losses in heat exhaustion, vomiting and mild cases of diarrhoea.

Normal saline: Isotonic; useful in dehydration and vomiting.

Darrow's solution: Malnutrition, severe diarrhoea.

Ringer's solution: Severe dehydration due to vomiting, diarrhoea.

Lactated Ringer's solution (with or without dextrose): Useful in dehydration; moderate acidosis and diarrhoea.

Sodium lactate solution: Metabolic acidosis, severe diarrhoea, ketosis, acute infection, malnutrition.

Isolyte M: To meet the daily needs.

Isolyte P: Provides more water than electrolytes for young animals.

Isolyte E: Same composition as plasma except that potassium and bicarbonate precursors are double. Useful as extracellular fluid replacement.

Electrolyte solutions: The electrolyte solutions are designed for daily water and electrolyte maintenance and also for the replacement of losses. Some of the solutions are described below:

1. ***Solution M:*** It is a maintenance solution with 5% dextrose and is administered in accordance with water needs. It is given in conditions requiring daily water and electrolyte maintenance. Sweating, water depletion due to the reduction in water intake and potassium deficit resulting from vomiting, diarrhoea and prolonged infusion of potassium free solutions and mild metabolic acidosis.
2. ***Solution E:*** This extracellular replacement solution has essentially the same composition as plasma except that the concentration of potassium and bicarbonate precursor doubled. It provides potassium, calcium, magnesium and bicarbonate in addition to sodium and chloride. Indicated in mild diarrhoea, excessive water intake, or sodium depletion, hyponatremia and metabolic acidosis.
3. ***Solution P:*** This pediatric maintenance solution with 5% dextrose is designed to provide the daily water and electrocyte maintenance requirement in young ones (in excessive water loss or mild metabolic acidosis, and when they are unable to concentrate urine).
4. ***Lactated Ringer's solution (Hartman's):*** It provides electrolytes at the approximate concentration of these electrolytes in plasma, while supplying a bicarbonate precursor (lactate) for the correction of mild acidosis. Lactate is rapidly metabolized to bicarbonate except in patients with poor liver function due to hepatic disease or anoxia due to shock, when blood lactate may already be elevated. Restoration of normal fluid balance following distributional shifts of extracellular fluid due to burns, fractures, infection, peritoneal irritation, cardiovascular emergency, diarrhoea and also other indications for this fluid.
5. ***Acetated Ringer's solution:*** In many clinical conditions lactate metabolism is impaired. In such situations the administration of Ringer's lactate solution will elevate serum lactic acid levels. Acetate is more efficiently metabolized in conditions associated with tissue hypoxia such as shock, because its metabolism requires less oxygen. In addition, it is metabolized primarily by muscle and other peripheral tissues in contrast to lactate which is metabolized largely by liver. Therefore, it is the preferred solution in metabolic acidosis associated with circulatory insufficiency and liver dysfunction.
6. ***Ringer's solution:*** It is frequently preferred to normal saline in treating dehydration because it contains potassium and calcium.
7. ***Sodium chloride solution:*** It is used during conditions in which chloride loss is greater than or equal to loss of sodium. Sodium chloride solution (5%) is useful in sweating, vomiting, diarrhoea and excessive water intake.
8. ***Potassium solution (lactated potassium saline injection - Darrow's solution):*** It is useful in cases of malnutrition, marked loss of gastro-intestinal secretions because of vomiting, diarrhoea, prolonged diuresis, metabolic alkalosis, overmedication with adrenocortical steroids, etc.
9. ***Dextrose saline:*** This primarily supplies calories and water, and at the same time sodium and chloride, the chief ions of extracellular fluid.
10. ***Dextrose solutions:*** It can be used in 2.5, 5, 10 and 20% solutions; it provides intravenous hydration, supplying immediately available water and carbohydrate to the starved and thirsty tissues. It is used in

prophylaxis and treatment of diarrhoea, starvation, vomition and high fever.

11. ***Plasma volume expander (6% dextrose in 0.9% sodium chloride):*** It increases the plasma volume by 10-15% and 15-20% if 500 and 1,000 ml are given intravenously respectively. It is indicated in shock due to decreased effective blood volume, such as occurring in haemorrhage, trauma, burns, severe dehydration and surgical procedures.

How to Calculate Fluid Requirement

The fluid requirement is calculated on the basis of total normal turnover of water plus replacement of the abnormal losses. An average turnover of water for mature animals should be 65 ml/kg body weight/24 hours and 130 ml of fluid/kg body weight/24 hours for immature animals of all species. *For example:* To maintain 20 kg dog around 1,300 ml fluid is required every day. To calculate abnormal losses the extent of dehydration should be estimated.

A. Symptoms of 4% fluid loss (due to diarrhoea) include leathery skin, slight moist mucous membrane, increased thirst. For this mild degree of dehydration a 20 kg dog requires fluid equivalent to 4% of its body weight, i.e. 0.8 litre.
B. In 8% dehydration (severe) there is lack of skin pliability and elasticity; skin is picked up, it will peak and stay. Both oral mucosa and tongue become dry; eye-balls are soft and sunken. A 20 kg dog requires 8% of its body weight of fluid, i.e. 1.6 litres of fluid. This amount should be added to the maintenance requirement, i.e. 1,300 ml daily for 20 kgs dog.
C. A 2-month-old (15 kg) 6% dehydrated dog clinically loses approximately 100 ml of water/kg body weight a day while undergoing treatment for diarrhoea.

The fluid requirement in 24 hours is as follows:

(i) Maintenance 130 ml × 15 kg = 1,950 ml
(ii) Replacement (6%) 100 × 15 kg = 900 ml
(iii) Continuing loss per 24 hours = 100 ml
Total fluid required for first 24 hours = 2,950 ml

How much fluid to use: The status of dehydration and fluid requirement for correction can be estimated with the help of PCV as below:

Body weight loss (%)	*PCV (%)*	*Fluid requirement , ml/kg body weight*
4-6	40-45	20-25
6-8	50	30-50
8-10	55	50-80
10-12	60	80-120

The percentage of loss of fluid can be assessed by the following "Rule of Thumb".

4-6 dehydration - No signs of dehydration

6-8 dehydration - Moderate dehydration with sunken eyes and 2 to 4 seconds skin fold test

8-12% dehydration - Severe dehydration, skin fold test 20-35 seconds. A loss of 12% fluid is life threatening.

Additional points to be considered:

1. Dehydration affects young animals faster than adults.
2. Old patients with chronic diseases require more water than other animals.
3. Animals need more fluid if they are active or the weather is hot and humid.
4. Drugs like corticosteroids and diuretics will change fluid and electrolyte requirements.
5. Animals that have been under various forms of anaesthesia may require additional water for a few days.

Rate of Administration

The rate of administration should be parallel to the severity of dehydration. Fluids should be administered rapidly at first (13-14 ml/kg body weight/hours) until urine flow is restored and then at decreased rates (10 ml/kg body weight/hour) until the condition improves. If urine is not voided by 1 hour reduce the rate to 1/3rd. Renal function should be wached. (Administer 1-25 ml of 50% glucose; urine should be checked for glucose which indicates filtration is occurring.)

The route of administration of fluids depends on:

(i) type of illness and severity of the condition;
(ii) degree of dehydration;
(iii) condition of the patient;
(iv) type of electrolyte imbalance;
(v) organic functions of the patient; and
(vi) time and equipment available.

1. ***Oral route:*** It is the easiest, most physiologic and economical route without strict attention to tonicity, volume and asepsis. Isotonic fluid is preferable.
2. ***Rectal route:*** Suitable for very young animals; warm water potassium, sodium and chloride are well absorbed.
3. ***Parenteral route:***
   (a) *Intravenous route:* Always prefer isotonic fluid, most versatile.
   (b) *Subcutaneous route:* Suitable for small animals. Contraindicated during oedema.
   (c) *Intraperitoneal route:* Asepsis is important.

TABLE 15: INTERPRETATION OF PACKED CELL VOLUME (PCV) AND PLASMA PROTEIN CONCENTRATION

I. Normal PCV with:	
(a) Low*	: Severe liver disease, gastro-intestinal protein loss, proteinurea.
(b) Normal*	: Normal values.
(c) High*	: Dehydration, masked anaemia, increased globulin synthesis.
II. High PCV with:	
(a) Low*	: Protein loss with splenic contraction.
(b) Normal*	: Splenic contraction, primary or secondary erythrocytosis, dehydration, masked hypo-proteinaemia.
(c) High*	: Dehydration.
III. Low PCV with:	
(a) Low*	: Recent blood loss, overhydration.
(b) Normal*	: Increased RBC destruction, decreased RBC production, chronic blood loss.
(c) 'High*	: Anaemia of chronic disease, lymphoproliferative diseases.

* Plasma protein

TABLE 16: ELECTROLYTE IMBALANCE IN SOME CLINICAL CONDITIONS

Conditions	*Water balance*	*Sodium*	*Potassium*	*Acid base*	*Calories*
1	*2*	*3*	*4*	*5*	*6*
Vomiting	Water loss	Na^+ loss	Urinary K^+ loss in exchange of H^+ ions	Loss of H^+ and Cl^- ions leading to alkalosis	-ve balance, if no food retained
Intestinal obstruction	Water loss	Na^+ loss	May be K^+ loss	Acidosis due to loss of bicarbonate	-ve balance usually
Diarrhoea	Water loss	Na^+ loss	K^+ loss	-do-	-ve balance, if malabsorption
Impaired prehension, starvation	Reduced intake	Reduced intake	Reduced intake	Often mild acidosis	Reduced intake
Oliguric renal failure (severe)	Normal (but may be overhydration)	Hyper-natraemia	Hyperka-laemia	Acidosis	-ve balance
Polyuric renal failure	Water loss	Na^+ loss	Rarely hypo-kalaemia	Acidosis, urinary bicarbonate loss	-ve balance
Haemorrhage	Water loss	Na^+ loss	K^+ loss	May be acidosis	

TABLE 17: COMPOSITION AND USE OF INTRAVENOUS FLUIDS (MMOL/LITRE)

Solution	*Tonicity*	*Calories/*	*Na^+*	*K^+*	*Ca^+*	*Cl*	*Lactate*	*Comments*	*Indication*
5% Dextrose	Isotonic	200	-	-	-	-	-	Causes glycosuria, may produce haemolysis Dilutes plasma Na^+. Therefore may produce oliguria.	Use to replace water loss
Normal saline (0.9%)	Isotonic	-	154	-	-	154	-	Large volume gives excess of chloride.	Useful in vomition and large chloride loss.
Ringer's	Isotonic	-	147	4	2.5	113	-	Provides K^+ and Ca^+	Better than saline for vomiting and for dehydration associated with alkalosis.
Lactated Ringer's (Hartmann's)	Isotonic	9	131	5	2.0	111	29	Approximate closely to composition of ECF, lactate metabolized to bicarbonate.	Fluid of choice for restoring ECF volume. Used for post-pyloric losses and whenever in doubt.
Sodium bicarbonate 5%	Isotonic		600	-	-	-	600	Provide 0.6 mmol/ ml	Used to correct metabolic acidosis add to infusion
Sodium bicarbonate 2.5%		-	300	-	-	-	300	Provide 0.3 mmol/ ml	Used to correct metabolic acidosis add to infusion.

TABLE 18: FLUID DEFICIENCY IN VARIOUS DISEASES AND THEIR THERAPY

Disease condition	*Fluid therapy*
Isotonic depletion	5% dextrose + Hartmann's solution (1 : 1).
Water depletion	5% dextrose for repair of deficit. N/5 dextrose-saline for maintenance, or 5% dextrose + Hartmann's solution (2 : 1).
Vomiting	0.9% saline or Hartmann's solution.
Diarrhoea	Darrow's solution for repair of deficits. N/5 dextrose-saline + 25 mEq/litre potassium or Hartmann's solution for maintenance.
Polyuric renal failure	5% dextrose for repair or N/5 dextrose-saline, sodium chloride and sodium bicarbonate orally.
Anuric renal failure	Start with N/5 dextrose-saline (+ calcium lactate) or 5% dextrose + sodium bicarbonate frequently.
Haemorrhage and post-surgical support	Blood if required. Plasma or plasma expander to restore circulating volume, then Hartmann's solution.

13

OPERATIVE SURGERY

The operation must be performed by a qualified Veterinary Surgeon/or a team of Veterinary Surgeons. Usually team of four persons, viz. surgeon, assistant surgeon, helper and an anaesthetits, are needed in major operation. All prerequisites like surgical pack, instruments, anaesthesia, tranquilizers, required medicines, suturing material, arrangements for blood/fluid transfusion and oxygenator should always be available in operation theatre. For the convenience of the surgeons some important operation, viz. amputation of dew-claw, docking of tail, amputation of ear, castration, exploratory laprotomy, caesarian section, hysterectomy, amputation of penis, removal of vaginal tumor, correction of diaphragmatic hernia, repair of umbilical hernia, catheterization of male dog, catheterization in bitch, application of plaster of paris in fracture of fore and hind limbs, and resection of mammary tumor has been described in detail. Necessary requisites like materials required, site of operation, surgical anatomy, restraining of the dog, surgical procedure and post-operative care for each operation has been provided in this chapter.

AMPUTATION OF DEW-CLAW

One dew-claw in the forelimb is normally present in dogs. Additional dew-claws are often found in the fore-limb and/or hind of limb and sometimes a cluster of 3-4 dew claws appears quite abnormal, hence to maintain a normal morphological appearance, owners prefer the removal of additional dew-claws from the limbs of their dogs.

Material required: It is a simple surgical management, for which general surgical pack, sedative, local anaesthesia, antiseptic lotion, soap, warm water, shaving machine and antiseptic dressing material are required.

Site of operation: About 2-3 cm area around the dew-claw is shaved, cleaned and painted with antiseptic lotion before the operation.

Surgical anatomy: Dew-claws are the normal or supranumerary phalanges present on the distal part of metacarpal and metatarsal bones. One normal dew claw on forelimb articulates with the metacarpal bone, while supranumerary are attached by fibrous tissue. For anatomical details see Fig. 111.

Restraint: The animal is secured properly in the recumbent position after the oral administration of a sedative. Local anaesthetic is infiltrated around the site of operation.

Procedure: An elliptical incision should be made around the dew claw with the help of a B.P. knife. The underlying tissue layers and fascia should be dissected to expose the metacarpal phalyngeal joint. The dew-claw should be removed with the help of a sharp incision on the joint, and the haemorrhage controlled by pressure with artery forceps or by ligation with catgut. The wound should be wiped clean, antiseptic drugs applied and closed with interrupted sutures. Finally dressing should be carried out with antiseptic drug, sterile pad and bandage daily till the wound is completely healed.

DOCKING OF TAIL

Docking of tail in dogs may be required either due to kennel rules for some breeds or clinical reasons. In certain breeds it is done to enhance the appearance, e.g. Dobermann pinscher, Boxer, Fox terrier, Irish terrier, and Cocker Spaniel.

Materials required: General surgical pack, sedative, local anaesthetics, docking knife, tourniquet, suturing material and antiseptic drugs.

Site of operation: As per requirement of kennels for various breeds in the case of healthy animals and about 2-3 cm behind the junction of diseased and healthy tissues in clinical cases.

Surgical anatomy: The tail is covered by hair, skin, fascia and muscles around the coccygeal bones.

Restraint: After oral administration of a sedative the animal should be properly secured in recumbent position on the operation table. The site of operation should be shaved, cleaned, and painted with an antiseptic lotion. Anaesthetic is infiltrated subcutaneously around the site of docking.

Procedure: After ascertaining the caudal articulation for amputation a tourniquet should be applied at a distance of 3-4 cm behind the site. The tail should be removed by forceful cutting with the help of a docking knife. The stump should be cleaned with antiseptic lotion and a sterile bandage tied tightly to check bleeding. The tourniquet should be removed after 2-3 hours of the operation. Daily antiseptic dressing is required until complete healing.

In the absence of docking knife, operation is performed by flap method. Two V-shaped incisions should be made on the dorsal and ventral aspects of the tail. The caudal articulation to be cut should be exposed by blunt dissection and joint cut with the help of a B.P. knife. The wound should be wiped with antiseptic lotion and then sutured joining the lips of flaps; antiseptic bandage is then applied.

AMPUTATION OF EAR/EAR CROPPING

Long and drooping ears are often found inconvenient for the pet and require surgical trimming. Surgical management is also required during mechanical tear and diseased conditions like haematoma on the inner or outer aspect of the ear (Fig. 112).

Materials required: General surgical pack, B.P. knife and blades, sedatives, anaesthetics and antiseptic dressing material.

Surgical anatomy: Ear is formed of skin, muscles, fascia and cartilage.

Restraint: The dog should be controlled in recumbent position after the oral administration of sedative. Local anaesthetic gets infiltrated subcutaneously at the base of ear.

Procedure: After close clipping of hairs, the surface of ear should be washed with soap and water, and painted with antiseptic lotion. The required portion of ear should be cut straight with the help of a sharp knife or a pair of scissors. Bleeding should be controlled with the help of artery forceps and stump dressed with antiseptic bandage. Dressing should be repeated daily until complete healing of the wound.

CASTRATION

The induction of surgical sterility in males is called castration. In dogs open system is followed.

Materials required: General surgical pack, sedative, local anaesthetics, general anaesthetics (for adult animals), suturing materials and antiseptic bandage materials.

Site of operation: A little anterior to the scrotum.

Surgical anatomy: The scrotum in dog is present on the posterior aspect of the inguinal region halfway below the anus. The epididymis is found on the dorsal border of lateral surface of the testis and its tail is palpable. The scrotal ligament between the tail of epididymis and scrotal wall is weak and destroyed during incision.

Restraint: Animal should be secured tightly in the dorsal position after the administration of sedative. The legs should be tied with metal poles provided on the four corners of operation table. Epidural anaesthesia should be used for young animals and short duration general anaesthesia for adult males.

Procedure: An incision should be made on the midline behind the bulbus glandis of the penis, followed by the testicles and spermatic cords. Each cord should be clamped with an artery forceps and ligated with chromic catgut above the forceps. The forceps are released and cords incised below the ligature. After cleaning the wound with the antiseptic lotion and applying antibiotics the skin should be sutured by interrupted sutures. Daily antiseptic dressing is carried until, it heals completely.

EXPLORATORY LAPAROTOMY

For the removal or surgical management of abdominal organs exploratory laparotomy is performed.

Materials required: General surgical pack, suturing materials, antiseptic dressing material and arrangements for general anaesthesia.

Site of operation: The site of operation is linea alba behind the xiphoid cartilage.

Restraint and procedure: The site of operation should be shaved and washed with soap and warm water usually one day before the operation. On the day of operation the site should be cleaned and painted with the antiseptic lotion, and then covered with a shroud having elliptical opening to expose the site of operation. After this an incision should be made with a sharp B.P. knife on the midline. The haemorrhage should be controlled by the use of artery forceps and ligation. The interlayers should be incised subsequently below the linea alba to minimize the haemorrhage. The peritoneum should be then elevated with the help of forceps and opened with straight scissors and its margins held along with abdominal wall with the help of Allis tissue forceps. After performing required operation of one or more abdominal organs the peritoneum should be sutured with the catgut. This should be followed by the suturing of fascia with catgut and the skin is closed with interrupted silk sutures.

Purpose of laparotomy: The exploratory laparotomy is a major operation and performed for the purposes of the correction of diaphragmatic hernia, splenectomy, gastrotomy, enterotomy, caecotomy, nephrotomy, cystotomy, ovariohysterectomy, ligation of oviducts in bitches, removal of ovaries or ovarian cysts in bitches, caesarian section in bitches, and urethrotomy in males.

CAESAREAN SECTION/HYSTERECTOMY

It is an emergency operation required to be performed during the dystocia for the removal of foetuses from the gravid uterus.

Materials required: As given for the exploratory laparotomy.

Site of operation: Normally 2 sites are used for the caesarean section viz.

(a) Abdominal mild-line behind the umblicus, and

(b) Parallel to the spine and 3-4 cm behind the costal arch-flank region in the paralumbar fossa.

Surgical anatomy: The gravid uterus is found either on the abdominal floor or sometimes between the supraomental space with the intestine.

Restraint: Same as given for the exploratory laparotomy.

Procedure: Laparotomy should be first performed as per the procedure described earlier. Then the nearest foetus in the gravid uterus should be located with the help of fingers. The entire uterus should be lifted through the abdominal incision and spread on the sterilized shroud. Sufficiently large longitudinal incision should be made on the free border of one gravid cornua near the corpus uteri. The foetuses and membranes are removed and wound sutured with catgut by continuous inverting type sutures after wiping the wound and cut edges with antiseptic lotion. After this the omentum and fascia should be closed by continuous sutures and skin by interrupted sutures. Daily antiseptic dressing is as usual carried until complete healing of the wound. Supportive therapy like parenteral administration of glucose saline and blood may be required in weak bitches.

AMPUTATION OF PENIS

Amputation of penis should be performed for surgical correction of neoplasia, paralysis of penis or traumatic injury.

Materials required: General surgical pack, general or local anaesthesia, sedative, suturing material, male catheter, torniquet and bone cutting forceps.

Surgical anatomy: The corpus cavernosum penis is dorsal and surrounded by heavy tunica albuginea. The glans penis is continuous with the corpus cavernosum urethra and covers the end of the penis. Penis is supplied by three arteries.

Restrain: The dog should be controlled in recumbent or in dorsal position. General or epidural anaesthesia should be used.

Procedure: Prepare the dog for surgical procedure by thorough washing. For identification of urethra, an urethral catheter should be passed. The prepuce should be retracted and should be held out of the way with stay sutures or fingers. A torniquet by rubber band should be applied either on proximal or distal to the bulb of the penis. Two incisions should be given with a scalpel to form a flap and dissected down the os penis and urethra. With the help of bone cutter, the os penis should be cut off as short as needed. The urethra should be long so that it would protrude from the end of the incision about 0.3-0.5 cm. The flaps should be sutured together using catgut (000) for interrupted stiches. Let the tip of the urethra protrude through the incision and split the end with two opposing scissors cuts.

After removing the catheter, the end of the urethra should be trimmed by rounding its corners and suture the two flaps in place using 4-0 or 5-0 catgut. The torniquet should be released and the stay sutures removed. The ventral midline of the prepuce should be split with scissors. The distance depends upon the length of the penis that remains and in every case should extend almost to the end of the remaining portion. By cutting with scissors, the sides of flaps carrying the incision forward enough along the mid-line of abdomen should be removed to create a smooth defeat. Mid-line incision should be sutured skin to skin, until the new preputial opening is reached, and form the new preputial orifice by suturing the edge of each side with the help of non-absorbed suturing material (000 or 4-0). These sutures pass through the mucous membrane and the skin. After completing the operation antiseptic dressing should be applied and antibiotic therapy should also be given to check the infection. After 1 week suture should be removed.

REMOVAL OF VAGINAL TUMOR

It is required to remove the fibroma, sarcoma, carcinoma etc. in female dog (Fig. 113).

Materials required: General surgical pack, general anaesthesia or epidural anaesthesia, suturing material etc.

Surgical anatomy: Vagina may be approached easily by opening of vulva. During operation handling of vagina should be very gentle as it is a very delicate organ of the body.

Restrain: The bitch should be controlled in ventral position and the hind quarter raised by putting padding under pelvis.

Procedure: The tumor should be cleaned for easy approach. Interior part of vagina (perineal region) may be incised for exposing tumor. Tumorous growth should be removed along with some healthy tissues. Antimosan compresses should be applied. The surgical wound should be dressed with antimosan solution for 1 week. Antimosan may be given 2 ml S/C for 5 days which will help to prevent the recurrence of vaginal tumor.

CORRECTION OF DIAPHRAGMATIC HERNIA

Diaphragmatic hernia may be found in either sexes of dog and require immediate repair.

Materials required: General surgical pack, endotracheal tube, Boyle's apparatus for anaesthesia, suturing material (non-absorbant) and antiseptic dressing.

Surgical anatomy: Thoracic and abdominal cavity are partitioned by the diaphragm. Diaphragm contains 3 openings, viz.

(i) Aortic opening,

(ii) Opening for caudal vena-cava, and

(iii) Oesophageal opening.

Visceral organs like liver and stomach are adjacent to diaphragm.

Restrain: Restrain the pet in dorsal recumbency. Anaesthetize through the endotracheal tube.

Procedure: A long cranial midline incision should be given through skin, connective tissue and abdominal wall. The filiform ligament should be trimmed from the edges of the incision. At the time of opening of the abdomen, the respiration of patient should be maintained by artificial means. The edges of the incision should be retracted and the slit explored in the diaphragm. In case there are adhesions of viscera to the margins of the slit, they should be removed by blunt dissection. Viscera should be returned to the abdomen in original position by gentle and slow traction. To close the bite/slit, the deepest suture should be placed first. An air-tight repair should be made and all bites should be closed. For suturing, 00 mild or medium chromic catgut on a small half circle taper needle sewing a lockstiches or mattress type of sutures are used. Air should be removed from the thorax to restore negative pressure. It may be obtained with the help of a syringe having 3-way valve. The needle should be inserted through an intercostal space. The abdomen should be closed in the usual manner. Infection should be prevented by using antiseptic dressing and antibiotic therapy. Artificial respiration should be continued until the pet start respirating normally.

REPAIR OF UMBILICAL HERNIA

To repair a hernial ring in pets.

Materials required: General surgical pack, suturing material.

Restrain: Restrain the animal in lateral recumbency.

Procedure: Umbilical sac should be opened with scissors and edges trimmed to expose fresh surface. Incision should be made bigger anteriorly and posteriorly and the edges trimmed with scissors to make an elliptical defect. Incision should be closed with interrupted everting mattress sutures with the help of catgut (0 or 00). These sutures may be inverting mattress and in any case should be pulled tight enough to close incision. The remaining part of the incision may be sutured in usual manner. This method cannot repair if the ring is too large.

CATHETERIZATION IN MALE DOG

Catheterization is used for collection of urine sample, in atony of urinary bladder, administration of various drugs and obstruction in urinary tract, etc.

Materials required: Catheter (metal, woven, teflon or rubber), syringe, lubricant, urine collection jar, required medication etc.

Surgical anatomy: Anatomy of tip of penis to urinary bladder must be known.

Restrain: Pet should be restrained in left lateral recumbency.

Procedure: Penis should be exposed by retracting the prepuce, pushing against the bulbus glandis. The penis should be kept out from prepuce by pressure against the bulb. Catheter should be inserted gently and slowly into urethral orifice to bladder. A water-soluble lubricant may be used on the catheter to lubricate it. When catheter approaches in the urinary bladder, the prepuce and penis should be released; and the urine collected with the help of sterile syringe. Care must be taken to avoid any injury during catheterization. After catheterization antibiotic solution may be instilled into the bladder as a precautionary measure.

CATHETERIZATION IN BITCH

Required for same functions as in male dog.

Materials required: Catheter (metal or woven), vaginal speculum, syringe, lubricant, urine collection jar, required medication etc.

Surgical anatomy: Anatomy of urogenital tract to urinary bladder must be known.

Restrain: Restrain the bitch in a standing position. In case an anaesthetic or sedative is used, lateral recumbency should be preferred.

Procedure: A small vaginal speculum should be lubricated with water-soluble lubricant and inserted into the vagina in a dorsal direction, avoiding damage to the clitoris. It may be pushed as far as it goes without thrust and the sliding piece withdrawn. This exposes the external urethral orifice which appears as a small cleft on the floor of the vagina at the end of speculum. The catheter should be inserted into the urethral orifice. The speculum should be removed when catheter enters the urethra. The catheter should be further pushed into the urinary bladder gently and slowly. In case of small or spayed bitches this method is very difficult unless a smaller speculum is available.

APPLICATION OF PLASTER OF PARIS BANDAGE

It is required in the fractured legs of pets.

Materials required: General surgical pack, plaster of paris bandage, general anaesthesia, muscle relaxant, analgesic, splints (wood, metal-strips, hard wave cloth or aluminium), Gordon's extendor, talcum powder, sterile - cotton and gauge and lukewarm water etc.

Surgical anatomy: Affected side of the leg. Plaster cast to immobilize the incorporate part of the joint below and above the fracture in the cast (Figs. 114, 115).

Restrain: Restrain the pet and administer a general anaesthesia.

Procedure: The fractured bones should be rearranged in original position as much as possible. The over-riding of fracture should be counterbalanced either with the use of muscle relaxant (curare) or by traction with traction tongs. To overcome the spasms of muscles Gordopn's extender should be used. If the pet has medium or long hair, the hair should be clipped and talcum powder applied to the affected part. To protect the bony sprayed as prominences sufficient paddings should be put and some soft material put under the claws and between the toes. At the time of padding one should keep in mind that overpadding must be avoided otherwise it may impair the immobilization by allowing the movements of fragments. Splints may be applied with the help of adhesive tape or bandage at right place. Plaster of paris bandage should be soaked in lukewarm water until bubbles stop appearing. The joint below and above the fracture should be incorporated in the cast. As per requirement toe pads may be covered or left uncovered. First 2 days the toes should be inspected several times; if there is swelling or it is too cold and constricted, plaster should be removed and reapplied. Radiograph should be taken at 15, 30 and 45 days to observe the formation of callus. Plaster should be removed when complete healing has taken place.

After removing the plaster, affected area should be messaged with talcum powder for a few days followed by wet massage (olive oil or sesame oil) to promote the blood circulation. The pet should be kept on light exercise till the limb becomes normal. After removing the plaster if the pet is still in pain and there is swelling over the affected part the analgesic and anti-inflammatory drugs should be given. Physiotherapy like hot fomentation with magnesium sulphate, or sodium chloride may be given, or wax and liquid paraffin (1 : 3) (lukewarm solution) should be applied. It should be repeated 2-3 times daily for 1 week. When the cast is on, there should not be any movement and immobility should be maintained under full anaesthesia until the plaster is hard.

RESECTION OF MAMMARY TUMOUR (REMOVAL OF MAMMARY TUMOUR)

Materials required: Surgical pack, suturing material, local or general anaesthesia.

Surgical anatomy: Anatomy of mammary gland must be known.

Restrain: Restrain the dog in dorsal reumbency.

Procedure: Various types of tumors are observed in bitches. It may be solitary nodules (single or multiple), cauliflower like growth etc. Incision should be given over the tumor through the skin and subcutaneous tissue. Pressure should be applied at the base of the nodule with one hand and the mass expressed, assisted by traction with the other hand. The connective tissue stalk should be clamped with haemostat and the tumor removed by cutting with the scissors. All infected and dead tissues should be removed and the connective tissue sutured with the help of 00 catgut. Skin incision should be sutured with the nonabsorbable 00 suture material. Antiseptic and antibiotic therapy should be given to prevent the infection.

COLLECTION OF BODY FLUIDS

I. Joint Puncture

Uses:

1. For the administration of therapeutic agents for the treatment of joint ailments.
2. To induce intra-articular anaesthesia.
3. To collect synovial fluid for diagnosis of joint affections.

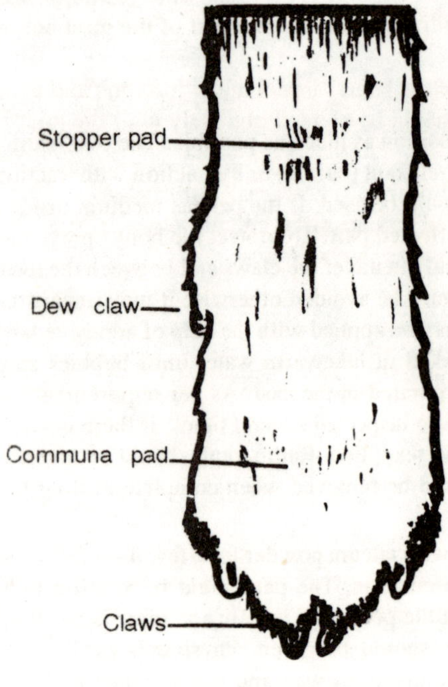

Fig. 111. Paw of a dog.

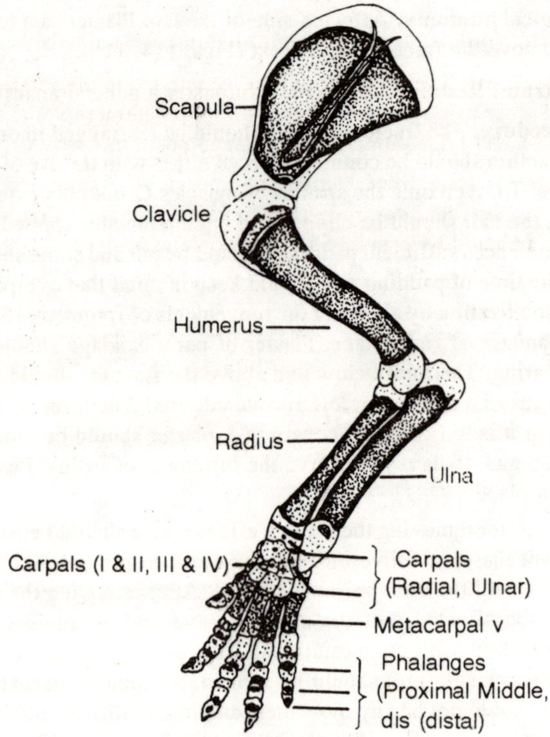

Fig. 114. The thoracic limb of a dog.

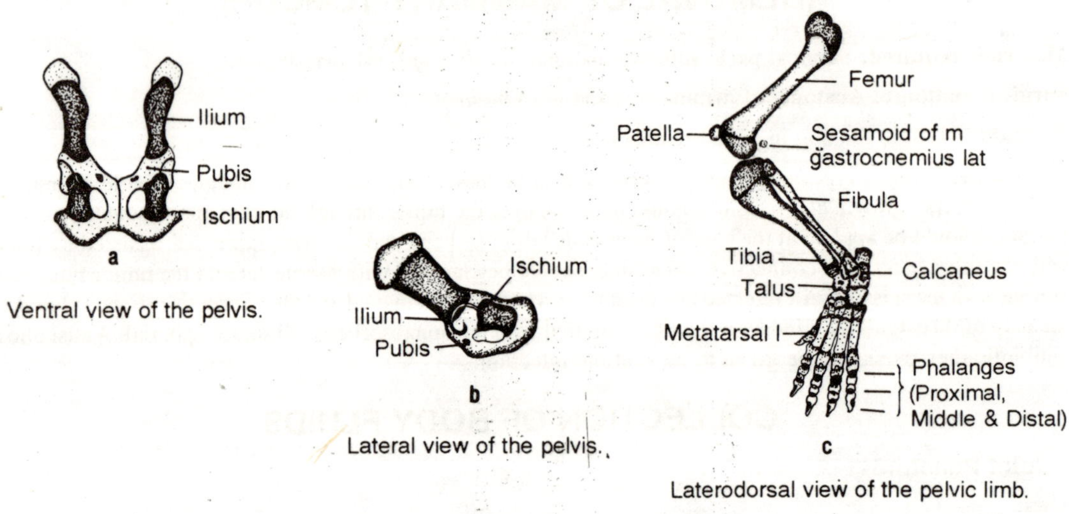

Ventral view of the pelvis.

Lateral view of the pelvis.

Laterodorsal view of the pelvic limb.

Fig. 115. The pelvic limb and girdle.

Shoulder joint: Generally applicable in large animals.

Elbow joint: The needle should be penetrated in the anterior part of the lateral aspect of the forelimb and must be slightly below the lateral condyle of the humerus. The needle should be pointed obliquely until the joint is pierced and joint should be in a flexed position.

Carpal or knee joint: This joint consists of 3 subjoints, viz. radiocarpal, intercarpal and carpometacarpal. Usually the first two joints are punctured. The joint should be flexed and the distal end of radius palpate. The needle should be penetrated at the dorsomedial aspect obliquely just below the radius.

Stifle joint: This joint has 2 synovial sacs; the first is femoro-patellar articulation and the second is femoro-tibial articulation (medial and lateral). The joint should be flexed for femoro-tibial sac puncture. A needle should be penetrate into medial or lateral to the patellar ligament half way between patella and tibial crest.

Joint puncture must be performed under aseptic conditions.

II. Puncture Sites of Different Organs

Paracentesis may be defined as surgical puncture of a cavity for the aspiration of fluid as of the abdominal or thoracic cavity. For these conditions it should be done aseptically so that infections may not take place.

Paracentesis thoracis or thoracocentesis: A simple method of performing paracentesis thoracis is to make use of an ordinary hypodermic syringe with a large bore needle. The seventh intercostal space on the left side and the sixth intercostal space on the right side, above the level of the point of the elbow of the respective site in the standing position is used. The needle should be introduced close to the anterior border of the rib concerned.

Paracentesis abdominis (Tapping the abdomen): The operation is close to the linea alba, or as close to it as possible, an inch or so behind the level of the umbilicus.

Liver biopsy: It is recommended to examine the extent of liver damage. Biopsy material should therefore be collected in liver diseases. It can be done through 11th and 12th intercostal space near to costal arch from the right side of the abdominal wall. It should be performed by a sharp pointed small bore trocar and cannula about 10-20 cm long with a screw thread at the blunt end to which a syringe of sufficient capacity can be attached to produce the necessary negative pressure for withdrawing the sample of liver. The pointed end of instrument should be penetrated through desensitized skin at the above-mentioned intercostal spaces and instrument inserted with a rotating action to reach liver surface. The trocar should be withdrawn and syringe attached. Insert it for about 2-5 cm and apply suction. The syringe is useful in discharging the core of liver from the canula after the biopsy is done successfully. Precaution should be taken to avoid damage of any other organ and blood vessels.

Paracentesis cardis (Heart puncture): The apex of the heart is at 6th intercostal space and the base of the heart at third rib. Site for puncture is at 4th to 5th intercostal space.

Pericardial paracentesis: The site for puncture is the same as for cardiac puncture.

Ocular paracentesis: The eye is generally punctured for removing the eye parasites. The technique is simple and can be performed with the help of a needle or eye lancet penetrating through limbus into the anterior chamber of the eye.

14

LEGAL PROVISION FOR PROTECTION OF DOGS

Dog owners often encounter situations requiring legal procedures. Indian penal codes and other acts provide enough provisions for the safety of pet dogs, cats and other domestic animals against offences.

Cruelty to animals act 1960 (Act LIX of 1960) - The act is called "The prevention of cruelty to animals Act 1960". It was passed on 26 December 1960.

This act is applicable throughout the Indian territory except the State of Jammu and Kashmir.

The owner of the animal is responsible for ensuring the well being of his domestic/pet animal, providing optimum normal conditions and not causing unnecessary pain or torture. Registration with competent board or authorities is essential for the use of experimentation or training the animal for shows, etc.

The Livestock Importation Act, 1898 known as Act No. IX of 1898 was passed on 12 August 1898 and ammended from time to time. This act provides procedure for the import of animals from other countries.

HINTS ON LEGAL PROVISION FOR SOME COMMON OFFENCES

Offence		*Protection under Indian Panel Code*
Injury, death drugs, vaccines.	Sections	44, 47, 51, 52, 53, 80, 81, 172, 173, 178, 192, 193, 197, 204, 269, 270, 271, 272, 273, 274, 275, 276, 284, 289, 304A, 326.
Bestality or Carnal Inter-course	Section	377
Cheating	Sections	415, 420
Mischief	Sections	427, 428, 429, 430

ROLE OF VETERINARIANS

Veterinarians are required to help in the administration of justice and help the Government. They are governed by enforcement of byelaws and enactment. A veterinarian may be called upon as a witness or as an expert. As an expert, he is required to investigate injuries, sudden death, perform postmortem examination and give a report, examine animal for age, identify soundness and disease for despatch of veterolegal material for chemical analysis and laboratory examination. They also issue a veterinary certificate.

PROCEDURE OF EVIDENCE IN COURT

An oath should be taken and the reports are to be read. On cross examination by the accused or prosecution the answer should be brief, relevant and to the point and related to the case. The expert opinion should be given with full confidence giving reasons. Before leaving the court, the veterinarian must get court certificate of attendance.

Following hints are given for various examination:

(a) ***Examination of animals for export:*** Before giving a certificate (proforma is given separately) the veterinary surgeon is required to undertake the following examination and tests on the animals intended for export by the Government of India at the request of the competent authority:

1. Soundness.
2. Laboratory tests for:
   (a) Rabies,
   (b) Canine distemper,
   (c) Infectious chronic hepatitis,
   (d) Tuberculosis, and
   (e) Brucellosis.
3. Vaccination against rabies, canine distemper, infectious canine hepatitis, leptospirosis and parvovirus.

B. ***Common causes of violent/sudden death:***

1. Poisoning - accidental or malicious.
2. Asphyxia or strangulation - cyanosed, collapse of lung, bruises on neck.
3. Drowning - a lot of water in thoracic cavity.
4. Heat stroke - due to humidity, over-crowding, deprivation of water.
5. Sun stroke - sunrays acting on cranium, high fever.
6. Lightening and thunder - burning of hair.
7. Electric shock - burning of hair and contact point.
8. Burning - big wounds.
9. Snake bite - bleeding and swelling, at bite point.
10. Accident - injury site, fracture etc.
11. Infectious diseases like canine distemper, rabies.

C. ***Common criminal injuries and offences against animals in India:***

1. Injuries due to assault with a weapon.
2. Lacerated wounds.
3. Incised wounds.
4. Stab and punctured wounds.
5. Gunshoot wound.
6. Offences connected with unnatural intercourse.

7. Offence regarding cruelty to animals.

D. ***Transmission of material for vetero-legal cases for examination by expert:*** Very often the veterinary officer has to deal with the case of poisoning in animals. In all such cases it is necessary to get the opinion of the expert and send the suspected material to the chemical examiner.

The poisons usually employed are arsenic, opium, datura, ratti, belladona and nux vomica.

If animals are brought alive, the symptoms may be observed. In arsenic poisoning there will be gastroenteritis, stupor in opsum, delerium, dryness of mouth, difficulty in swallowing and dilation of pupil (4 Ds). In belladona and ratti poisoning toxic symptoms are found. In all such cases, every care should be taken to wash the stomach and the washed material should be properly despatched to the laboratory. The material should be put in a wide mouth bottle, corked and sealed in the presence of witnesses (Sarpanch etc.). The container should be packed in a box and despatched by registered post. No preservative should be added to the material. Detailed history and symptoms should be sent.

In case of dead animals a note on the general condition of the animal should be submitted. Identification of the animal, date and time of death and post-mortem and detailed report of postmortem findings should be recorded. Stomach and a portion of small intenstine with contents should be collected. Pieces of liver and kidneys should also be properly despatched.

WRITING OF REPORTS

Veterinary officers in some of the cases are required to give the certificate of soundness or any examination conducted by them. They have to issue the reports, notify and confirm scheduled disease. Sometimes, the report and certificates of professional character may have to be issued which may be produced in the court of law.

The following reports are generally issued:

(a) Post-mortem examination;

(b) Examination of blood, faeces, urine, pus, milk samples, etc.

(c) Falsification of flesh, and

(d) Poisoning.

False or improper report or certificate should not be issued.

The following procedures may be adopted in writing the certificates and reports, based on ones own examination.

1. ***Description of the animal:*** Species, breed, colour, sex, age, identification marks, birth marks, size, weight, registration number, insurance number etc. are to be given. If the carcass has been submitted, all these details are to be given.
2. Any laboratory tests conducted are to be mentioned.
3. Name of the owner and his father's name and address.
4. Date and time of examination.
5. Examination report, which should give the details of injury, if any. The site of injury should be correctly mentioned. In post-mortem examination, all abnormalities should be recorded system-wise.
6. ***Opinion:*** The veterinary surgeon should record his opinion about injury, whether mild or serious, and also the nature of the weapon whether blunt, sharp, pointed etc.
7. Signature and seal with date.

Make duplicate reports. One copy should be kept for records.

PROTO TYPE OF REPORT

This is to certify that I have today personally examined at the request of Mr/Ms ____________________
S/o/D/o Shri ____________________ resident of the ____________________
animal/carcass answering the descriptions given below and found the undermentioned injuries/lesions/ laboratory findings on its body/carcass.

Description of Animal:

(a) Species ____________________

(b) Breed ____________________

(c) Sex Male/Female ____________________

(d) Colour ____________________

(e) Identification mark ____________________

(f) Size ____________________

(g) Weight ____________________

(h) Birth mark ____________________

(i) Registration number ____________________

(j) Insurance number ____________________

(k) Pedigree ____________________

Injuries/Lesion/Lab findings:

1. ____________________
2. ____________________
3. ____________________
4. ____________________

Opinion:

In my opinion the lesions/injuries (1), (2), (3) etc. are simple/serious and seem to have been caused by sharp/ blunt/external violence/accident/poisoning.

Date:

Signature of Veterinary Surgeon
Seal

Signature of person to whom
the report was issued.

CERTIFICATE OF IDENTIFICATION

This is to certify that I have examined the following pet (details given below) at the request of Mr/Ms ______________________ S/o/D/o Mr ______________________ resident of ______________________ in detail.

THE DETAILS OF THE PET INCLUDING IDENTIFICATION CHARACTERISTIC

Owner's Name and Address ______________________

Pet's name ______________________

Reg. No. (if any) ______________________

Species ______________________

Breed ______________________

Sex ______________________

Age ______________________

Colour ______________________

Identification mark ______________________

Birth mark ______________________

Insurance No. (if any) ______________________

Pedigree (i) Sire - GS - GGS ______________________

(ii) Dam - GD - GGD ______________________

(GS = Grand sire, GD = Grand Dam, GGS = Great grand sire, GGD = great grand dam).

Language used with the pet:

Feeding system followed:

I ______________________ sign this certificate on this day of ________ month ________ year ________ (in words).

Date:

Veterinary Surgeon

Seal

CERTIFICATE OF SOUNDNESS

This is to certify that I have examined the pet(s), the details of which are given below belonging to Mr/Ms ______________________ S/o/D/o Mr.______________________
resident of ______________________ to the best my capabilities and skill for soundness.

Description of pet:

Owner's name and address ______________________

Pet's name ______________________

Reg. No. (if any)______________________

Species ______________________

Breed______________________

Sex ______________________

Colour______________________

Identification mark ______________________

Birth mark______________________

Insurance No. (if any) ______________________

Pedigree: (i) Sire - GS - GGS ______________________

(ii) Dam - GD - GGD______________________

Language used with the pet

Feeding system followed:

(i) The general health status of the animal is excellent, very good, good, fair, poor.

(ii) The pet is fit/not fit for keeping.

(iii) The animal has temporary defect which may or may not lead to unsoundness. Therefore a further examination is needed on date ______________________

(iv) The animal is suffering from ______________________(disease).

In my opinion the health and general condition of the animal is good/bad at the time of examination.

The animal described above is sound/unsound.

I ______________________ sign this certificate on this day of ______________________

month_______ year (in words).

Date:

Veterinary Surgeon

Seal

CERTIFICATE OF SICKNESS

This is to certify that the pet(s) described below has been examined by me at the request of Mr/Ms ____________________ S/o/D/o Mr ____________________ resident of ____________________ (place) ____________ on ____________ (date).

Description of pet:

Owner's name and address ____________________

Pet's name ____________________

Reg. No. (if any) ____________________

Species ____________________

Breed ____________________

Sex ____________________

Age ____________________

Colour ____________________

Identification mark ____________________

Birth mark ____________________

Insurance No. (if any) ____________________

Pedigree: (i) Sire - GS-GGS ____________________

(ii) Dam - GD-GGD ____________________

Language used with the pet ____________________

Feeding system followed: ____________________

In my opinion the pet is suffering/not suffering from ____________________.
The reason for the findings are:

(i) ____________________

(ii) ____________________

(iii) ____________________

(iv) ____________________

I sign this certificate on this day ________ month ________ year ________ (in words).

Date:

Veterinary Surgeon

Seal

HEALTH CERTIFICATE OF PET FOR EXPORT

This is to certify that I have personally examined the animal of Mr/Ms ____________________
S/o/D/o Mr. ____________________ resident of ____________________
to the best of my ability and satisfaction, and the animal show(s)/does not show evidence of any infectious/ contagious disease, at present.

Description of Pet:

Owner's name ____________________

Pet's name ____________________

Reg. No. (if any) ____________________

Species ____________________

Breed ____________________

Sex ____________________

Age ____________________

Colour ____________________

Identification mark ____________________

Insurance No. (if any) ____________________

Pedigree: (i) Sire - GS-GGS ____________________

(ii) Dam - GS-GGD ____________________

Language used with pet ____________________

Feeding system followed ____________________

Test conducted:

(i) Clinical examination
(ii) Haematological
(iii) Biochemical
(iv) Faecal
(v) Serological
(vi) Urine
(vii) X-ray
(viii) E.C.G.
(ix) Animal found/not found positive for disease(s)
(x) Animal is vaccinated against:
Specially for rabies, canine distemper, leptospirosis, infectious canine hepatitis, tuberculosis, Parvo and Brucellosis.

Rabies on ____________________

Canine distemper on ____________________

Infectious canine hepatitis on ____________________

Parvo virus on ____________________

Leptospirosis on ____________________

The animal is pregnant/not pregnant on date ____________________

Any other information ____________________

I ____________________ sign this certificate on this day of ______ month ______ year ____ (in words).

Date:

Veterinary Surgeon
Seal

CERTIFICATE OF QUARANTINE

This is to certify that the pet described below was kept in quarantine for 10 days/1 month/2 months/3 months under direct observation of a qualified veterinarian.

Dr. ____________________

2. The animal was vaccinated against
   (i) ____________________ (ii) ____________________
   (iii) ____________________ (iv) ____________________
3. The animal was found negative for diseases
   (i) ____________________ (ii) ____________________
   (iii) ____________________ on testing at the time of examination (notifiable and schedule diseases).
4. The animal was suitably treated against ecto- and endo-parasites during quarantine period.
5. The animal was accompanied with valid health certificate by a qualified veterinarian of the government of ____________________ (country).
6. The animal is not liable for detention in quarantine.

Description of animal:

Owner's name and address: ____________________
____

Pet's name ____________________

Reg. No. (if any) ____________________

Species ____________________

Breed ____________________

Sex ____________________

Age ____________________

Colour ____________________

Identification mark ____________________

Birth mark ____________________

Insurance No. (if any) ____________________

Body weight ____________________

Height ____________________

Pedigree: (i) Sire - GS-GGS ____________________

(ii) Dam - GD-GGD ____________________

Language used with pet ____________________

Feeding system followed ____________________

Country from which imported ____________________

Date

Signature of Veterinary Officer
Name and Seal
Countersigned by Chief Vety. Officer
(Quarantine Officer)

SURGICAL RISK NOTE BY OWNER

I ____________________ S/o/D/o Mr ____________________ resident of ____________
hereby declare that the animal (species, breed, age, sex, colour) ______________ is owned by me and I take full responsibility for the complications and risk involved in anaesthesia/surgery (operation) of this animal for the disease ______________ I am willlingly giving my consent for necessary surgery to be performed on the animal and will not hold Veterinary Assistant Surgeon/authorities responsible for any untoward happening.

Signature of the Owner

Date ______________________________ Name ____________________

Name of Veterinary Hospital ______________________ Address ____________________

____

Name of Veterinary Assistant Surgeon ______________________________

Counter signed ______________ Veterinary Assistant Surgeon

Seal

CERTIFICATE OF CASTRATION/SPAYING

Certified that I have examined the stud/bitch ____________________ details given below belonging to Mr/Miss ____________________ S/o/D/o Mr ______________ resident of ____________

Description of Pet:

Owner's name and address ______________________________

Pet's name ______________________________

Reg. No. (if any) ______________________________

Species ______________________________

Breeds ______________________________

Sex ______________________________

Age ______________________________

Colour ______________________________

Identification mark ______________________________

Birth mark ______________________________

Insurance No. (if any) ______________________________

Pedigree: (i) Sire - GS-GGS ______________________________

(ii) Dam - GD-GGD ______________________________

Language used with pet ______________________________

Feeding system followed ______________________________

*(i) The animal has been effectively castrated/spayed by an approved method and in manner by me.

*(ii) The animal was already found to have been effectively castrated/spayed after examination.

In my opinion the animal is not capable of propagating its kind.

I Dr. ______________ sign this certificate on this day of ______ month ________ year _____ (in words).

Date: Veterinary Surgeon

Seal

RISK NOTE FOR EUTHANASIA BY OWNER

I____________________ S/o/D/o Shri __________________ resident of ____________________ hereby undertake that the animal____________________ (species, breed, sex, age, colour, identification mark), belongs to me. The animal is suffering from _____________as declared by_______________ (Veterinary Officer). I as owner, give full authority to the Veterinary Officer or his authorized representative to destroy/kill the animal (or euthanasia) in a manner the veterinary officer deems fit.

I am willingly giving my consent for the destruction of the animal and the veterinary surgeon/any authority shall not be responsible for the said euthanasia (killing).

This is further certified that the animal has bitten/not bitten any animal/person(s) during last 15 days and to the best of my knowledge is/not suffering from rabies.

Date

Place

Signature

Name of the Owner

Address

Countersigned by Veterinary Assistant Surgeon

Seal

CERTIFICATE OF FITNESS FOR DESTRUCTION OR EUTHANASIA

Certified that the following pet has been thoroughly examined by me. The animal is more than 15 years of age. It has become permanently unfit and/or unserviceable. The animal is suffering from __________________ (incurable/infectious/contagious disease(s)).

The animal may be destroyed in the manner the veterinary surgeon deems fit. This is also certified that the animal is suffering/not suffering from rabies.

Description of the pet:

Owner's name and address ______________________________

Pet's name ______________________________

Reg. No. (if any) ______________________________

Species ______________________________

Breed ______________________________

Sex ______________________________

Age ______________________________

Colour ______________________________

Identification mark ______________________________

Birth mark ______________________________

Insurance No. (if any) ______________________________

Pedigree: (i) Sire - GS-GGS ______________________________

(ii) Dam - GS-GGD ______________________________

Language used with pet ______________________________

Feeding system followed ______________________________

Consent of the owner has already been obtained.

I Dr.________________ sign this certificate on this day of_______ month ________year (in words).

Date

Veterinary Surgeon

Seal

Appendix-1

DOG SHOW

The beauty of a dog lies in its purity of breed, good health, clean coat and intelligence. All over India, various dog shows are conducted to judge these essential qualities in a dog. Dog shows are a kind of beauty contest for dogs. Knowledge about various qualities of each pure breed of a dog is necessary to prepare a dog for the show. Various breeds of dog differ in their morphological conformation. The kennel clubs of India have formulated a class rule of dog as per their specifications.

Registration of Dog

Before a dog can be shown at any dog show held under Kennel Club of India (KCI) rules it must be registered at the Kennel Club of India. The pet owner must enter in the registered form, accompanying all schedules in respect of dog shows, the particulars of the dog be proposes to show. Without registration a pet or change of ownership may lead to disqualification, and may have even more serious problems. Dog lovers should have a copy of rules and regulations of KCI, which may help them during the shows.

Preparation for Show

The preparation of a dog for the show requires considerable experience and expertise. The dogs should be got trimmed by an expert. It should be clean and in good optimum health. Ideal condition for any particular breed is best understood by observing the winning exhibits at various dog shows. Generally, a dog shown should have a little fat on it in keeping with the correct scales provided to that particular breed. Cleanliness is essential for giving an overall good appearance to a dog. The breeds possessing hard coat should be seldom given bath and the last bath should be given two or three days before the show. In certain breeds, it is better for a dog to wear a light coat during the period between the final bath and the show to prevent it from becoming dirty again. The breeds where hard coat is not a necessity, they may be given a bath the evening before the show. All white-coated dogs should have dry cleaner (dog cleaning powder) well rubbed into their coats on the morning of the show.

Trimming and Grooming

The dog may be trimmed by an expert. Several breeds are groomed before the show but the most extensive work is carried out on the terrier species.

Generally, the old coat is easily removed in the early summer and in the late autumn. The new coat coming through thick and close will prevent the dog from feeling the cold in the coming winter.

During trimming, only the finger and thumb should be employed, pulling the hair in the direction of the lay of the coat. The use of a knife results in the cutting of hair, whereas the finger and thumb method ensures the removal of only dead hair and the final appearance is greatly enhanced. The use of clippers should not be permitted, except in French Poodle. The fingers may be rubbed with powdered resin or ordinary household whitening powder. Efforts should be made to pluck evenly and to avoid patchiness. The dog should not be trimmed too closely. Every effort should be made to maintain the smart appearance by attention during the regular grooming. Show dogs need considerably more attention in this way than do other dogs.

The object of trimming and grooming its to display the outline of a dog to perfection, and to accentuate certain features that are thought to be desirable (for details see Chapter 4).

Transportation of Dog for Show

Before despatching the dog by rail, the route and time of arrival should be enquired. If the journey is long, water may be made available enroute.

The larger breeds may be sent loose with collar, chain and muzzle. For the smaller breeds a strong travelling box with peaked roof and air holes in the top and on each side should be used. The box should have a stout guard rail by round standing from the side about an inch and a half (4 cm); this proves useful when the box is carried, and prevents the piling up of luggage tight against the box. Painted upon the box in large letters should be the words "Valuable Live Dog". The journey may preferably be arranged in the night. Aggressive dog may be mildly tranquilized. Dog may also be transported by ship, plane, bus and taxi (for details see Chapter 4).

Veterinary Examination at Shows

Clinical examination of the dog is conducted by the qualified veterinarians at the show to rule out any infectious disease, and ectoparasitism. Dogs with ectoparasites, eczema etc. are refused entry at the show. The dog may get infection at the show as the overcrowding during examination may help to disseminate infection. For this reason, it is better to reach for the show well in advance to avoid rush during examination. It is advisable to give bath to all the dogs with antiseptic soap after a show.

In the Ring

It is important to train the dog to show in a lively, alert manner and in a way to disguise any faults. The dog should be regularly taught to walk in a wide circle and to stand in the position which will show him off to the best advantage. A lead of 3 ft (90 cm) or so should be used, and held loose enough to maintain gentle control of the dog.

The best time for the training is just prior to the principal meal. The trainer should provide himself with tit-bits to induce and to reward good behaviour; small pieces of hard-boiled goat or sheep liver or dog biscuits (containing meat extract) are ideal for this purpose.

To prevent the dog from getting nervous when handled by strangers, the services of friends should be enlisted. The aim should be to get the dog interested in his work and train him in such a way that its attention is on his master and he behaves well (for details see Chapter 4).

The exhibitor, in turn, must play his part well and concentrate his attention solely on the judge and on his own dog. After the judge has examined the dog, the exhibitor should allow the dog to stand at ease but while the judge is examining him and during the parades, the dog should be "on his toes".

Toy dogs which usually suffer from slight stomach trouble after a show, may be given a few doses of a mild laxative.

Procedure to Conduct a Dog Show

Entry Fees: It is charged as per Kennel Club Rules.

Address of Kennel Club who is conducting the dog show must be given in full.

Eligibility

Only dogs registered with K.C.I. may compete. Monorchid and cryptorchid dogs will not be allowed to compete. Bitches in season shall be allowed to participate in the breed shows only.

Rules

The decision of the Dog Show Committee is final, subject to appeal only to the K.C.I. Should objections arise which are not provided for in the rules, the decision of the Committee will be final. Any breach of the rules and/ or K.C.I. Regulations will render the exhibitor liable to disciplinary action by the Committee. Exhibitors are also liable for any damage done by them, or their servants or their dogs. The Committee reserves the right to refuse or accept any entry without assigning any reason.

Veterinary Examination

All dogs must be passed by the veterinary doctor present at the gate and certified fit by him before admission into the Dog Show.

Objections

Only after depositing prescribed fee may be entertained.

Precautions

Exhibitors shall make themselves familiar with the K.C.I. Rules and Regulations for shows, copies of which may be obtained from the Secretary, K.C.I. on payment of the stamp or cash.

Penalty

All willful misrepresentations regarding ownership, age, name, pedigree etc. of dogs entered and prepared for exhibition in contravention of the K.C.I. regulations will be liable to disciplinary action by the Committee.

Dogs that are not present in the ring when their classes are judged will be deemed to have been absent.

Various Classes of Dog Show

(a) ***Puppy Class:*** In this only dogs of 4 months and not exceeding one year on the first day of the Show can compete; date of birth, sire and dam must be shown on the entry form.

(b) ***Junior Class:*** In this only dogs of 9 months and under 18 months on the first day of the Show can compete. Date of birth, sire and dam must be shown in the entry form.

(c) ***Maiden Class:*** In this no dog which has won any prize in any class at any Dog Show can compete.

(d) ***Novice Class:*** In this no dog which has won a First Prize in any class other than Puppy can compete. Maiden Limit at a Championship or Open Shows.

(e) ***Limit Class:*** In this no dog which has won First Prizes in all Open and Limit Classes at Championship Open Shows can compete.

(f) ***Special Limit Class:*** This is similar to an Open Class say that no dog which has won three Challenged Certificates can compete.

(g) ***Bred in India Class:*** This is a class in which only dogs bred and begotten in India, shall be eligible. Dogs begotten abroad and born in India or on the voyage out or imported dogs under Regulations for Registration.

(h) ***Open Class:*** This competition is confined to a breed or to a variety of a breed classified as such by K.C.I. All dogs of that breed or variety of breed may compete in this show.

(i) ***Brace:*** In this class 2 exhibits of the same breed or a variety of a breed (either sex) being the property of the same owner can compete provided such exhibits are entered in one or more of their breed classes.

(j) ***Team:*** Team class is one in which 3 or more exhibits of the same breed or variety of a breed (either sex or both) being the property of the same owner can compete provided such exhibits are entered in one or more of their Breed Classes.

(k) ***Variety Class:*** In this class more than one breed or variety of a breed are entered for competition.

(l) ***Litter Class:*** Puppies not less than 2 in number, of one of the same litter being not less than 45 days are not more than 4 calendar months of age on the first day of the dog show. A litter shall be exhibited by one breeder only and not more than one entry can be made for one class.

(m) ***Champion Class:*** In this class dogs which have qualified for the title champion with accordance with the regulations can compete.

(n) ***Field Trial Class:*** For this class only dogs that have won a prize or certificate or Diploma or merit in actual competition at a recognized field trial may compete.

(o) ***Veteran:*** In this class only dogs not less than 7 years old on the first day of the show can compete.

TYPE OF BREED AND OBEDIENCE CLASSES FOR DOG SHOW

(Classification shown by letters)

Dogs	*Bitches*	*Obedience Classes*
A Puppy	I Puppy	C-1 Pre-beginners
B Junior	J Junior	C-2 Beginners
C Maiden	K Maiden	C-3 Novice
D Novice	L Novice	C-4 Class 'A'-Under Graduate
E Limit	M Limit	C-5 Class 'B' Graduate
F Special Limit	N Special Limit	C-6 Class 'C'-Open
G Bred in India	O Bred in India	C-D Companion Dog
H Open	P Open	

List of Variety Classes

A.V. 1 Any Variety Litter

A.V. 2 Any Variety Puppy (4-6 months)

A.V. 3 Any Variety Puppy (6-12 months)

A.V. 4 Any Variety Junior (9-18 months)

A.V. 5 Any Variety Bred in India

A.V. 6 Any Variety Open

A.V. 7 Any Variety Sporting

A.V. 8 Any Variety Non-Sporting (Othern than Toy)

A.V. 9 Any Variety Toys

A.V. 10 Any Variety Terrier

A.V. 11 Any Variety Gun Dogs

A.V. 12 Any Variety Imported

A.V. 13 Any Variety Brace

A.V. 14 Any Variety Bred by the Exhibitor

A.V. 15 Any Variety Property of a member of O.K.C.

A.V. 16 Any Variety Owned and handled by exhibitor

A.V. 17 Any Variety Handled by a lady

A.V. 18 Any Variety Team

A.V. 19 Any Variety Veteran--7 years or above

A.V. 20 Any Variety Indian Breed

A.V. 21 Hound Group

A.V. 22 Any Variety

Important Points to be kept in mind by owners and/or Organisers:

(i) No dog shall be eligible to compete in a Variety Class unless it is entered and competes in at least one of its breed classes.

(ii) A dog imported from abroad shall not be eligible to be entered in any class except Open Junior and Puppy.

(iii) A dog may be entered in Obedience classes only, without being entered in any Breed Classes.

(iv) **Best in Show:** All exhibits that have been awarded a.c.c. or Reserve c.c. at this show shall be eligible to compete for Best in Show.

(v) A dog which is entered in Obedience Classes only shall not be eligible to compete for Best in show.

(vi) Should any Judge or judges be prevented from fulfilling his engagement, the committee has the right to appoint substitutes.

(vii) No refund of the fees will be made if a dog entered for a show is prevented from being exhibited at the show due to any cause whatsoever.

(viii) **In Obedience:** The same dog cannot compete in more than two tests. Dog entered in class 'C' may not compete in any other class. One handler can only handle one dog per class.

(ix) **Reserve Challenge Certificates:** Not withstanding the right to Award Challenge Certificates the right to Award Reserve Challenge Certificates shall also be given in such cases where a Challenge Certificate has already been awarded to a Dog/Bitch or to both. The Dog/Bitch in that respective breed classes beaten by the Dog/Bitch awarded the Challenge Certificate shall also be called in for a Reserve Challenge Certificate.

RULES OF THE KENNEL CLUB OF INDIA

The Kennel Club of India is affiliated to the Kennel Club, London, 1900, and following are the Regulations for Registered Kennel Clubs in India which is essential for each Club.

1. No Dog Club or Society shall be recognized by the Kennel Club of India until it has been registered in the books of the Kennel Club of India.
2. Application for registration shall be made to the Committee of The Kennel Club of India accompanied by the following:
   - (i) Copy of the notice or advertisement calling a Meeting for the purpose of forming the Club.
   - (ii) Copy of the proceedings of such Meeting signed by the Chairman and Secretary, together with a list of members present at the Meeting:
     - (a) In the Case of All-India Specialist Clubs, a list of members who have agreed to join the Club.
   - (iii) Copy of the proposed Rules of the Club for approval.
   - (iv) A list of the Official and Committee with their addresses.
3. The prescribed fee for Registration of a Club must accompany the application. No name or title of a Club shall be accepted for registration which is similar to a name or title already registered, or which is a colourable imitation thereof, or is calculated to mislead. The Club shall notify on all printed matter below its own name or title "Registered under K.C.I. Regulations".
4. The application, if received by the Kennel Club of India, not later than the 15th of any month, shall be published in the Indian Kennel Gazette for that month, if later for the following month; and it shall be submitted to the Committee for approval together with the objections, if any, received with regard to same.
5. Registration of a Club shall only be granted if the Rules of the Club recognize. The Kennel Club of India is the ruling body for Kennel affairs in India and the final Court of Appeal as provided in K.C.I. Show Regulations. All proposed alterations and amendments to the Rules shall be subject to the approval of the K.C.I. Committee.
6. A copy of the K.C.I. Regulations for Registered Clubs, shall be printed and bound in the Rules of every Registered Club, and every Registered Club shall supply a copy of the Rules to each of its Members on joining; and at any time thereafter on payment of a fee to be fixed by each Club. (Note - If desired the K.C.I. Committee will supply standard size copies of these Regulations for binding up in Club Rules, at the actual cost of printing).
7. All Challenge Cups and Trophies donated to any Club or Show, and all other assets shall be deemed to be held in trust by such Registered Club or Show for the benefit of exhibitors, and shall be vested in the Committee of The Kennel Club of India, and shall be made over to the K.C.I. Committee, in the event of the Club or Show ceasing to function. The K.C.I. Committee shall in each eventuality, hold all such assets in trust for any future Club or Show that may be instituted having the same or similar objects.
8. The K.C.I. Committee shall not sanction the Registration of a second Club, in any area (such as the Presidency Towns or any Provincial area), or in any Breed, without first referring any application to the

existing Club in such area or Breed. This regulation shall not, however, make it illegal for the Kennel Club of India to allow the formation and registration of a new Club, in the interest of dog owner, breeders and exhibitors, in any area or Breed, should be existing Club in such area or Breed be struck off the Register of The Kennel Club of India.

9. Every Registered Club shall publish annually a complete list of Members either in its annual Show catalogue, or where no Show is held, in the Annual Report; such list shall be circulated to all Members of the Club concerned and submitted to The Kennel Club of India with the maintenance fee.

10. The rules of the Club, together with a list of the Officers and Committee and a copy of the Accounts for the last completed year, must be supplied to the Kennel Club of India in each year, not later than 60 days after the close of the Club's official year. These shall be accompanied by a Certificate signed by the Chairman and Secretary of the Club showing:

    (a) The number of Members on its books at the close of the year; and if required a list of Members with their addresses at any time.

    (b) The name of the Bank and branch in which the funds at credit of the Club are deposited.

    (c) The name of the firm in whose care the Challenge Cups and Trophies owned by the Club care deposited for safe custody.

    (d) The place where the Club's Show gear and other property is stored.

11. Every Registered Club, shall pay to the Kennel Club of India an annual Maintenance Fee as prescribed for every 50 members or part of 50 members. The payment of such Maintenance Fee shall entitle the Club to nominate one Delegate on the Committee, who shall have power to act and vote on all matters arising out of or in connection with K.C.I. Regulations. Every such Delegate shall be deemed to officially represent the Club by which he/she has been nominated.

12. The Delegate shall be elected by the vote of Members at a General Meeting of the Club, or as provided in the Club Rules for the election of the Officers of the Club, and shall be recorded in the minutes, a copy of which signed by the Secretary and the Chairman, shall be forwarded to the Kennel Club of India.

13. The term of office of a Delegate shall be one year. In the event of a vacancy occurring during a Delegate's term of office, a successor may be similarly elected for the unexpired period of the term. All Delegates so elected shall be subject to the approval of the Committee of The Kennel Club of India.

14. A Registered Club shall be completely autonomous in the management of its affairs and shall act generally as co-trustee with the Committee of The Kennel Club of India for the exhibiting public in its area or Breed; it may organize and hold Dog Shows and Dog Trials with the sanction of The Kennel Club of India and award there such Prizes and Special Prizes as the members may decide.

15. A Registered Club may receive and adjudicate upon all complaints and charges as between Member in respect of Exhibitors at its Shows, in accordance with its own Rules and the K.C.I. Regulations; provided that in all cases, an appeal against the decision of any Club shall lie to the Committee of the Kennel Club of India, if posted within 30 days. A copy of the proceedings in respect of any complaint, or charge or objection, shall be immediately forwarded to the Kennel Club of India together with any other information that may be required.

16. All cases under K.C.I. Show Regulation No. 12 (Objections), or No. 13 (Disqualifications), or No. 17 (Suspensions), or any disqualification or expulsion or suspension of a member or an exhibitor for any fraudulent or discreditable conduct, or any irregular conduct in connection with Dogs, Dog Shows or Trials must be immediately reported by the Secretary of such Club to the Committee of the Kennel Club of India, with full particulars of the case, and a copy of the proceedings in respect of the same.

17. Any person against whom a decision is given by any Club or Show Committee shall be served by such Club or Show Secretary with a copy of such decision and shall be informed that he/she has the right of appeal to the Committee of the Kennel Club of India provided the same is posted within 30 days accompanied by a prescribed fee as laid down in K.C.I. Show Regulations. No disqualification or suspension shall have effect unless and until confirmed by the Committee of The Kennel Club of India.
18. No person disqualified or suspended under K.C.I. Regulations may be elected or remain a member of any Registered Club. Should any such person be retained on the list of Members of any registered Club, the Officials of such Club shall be liable to be proceeded against under Regulations 17 of the K.C.I. Regulations for Shows.
19. Registered Clubs and Shows may report to The Kennel Club of India the name of defaulters or any person indebted to the Club to Show; and no person who is indebted to The Kennel Club of India, or to any Registered Club or Show, shall be eligible to judge or compete or win a prize at, or take any part in a Show, or Dog Trials, held under permission of The Kennel Club of India. The K.C.I. Committee shall have the power to punish the names of owners and addresses and description of such defaulters, as provided in K.C.I. Show Regulation.
20. All official communication from The Kennel Club of India shall be recorded by the Club for future guidance. Copies of all Members' Circulars and of important proceedings of the Club shall be sent to the Kennel Club of India for record.
21. Any Club which fails to comply with the K.C.I. Rules and Regulations, or whose returns under these Regulations are not submitted by due date may be struck off the Register, unless good cause be shown for such failure or delay. All Officers and Members of any Registered Club struck off the register of The Kennel Club of India continuing as Officers or Members of such Club, and all Officers and Members of any Dog Club Society, or Association, which is not registered by the Kennel Club of India shall be disqualified from judging, competing, winning a prize, making an objection, or taking any part at a Show or Dog Trials held under the permission of the Kennel Club of India. Such qualifications shall also apply to all Dogs registered in the name of, or owned by any person disqualified under this Regulation.
    (a) The K.C.I. Committee shall have power to remove any disqualification under this Regulation.
    (b) The K.C.I. Committee shall have power to reinstate any Club struck off the register.
22. In the event of a Club or Show being wound up, a final statement of the accounts with a report as to the disposal of all property and assets of such Club or Show shall be rendered to The Kennel Club of India for record. The Committee of The Kennel Club of India shall be empowered under these Regulations to take over and to sue for and recover any Challenge Cups, Trophies and other assets of any Registered Club or Show whose Committee may have ceased to function, or which may be struck off the Register.
23. An amendment made by the club from time to time should be obtained and followed.

ENTRY PROFORMA FOR REGISTRATION IN A DOG SHOW

Closing Date__________

Read the Schedule and K.C.I. Regulations for Show carefully.

Name of Kennel Club:
Address:
(Registered Under Kennel Club of India Regulations)
Note: Form should be typed or written in BLOCK LETTERS

Name of Dog and Description	*K.C.I. Registration No.*	*Breed*	*Sex*	*Sire*	*Dam*	*Date of Birth*	*Name of Breeder with Address*	*Imported or Bred in India*	*Breed No.*	*Entered in Class*		*Any other information*
										Breed Classes Litters	*Variety Obedience Classes*	

DECLARATION BY OWNERS

N.B. Sec's for Office Use Only

	Dogs	Entries	Fees
Brought Forward			
On this Form			
Carried Forward			

Fees-Remitted with this form:

Entry Fees Rs. __________

Total Rs. __________

Remitted by (D/D/Money Order/Indian Postal Orders/Cash).

I/We hereby certify that the dog(s) entered above is/are my/our bonafide property and I/We enter them at my/our own risk and that the dog(s) entered on this form is/are registered in India only with the Kennel Club of India.

I/We undertake to abide by the Rules and Regulations and Bye laws of the Kennel Club of India and of this Show and I/We declare that the dog/s entered has/have not suffered from or been exposed to the risk of Distemper or any contagious or infectious disease for the six weeks prior to exhibition and I/We will not show them if they incur such risk between now and the day of the Show or if they have been inoculated within fourteen days prior to the show.

Signature __________ Dated __________

Name Mr./Ms. __________

Address __________

NOTES FOR EXHIBITORS

1. All dogs must be first registered with the Kennel Club of India.
2. If a Registration Certificate has been lost a Certified Copy may be obtained.
3. Transfer of ownership must also be registered.
4. Entries cannot be accepted unless accompanied by Entry Fees in full.
5. For definition of Classes, Puppy, Novice, Limit and open, etc. see K.C.I. Reg. in Schedule.

Receipt No.__________ Dated __________

THE KENNEL CLUB OF INDIA **APPLICATION FOR REGISTRATION OF A SINGLE DOG**

(Founded 1896-Affiliated to the Kennel Club, London, 1900) (See Regulations 11, 12 (a), 16 and 17 of K.C.I. Regulation for Registn.)

K.C.I. Form C/I

Please write in BLOCK LETTERS or TYPE ALL NAMES and read the NOTES on reverse VERY CAREFULLY before filling in the form

FOR OFFICE USE ONLY

Regn. No. ______
Regd. No. ______
Fee Rs. ______ by ______
Paid on ______
Receipt No. ______

Breed or Variety ______ Sex ______

House or Pet Name ______

N.B.—The dog may be registered in the first name applied for, if available but owners must add two alternatives in case it is not, or the application may be returned. In the event of any of the names applied for being inadmissible, the K.C.I. will select a name, if the applicant marks X in the square of the right and such name shall be the { } registered name.

Name Applied (1) ______ (2) ______ (3) ______
Date of Birth ______ Colour and Markings ______
Sire ______ K.C.I. No ______ G. Sire ______ K.C.I. No. ______
Owner of Sire ______ G. Dam ______ K.C.I. No. ______
Dam ______ K.C.I. No. ______ G. Sire ______ K.C.I No. ______
Owner of Dam ______ G. Dam ______ K.C.I. No. ______

*** Breeder Mr/Mrs/Miss**
Breeder's Address ______

* Breeder means the person who is the owner of the dam at the time of its whelping, unless a registration varying this definition has been effected under regulation No. 25 (Loan of bitch for breeding purposes).

"Bred in India" means that a dog is bred and begotten in India. Pups begotten abroad and born in India or on the voyage out, shall be deemed to be "Imported".

Bred in India or Imported from ______

1. IMPORTED DOGS: Only in the case of an imported dog please fill in the particular required and mark X in box against (a) or (b) whichever is applicable and strike out the other (See Regulation 16 and Note 1 (iii) on reverse).

[ ] (a) Certified Pedigree No............ dated........ issued by the......................... Kennel Club sent in original to be returned/photostat copy (to be retained) attached.

2. PROVISIONAL REGISTRATION: If the dog is to be registered provisionally mark X in the box on the left. (See Regulation 17 and Note 1 (iv) on reverse.

DECLARATION TO BE SIGNED BY OWNER/S (SEE NOTE 5 ON REVERSE)

I/We hereby declare that the above dog is solely and unconditionally my/our property and that the particulars given are true to the best of my/our knowledge and belief. I/We further declare that I/We are not suspended or disqualified or indebted to the Kennel Club of India or any Registered Club or Dog Show or Dog Trial or Working Trial or Field Trial. In making this application I/We agree to be bound by the Kennel Club of India Rules and Regulations and Bye laws as may be amended and in force from time to time and I/We do hereby acknowledge the jurisdiction of the Committee of the Kennel Club of India as the governing body for canine affairs in India and the Final Court of Appeal or Umpire, on all questions or disputes or complaints or reports of any kind whatsoever arising in respect of Registered Clubs. Dog Shows, Dog Trials, Working Trials and Field Trials and of the Registration or Transfer of name of any Dog or dogs and of any transaction in respect of breeding or sale or pedigree of any dog or dogs, and I/We hereby expressly agree that the decision of the Committee upon any question or dispute or complaint or report shall be final and binding on me/us. The dog has not been previously registered in India.

Date ______
Name/s Mr Mrs Miss ______
Address Reply for ______

9. Balar Kalvi Nilayam Avenue,
Off. Ritherdan Road,
Madras-600 007.

Signature/s of Owner/s ______

This form duly completed and signed, should be sent together with the requisite fee to
Secretary:
The Kennel Club of India

Note: All the particulars required should be entered on the form. When any particulars cannot be given the word "UNKNOWN" must be written. If the Registration Certificate is to be sent by Regd. Post, please add Rs. 10/- to your Remittance.

PLEASE READ THE FOLLOWING NOTES VERY CAREFULLY BEFORE FILLING IN THIS FORM

This application for Registration Form—K.C.I. Form C/1—should be used in the following cases:

(i) For Registration of a SINGLE DOG from a litter [Reg. 12(a)].

(ii) For Registration of a Dog whose breeding (Sire, Dam, Date of Birth etc.) is known partly or fully.

A CERTIFICATE OF OPINION in the prescribed form (K.C.I. Form B) duly filled in and signed by the owner and by a judge whose name is on the panel of judges of the K.C.I. of competent to judge the breed, or by a person who is authorised in this behalf by the Committee or Secretary of the K.C.I. or in the absence of a Certificate of Opinion a CERTIFIED PHOTOGRAPH of the dog must accompany the application. A separate Application Form and a Certificate of Opinion or Certified Photograph must be submitted for each dog. (Reg. 11).

(iii) For Registration of a DOG imported from abroad, either of the following documents must accompany the application; if the dog is registered abroad a CERTIFIED PEDIGREE (Export Pedigree) issued by the KENNEL CLUB of the country of export in original which will be returned with a photostat copy of the same, which will be retained. A separate application must be submitted for each imported dog. The particulars required should be retained. A separate application must be submitted for each imported dog. The particulars required should be filled in on the form (See item 1 (a) and (b) below the column-Bred in India or imported from-on reverse). (Reg. 16).

(iv) For Registration of a dog PROVISIONALLY the owner should mark X in the appropriate box on reverse. (See item 2 below the column Bred. in India or imported from ____________ (Reg. 17).

(v) For Re-registration permanently of a dog previously registered provisionally. The applicant should indicate on the top of the form the Provisional Registration number granted to the dog and returned the Provisional Registration Certificate along with the form.

If there are MORE than one DOG from ONE and THE SAME LITTER to be registered in the name/s of the SAME PERSONS (i.e. SIRE, DAM, DATE OF BIRTH OF THE DOGS TO BE REGISTERED and THE NAMES OF THE PERSON/S identical) or if a litter of Puppies is to be registered by the BREEDER at the reduced fee of Rs. 10/- per puppy, K.C.I. Form C2—PINK Form. Application for Registration of more than one dog from the same litter-obtainable free on application to the Secretary, K.C.I. SHOULD BE USED (Reg. 12 (b) and 15).

REGISTRATION FEE:

(i) The FEE for REGISTRATION of a dog Bred in India is Rs. 20/- if BOTH PARENTS are registered with the K.C.I. or if only one are neither parent is registered or unknown for fee is Rs. 25/-.

(ii) The FEE for REGISTRATION of a dog imported from abroad is Rs. 20/- provided the documents required under Regulation 16 are submitted (See note I (iii) above). In all other cases the FEE will be Rs. 25/-.

(iii) The FEE for REGISTRATION of a dog—imported or bred in India—PROVISIONALLY is Rs. 20/-.

(iv) The FEE for REGISTRATION permanently of a dog previously registered PROVISIONALLY is the same as in item (i) or (ii) whichever is applicable.

NAMING THE DOG: Before choosing the name for the dog to be registered the owner is requested to note CAREFULLY the following CONDITIONS and to give TWO ALTERNATIVE NAMES in addition to the first choice, so that in case the first name applied for is inadmissable, the dog may be registered in one of the two alternative names given.

(i) A dog NEED NOT BE REGISTERED in its pet or house name or in the name by which it is called. The pet or house name or the name to which the dog responds has NO connection whatsoever with its REGISTERED NAME which should be used in pedigrees and other documents and when the dog is entered at a Dog Show or Dog Trial etc.

(ii) The names of notable persons, titles, kennels, countries, large towns, common names well known dogs abroad, or numbers in figures or words should not be selected. (Reg. 13(c)).

(iii) A name or names excluding a Registered Prefix/Affix shall not exceed TWENTY-FOUR letters except that in the case of an imported dog registered abroad the same shall be registered in its original name (Reg. 13 (e) and (g)).

(iv) A word or words SHALL NOT be used in the name of MORE THAN ONE DOG unless the same is registered as a PREFIX/AFFIX Reg. 13 (b). If the owner has already used a particular word or words in the name of a dog registered by him previously, he cannot use the same word or words again unless he registers the word or words as his Prefix/Affix (Reg. 14). The main advantages of registering a word or words as a Prefix/Affix are (a) it serves as in indication that the dog has been bred and or registered by a particular person, (b) it cannot be used by any other person except by the registered owner thereof, and (c) choosing and names becomes more easy.

(v) Application for Registration of PREFIX/AFFIX must be made in the prescribed form and the FEE for REGISTRATION of a PREFIX/AFFIX is Rs. 250/- and is for life.

The dog mentioned on reverse must be solely and unconditionally the property of the applicant, and the DECLARATION must be signed by him. In case of JOINT OWNERSHIP the names of ALL the owners must be given and the DECLARATION must be signed by ALL the owners.

THIS FORM DULY FILLED IN AND THE DECLARATION SIGNED WITH DATE SHOULD BE SENT ALONG WITH THE REQUISITE FEE—(Rs. 20/- or 25/- as the case may be—(See 3 above)—by I.P.O. or M.O. (the M.O. postal receipt should be attached to the Application Form for reference) or to THE SECRETARY, KENNEL CLUB OF INDIA, 9, Balar Kalvi Nilayam Avenue, Off. Ritherdan Road, Madras-600007.

The Registration of a dog will be published in the issue of The Indian Kennel Gazette for the month following the month of registration or in later issue. If the owner is not a regular subscriber and wishes to have a copy of the I.K.G. in which the registration of his dog will appear, he may remit Rs. 4/- EXTRA towards the cost of the same along with the FEE for REGISTRATION of the dog.

The annual subscription to Indian Kennel Gazette is Rs. 45/- which includes the Annual Number issue which is an enlarged and pictorial edition and priced Rs. 20.00 for non-subscribers. Subscriptions may commence from any month. All communications and remittance regarding the journal should be addressed to The Secretary, K.C.I.

POPULAR DOG SHOWS IN INDIA

Dog shows are organised in different states mostly in big cities and most of the people living at remote places are usually unaware with such activities. The dog is a beautiful creature and owners feel proud when their pets are listed in winners. A brief information about some important clubs organising dog shows is given for the convenience of dog lovers.

1. Andhra Pradesh Kennel Club
   Mr. R.K. Bakshi
   Hony. Secretary, Andhra Pradesh Kennel Club
   1/2 Vallabhadas Building, Nampally
   Hyderabad-500 001.

2. Bihar Kennel Club
   Mr. K.B. Sinha
   Hony. Secretary, Bihar Kennel Club
   Tata Iron & Steel Co., Ltd.
   Jamshedpur-831 001.

3. Bombay Presidency Kennel Club
   Mrs Sheila Naharwar
   Hony. Secretary
   Bombay Presidency Kennel Club
   1-B-1, Giriraj Anstey Road
   Bombay-400 026.

4. Calcutta Canine Club
   Mr. Partha Sekhar Chatterjee
   Hony. Secretary, Calcutta Canine Club
   92, Garpar Road
   Calcutta. Phone-35-5724.

5. Calcutta Kennel Club
   Mr Dulal Chandra Banerjee
   Hony. Secretary, Calcutta Kennel Club
   18/12, Raja Raj Ballav Street
   Calcutta-700 007.

6. Calicut Kennel Club
   Mr. T.A. Rajagopal
   Hony Secretary
   Raj Kamal, Calicut-4.

7. Chandigarh Kennel Club
   Major Trilochan Singh
   Hony. Secretary, Chandigarh Kennel Club
   1156, Sector 33-G, Chandigarh.

8. Coimbatore Kennel Club
   Mr. M. Udaychander
   Hony Secretary, Coimbatore Kennel Club
   699, Ananashi Road
   Coimbatore-144 003.

9. Delhi Kennel Club
   Mr. P.S. Shandilya
   Hony. Secretary, Delhi Kennel Club
   3500, Kucha Lalman
   Delhi Gate, Delhi-110 006.

10. Doon Valley Kennel Club
    Dr. A.K. Aggarwal
    Hony. Secretary
    Doon Valley Kennel Club
    11/1, Lytton Road
    Dehra Dun-248 001.

11. Gujarat Kennel Club
    Dr. R.S. Gaekwad
    Hony. Secretary
    Gujarat Kennel Club
    Madhav Bagh, Makarpura Road
    Vadodra-390 009.

12. Haryana Kennel Club
    Dr. K.K. Saxena
    Hony. Secretary
    Haryana Kennel Club
    Shop 3G/34, New Market
    Near Police Post No. 3
    N.I.T., Faridabad.

13. Kanpur Kennel Club
    Mr. P. Shukla
    Hony. Secretary
    Flat No. 21, II Floor
    Naveen Market
    Kanpur-308 001.

14. Kohinoor Kennel Club
Major V.P. Singh
Hony. Secretary
Kohinoor Kennel Club
14, Model Town, Jalandhar-144 003.

15. Madras Canine Club
Mr. C. V. Sudarsan
Hony. Secretary
Madras Canine Club
17, Mukathal Street, Madras-600 007.

16. Mysore Kennel Club
Mrs. A. Gopinath
Hony. Secretary
Mysore Kennel Club
3/1, Cornwell Road, Langford Garden
Bangalore-560 025.

17. Noida Kennel Club
Mr. R. Shanker Rao
1472, Arun Vihar, Sector 37
NOIDA-201 303 (UP).

18. North of India Kennel Club
The Secretary
North of India Kennel Club
H/9, Green Park Extension
New Delhi-110 016.

19. Orissa Kennel Club
Dr. S.K. Ray
Hony. Secretary, Orissa Kennel Club
Qr. No. 3R-33, Agriculture Colony
Bhubaneshwar-751 003.

20. Oudh Kennel Club
Mr. Awadh Narain Srivastava
Hony. Secretary, Oudha Kennel Club
Room No 501, Carlton Hotel
Shahnajaf Road, Lucknow-226 001.

21. Palghat Kennel Club
Mr. K. Mohanchandran
Hony. Secretary, Palghat Kennel Club
C/o Instrumentation Ltd., Palghat-678 623.

22. Poona Kennel Club
Captain Sunny Jacob
Hony. Secretary, Poona Kennel Club
B-6, Hermes Park Society (R)
Bund Garden Road, Pune-411 001.

23. South of India Kennel Club
The Hony. Secretary
South of India Kennel Club
Oak End, Ootacamund-643 001
Nilgiris.

24. Tristar Kennel Club
Mr Rajinder Malhotra
Hony. Secretary, Tristar Kennel Club
87, Maharana Pratap Marg
Ambala Cantt-133 001. Phone: 21231 and 22677.

25. Vishakapatnam Kennel Club
Dr. Narasimha Prasad
Hony. Secretary
Vishakapatnam Kennel Club
49-46-4C Devi Nilayam, Akhayyaapalam
Vishakapatanam-530 016.

Appendix-2

DOG INSURANCE SCHEME

The loss of canine population either by disease or accident leads to economic deterioration of individual owner/ dog keeping organizations. Keeping this in view and the interest of dog lovers, various Insurance Corporations have come forward with various schemes to cover the death/accident risk of dog. The insurance Scheme has proved to be a boon for dog keepers.

Having insured the dog(s), the dog owner can cover the losses occurring due to sudden death, diseases, accidents or natural calamities. The procedure and requirements for the insurance of dog(s) by the United India Insurance Company Limited, 24, Whites Road, Madras-600014, has been given in detail as an example. These are nearly the same with other insurance companies also, but with some modifications. Almost similar procedures are followed by other Insurance Companies.

The salient features are as under:

Type of Dogs Covered

Pure or crossbreed pet dogs, watch dogs, hunting dogs and sheep dogs are covered under this scheme.

Age Group

Dogs above 3 months of age will be covered for Insurance.

Sum Insured

If insurance is taken at the time of purchase, the purchase price paid will be taken as the sum insured. Proof must be submitted to the Company as to the value paid at the time of purchase. In other cases, the value of the dog should be certified by Kennel/Canine Club. In the absence of such clubs the value of the dogs should be given by a veterinary doctor who is approved by the clubs or is well-versed in the pedigree of dogs.

Premium Rate

(a) The premium rate is 5%.

(b) To cover the risk of breeding and whelping extra premium of 1% should be paid.

Duration of Policy

The duration of the policy is for 1 year. It can be renewed annually.

Scope of Cover

The policy provides indemnity in the event of death of insured dogs due to accident or disease contacted during the period of policy subject to the following exclusions:

(a) Surgical operations other than that required due to accident or diseases occurring during the period of the cover and castration.

(b) Malicious or wilful injury or neglect, unskilful treatment or use of dogs for purpose other than stated in the policy without the consent of the Company in writing.

(c) Disease contacted prior to commencement of risk.

(d) Transport by air and sea.

(e) Theft or clandestine sale of the injured dog.

(f) Total or partial disabilities of any type whether permanent or temporary, is not covered under the policy.

(g) Breeding and whelping risk. It can be covered under the policy by paying extra premium @ 1%.

(h) The diseases like distemper, rabies, viral hepatitis, leptospirosis will be covered only when proper inoculation/vaccination are given at appropriate age. Certificate to that effect from a veterinary doctor should be provided to the Company.

(i) War, invasion, act of foreign enemy, hostilities (whether war be declared or not), civil war, rebellion, revolution, insurrection, mutiny, tumult, military or usurped power or any consequences thereof or attempt there at.

(j) The indemnity or compensation provided by this policy shall not apply to nor include any accident, loss, destruction, damage or legal liability directly or indirectly caused or contributed to by or arising from nuclear weapons material.

Veterinary Examination

The dogs must be identified suitably and sufficiently by artificial means. Natural identification marks should be clearly given in the proposal and veterinary report. The report of a veterinary surgeon giving details about the age, identification marks, health of the dog and protective inoculation must be given to the company.

Claim Procedure

The claimant has to furnish information in the following forms:

(a) Duly claimant completed livestock claim form.

(b) Veterinary Death Certificate on Company's form.

(c) Post-mortem Examination Report if required by the Company.

Liability Extension - Dog Insurance

(Third party liability cover under Dog Insurance)

"Notwithstanding what is stated herein to the contrary, it is hereby declared and agreed that the within mentioned policy is extended to cover liability arising out of pet dog to third parties to the extent of Rs. 10,000 only.

In consequence whereof, an additional premium of Rs. 20/- is charged to the insured.

FORMAT FOR DOG INSURANCE

PROPOSAL-CUM-POLICY WITH RECEIPT AND VETERINARY CERTIFICATE

Name of Insurance Company ______________________________

____

____

Please affix here a recently taken passport size Photograph of the dog with owner's Signature

Whereas the Insured named in the Schedule here to has made to (United India Insurance Co. Ltd.), herein after called "Company" a proposal and declaration which shall be the basis of this contract and is deemed to be incorporated herein for the Insurance hereinafter contained and has paid or agreed to pay the premium stated herein.

The Company hereby agrees subject to the terms, provisions, conditions contained herein or endorsed or otherwise expressed here on that if any dog described in the Schedule and belonging to the Insured shall die from any disease or accident (Including fire and lightning) contacted or occurring during the period of Insurance stated herein or any subsequent period in respect of which the Insured shall have paid or agreed to pay and the Company shall have accepted or agreed to accept the premium required for the renewal thereof, the Company will pay to the Insured, after receipt of proof of death satisfactory to the Company, the loss which the Insured shall suffer by death or such dog not exceeding the Sum Insured shall there of as stated in the Schedule hereto or its Market value at the time of loss which ever is less.

Agency Policy No.

Schedule

Insured
- Name
- Address
- Business or Occupation

Period of Insurance ***To*** ***Both days Inclusive***

Breed	***Coat type, sex, colour and distinguishing marks***	***Date of birth and age in months***	***Height***	***Purpose for which kept***	***Date of last whelping (in case of females)***	***Present market value***	***Sum Insured***

Total sum Insured : Rupees

Please enclose the photostat copy of the pedigree certificate issued by Kennel Club.

1. Where is/are the dog/s housed?
2. (a) Have you any other pedigree dog?
   (b) Are they insured? If so give full details, if not why?
3. Since how long is/are the dog/s under your possession?
4. (a) Is/are the dog/s sound and healthy?
   (b) Give full particulars of defects and ailments, if any?
5. How many dogs have you lost during the last three years? If so state the causes and dates of death.

I/We hereby declare that the details given in the Schedule and the Photostat copy of the Pedigree Certificate are true and that all the dogs are correctly described, are sound, in good health and free from vice and that they are and shall be used solely for the purpose above stated and are well cared for and regularly fed.

Place

Dated (Signature of the Insured)

I Certify that I have this day examined the dog(s) described above and that the particulars given therein are correct and the dog(s) is (are) in sound good health and free from vice. I also certify that the dates of vaccination as given below and in the vaccination certificate-cum-health card maintained by the President, Kennel Club are true and correct. I further declare that there is no contagious or infectious disease prevalent in the place of housing of the dog or its vicinity.

Names of diseases	*Dates of vaccination of vaccine*	*Brew No., and source of receipt*
1. Rabies		
2. Distemper		
3. Hepatitis (Canine Viral Hepatitis)		
4. Leptospirosis		

Signature of the Veterinary Surgeon

Place Name

Date Address

Issued Office Policy No

Stamp

Received with thanks from Shri ____________________ a sum of Rs. __________ (in words) by cash/cheque No. dated __________ drawn by ________ Bank on account of premium under dog Policy No.

Rs. ____________________

Place

Dated

For United India Insurance Co. Ltd.

Authorised Signatory

EXCEPTIONS

Provided always that the Company shall not be liable in respect of Death Directly or Indirectly Caused by or arising out of or resulting from.

1. Surgical operations other than required due to accident or disease occurring during the period of cover.
2. Malicious or wilful injury or neglect or unskilful use of dog for the purpose other than stated in the policy without written consent of the Company in writing.
3. Diseases contracted by the dog prior to commencement of risk or within 15 days from the date of commencement of risk.
4. Intentional slaughter of the dog except in cases where destruction is necessary to terminate incurable suffering on humane consideration on the basis of certificate issued by a qualified Veterinary Surgeon or in cases where destruction is resorted to by order of lawfully constituted authority.
5. Famine.
6. Transport by Air and/or Sea.
7. Rabies, Canine distemper, Canine viral hepastitis, Leptospirosis. These diseases are covered by the policy if the dog/s is/are successfully vaccinated and re-vaccinated in the appropriate age and interval and necessary veterinary certificates are supplied to the company.
8. Act of whelping.
9. Theft or clandestine sale of dog/s.
10. Partial or total disability of any kind whether temporary or permanent.
11. War, invasion, act of foreign enemy, hostilities (whether war be declared or not), civil war, rebellion, insurrection, mutiny, tumult, military or usurped power or any consequences thereof or attempt thereat.
12. The indemnity or compensation provided by this policy shall not apply to nor include any accident, loss, destruction damage or legal liability directly or indirectly caused by or contributed to by or arising from nuclear weapons material.
13. The indemnity or compensation provided by this shall not apply to any consequential loss or legal liability or any kind or description.

CONDITIONS

1. If there shall be any incorrect or untrue statement in the proposal herein referred to or if the insured shall not state any material fact or circumstance at the time of proposal or afterwards, or at the commencement of the risk hereunder or on any alteration on extension or renewal of this policy or on the insured making any claim hereunder or if he shall make any false or fradulent claim or shall fail in any particular to observe and perform the terms and conditions hereof, this policy shall be void and all premium paid hereon shall be forefeited to the Company.
2. Every dog must be sound and in perfect health and free from any injury at the time of the proposal for insurance, or for any renewal, addition or substitution and must also remain sound and be in perfect health and free from any injury at the time of payment of the premium or balance thereof.
3. The insured shall permit any authorised representatives of the Company at all time to inspect the dogs at the premises of the insured, shall furnish any information which they may require and shall comply with all reasonable regulations and direction from time to time made and given by the Company.
4. The insured shall at all times exercise all reasonable care and shall see to it that every dog insured has sufficient and proper food, water and shelter and shall keep secure all fences, yards, sheds and kennels if any and shall use and exercise every precaution in regard to these and in every manner provide same care and attention as if no insurance has been affected.

5. In the event of illness or accident the insured shall, at his own expense, immediately obtain the services of a qualified Veterinary Surgeon and cause the animals to be properly treated.
6. On the death of any dog hereby insured the insured shall, within twelve hours give notice thereof by telegraph to the Company at the office which has issued the policy, and shall give the Company an opportunity of inspecting the carcass by not removing cutting or parting with it until at least the expiration of twenty four hours after such notice shall have been received by the Company. The insured shall also within fourteen days furnish the Company such information accompanied by such veterinary certificates and satisfactory proof as to the death, identity and value of the dog as the Company may require.
7. If and when any claim under this policy is made and there is any other insurance by whomsoever affected covering the same dog, the Company shall contribute only its retable proportion.
8. If death of the dogs hereby insured shall be due to the negligence, carelessness or wrong-doing of any person, the insured shall not claim or accept any compensation from such persons but shall at once give to the Company all necessary information and assistance to enable the Company to secure such compensation and it shall be absolutely the right of the Company to sue in the name of the person and recover compensation from the persons causing the death and any money or other compensation which shall be recovered shall belong to the Company will indemnify the insured against all costs and expenses so incurred with its written consent.
9. The company may cancel this policy by sending seven days notice by registered letter to the insured at his last known address and in such event will return to the insured the premium less the pro rata portion thereof for the period the policy has been in force or the policy may be cancelled at any time by the insured shall be entitled to return of the premium less Premium at the Company Short Rates for the time the policy has been in force.
10. If any difference shall arise to the quantum to be paid under this policy (liability being otherwise admitted) such difference shall be referred to arbitration in accordance with the provision of the Arbitration Act, 1940, as amended from time to time and for the time being in force. It is clearly agreed/understood that no difference or dispute shall be referrable to arbitration as herein before provided if the Company has disputed or not accepted liability under or in respect of this policy it is also hereby further expressly agreed and declared that if the Company shall disclaim liability to the insured for any claim hereunder and such claim shall not within 12 calendar months from the date of disclaimer have been made and subject matter of a suit in a court of law than the claim shall for all purpose be deemed to have been abandoned and shall not thereafter be recoverable hereunder.

PROHIBITION OF REBATES

The following is copy of Section 41 of the Insurance Act, 1938.

(a) No person shall allow or offer to allow either directly or as an inducement to any person to take out or renew or continue an insurance in respect of any kind of risk relating to lives or property in India any rebates of premium shown on the policy nor shall any person taking out or renewing or continuing a policy accept any rebate, except such rebate, as may be allowed in accordance with the published prospectus or table of the insured. Provided that acceptance by an insurance agent of commission in connection with a policy of life insurance taken out by himself on his own life shall not be deemed to be acceptance of a rebate or premium within the meaning of this sub-section if at the time of such acceptance the insurance agent satisfied the prescribed conditions establishing that he is a bonafide insurance agent employed by the insurer.

(b) Any person making default in complying with the provision of this Section shall be punishable fine which may extend up to five hundred rupees.

CERTIFICATE OF VACCINATION-CUM-HEALTH CARD FOR DOGS

1. Name of owner ____________________
2. Address ____________________
3. Occupation ____________________

DESCRIPTION

1. Name of the dog ____________________
2. Breed of the dog ____________________
3. Date of birth ____________________
4. Age in months ____________________
5. Colour ____________________
6. Sex ____________________
7. Distinguishing marks ____________________

PHOTOSTAT COPY OF THE PEDIGREE CERTIFICATE SHALL BE ENCLOSED

The undersigned declares herewith that on the dates specified, he has carried out vaccinations against Rabies, Canine distemper, Canine viral hepatitis, Leptospriosis in the dog described above and that the vaccinated animal was examined clinically prior to inoculation and found to be healthy.

S. No.	***Name of diseases***	***Date of basic vaccinations and revaccinations***	***Name of vaccines used and source of receipt***	***Brew No. batch No.***	***Dates of receipt of vaccines***	***Due date for next vaccinations***
1.	Rabies					
2.	Distemper					
3.	Canine Viral Hepatitis					
4.	Leptospirosis					

Place

Date

Signature of Veterinary Surgeon

Name

Address

DETAILS OF SPECIFIC ILLNESS

Date	*Symptoms*	*Diagnosis*	*Particulars of treatment given*	*Remarks*

Date　　Signature of Attending Veterinarian

Place　　Name

Address

Dog Claim Form

Policy No.__________

Claim No. __________

Name of Insurance Company __________

The issue of this form is not to be taken as an admission of liability.

Name of Insured (in full) __________

Address __________

Occupation __________

DESCRIPTION OF ANIMAL CLAIMED FOR

Species/ Breed	*Tag/ Brand No.*	*Sex*	*Colour*	*Natural Identification marks*	*Age*	*Value prior to illness*

1. When was the animal first seen ill.
2. When was notice sent to Veterinary Surgeon.
3. When first and last seen by Veterinary Surgeon.
4. Dates of attendance.
5. Name and Address of Veterinary Surgeon who attended.
6. Place of death with date and hour.
7. Cause of death.

   If from disease, how do you account for it? If from accident, how did it occur and who was in charge? If operated upon accidental nature of operation, date of operation and also name of surgeon.
8. Purpose for which used or employed when last at work.
9. Did you breed or buy the animal.
10. Date of last parturition?
11. If brought, state

    (a) From whom (a)

    (b) Date of purchase (b)

    (c) Price paid (c)
12. Amount of claim.
13. Is the animal insured elsewhere?

    Are you receiving compensation from any other source? If so from whom.
14. (a) If animal has not died, describe the nature of injury/disease and state when it occured and its duration.

    (b) Has this injury/disease resulted is permanent incapacity to conceive or breed or guard work?

    (c) What steps were taken by you after the injury/disease was noticed to prevent the permanent incapacity to conceive or guard work or breed.
15. When was premium paid?

I/We the above named do hereby to the best of my/our knowledge and belief warrant the truth or the foregoing statements in every respect and affirm that proper treatment and care was given to the animal. I/We agree that if I/We have made or in any further declaration the Company may require in respect of the said accident shall make any false statement or any suppression or concealment the Policy shall be void and all rights to recover thereunder in respect of past or future accidents shall be forefeited.

Date Signature of Insured ______________________

Name and Signature of Witness ______________________

Private and Confidential

Policy No. ______________

Claim No. ______________

Name of Insurance Company ______________

Dog Claim

VETERINARY CERTIFICATE

To

Address of Insurance Company

I hereby certify that the animal described below, the property of Mr ______________ of ______________ died on the __________ 19...

DESCRIPTION OF ANIMAL

Sex	*Tag. Brand No.*	*Name*	*Breed*	*Colour*	*Marks*	*Age*	*Value prior to illness*

1. Did you make a post-mortem? If so, give detailed report on reverse of form
2. Cause of death.
3. If from disease how do you acccount for it?
4. If from accident, where did it occur and nature of injuries?
5. If from an operation, give date and nature of operation.
6. Had animal every care and attention?
7. Did you examine for Insurance and did you identify the animal?
8. (a) If animal has not died, describe the nature of injury/disease and state when it occurred and its duration.
   (b) Has the injury/disease resulted in permanent incapacity to conceive or guard work or breed?
   (c) Did you treat the animal for the injury/disease and if so, what was the nature of treatment given to prevent the permanent incapacity to conceive or breed or guard work?

I hereby warrant the truth of my answers respecting the above animal's death and I know of no material information which has been withheld.

Signature

Date

Qualifications

Address

Seal

The form should be completed without delay and forwarded direct to the Company.

POST-MORTEM REPORT OF DOG

Name of Insurance Company ______________________

1. Name of the owner ______________________
2. Place of death ______________________
3. Description of animal ______________________

   Species ______________ Natural identification mark ______________

   Breed ______________

   Age ______________ Brand No./Ear Tag. No. ______________

   Height ______________ Colour ______________

   Tail ______________
4. Date and time when disease started ______________________
5. Date and time of death ______________________
6. Date and time of P.M. ______________________
7. Is rigor mortis present ______________________
8. General condition of body (Note anything abnormal) ______________________
9. Note discharge from orifices ______________________
10. Conditions of mouth, tongue and teeth ______________________
11. Condition of eyes ______________________
12. Condition of brain ______________________
13. Condition of pharynx and larynx ______________________
14. Condition of trachea and bronchi ______________________
15. Thoracic cavity (Note any fluid, its colour and quantity) ______________________
16. Condition of pleura ______________________
17. Condition of lungs ______________________ (Note size, colour, hardness and look for tumors, cyst and parasite etc.)
18. Pericardial sac. (Note: if any fluid, quantity and colour) ______________________
19. Condition of pericardium and endocardium ______________________
20. Condition of heart ______________________
21. Abdominal cavity (Note if any fluid, quantity and colour) ______________________
22. Stomach (Condition of mucous membrane and presence of parasite) ______________________

23. Intestine large and small ______
(Colours of mucous membrane and presence of parasite)

24. Condition of liver ______
(Colour, hardness and look for cyst, parasite etc.)

25. Portal vein (Parasite) ______

26. Condition of spleen ______
(Size, pulp and colour)

27. Condition of kidneys ______
(Size, colour and look for calculii)

28. Condition of rectum ______

29. Condition of uterus ______
(State of pregnancy)

30. Condition of urinary bladder ______
(Colour, quantity of urine look for calculi)

31. Cause of death ______

Veterinary Surgeon

Dated ______ Full Name ______

(Seal)

Appendix-3

ANATOMICAL DETAILS

The body of dog may be divided into the following three parts for convenient identification of the various points of the body.

A. ***Face:*** It includes lower lip, upper lip, lower jaw (mandible), upper jaw, mouth, nostrils, stop (nasal ridge), dome, poll, cheek, eyes, ears and jowl.

B. ***Pectoral region or anterior half:*** It includes neck, crest, mane, shoulder, wither, breast, brisket, chest, back, belly, umbilicus, point of shoulder, point of elbow, arm, forearm, wrist, fore paw, toes and nails.

C. ***Pelvic region or posterior half:*** It includes flank, loin, rump, hip, buttock, anus, thigh, stifle, hock joint, hind paw, toes and nails. In addition to these some other points of posterior region are the dock or root of tail, tail, scrotum, prepuce and penis.

N.B. In bitch external male genitalia are replaced by vulva situated below the anus.

Parts of Eye

The eye is an important sensory organ which requires careful examination at the time of grooming. The various points of the eye are: eye lashes, eye brow, upper lid, lower lid, inner canthus and outer canthus.

A. BONES OF SKELETAL SYSTEM OF DOG

Type of bone	*Total average number of bone*
Axial Skeleton	
Vertebral column	50
Skull and hyoid	50
Ribs and sternum	34
Appendicular Skeleton	
Pectoral limbs	90
Pelvic limbs	96
Heterotopic Skeleton	
Os penis	1
Total bones	321

B. COMPARATIVE OSTEOLOGY OF DOG

Bone	***Dog***
1. Vertebral Column	C7 T13 L7 S3 Cy 20-23
2. Ribs	13 pairs
3. Anterior/Forelimb	
(i) Shoulder girdle	Scapula
(ii) Arm	Humerus
(iii) Forearm	Radius and ulna
(iv) Manus	(i) Carpals: 7 bones 3 proximal row (Radial and intermediate fused) and 4 in distal row 5 metacarpals are present and the first is shortest (iii) Digits: Five digits, each comprises three phalanges. Nine volar sesamoid are present. Two at each metacarpophalangeal joint of chief digits and one the joint of the Ist digit.
4. Posterior/Hind Limb	
(i) Pelvic girdle	Two os coxae, each os coxae consists of three bones (ilium, ischium and pubis)
(ii) Thigh	Femur
(iii) Leg	Tibia, Fibula and Patella
(iv) Pes	(i) Tarsals: Seven bones, two in proximal row (Tibia and Fibula), one central tarsal and four in distal row (1st, 2nd, 3rd and 4th) (ii) Metatarsals: Five metatarsal present. First shortest (iii) Digits - The first digit is mostly absent. If present it contains one or two phalanges. Other digits and phalanges are similar to fore limb.

C. JOINTS OF FORE AND HIND LIMBS OF DOGS

Name of the joint	*Articular surfaces/bones which form the joint*
Fore limb (Fig. 114)	
(Thoracic limb)	
1. Shoulder joint	(a) Glenoid cavity of scapula
	(b) Head of the humerus.
2. Elbow joint	(a) Trochlear surface formed by the condyles of the humerus.
	(b) Glenoid cavities and ridge on the proximal extremity of the radius together with the semi-lunar notch of the ulna.
3. Carpal joint	(a) Radiocarpal or antibrachio-carpal joint. Formed by the digital end of the radius and the proximal row of the corpus.
	(b) Intercarpal joint: Formed by the two rows of the carpus.
	(c) Carpo-metacarpal joint: Formed by the digital row of the carpus and the proximal ends of the metacarpal bones. It is the metacarpophalangeal articulation.
4. Fetlock joint	It is formed by the distal end of the large metacarpal, the proximal end of first phalanx and the proximal sesamoid bones.
5. Pastern joint	This is the proximal inter-phalangeal articulation and is formed by the distal end of the first phalanx and the proximal end of the second phalanx.
6. Coffin joint	This is the distal inter-phalangeal articulation and is formed by the distal end of second phalanx, proximal end of the third phalanx and the distal seasamoid.
Hind Limbs (Fig. 115)	
(Pelvic limb)	
1. Hip joint	Formed by the acetabulum of os coxae and the head of femur.
2. Stifle joint	Formed by two joints-femoropatellar and the femoro-tibial. The first one is formed between the trochlea of the femur and the articular surface of the patella.
	The second is formed between the condyles of the femur, proximal end of the tibia and anterior semilunar cartilages.
3. Hock joint	
(a) Tibio-tarsal joint	Formed by distal end of tibia and proximal row of tarsus.
(b) Inter-trasal joint	Formed by two rows of tarsals.
(c) Tarso-metatarsal joint	Formed by distal row of tarsals and proximal row of metatarsal.
4. Fetlock joint	Similar to forelimb.
5 Pastern joint	Similar to forelimb.
6. Coffin joint	Similar to forelimb.

N.B.: Various body points of a dog to be considered during judging and surgical operations (Fig. 116), and bones of skeletal system (Fig. 117) as in A.

D. Teeth at a Glance in Dog

Dentition and Ageing

Like other mammalian species dogs also possess temporary milk (deciduous) teeth, which include incisors, canine and premolars and permanent teeth and additional molars (Fig. 118).

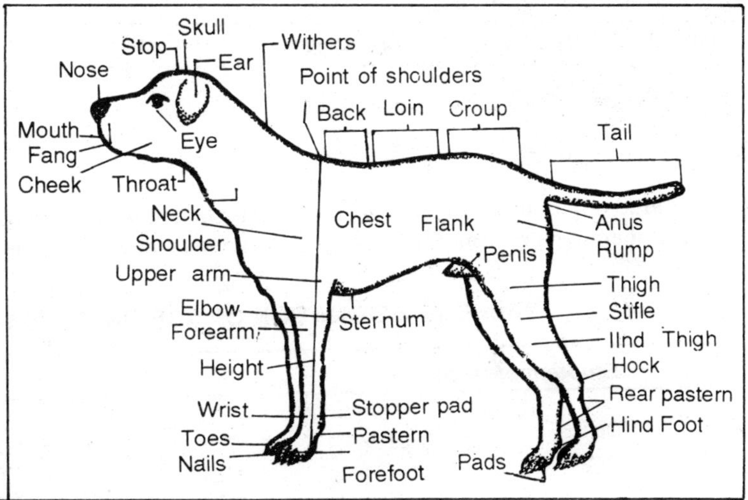

Fig. 116. Various body points of a dog

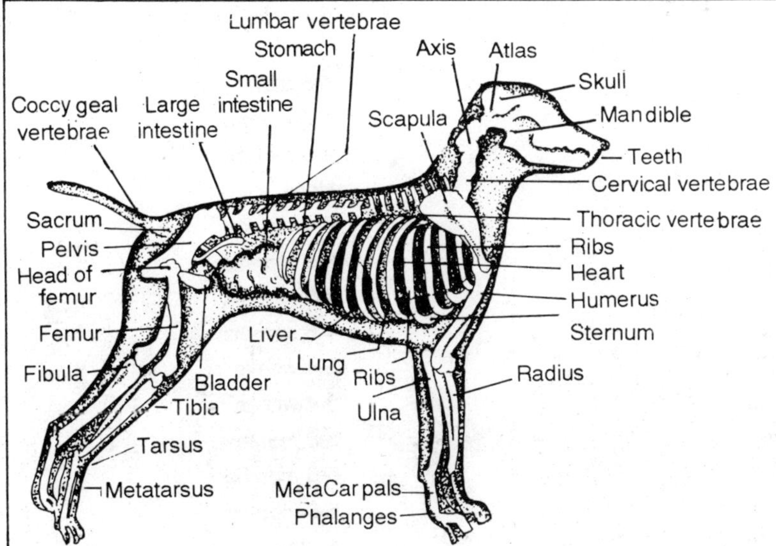

Fig. 117. Skeleton and important body organs of the dog

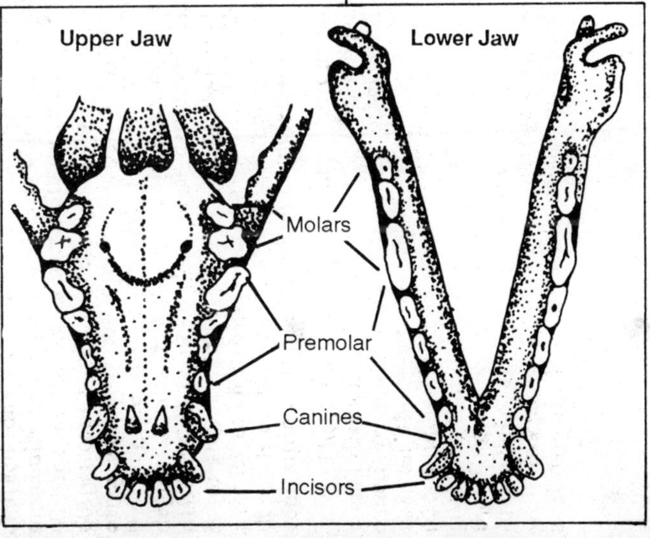

Fig. 118. The pattern of teeth in dog,

1. Dental formula of temporary teeth

$$2I\frac{3}{3}\ C\frac{1}{1}\ P\frac{3}{3}\ M\frac{0}{0} = 28$$

2. Dental formula of permanent teeth

$$2I\frac{3}{3}\ C\frac{1}{1}\ P\frac{4}{4}\ M\frac{2}{3} = 42$$

Large variation has been observed in the eruption of teeth in the dogs kept under different management. The age at eruption of teeth (Table 19) is not a good guide for the estimation of a dog's age.

TABLE 19: ESTIMATION OF AGE ON THE BASIS OF TEETH

Eruption of teeth	*Dog*
Di 1	4 weeks
Di 2	4 weeks
Di 3	4 weeks
Di 4	
I_1	4-5 months
I_2	4-5 months
I_3	4-5 months
I_4	None
DC	3-4 weeks
C	5-6 months
DP-1	4-5 months
DP-2	4-6 months
DP-3	3-4 weeks
DP-4	3-4 weeks
P 1	5-6 months
P 2	5-6 months
P 3	5-6 months
P 4	4-5 months
M 1	4 months
M 2	4.5-6 months
M 3	6-7 months

Appendix-4

PET - HEALTH CARD

Owner's name and address ____________________

____

Telephone No. ____________________

Name of pet ____________________

Clinician's name & Add. ____________________

Telephone No. ____________________

Species ____________________

Breed ____________________

Photograph

Sex ____________________ Date of birth ____________________

Place of birth ____________________

Identification mark ____________________

Birth mark ____________________ Colour ____________________

Registration No. (if any) ____________________ Insurance No. (if any) ____________________

Pedigree ____________________ Dam ____________________

Sire ____________________

Language used with pet ____________________

Feeding system followed ____________________

HEALTH STATUS

Date of check up	*General appearance*	*Behaviour*	*Clinical status*	*Sign. of Vet.*

BREEDING RECORD OF BITCH

S.No	*Name of sire*	*Date of covering*			*Date of whelping*	*Pup born*		*Pup died*		*Remarks & Sign. of Vet.*
		I	*II*	*III*		*M*	*F*	*M*	*F*	

BREEDING RECORD OF MALE DOG

S.No.	*Name of dam*	*Date of mating*			*Pup born*			*Pup died*			*Remarks and Sign. of Vet.*
		I	*II*	*III*	*Date*	*M*	*F*	*Date*	*M*	*F*	

VACCINATION SCHEDULE (FOR DETAILS SEE BELOW)

Sl. No	*Date*	*Nature*	*Batch No.*	*Administration*	*Next due date*	*Sign. of Ven.*

INOCULATION SCHEDULE

Disease		*Vaccine*	*Inoculations*		
			First	*Second*	*Booster*
Rabies	(i)	Flury (LEP, freeze dried) Rabies vaccine	4th to 6th month (freeze dried) Rabies vaccine	6 months after first inoculation	Annual
	(ii)	Rabies vaccine	4th week of life	1 year after Ist inoculation	Biennial
Canine distemper		Modified live virus canine distemper vaccine	Before 9th week of life	12th week of life	16th week of life
Parvovirus disease		Parvovirus vaccine	6th to 8th week of life	After 12th week of life	Annual
Rabies, canine distemper leptospirosis and canine hepatitis		Penta dog vaccine	7th to 10th week of life	11th to 14th week of life	After 1 year of second injection; later annually
Canine distemper, hepatitis and leptospirosis		Candur DHL vaccine	7th to 9th week of life	12th to 14th week of life	After 1 year; later annually
		Caniffa vaccine	7th to 9th week of life	12th to 14th week of life	Annually
C.D; Adenovirus type-2, Hepatitis, Parainfluenza, Parvovirus, *Leptospira canicola* and *L. icterohaemorrhagiae*		Adenomune-7	7th to 9th week of life	12th to 14th week of life	Annually

DEWORMING

Sl. No.	Date of deworming	Dewormer used	Administration	Next due date	Sign. of Vet.

ECTOPARASITICIDAL SPRAY

Sl. No.	Date of spray	Drug used	Concentration of drug	Next due date	Sign. of Vet.

THERAPEUTIC REGIMEN

Date	Disease	Treatment	Progress	Remarks and Signature of Vet.

Laboratory Investigation

(Punch Laboratory investigation report)

A *Haemato-biochemical profile:*
B *Urine analysis:*
C *Faecal examination:*
D *Skin scraping examination:*
E *Electrocardiogram:*
F *X-ray:*
G *Microbiological examination:*
H *Others:*

DISTINGUISHED WORKS/AWARDS

Date	Type of work/award	Place

WEIGHT AND HEIGHT RECORD

S.No.	Date	Weight (kg)	Height (cm)	Increase		Decrease		Remarks and Sign. of Vet.
				Wt. (kg)	Ht. (cm)	Wt. (kg)	Ht. (cm)	

Appendix-5

PRESCRIPTIONS USED IN CANINE PRACTICE

A. PRESCRIPTIONS WRITING

A prescription order is a physician's instructions to a pharmacist for medicinal substances for a patient. It includes directions to the pharmacist regarding the preparation and to the patient regarding the use of medicine.

Choice of language: Years ago prescriptions were written exclusively in Latin. But today it is strongly recommended that prescription orders be written entirely in English in view to avoid errors. Most common abbreviations used in order are as under.

ABBREVIATIONS USED IN PRESCRIPTION WRITING

Abb.	*Latin word*	*English meaning*
$\bar{a}$	(ante)	before
$\bar{a}\bar{a}$	(ana)	of each
a.c.	(antecibum)	before meals
ad.	(ad)	to, up to
ad. lib.	(ad libitum)	freely as wanted
aq.	(aqua)	water
bid	(bis in die)	twice a day
C.	(congius)	gallon
$\bar{c}$	(cum)	with
cap.	(Capula)	capsule
div.	(divide)	divide
dos.	(dosis)	dose
eq. pts.	(equalis partes)	equal parts

Ft.	(Fiat)	make
g, gm, Gm.	(Gramme)	gram
gr.	(grains)	grain
gtt.	(gutta)	drop
h.	(hora)	hour
haust.	(haustus)	drench
M.	(Misce)	mix
no.	(numero)	number
n.r.	(non repetatur)	do not repeat
O.	(octarius)	pint
o.d.	(omnie die)	daily
o.h.	(omnie hora)	per hour
P.c.	(Post cibum)	after meals
Pil	(Pilula)	pill
P.r.n.	(Pro re nata)	as needed
pv.	(pulvis)	powder
q.h.	(quaquae hora)	every hour
Q.I.D.	(quarter in die)	four times in a day
q.s.	(quantum sufficit)	as much as needed
q. 3h.	(quaque 3 hora)	every three hours
s.	(sine)	without
s.i.d.	(semel in die)	once a day
Sig. or S.	(Signa)	write on the label
sol.	(solution)	solution
s.o.s.	(Si opus sit)	if necessary
ss	(Semise)	half
stat.	(Statim)	immediately
Syr.	(Syrups)	syrup
tab.	(tabella)	tablets
t.i.d.	(ter in die)	3 times a day
Tinct., tr.	(tincture)	tincture
cing.	(unguentum)	ointment
P/o	(Per os)	orally
I/M		intramuscular
I/V		intravenous
I/P		intraperitoneal
S/c		subcutaneous
I/u		intrauterine
I/A		intra-arterial

Parts of Prescription

1. Date
2. Name and address of the patient
3. **Superscription:** Consists of Rx - stands for recipe, take thou. The stroke has been considered an ancient invocation to Jupiter.
4. **Inscription:** It is the body of prescription order and contains the name and amount of each ingredient, written in official language. The order of the ingredients, should there be more than one, is as follows:
    - (a) Basis - Principle drug - gives chief action.
    - (b) Adjuvant - drug increases the action of principle drug.
    - (c) Correction - corrects undesirable effects of the basis of adjuvant.
    - (d) Vehicle - agent used as solvent in the solution.
5. **Subscription:** Contains directions to the pharmacist, while usually consists in short sentence as, make a solution etc.
6. **Signature:** Derived from "Latin (sig,s) signa" meaning write, mark. It consists directions to the patient that should always be written in English.
7. **Prescriber's signature:** Signature at bottom of the blank and last name in full with ink or pencil.

A Sample Prescription Form

1. Reg. No.__________ Dated __________
   Doctor's name with degree and address
2. Client's name __________ Address __________

   Patient __________ Age __________ Sex __________
3. R_x
4. Basis (Principle drug) __________
   Adjuvant __________
   Corrective __________
   Vehicle __________
5. Make and divide into three equal parts.
6. As one tablet daily for three days.
7. __________

Signature with Degree

Incompatibility: Prescription incompatibilities arise only from the carelessness or ignorance of the prescriber which may nullify the desired therapeutic effect. These incompatibilities may be as follows:

(a) *Therapeutic Incompatibility:* Occurs when drugs having antagonistic action are administered simultaneously as physostgmine (Iris constrictor, and atropine (Pupil dialator).

In another view, i.e. *Synergestic action* e.g. Morphine, if used as preanaesthetic following the administration of pentobarbital reduces anaesthetic dose of later administered drug.

(b) *Chemical Incompatibility:* It arises from interaction of compounds during or following their compounding in a prescription resulting in production of toxic substances as chloral hydrate plus alkali gives chloroform.

(c) *Pharmaceutical Incompatibility:* It arises from a lack of miscibility, i.e. the ingredients are not mutually solúble (oil in water).

CONVERSION TABLES REQUIRED FOR THERAPEUTIC PURPOSES

British Measures and Metric Equivalents

Weight	1 grain	0.0648 gramme
	1 ounce	28.350 grammes
	1 pound	0.4536 kilogram
	1 hundred weight (110 lb.) cwt	50.8 kilogram
	1 ton (2,240 lb)	1016.0 kilograms
	1 milligramme	0.015 grain
	1 centigramme	0.154 grain
	1 gramme	15.432 grains
	1 kilo gramme	2.2046 lb
	1 quintal	1.968 Cwt
Linear	1 inch	25.4 millimetres
	1 foot	0.3048 metre
	1 yard	0.9144 metre
	1 mile	1.6093 kilometres
	1 millimetre	0.0394 inch
	1 centimetre	0.3937 inch
	1 metre	39.370 inches
	1 kilometre	1093.63 yards
Measure	1 gill	1.42 decilitres
	1 pint	0.57 litre
	1 quart	1.136 litres
	1 gallon	4.546 litres
	1 bushel	36.37 litres
	1 quarter	0.29 kilolitre
	1 centilitre	0.07 gill
	1 litre	1.761 pints
	1 hecto litre	2.75 bushels
	1 kilo litre	3.44 quarters.

British Weights and Measures

12 inches	1 foot
3 feet	1 yard
220 yards	1 furlong
8 gills	1 mile

	4 gills	1 pint
	2 pints	1 quart
	4 quarts	1 gallon
	16 drams	1 ounce
Weight	16 ounces	1 pound
	14 pounds	1 stone
	8 stone	1 Cwt
	20 Cwt	1 ton

Metric Weights

The unit of weight is the kilogram (1 seer 6 tolas or 68 tolas) or 2 lb 30 ZS

Sub Units	
10 milligrams	1 centrigramme
10 centigrams	1 decigram
10 decigrams	1 gram
10 grams	1 hectogram
10 hectograms	1 kilogram
Multiples	
100 kilograms	1 quintal
10 quintals or 1,000 kilograms	1 metric tonne
Volume	
1 cubic centimetre	0.06102 cubic inch
1 cubic metre	35.3145 cubic feet
	1.3079 cubic yard
1 cubic inch	16.3872 cc
1 cubic feet	0.02832 cubic metre
1 cubic yard	0.7646 cubic metre
Capacity	
1 ml	16.23 minims
	0.2705 fluid dram
	0.0338 fluid ounce
1 litre	2.1134 pints
	1.0567 quarts
	1,000 ml
1 Minin	0.06 ml
1 Fl. dram	3.697 ml
1 Fl. ounce	29.573 ml
1 pint	473.168 ml
1 quart	946.33 ml
1 teaspoonfull (tsf)	5 ml
1 dessertspoonfull	10 ml
1 tablespoonfull (tbsf)	15 ml
1 wine glass full	200 ml
1 glass full	250 ml

DOSE EQUIVALENT TABLE: APPROXIMATE EQUIVALENT CONVERTING DOSES IN THE IMPERIAL SYSTEM INTO THE METRIC SYSTEM

Pounds and ounces			*Pints and fluid ounces*		
Pounds	***Ounces***	***Grams***	***Pints***	***Fluid Oz***	***Litres***
1	16	500	$1^3/_4$	35	1
$^3/_4$	12	350	1		0.6
½	8	250	$^3/_4$	15	0.44
$^1/_4$	4	125	-	6	0.175
-	3½	100	-	4	0.12
-	2	60	-	2	0.06

DOSE EQUIVALENT TABLE: APPROX. EQUIVALENT CONVERSING PER POUND BODY WEIGHT OF DOSES OF DRUGS TO PER KILO GRAM BODY WEIGHT FOR THERAPY

Milligram per kilogram body-weight	*Milligrams per pound body weight*	*Grain per pound body weight*	*Milligrams per pound body weight*	*Milligrams per kilogram body weight*	*Grains per pound body*
1	*2*	*3*	*4*	*5*	*6*
0.1	0.05	1/100	50	23	3/8
1	0.45	1/140	70	32	1/2
2	0.9	1/72	80	36	3/5
3	1.4	1/50	100	35	3/4
4	1.8	1/36	120	54	4/5
5	2.3	1/28	150	68	1
6	2.7	1/24	200	91	1.2/5
7	3.2	1/20	220	100	1.1/2
8	3.6	1/18	250	110	2
9	4.0	1/16	300	135	2
10	4.5	1/14	400	180	3
15	7	1/10	500	225	3.1/2
20	8	1/7	600	270	4
25	11	1/6	700	320	5
30	14	1/5	800	360	5.1/2
40	18	1/4	900	410	6
45	20	1/3	1 gm	450	7

Note: For conversion - mg/kg to mg/lb, multiply by 0.45; mg/kg to grains/lb., multiply by 0.007; mg/kg to grains/lb, multiply by 0.015; grains/lb to mg/kg, multiply by 65; and grains/lb to mg/kg, multiply by 14.3.

The factors are approximate, but sufficiently accurate for dosage purpose.

Dose of Medicament given by Different Routes

Stomach dose	=	1
Rectal dose	=	2
Intramuscular	=	1/5-1/10
Subcutaneous	=	1/10
Intratracheal	=	1/20
Intravenous	=	1/25-1/50

CALCULATION OF DOSES FOR PER KG BODY WEIGHT FOR DOGS (APPROX.)

Take the minimum prescribed dose for 6.0 kg body weight dog as standard.

Body weight in kg	*Level of dose*
1	1/6 of the dose
2	1/4
4	2/3
6	Minimum dose
8	4/3
10	5/3
12	2
14	7/3
16	7/3
18	11/4
20	3
More than 20	10/3

CALCULATION OF DOSES FOR DOG ON THE BASIS OF AGE (APPROX.)

Age	*Level of dose*
Below one month	1/16th part
One month of 1-1/2 months	1/8th part
One and half months to 3 months	1/4th part
Three to 6 months	1/2 part
6 months and above	1 part

Fahrenheit (°F) and Centigrade/Celcius (°C) Table

To convert °C into °F, Multiply by 9/5 then add 32

To convert °F into °C, subtract 32 then multiply by 5/9

Example: (a) 20° C x 9/5 = 36 + 32 = 68° F

(b) 104° F - 32 = 72 x 5/9 = 40° C

°F	°C	°F	°C	°F	°C
210	100	99	37.2	80	26.7
200	93.3	98.4	36.9	78	25.6
150	65.6	98	36.7	76	24.4
112	44.4	97.5	36.4	74	23.3
110	43.3	97	36.1	72	22.2
108	42.2	96.5	35.8	70	21.1
106	41.1	96	35.6	68	20.0
105	40.6	95.5	35.3	66	18.9
104	40.0	95	35.0	64	17.8
103	39.4	94	34.4	62	16.7
102	38.9	92	33.3	60	15.6
101.5	38.6	90	32.2	58	14.4
1C1	38.3	88	31.1	56	13.3
100.5	38.1	86	30.0	54	12.2
100	37.8	84	28.9	52	11.1
99.5	37.5	82	27.8	32	0

B. COMMON PRESCRIPTIONS

After the diagnosis of disease it is very important to select an appropriate line of treatment. For this purpose it is essential to write a concise but self explanatory prescription for the pharmacy for dispensing the drugs. The prescription should also show the sequence of drugs, dose, interval, route of administration and duration of treatment. The prescription should also contain the details of animals, name and address of owner and should be duly signed by the veterinary doctor with date. In this chapter informations about proprietary drugs of some leading firms have been given for the use of practitioners. This is followed by an alphabetic list of therapeutic agents along with dose, route of administration and duration of the treatment.

1. MEDICINES USED IN INFECTIOUS DISEASES

(a) Antibiotics

(i) Name: Achromycin (Cyanamid)
Composition: Tetracycline hydrochloride
Dosage: 4-10 mg/kg BW I/M, daily
Packing: 100 mg and 500 mg vials

(ii) Name: Albercillin Vet (Inga)
Composition: Ampicillin trihydrate

Dosage: 5-10 mg/kg BW I/M or I/V
Packing: 250 mg and 1,000 mg vials

(iii) Name: Campicillin (Cadila)
Composition: Ampicillin sodium
Dosage: 5-10 mg I/M or I/V
Packing: 500 mg and 1,000 mg vials

(iv) Name: Combiotic - V (Pfizer)
Composition: Procainepenicillin G, 1,500,000 units, sodium penicillin G - 500,000 units; streptomycin sulphate - 2.5 g
Dosage: 5-10 mg/kg BW
Packing: To each vial add 8.4 ml of distilled water

(v) Name: Crys - 4 Veterinary (Sarabhai)
Composition: Small dose procaine penicillin G-300,000 units and crystalline sodium penicillin G-100,000 units
Dosage: 1/2 to 1 vial I/M as per size
Packing: Box of 25 vials

(vi) Name: Dicrysticin-S Vet (Sarabhai)
Composition: Small dose 300,000 and 100,000 units of PPG and sodium penicillin with 0.5 g of streptomycin sulphate
Dosage: 200,000 units/5 kg BW I/M
Packing: 0.5 gm and 2.5 gm vials

(vii) Name: Gentavet (PCI)
Composition: Each ml contains 50 mg Gentamicin sulphate
Dosage: 4.4 mg/kg BW BID on first day followed by OD I/M or I/V
Packing: 2 ml and 5 ml vials

(viii) Name: Hostacycline (Hoechst)
Composition: 5 g tetracycline HCl in 100 g hostacycline
Dosage: @ 1 g/kg BW orally
Packing: 100 g bottles/sachets

(ix) Name: Lisarin (Sarabhai)
Composition: Gentamicin sulphate 40 mg/ml
Dosage: 3-5 mg/kg BW BID on day 1 and OD on following days I/V, I/M or S/C
Packing: 2 ml vials

(x) Name: Microvet (PCI)
Composition: 100 mg oxytetracycline HCl/ml
Dosage: 7-11 mg/kg/BW/day, I/M
Packing: 5 ml x 1 ml ampoules

(xi) Name: Oxysteclin (Sarabhai)
Composition: 50 mg Oxytetracycline dihydrate/ml
Dosage: 1 ml/10 kg BW I/M, I/V or S/C
Packing: 10 ml, 30 ml, 100 ml vials

(xii) Name: Phenivet (PCI)

	Composition:	125 mg of chloramphenicol/ml
	Dosage:	10-30 mg/kg BW I/M
	Packing:	5 ml x 2 ml ampoules and 10 ml and 30 ml vials
(xiii)	Name:	Primicin - vet (HAL)
	Composition:	40 mg/ml of gentamicin sulphate
	Dosage:	2-4 mg/kg BW I/M, I/V or S/c
	Packing:	10 ml and 30 ml vials
(xiv)	Name:	Stancillin (Sarabhai)
	Composition:	Each 5 ml provides 125 mg of ampicillin trihydrate
	Dosage:	4-12 mg/kg BW, I/M
	Packing:	30 g bottle
(xv)	Name:	Steclin (Sarabhai)
	Composition:	500 mg vial contains 500 mg tetracycline - hydrocloride, 200 mg xylocaine, 1,500 mg vitamin C and 235 mg magnesium chloride
	Dosage:	4-10 mg/kg BW I/M
	Packing:	500 mg vial
(xvi)	Name:	TM-Liquid (Pfizer) Infection
	Composition:	50 mg Oxytetracycline HCl/ml
	Dosage:	5-15 ml for 4-5 days in drinking water
	Packing:	10 ml, 30 ml and 100 ml vials. Terramycine is also available in the form of tablets and injectable solution
(xvii)	Name:	Vetnicol (ACI)
	Composition:	Chloramphenicol 125 mg and lignocaine hydrocloride 1% W/V/ml
	Dosage:	20-30 mg/kg BW I/M
	Packing:	30 ml vial
(xviii)	Name:	Vetampin (Wockhardt)
	Composition:	1 g Ampicillin sodium
	Dosage:	5-10 mg/kg BW I/M or I/V
	Packing:	1 g vial
(xix)	Name:	Wolicyclin (Wockhardt)
	Composition:	100 mg oxytetracycline HCl/ml
	Dosage:	Streptomycin 10 mg/kg BW I/M, I/V or S/C
	Packing:	30 ml vial
	Others:	Cap, Duoclox and syrup (FDC), Penglobe (astra), and inj. Ivimicin (FDC) Eltocin (IPCA) Althrocin, wymox Ampitum sulphate (FDCV) and Mikacin (Aristo).

(b) Sulphonamides

(i)	Name:	Bactrisol bolus (Alved)
	Composition:	200 mg trimethoprim BP (Vet.), 1,000 mg sulphadiazine BP (Vet)
	Dosage:	30-50 mg/kg BW orally for 5 days
	Packing:	10 and 100 boluses
(ii)	Name:	Chemozine bolus (PCI)
	Composition:	1.0 g sulphadiazine, 0.2 g trimethoprim

Dosage: 20 mg/kg BW BID orally
Packing: 5 x 4 tablets

(iii) Name: Coccil liquid (Akelvi)
Composition: Sulphadimidine sodium B Vet C 12.5%
Dosage: 150 mg/kg BW on day 1 followed by 75 mg/kg BW for 4-5 days
Packing: 450 ml bottle

(iv) Name: Diadin injection (Pfizer)
Composition: 0.333 mg/ml of sulphadimidine sodium (33.33%)
Dosage: 3 ml/5 kg BW followed by 1.5 ml/5 kg
Packing: 100 ml bottle

(v) Name: Oriprim injection (Cadila)
Composition: 160 mg trimethoprim I.P. and 800 mg sulphamethoxazole IP/3 ml
Dosage: 1 ml/20 kg BW I/M
Packing: 5 x 3 ml ampoules. Also available in the form of tablets and boluses

(vi) Name: Robatran Vet Granules (TTK)
Composition: Trimethoprim 80 mg and sulphamethoxazole 400 mg/5 g
Dosage: 10-20 g/daily orally
Packing: 100 g and 500 g.

(vii) Name: Sulpha bolus (Sarabhai)
Composition: Each bolus contains 5 g sulphadimidine
Dosage: 1 g/5 kg BW orally followed by 1/2 dose
Packing: 10 boluses of 5 g each

(viii) Name: Trinamide (M&B)
Composition: Sulphadimidine, sulphadiazine and sulphapyridine in equal parts (and powder)
Dosage: 1 g/7 kg BW initially followed by 0.5 g/7 kg BW
Packing: 10 g x 5 g embets

(ix) Name: Vesadin (M&B)
Composition: Sulphadimidine sodium B. Vet. C. 33.3%
Dosage: 6 ml/9 kg BW. The initial dose should be given BID and followed by half dose
Packing: 100 ml vial
Others: Supristal tabs, Triglobe tabs, Anrima tabs Bactrim tabs, Ciplin tab, Biofloxin, Eradacil etc.

2. MEDICINES USED IN GASTROINTESTINAL DISORDERS

(a) Antidiarrhoeals

(i) Name: Achromycine vet doser (Cynamid)
Composition: 100 mg tetracycline/ml
Dosage: 0.5 ml/1-2 kg BW daily
Packing: 10 ml bottle

(ii) Name: Gastina (Glaxo)
Composition: Each tablet contains streptomycin sulphate 250 mg, neomycin sulphate 100 mg, vitamin A 25, 000, IU

	Dosage:	1-2 tablets BID for 3 days
	Packing:	20 tablets bottles
(iii)	Name:	Lomotil (Searle)
	Composition:	Diphenoxylate 2.4 mg, atropine sulphate, 0.025 mg
	Dosage:	1 tab., bid for 3-5 days
	Packing:	10 x 10 tablets
(iv)	Name:	Orazol (ACI)
	Composition:	Each 5 ml contains Metronidazole IP-40 mg, Pectin - 20 mg, light Kaolin - 1.0 g furazolidone BP - 30 mg
	Dosage:	5 ml, 2-3 times daily for 3-4 days
	Packing:	60 ml bottle
(v)	Name:	Pesulin (Cadila)
	Composition:	Each 15 ml contains phthalylsulphathiazole 1 g. pectin 0.15 g and kaolin 3 g
	Dosage:	15-30 ml BID
	Packing:	100 ml, 450 ml bottle
(vi)	Name:	Stopit (Arex)
	Composition:	Calcium carbonate 12%, kaolin 20%, sodium bicarbonate 4%, magnesium carbonate 6% sulphaguanidine 10%, tamarindectin 25%
	Dosage:	1 TSF thrice daily
	Packing:	80 g
(vii)	Name:	Thalazole (M & B)
	Composition:	Pthalylsulphathiazole B. Vet. C.
	Dosage:	1 g/7 kg BW, BID for 7-8 days
	Packing:	10 g x 5 g tablets
(viii)	Name:	Quixalin bolus (Sarabhai)
	Composition:	Each bolus contains 1.5 g Haloquinol
	Dosage:	1/2 to 1 bolus per day orally
	Packing:	25 boluses

Other drugs like Bonnisan, Diadisco, Diarex, Neftin, Flagyl, Furoxon, Isabgol husk tablets, Dependal M and stat can be used.

(b) Laxatives and Purgatives

(i)	Name:	Cremaffin (Boots)
	Composition:	Milk of magnesia 11.25 ml and liquid paraffin 3.75 ml/15 ml
	Dosage:	1-2 TSF BID for 2-3 days
	Packing:	210 ml
(ii)	Name:	Glaxena (Glaxo)
	Composition:	Senna powder : 600 mg/tablet
	Dosage:	1-2 tab BID as needed
	Packing:	10 tablets
(iii)	Name:	Senade (Cipla)
	Composition:	13.5 mg Senna extract

Dosage: 1-2 Tab., bid as needed

Packing: 10 tablets strip

(iv) Name: Dulcolax (German Remedies)

Composition: Bisacodyl 5 mg

Dosage: 1-2 tablets BID or TID as required. Suppository form is also available

Packing: 100 x 10 tablets and 250 tablets

(ii) Name: Agarol (Warner)

Dosage: 2-4 T.S.F. daily

Other drugs used include Impecdon, Isabgole Husk, Magnesium Sulphate and Castor oil etc.

(c) Enzymes: Used in indigestion and dyspepsia etc.

(i) Name: Bestozyme (biological evans)

Composition: Fungaldiastase 150 mg; Papain 25 mg; thiamine mononitrate 2 mg; ribofla-vin 1 mg; niacinamide 20 mg; hematropin 1 mg; methylpolysiloxane 20 mg; activated charcoal 75 mg; chitrak moola extract 10 mg; mehndi extract 20 mg; Karela extract 10 mg; Katuk extract 20 mg; pachamrit parpati 10 mg

Dosage: 1-2 tablets TID for 5 days

Packing: 30 tablets

(ii) Name: Lupizyme (Lupin)

Composition: 5 ml contains fungal diastase (1 : 50) 750 mg; pepsin (13,000) 12.5 mg; riboflavin 0.5 mg; thiamine HCl 4 mg; dipantothenyl alcohol 3 mg; Vitamin B12 4 mcg; niacinamide 12.5 mg; sorbital 220 mg

Dosage: 1 T.S.F., TID for 5 days

Packing: 110 and 450 ml.

(iii) Name: Panzynorm (German Remedies)

Composition: Pancreatin 100 mg; bile extract 40 mg and dry stomach extract 100 mg

Dosage: 1-2 tablets TID as needed

Packing: 25, 100 tablets

(iv) Name: Bilamide (Ethnor)

Composition: Pyridine - 3 carboxylic acid - N-hydroxymethylnicotinamide 0.5 g

Dosage: 1/2 to 1 tablet BID as needed

Packing: 30 tablets

(v) Name: Takazyme (Parke Davis): Contains takadiastase 8%; mag. trisillicate light 16%; mag. trisillicate 66.3% powder

Dosage: 3-5 g BID as needed

Packing: 57 g and 142 g powder

(vi) Others: Molzyme tabs (FDC), Methozyme (Abhilpharma) and Vitapepsin (Siri pharma)

(d) Antacids

(i) Name: Gelusil MPS Liquid (Warner)

Composition: Each 5 ml contains: methypoly siloxane 50 mg, magnesium hydroxide 250 mg, dried aluminium hydroxide gel 250 mg

Dosage: 1-2 TSF 2-3 times as needed
Packing: 170 ml and 400 ml bottles

(ii) Name: Paractol (German Remedies)
Composition: Methyl polysiloxane 250 mg
Dosage: 1/2-1 tablet BID as needed
Packing: 10 x 6 tablets

(iii) Name: Gelusil (Warner)
Composition: Dried alum hydroxide gel 0.25 g, magenisium trisilcate 0.5 g
Dosage: 1/2-1 tablets BID as needed
Packing: Strips of 10 tablets

(iv) Name: Gelusil liquid (Warner)
Composition: 5 ml contains magnesium trisilicate 0.5 g; dried aluminium hydroxide gel 0.25 g
Dosage: 1-2 TSF, 2-3 times daily as needed
Packing: 170 ml, 400 ml bottles

(v) Name: Gelusil MPS tabs (Warner)
Composition: Mag. hydroxide 250 mg; methyl-polysiloxane 50 mg and dried aluminium hydroxide gel 250 mg
Dosage: 1/2-1 tablet BID as needed
Packing: Strip of 10 tablets

(vi) Name: Almacarb (Glaxo)
Composition: Dried alum. hydroxide gel 235 mg; magnesium carbonate light 50 mg; activated methyl polysiloxane 40 mg; deglycirrhizinized liquorice 380 mg
Dosage: 1-2 tablets BID as needed
Packing: Strip of 10 tablets

(vii) Name: Cimetidine (Cipla)
Composition: Cimetidine 200 mg/tab
Dosage: 1-2 tablets BID as needed
Packing: Strip of 10 tablets

(viii) Name: Digestone (Anuja)
Composition: Harda 300 mg; triphla 150 mg; chitrak 100 mg; kalimirch 50 mg; sunth 75 mg; vidanga 100 mg; shankh bhasam 75 mg; gulvel 100 mg
Dosage: 3-4 g daily
Packing: 100 g
Others: Famofast, 20, 40 (FDC), Actriol, allujel DF, Alucinol, Aludrox, Anital, Digene Gel, Divol forte susp, Disitox MPS, Dopcid, Silox forte gel.

4. MEDICINES USED IN UROGENITAL TRACT DISORDERS

(a) Drugs acting on uterus

(i) Name: Oxytra (HAL)
Composition: Each tablet contains 500 mg of oxytetracycline HCl IP
Dosage: 1/4-1/2 tablets IU

Packing: 5 and 25 x 500 mg tablets

(ii) Name: Aqueous iodine solution IP (Ethicare)

Composition: 5% w/v iodine and 10% W/V potassium iodine (equal to 50 mg free iodine) and 130 mg of total iodine/ml

Dosage: 5 ml of aqueous iodine solution in 250 ml water by I/U irrigation

Packing: 100 ml, 400 ml and 500 ml bottles

(iii) Name: Bactrisol bolus : (Alved)

Composition: Bolus contains: Sulphadiazine BP (Vet) 1,000 mg; trimethoprim BP (Vet) 200 mg

Dosage: 125 mg/kg BW for 5 days (give intra uterine)

Packing: 10 and 100 boluses

(iv) Name: Lisarin (Sarabhai)

Composition: 40 mg Gentamicin/ml

Dosage: Injected intra uterine

Packing: Available as 2 ml vials

Name: Himidin (HAL)

Composition: Sulphadimidine IP 5 g

Dosage: Administered intra uterine

Packing: 10 and 50 x 5 g tablets

(vi) Name: Duvadilan (Duphar)

Composition: Isoxsuprine HCl 5 mg/ml

Dosage: Intra uterine infusion

Packing: Available as 2 ml vials

(vii) Name: Odine - 10 (ACI)

Composition: 10% w/v povidone iodine USP

Dosage: Intra-uterine infusion

Packing: 100 ml bottles

(viii) Name: TM-Animal formula tablets (Pfizer)

Composition: 500 mg of Oxytetracycline HCl/bolus

Dosage: 1/2-1 bolus intra uterine

Packing: 4 x 4 tablets

(ix) Name: Steclin bolus (Sarabhai)

Composition: Tetracycline HCl 500 mg

Dosage: 1/4 to 1/2 bolus I/U

Packing: 16 boluses

Other drugs used in female reproductive systems are: Mixtures like Gyanomin Bhanjna and Aloe compounds are useful, Lukol tablet (Himalaya) 1-2 for 10 days. Other than these Prajna Capsule, Epidosin-vet, Myron-vet, Replanta, Syntocinon, Oxytocin (2 or 5 ml amp) and Vetoestrol can also be tried.

Drugs used to prevent threatened abortion

Name: Duvadilan

Composition: Isoxsuprine Hcl

Dose: 2 tab, 3-4 times daily after meals, reduce following improvement

2 Tidilan: 1 tab 3-4 times daily.

Spastic disorders of uterus

1. Name: Bardase:
   Composition: Phenobarbulone 16 mg hyoscyamine 0.1 mg hyoscyamine hydrobromide 7 mg atropine SO4 - 20 mcg, taka diastase - 0.16 gm
   Dose: 1 tab, tid
2. Buctocin: ½ - 1 tab 5 times a day, (desamino-ocytoun 50 IU)
3. Buscopan: 2 tab, 3-5 times a day
   Composition: Hysocine-n-butylbroud long
4. Metherone:
   Composition: Methylergorovine maleate 0.2 mg per ml
   Dose: 1 ml S/C, I/M

Drugs used to Prevent Post-Partum Haemorrhage/Bleeding

1. Ingagen-M:
   Composition: Methylergometune maleate 0.2 mg per ml
   Dose: 1 ml I/M 1 ml every 2-4 hours required
2. Methergin: Methylergonovine maleate - 0.125 mg
   Dose: 0.2 mg I/V or 0.1 to 0.2 mg I/V repeated at intervals not less than 2 hours
3. Metherone:
   Composition: Methylergonovine maleate 0.2 mg per ml
   Dose: 1 ml S/C, I/M or I/V, also tabs - 1 tab TID for 5-7 days
4. Pitocin: Oxytocin 5 m per ml 0.5 I/V method of choice
5. Syntocinon:
   Composition: Synthetic oxytocin 11 m per ml
   Dose: 1 iμ infusion in 5% destrose at induction or enhancement of labour

(b) Drugs acting on male reproductive system

(i) Name: Tentex fort (Himalaya)
   Composition: 1 tablet daily for 7 days
   Packing: 10, 50, 100 and 250 tablets

(ii) Name: Saxon (Indian Herbs)
   Dosage: 2-3 g/daily
   Packing: 250 g and 1 kg pack

(iii) Name: Fortege (Alarsin)
   Dosage: 3-6 tablets/daily for 10-15 days
   Packing: Bottles of 100 and 1000 tablets

(iv) Name: Himcolin cream (Himalaya)
   Dosage: Tones up the erection of penis, produce vascular engorgement by active vasodialation, help in maintain the coitus. Poor erectile power due to advancing age or over indulgence, functional impotence. Massage once or twice a day a little himocolin on the penis and the pubic region. Continue this treatment for 15-20 days. Himcolin should not be washed off immediately after use. Allow an hour between application

of himcolin and sexual intercourse. Simultaneous administration of tentex fort tablets produces results faster.

Packing: 7 gm and 21 gm

Other then these drugs Gerifort and Speman (Himalaya) 1 tablet BID or TID for 7 days.

(c) Diuretics

(i) Name: Bangshil (Alarsin)
Dosage: 5 tablets BID for 10 days
Packing: 100 tablets

(ii) Name: Di-Ademil (Sarabhai)
Composition: Hydoflumetizol 25 mg/tablets
Packing: Bottle of 20 and 100 tablets

(iii) Name: Diamox (Cyanamid)
Composition: Acetazolamide 250 mg
Packing: Strip of 10 tablets. Contraindicated in renal failure

(iv) Name: Diural (Alembic)
Composition: Frusemide 40 mg/tablets
Packing: Strip of 10 tablets

(v) Name: Diural injection (Alembic)
Composition: 10 mg of frusemide/ml
Packing: 2 ml ampoules

(vi) Name: Kenty (ACI)
Composition: 25 mg of nandroline phenyl propionate BP and 9% v/v benzyl alcohol
Dosage: 25-50 mg/every fortnight
Packing: 3 ml x 1 ml ampoules

(vii) Name: Kinex injection (Unique)
Composition: 20 mg of frusemide/ml
Packing: 2 ml ampoules

(viii) Name: Lasix tablet and injection (Hoechst)
Composition: 40 mg and 20 mg/ml of frusemide respectively
Packing: 2 ml ampoules and strip of 10 tablets

(ix) Name: Nephpril (Pfizer)
Composition: Polythiazide 1 mg tab

(x) Name: Stonil (Indian Herbs)
Dosage: 2.5-4 g
Packing: 100 g and 1 kg pack
Others: Ridema inj and Aldacetone

(d) Urinary anti-infectives

(i) Name: Albercillin (Inga)
Composition: Ampicillin trihydrate 250 mg or 1.0 g
Dosage: 2-7 mg/kg BW, I/V

(ii) Name: Roscillin (Ranbaxy)
Composition: Ampicillin 500 mg, 1.0 g and 2.5 g
Dosage: 2-7 mg/kg BW, I/M or I/V\

(iii) Name: Vetampin (Wockhardt)
Composition: Ampicillin 500 mg, 1.5 g
Dosage: 2-7 mg/kg BW, I/M or I/V

(iv) Name: Broadacillin (Alchem)
Composition: Ampicillin 250 mg, 500 mg
Dosage: 2-7 mg/kg BW, I/M or I/V

(v) Name: Campicillin (Cadila)
Composition: 250, 500 and 1,000 mg of ampicillin solution
Dosage: 4-10 mg/kg BW, orally; 2-7 mg/kg BW, parentrally

(vi) Name: Eskaycilin (Eskay lab)
Composition: 500 mg ampicillin sodium

(vii) Name: Cystone (Himalaya)
Composition: 1 tablet TID
Packing: 50, 100, 250 and 500 tablets

(viii) Name: Lisarin (Sarabhai)
Composition: 40 mg/ml of gentamicin I/M or I/M
Packing: 2 ml ampoules

Other than the above preparations Trimethoprim, sulphamethoxazole preparations, Chloramphenicol preparations, Duoclox - cap dry syrup, uroflox, norfa tab, furadantin tab and syrup can be used.

(e) Local and systemic drugs for urethral conditions

(i) Name: Flagyl (M & B)
Composition: Metronidazole 200 mg, 400 mg tablet
Indication: For Trichomanas vaginalis infection

(ii) Name: Gynosan (SG-Pharma)
Composition: Chloroquinaldol 200 mg tablet

(iii) Name: Dienoesterol cream (Ethnor)
Composition: Dienoestrol 0.01% w/w
Contraindicated in pregnancy and lesions of vulva and vagina
Packing: 30 g tube with applicator

(iv) Name: Triple sulpha (Ethnor)
Composition: Sulphathiazole 3.42% w/w/; sulphacetamide 2.86% w/w; N-benzyl-sulphanilamide 3.70% w/w; Urea 0.64% w/w
Packing: 30 g tubes with applicator

(v) Name: Sulpha cream (Stadmed)
Composition: Sulphacetamide 2.86%; sulphadimidine 2.86%; sulphadiazine 2.70%
Packing: 30 g and 60 g tubes with applicator
Others: Arflur - 50, 100 - Arrlur-sr (FDC)

4. DRUGS ACTING ON RESPIRATORY SYSTEM

(a) Respiratory stimulants

(i) Name: Coramine (Ciba)
Composition: Nikethamide 25% in aqueous solution
Dosage: Used I/M or I/V as injection 0.5 to 1.5 ml as per size of dog
Packing: 2 and 5 ml ampoules

(ii) Name: Coramine tablets (Ciba)
Composition: Nikethamide 2 mol + 1 mol of thiocyanate orally. Each tablet contain 0.4 g. Coramine drops are also available

(iii) Name: Restimulen (SG Pharma)
Composition: 1.5 ml contains - ethyl-butanide 112.5 mg, propylbutanide 112.5 mg
Dosage: 0.5 to 1.5 ml I/V, I/M or S/C

(iv) Name: Restimulen drops (SG Pharma)
Composition: 100 ml contain 7.5 g of Ethylbutanide and prophylbutanide each
Dosage: 5-10 drops TID orally
Packing: 15 ml drops

(v) Name: Cardiazol (Bohringer-K)
Composition: Leptazole 100 mg/tablet
Dosage: 1 Tab orally
Packing: 10 tablets

(vi) Name: Cardiazol injection (Bohringer-K)
Composition: 100 mg Leptazole/ml
Dosage: 0.5-2 ml, I/V or I/M
Packing: 5 ml and 30 ml vials

(vii) Name: Cardiazol liquid (Bohringer-K)
Composition: 100 mg/ml of leptazole
Dosage: 1-3 ml orally
Packing: 10 ml and 100 ml bottles

(b) Expectorants and cough suppressants

(ii) Name: Avil expectorant (Hoechst)
Composition: 5 ml contains: pheniramine maleate 15 mg; ammonium chloride 125 mg; menthol 1.14 mg
Dosage: Given orally twice or thrice daily - one TSF each time

(ii) Name: Capramin (Glaxo)
Composition: Phenylphrine HCl - 2 mg; caffeine 30 mg; phenacitine 160 mg; acetyl salicylic acid 230 mg; chlorpheneramine maleate 2 mg
Dosage: Given orally 1 tablet BID or TID for 5 days

(iii) Name: Aminophylline injection (Harson Lab)
Composition: 10 ml contains 250 mg aminophylline
Dosage: 1-3 ml given by slow I/V injection only

Packing:	10 ml ampoules
(iv) Name:	Caflon (Indian herbs)
Dosage:	2-4 g orally
(v) Name:	Cofgon (Indian herbs)
Dosage:	2-4 g
(vi) Name:	Corex (Pfizer)
Composition:	5 ml contains chlorpheniramine maleate 4 mg; codein phosphate 10 mg; Ephedrine HCl 5 mg; Sodium citrate 150 mg; and menthol 0.1 mg
Dosage:	Given orally twice or thrice daily depending on the need
	Other medicines which may be used include Phensedyl (M & B), zeet expectorant (Alembic), Glycodine (alembic), Benadryl (Parke Davis), elcof (Vesper India), Lupihist (Lupin), Hystalin cough syrup; Lastuss, LA, salmodil expectorant (FDC)

(c) Liniments and ointments effective in respiratory system

(i) Vicks Vaporub (Richadrson Hindustan) for local application and for inhalation.

(ii) Vicks inhaler (Richardson Hindustan) for inhalation.

(iii) Dabrub (Dabur) to be applied locally in the chest region.

(iv) Halls' cold rub ointment (Warner Hindustant) apply under nose, rub vigorously on throat and chest.

5. DRUGS FOR MUSCULOCUTANEOUS DISORDERS

(a) Non-steroid anti-inflammatory substances

(i) Name:	Oxalgin (Cadila)
Composition:	Contains Oxyphenbutazone IP 0.5 g; analgin IP 2.5 g
Dosage:	1/4-1/2 bolus twice daily, orally
(ii) Name:	Novalgin (Hoechst)
Composition:	Analgin 500 mg/ml
Dosage:	2-5 ml I/M, I/V twice daily or as per need. Tablets are also available
(iii) Name:	Baralgan (Hoechst)
Composition:	Contains Analgin 0.5 g with small amounts of spasmolytics
Dosage:	2-5 ml I/M or I/V. tablets are also available
(iv) Name:	Ronalgin (Ranbaxy)
Composition:	Each ml contains analgin 500 mg
Dosage:	2-4 ml twice daily I/M
(v) Name:	Kebutacine (ACI)
Composition:	Each ml contains phenyl butazone 200 mg; lignocaine HCl 10 mg
Dosage:	1-2 ml by deep I/M
(vi) Name:	Esgipyrin (SG Pharma)
Composition:	Phenylbutazone sodium 150 mg and amidopyrin 150 mg/ml with 1% lidocain
Dosage:	0.5 to 1 ml I/M Esgipyrin. Tablets are also available
	Other than these, medicines which may be used include algesin injection and tablet

(Alembic), Banghshil tablet (Alarsin), Butadex tablet (Cadila), Rumalaya tablet and cream (Himalaya), Zolandin tablet and injection (SG Pharma), Sugarnil tablet (SG Pharma), Tendril, anaflam; Deflam and Ultragesic (Siris Pharma).

(b) Muscle relaxants

(i) Name: Duodil tablets (Duphar)
Composition: Diazepam 5 mg and paracetamol 500 mg per tabs
Dosage: 1 tab BID

(ii) Name: Epidosin (TTK)
Composition: Contains valethamate bromide NF 10 mg/ml
Dosage: 5-10 mg/kg by I/M route

(iii) Name: Flaxedil (M & B)
Composition: 4% w/v gallamine triethiodide
Dosage: 1-2 mg/kg BW by I/V injection only

(iv) Name: Neo-octinum injection (Bohringer-K)
Composition: 0.06 g of Octinum amidosulphonate and 0.08 g of Octinum-D-amido-sulphonate/ml
Administration: By intramuscular route
Packing: 1 ml ampoules
Others: valium - (Roche), carisoma tab, Paraton and Robinax.

(c) Rubefacients

(i) Name: Iodex Vet ointment (EskayEf)
Composition: Iodine 4% w/w and methyl salicylate 5% W/W in petroleum base

(ii) Name: Iodyl Vet ointment (Sarabhai)
Composition: Iodine 4.7% and methyl salicyllate 5.9% w/w in non-staining emollint base
Packing: 100 g ointment tube

(iii) Name: Medicream (Rallis)
Composition: Each gram contain 0.03% adrenaline bitartrate, 1% methyl-nicotinate; 2.5% Mephenesin, 8% methyl salicylate, 2% chlorpheniramine maleate and 2% menthol
Packing: 30 g cream tube.

(iv) Name: Iodobal (Balloun)
Composition: 5% iodine and methyl salicylate 5% w/w
Packing: 200 g ointment tube

(v) Name: Rubriment (German Remedies)
Composition: Benzylincotinate - 1.5% Salicylic acid derivative 2%
Packing: 50 ml liniment

Other than this Sloan's liniment, Multigesic cream (Nicholas), Thrombophob ointment (German Remedies), Sensur cream and Relaxil ointment may be used.

6. EYE AND EAR MEDICINE

(a) For eyes:

(ii) Name: Betnesol eye/ear (Glaxo)
Composition: Betamethasone sodium phosphate 0.1%
Dosage: Ointment: Apply every 4-6 hours
Drops: 1-2 drops every 4-6 hours
Packing: Eye ointment and drops

(ii) Name: Betnesole - N. eye/ear (ointment and drops) (Glaxo)
Composition: Betamethesone sodium phosphate 0.1%; neomycin sulphate 0.5%
Dosage: Local application/instillation in eye/ear
Packing: 3 g ointment, 3 ml vial

(iii) Name: Cambison (Hoechst) eye ointment
Composition: Predniso lone 0.25%; neomycin HCl equal to 0.16^ base, and surfan 0.30%
Packing: 3-5 g tube

(iv) Name: Chlorocort (Parke Davis)
Composition: Chloramphenicol 1%, hydrocortisone acetate 0.5%
Packing: 3.5 g tube

(v) Name: Aplicaps (Parke-Davis)
Composition: Chloramphenicol
Administration: Instill into eyes

(vi) Name: Dexacol eye drops (ACL)
Composition: Chloramphenicol 1% w/v, dexamethasone 0.1% w/v
Packing: 5 ml vials

(vii) Name: Garamycin eye ointment (Fulford)
Composition: Gentamicin sulphate equal to 3 mg gentamicin/g
Packing: 3 g ointment tubes

(viii) Name: Genticin drops (Nicholas)
Packing: 3 ml vials

(ix) Name: Safracort (Roussel)
Composition: Soframycin (framycetin sulphate) 1%; hydrocortisone acetate 1%.
Packing: 3 ml vials

(x) Name: Soframycin opthalamic ointment (Roussel) and drop
Composition: Soframycin (framycetin sulphate) 0.5%
Administration: 2-3 application needed daily
Packing: 5 ml vials

(xi) Name: Vanmycetin eye drops (FDC)
Packing: Chloramphenicol 0.4%
Administration: Instill 1-2 drops 2-4 times daily into affected eyes.
Packing: 5 ml vials

Albucid eye drops (10%) (Nicholas), cellumide eye drops 20% (Alembic), gencyl eye ointment/drops (IDPL): nebasulf eye ointment (Pfizer), neosporin eye drops

(B.W.); Dexona eye drop (Cadila), Locula 10% (East India), Chlorocort applicaps (Parke-Davis) Decadron eye drops (MSD) Terramycin eye ointment (Pfizer) Pyricort, pyrimon, bactigen, can also be used.

(b) Medicines for ears

(i) Name: Betnesole eye/ear (Glaxo)
Composition: Betamethasone sodium phosphate 0.1%
Packing: Ointment/drops

(ii) Name: Betnesole N-eye/ear (Glaxo)
Composition: Betamethasone 0.1% neomycine sulphate 0.5%

(iii) Name: Chloromycetin ear drops (Parke-Davis)
Composition: 5% Chloramphenicol
Packing: 5 ml vials

(iv) Name: Dexona eye/ear drops (Cadila)
Composition: Dexamethasone sodium phosphate 0.1%; Neomycin Sulphate 0.5%; banzalkonium chloride in isotonic solution 0.2%
Packing: 2.5 ml vials

(v) Name: Genticin drops (Nicholas)
Composition: Gentamycine 3,000 I.U./ml of Gentamycin
Packing: 3 ml vials

(vi) Name: Otek-ac-ear drops(FDC)
Composition: Prenesolone 0.5%; lignocaine HCl 2%; phenylmercuric nitrate 0.2%, acetic acid 2%
Dosage: 4-5 drops in each ear
Packing: 5 ml vials

Other drugs like Sofracort ear drops (Roussel), TM eye/ear (Pfizer) and Otek-P (FDC) Pyricort eye/ear drops. Norzen eye/ear drop, Butox can also be used.

7. MEDICINE USED FOR PARASITIC DISEASES

(a) Endoparasiticidal Medicines

See Chapter: Endoparasitic Diseases

(b) Ectoparasiticide medicines

(i) Name: Ascabiol (M & B)
Composition: 25% emulsion of benzyl benzoater in water or oil
Application: Applied 1-2 times daily for 3-6 days on skin
Packing: 125 ml and 1 litre

(ii) Name: Asuntol 50 (Bayer) powder/liquid
Composition: 0, 0-dietyl-0-(chloro-4 methyl-7 Coumarinyl) - Phosphorothioate
Application: Spray/dust on the body surface after tying the mouth or putting on a mouth muzzle

(iii) Name: Cream of gamma benzenehexachloride and proflavine b. Vet. C. (Ethicare)
Composition: 0.1% pure gamma isomer BHC and 0.1% proflavin sulphate

	Packing:	200 g Jars
(iv)	Name:	Ectozide dusting powder (Balloun)
	Composition:	Gamma BHC B.P. Vet. 0.6% w/w
	Application:	Dusted on the affected areas of body
	Packing:	50 mg container
(v)	Name:	Ethnoscab cream (Ethnor)
	Composition:	1% Gamma BHC
	Application:	Applied on affected parts after bathing and left for 8-12 hours, then thoroughly washed
	Packing:	20 or 50 g tubes
(vi)	Name:	Herwex (B.B. Bhawan)
	Composition:	*Ageratum coneyzoides, Azadirachta indica, Acoruscalamus, Flcus-religiosa, B. aristate Bhilavia,* campher, cassiatar and viscid base
	Packing:	50 g and 1 kg tin
(vii)	Name:	Himax (Indian herbs)
	Application:	Apply 2-3 times daily
	Packing:	50, 250 and 1,000 g pack
(viii)	Name:	Jadit (Hoechst) liquid and ointment
	Composition:	Buclosamide 10%, Salicylic acid 1%
	Packing:	20 g or 20 ml tube for fungal diseases
(ix)	Name:	Jadit-H (Hoechst)
	Composition:	Buclosamide 10%, salicylic acid 2% and hydrocortisone 0.5%
	Packing:	5 g tube
(x)	Name:	Lorexane cream (ICI)
	Composition:	1% w/w Gamma BHC I.P. and 0.5% w/w chlorhexidine gluconate B.P.
	Packing:	30 g and 50 g tubes
(xi)	Name:	Pestoban (Indian Herbs)
	Composition:	5% Chinomoss, 3% Chin Spara, 2% zinc-oxides, 90% purified tale/use externally
	Packing:	100 ml, and 5 litres

Other medicines which can be used include Durmux cream (Agasthar), Mycostatin ointment (Sarabhai), Priya Dog powder (Priya), Scabalcid (Fair deal), Scabitex (Balloun), Tetmosol solution (ICI), Tinaderm and Quadriderm (Fulford), Grisovin-FP (Glaxo) and Grivin (CFL Pharma), Butox (1 : 250-500) solution (Hoechst) and 1% solution of Kilex carbaryl 50% W.P. Mycoderm dusting powder (FDC), Notix talc, Notix scrub (Pet care).

8. TOPICAL ANTI-INFECTION PREPARATIONS

(a) Anti-infective preparation without steroid

(i)	Name:	Cetrimide Cetavelon concentrate PC (ICI)
	Composition:	Centrimide IP 17.5%, rectified spirit 6.7-8.5% v/v of absolute alcohol
	Packing:	100 ml pack

(ii) Name: Fairgenol (FDC)
Composition: Dichloromethoxylenol BPC 1.88%, terpineol BPC 2%
Packing: 1 litre can

(iii) Name: Furacin vet powder (Eskey Ef)
Composition: 0.2% W/W nitrofurazone B.Vet. C. in soluble base
Packing: 10 g powder in vial

(iv) Name: Furacine-vet cream (Eskey Ef)
Composition: 0.1% W/W nitrofurazone B. Vet. C. in soluble base
Packing: 28 g tube and 500 g jars

(v) Name: Odine - 10 (ACI)
Composition: 10% W/V Povidone iodine USP
Packing: 100 ml bottle also odine - 1 - 450 ml bottle

(vi) Name: Pivipol (Arex)
Composition: 1% Povidone iodine (0.1% available iodine)
Packing: 100 ml and 450 ml bottle

(vii) Name: Savlon (ICI)
Composition: Chlorhexidine gluconate BP 1.5 W/V and cetrimide BP 15% w/v
Packing: 50, 100, 1000 ml bottles also savlon cream, 15, 30 and 450 g tube

(viii) Name: Spectrocin ointment (Sarabhai)
Composition: Neomycin sulphate 2.5 mg; gramicidin 0.25 mg of ointment
Packing: 15 g tube

Other preparations which may be used include Chloromycetin Topical (Parke-Davis), Dettol and Dettol Cream (Richett and Colman), M & B antiseptic cream, Nebasulf powder and cream (Pfizer), Livoderm (Rallis), Mitigal (Bayer), Rericort (Themis chemicals), Bedional gel (Bayer), Gegicain ointment (S.G. Pharma), Phenergan cream (M & B) and mycoderm powder (FDC).

(b) Topical steroid preparations

(i) Name: Betnovate (Glaxco)
Composition: 0.12% betamethsone velerate
Packing: 5 and 15 g cream or ointment

(ii) Name: Betnovate - N (Glaxo)
Composition: 0.12% Betamethasone velerate and 0.5% neomyhcin sulphate
Packing: 5 and 15 g tube

(iii) Name: Betnovate - C (Glaxo)
Composition: 0.12% betamethasone and 3% chinoform
Packing: 5 or 15 g tube

(iv) Name: Cambisone eye/ear ointment (Hoechst)
Composition: 0.25% Prednisolone, 0.16% of neomycin and 0.03 bis (2 methyl-4 aminoguinolyl - 6) carbamide HCL
Packing: 5 g tubes
Application: Apply 2-3 times daily till effective

(v) Name: Drobin - HC (Allenburrys)
Composition: 1.15% dithranol; 1.55% salicylic acid; 5.3% coatar solution and 0.5% hydrocortisone
Packing: 3 g tube

(vi) Name: Terracortil skin ointment (Pfizer)
Composition: 30 mg of OTC HCl and 10 mg of hydrocortisone/g
Packing: 5 g tube
Application: 2-3 times daily to affected part
Other steroid containing ointments include Dexaquin ointment (Cadila), Kennaderma (Sarabhai) and Sofradex (Roussel) cream, Cotarye N cream.

(c) Drugs used in mycotic diseases

See Chapter on mycotic diseases.

(d) Canine soaps/shampoo/talcum powder

(i) Name: Tetmosol soap (ICI)
Composition: 5% tetra ethyulthiuream monosulphide
Packing: 85 g soap

(ii) Name: Monosulfiram "Tetmosol" medicated soap (ICI)
Composition: 5% w/w Monosulfiram BP
Packing: 85 g soap

(iii) Name: Cetrilak soap (Shalaks)
Composition: Cetrimide
Packing: 80 g soap

(iv) Name: Priya dog soap (Priya)
Composition: Neem oil
Packing: 110 g soap

(v) Name: Neem dog soap (Calcutta Chemicals)
Packing: 100 g soap
Others: Canifur shampoo (Cadila), Notix scrub for bath Notix - talc (Pet care) butox for bath (1:250 sol.) (Hoechst) Blaze (Indian herbs) and G.B.H.C. Soap (Shalaks)

9. MEDICINES USED IN POISONINGS

(i) Name: BAL injection (Boots)
Composition: 100 mg of dimercaprol
Packing: 12 ml x 2 ml oily ampoules
Contraindicated in iron and lead poisoning. Used in toxicity as gold, arsenic, bismuth, mercury, thalium, nickel and antimony

(ii) Name: Lipomid (Cipla)
Composition: 500 mg of clofibrate
Indications: Indicated in lipidemias and contra-indicated in pregnancy, renal and hepatic dysfunctions

(iii) Name: Nivpharm (Curewell)

Composition:	Each ml contains Galanthamine hybroflomide and 1.0 mg 2.5 mg, 5 mg and 10 mg of it
Indications:	Indicated in morphine and pathedine poisoning
	Contraindicated in epilepsy, muscular rigidity and cardiac decompensation
Packing:	1 ml ampoules
(iv) Name:	Oricitral (Pharma Research)
Composition:	1.38 g of disodium hydrogen citrate/5 ml
Indication:	To render urine alkaline
Administration:	Given orally
Packing:	10 ml and 500 ml bottles
(v) Name:	Pralidoxine nethane sulphonate (Unichem)
Composition:	1 g pralidoxine methane sulphonate
Indication:	Organo phosphorus poisonings
Administration:	By slow I/V injections
(vi) Name:	Citralka liquid (Parke Davis)
Composition:	1.53 g of disodium, hydrogen citrate per 5 ml
Administration:	Given orally
Packing:	114 ml and 456 ml bottles
	Also see chapter on poisoning for detailed treatment

10. DRUGS AFFECTING CENTRAL NERVOUS SYSTEM

(a) Analgesics and antipyretics

(i) Name:	Esgipyrin-N5 (SG Pharmaceuticals)
Composition:	5 ml contains 750 mg phenyl-butazone; 750 mg analgin; 50 mg lignocaine HCl
Dosage:	1-5 ml by I/M route
Packing:	Available as 5 ml x 2, 10 ml and 50 ml ampoules
(ii) Name:	Feva (ACI)
Composition:	150 ml paracetamol IP and 1% lignocaine HCl/ml
Dosage:	2 ml twice daily by I/M route
Packing:	30 ml R C vialls
(iii) Name:	Novalgin Vet. (Hoechst)
Composition:	500 mg analgin/ml
Dosage:	1-5 ml by I/V or I/M routes
Packing:	Available as 10 ml and 30 ml vials
(iv) Name:	Oxalgin Vet. (Cadila)
Composition:	0.5 g Oxyphenbutazone, 2.25 g analgin
Dosage:	1/4 to 1/2 bolus orally
(v) Name:	Valgin (ACI)
Composition:	0.5 g analgin and 1.0% lignocaine HCl IP
Dosage:	2-3 ml by I/M route
Packing:	30 ml and 100 ml vials

(vi) Name: Valginate injection (TTK)
Composition: 2 mg valethamate bromide NF 0.5 g analgin IP
Dosage: 1-5 ml by I/M route
Packing: 10 ml and 30 ml vials

Some indigenous and other preparations which can be used include Feverdon (Vet's Frama); Herbina (Indian herbs), Pyrosen Powder (Balloun), Pyrovet (Agasthaj), metacin (Themis Pharmaceuticals), Arflur - 50, 100 (FDC), Armol, Ultragesic, Baralgan, Cibalgin Crocin, Ibugesic, Ibugesic Plus, Disprin, Dolopar, Norgesic, Brufen, Ibucon.

(b) Sedatives and tranquilizers

(i) Name: Eskazine (Eskay Ef) - tablets and injection
Composition: 1 mg/ml of trifluoperazine HCl
Administration: Tablets given orally and I/M or I/V injection
Packing: Tablets - 1 mg and 5 mg, Injection 5 ml and 1 ml ampoules

(ii) Name: Soneryl (May and Baker)
Composition: 100 mg/tablet of butobarbitone
Dosage: 1-3 tablets as per BW
Packing: Strips of 10 tablets of 100 mg each

(iii) Name: Largactil (May and Baker) Injections and Tablets
Composition: Chlorpromazine B.Vet. C as 2.5% and 5% solution and 10 mg, 25 mg, 50 mg and 100 mg tablets
Dosage: 5 mg/kg BW daily, orally. 2-3 mg/kg BW daily I/V or I/M
Packing: 10 x 10 mg, 10 x 50 mg, 10 x 25 mg and 10 x 100 mg strips; injection available as 2.5% - 10 x 1 ml or 10 x 2 ml ampoules. 5% - Boxes of 10 x 5 ml ampoules

(iv) Name: Calmpose injection (Ranbaxy) and tablets
Composition: 5 mg/ml of diazepam
Administration: Given I/M or I/V or orally
Dosage: 1-2 tablets BID orally or 1 ml I/M
Packing: Injections - 6 x 2 ml; tablets - 5 mg each

(v) Name: Geriforte (Himalaya)
Dosage: 1-2 tablets twice daily for 15 days then 1 tablet daily
Packing: 100 tablets

(vi) Name: Ketamine HCl
Composition: 100 mg/ml of Ketamine hydrochloride
Dosage: 5 mg/kg BW
Administration: By I/M route
Packing: 5 ml and 10 ml vials

(c) Antiemetics/Anti-nauseants

(i) Name: Eskazine (Eskay Ef)
Composition: 1 mg of trifluperazine hydrochloride
Packing: 5 x 1 ml ampoules

(ii) Name: Stemetil injection (M & B)
Composition: 12.5 mg/ml of prochlorprazine
Administration: Deep I/M injection
Dosage: 1/2-1 ml I/M
Packing: 10 x 1 ml ampoules

(iii) Name: Siquil (Sarabhai)
Composition: 20 mg/ml of triflupromazine HCl
Dosage: 1-2 mg I/V or 2-4 I/M
Packing: 1, 2, 5 ml ampoules

(iv) Name: Avomin (M & B)
Dosage: 1 tablet BID or TID

(v) Name: Emenil (Asira-IDPL)
Composition: Metoclopramid HCl 10 mg
Indications: Pregnancy
Dosage: 4 tablets strips

Other then the above injections tablets available under the same brand names can be used. Cinzan 25 (FDC), Diligan, Domstal, Emidoxyn, Marzine, Perinorm, Reglan and Pregnidoxin.

(d) Anticonvulsants

(i) Name: Gardenal (M & B)
Composition: Phenobarbitone 30 mg, 60 mg and 100 mg/tablet
Dosage: Dog: 30-300 mg orally as per BW
Cat: 15-60 mg daily as per BW
Packing: 10 x 30 mg, 10 x 60 mg and 10 x 100 mg

(ii) Name: Mysolin tablet (ICI)
Composition: 0.25 g/tablets of primidon
Dosage: 250 mg/5 kg BW, twice daily
Packing: 10 and 100 tablets

Others include Epsolin (Cadila) tablets and injections, Eptoin (Boots) Garoin (M and B) tablets Epilan (AFD) Valparin (Torrent) Epilex, Epital, Garoin, Mezapin, Phenytal, Valprol.

11. MEDICINES FOR CARDIOVASCULAR DISORDERS

(a) Vasoconstrictors

(i) Name: DHE injections (Inga Laboratories)
Composition: 1 mg/ml of dihydroergotamine methane sulphonate
Packing: 1 ml ampoules and as 1 mg tablets

(ii) Name: Nor-drin (Unichem)
Composition: 2 mg/ml of laverterinol (adrenaline)
Administration: I/V injection
Packing: 2 ml ampoules

(iii) Name: Adrenaline tartrate injection (Harson)
Composition: 1 : 1,000 of adrenaline tartrate
Administration: I/V of I/M injections
Packing: 1 ml ampoules

(b) Haemostatics

(i) Name: Revici (Kee-Pharma)
Composition: 200 mg of N-butanol and /W% mg of citric acid
Administration: I/M or slow I/V injection
Packing: 5 ml ampoules

(ii) Name: Styptobion (E. Merck)
Composition: 100 mg of Rutin; 20 mg of K6; 100 mg of ascorbic acid per tablet
Packing: 10 x 2 ml box of injections

Others inclulde Unipamba used for all haemorrhagic conditions (Unichem), Bothropase 1 ml amp. (Juggat Pharma): Stadrin CKP 10 tablets strips (Medinex) C.V.P. tab. claudene, Gynal C.V.P., Hemocid, Styptocid etc.

12. GENERAL TONICS

(a) Tonics

(i) Name: Livogen tonic (Glaxo)
Composition: Each 50 ml contains 7.3 g liver extract; 2.0 g yeast and high concentrations of Vitamin B_1 B_6 and B_{12}
Dosage: 5 ml daily orally
Packing: 450 ml bottles

(ii) Name: Livogen injections (Glaxo)
Composition: 25 mg B_1; 5 mg panthenol; 1.37 mg riboflavin; 100 mg nicotinamide; 5 mg B_6; 30 microgram cyanocobalamine; 15 mg Choline Chloride, 8 g liver extract equivalent to 2 mcg B_{12} and 1% w/v lignocaine HCl
Dosage: 1-2 ml by deep I/M or S/C
Packing: 10 ml vials

(iii) Name: Macrabin Injection (Glaxo)
Composition: 1000 mcg/ml of B_{12}
Dosage: 1-2 ml daily by I/M injection
Packing: 5 ml ampoules

(iv) Name: Vibelan injection (Glaxo)
Composition: 2.5 mg thiamine; 4.1 mg riboflavin; 100 mg nicotinomide; 5 mg d-panthenol; 2.5 mg B_6 and 5 mg lignocaine HCl/ml
Dosage: 3-5 ml daily by deep I/M injection
Packing: 30 ml vials

(v) Name: Neuroxin - 12 (Cadila)
Composition: 30 mg thiamine; 13.75 mg ribolavin and 500 mcg of vit B_{12}/ml
Dosage: 2-3 ml/day by I/M injections

Packing: 10 ml vials

Other preparations include Beckom L (Wockhardt), Conciplex (Concept) Belamyl injection (Sarabhai) Liverjet, Liver-B (ACI, vitcofol injections (FDC), Neuropick, ABDEC drops, aneudox 12 inj, Becosules, Becozyme Forte, Beta vite forte, Betonin, Bebidox, Cobadex fort, Multivitaplex forte, Neurobion, Stress cap, Winstress, toniazol, Mecal vit

(b) Parenteral vitamins and minerals

(i) Name: Berin (Glaxo)
Composition: 100 mg thiamine
Dosage: 1 ml daily for 3 days by I/M route
Packing: 10 ml pack

(ii) Name: Calboral (May and Baker)
Composition: 83 parts calcium gluconate and 17 parts boric accid as 25% solution
Dosage: 2-5 ml by S/C or I/V or both routes
Packing: Bottles of 450 ml

(iii) Name: Beekom-L (Wockhardt)
Composition: Thiamine I.P. = 25 mg; riboflavin phosphate BPC = 1.5 mg; Vit. B6 I.P. = 5.0 mg; Cyanocobalamine 50 mcg; niacinamide = 50.0 mg; Choline chloride = 25.0 mg; phenol IP = 0.5% ml
Dosage: 2-3 ml by I/M or S/C route and available as 30 ml vials

(iv) Name: Calcium magnesium borogluconate (Sarabhai)
Composition: 100 ml contains calcium gluconate monohydrate 17.98 g; dextrose - 16.75 g; magnesium hypophosphite 0.621 g; boric acid 1.8 g
Dosage: 2-5 ml slowly by I/V route
Packing: Bottle of 450 ml

(v) Name: Calcium borogluconate injection B.Vet. C. (Wockhardt)
Composition: 400 ml contains 25% calcium borogloconate w/v; 0.1% chlorocresol BP
Dosage: 2-5 ml given by slow I/V
Packing: Bottle of 450 ml

(vi) Name: Calcium (Sandoz) + Vit C 500 mg (Sandoz)
Composition: 1 ml contains 137.5 mg calcium gluconogalacto gluconate + Vit C 50 mg
Administration: By slow I/V or I/M route
Packing: 5 ml and 10 ml ampoules

(vii) Name: Calci - ostelin B_{12} (Glaxo)
Composition: 1 ml contains 137.5 mg of calcium gluconolactobinate; 500 IU Vit D_3 and 50 mcg Vit B_{12}
Dosage: 0.5-1 ml daily by I/M route
Packing: RC vial of 15 ml

(viii) Name: Macrabin (Glaxo) - 1,000
Composition: 1 ml contains 1,000 mcg of vit B_{12}
Dosage: 1 ml for 3 day by I/M route
Packing: 5 ml vials

(ix) Name: Prepalin forte (Glaxo)
Composition: 2 ml contains 6,00,000 IU of Vit. A
Dosage: 2 ml on alternate days for 3 times
Packing: 6 x 2 ml ampoules

(x) Name: Neurobion (E. Merck) injection
Composition: 1 ml contains 33 mg thiamine; B_6-33 mg and 333 mcg vit B_{12}
Dosage: 1-3 ml on alternate days for 4-5 times
Packing: 10 ml x 3 ml packs

(xi) Name: Kemicrocal (ACI)
Composition: Each ml contains Colloidal calcium 0.5 mg; calceferol (D_3)-5,000 IV and 50 mcg Vit. B_{12}
Dosage: 1-2 ml given by I/M route only
Packing: 10 ml vials

(xii) Name: Vibelon injection (Glaxo)
Composition: 1 ml contains 25 mg vit. B_1; Vit B_6-2.5 mg; 4.1 mg vit B_2; nicotinamide 100 mg; D-panthenol andlignocaine - 5 mg
Dosage: 1-3 ml daily by deep I/M route
Packing: 30 ml RC vials

(xiii) Name: Tonophosphan (Hoechst)
Composition: Sodium salt of 4-dimethyllamino-2
Dosage: 1-3 ml by I/M or I/V or S/C route
Packing: 5 x 5 ml pack and 30 ml RC vials

(c) Iron preparation

(i) Name: Imferon (Rallis)
Composition: Iron dextran injection equal to 50 mg of elemental iron per ml
Packing: Available as 10 ml ampoule for I/V use and 10 ml multidose vial for I/M use

(ii) Name: Rubraplex (Sarabhai)
Composition: 5 ml contains 38 mg elemental iron; 1 mg B_1; 1 mg B_2; 5 mg niacinamide; B_{12} 4 mcg; B_6 0.5 mg; d-panthenol 1.5 mg and alcohol-12%
Packing: Available as 10 ml ampoule for I/V use and 10 ml multidose vial for I/M use

(iii) Name: Vitcofol (FDC) injection and also available vitcofoliron syrup
Composition: 500 mcg cyanocobalamine; 0.2 g miacinamide and 15 mg ollic acid per ml
Administration: Given by I/M route
Packing: 5 ml and 10 ml vials

(iv) Name: Folinate B_{12} liquid (Alembic)
Composition: 10 ml contains 15 mcg B_{12}; 1.0 mg folic acid and 250 mg ferrous fumerate
Packing: Bottles of 100 ml, 250 ml and 450 ml

Other preparations include Hematic (Ethicare) Uniferon (Unichem) Ferroglobin syrup (chemidoc Enterprises) Shark Ferrol, Fefol (SK&F), ferrocalcium (Spencers) Raricap (Ethnor).

(d) Oral Feed Supplements

(i) Name: Beplex liquid (Anglofrench)
Composition: 5 ml contains 3.75 mg vit B_1; 1.25 mg vit B_2; 0.62 mg pyridoxine HCl; 1.25 mg D-panthenol, 37.50 mg niacinamide; 6.25 mcg vit B_{12}; and 5.00 mg DL methionine
Dosage: 5 ml daily orally
Packing: 100 ml bottles

(ii) Name: Bony - Vet (Arex)
Composition: 4.65 mg colloidal calcium; 7 mg Calcium gluconate; 3,000 IU vit. A; 1,000 IU vit D_3; and 5 mcg vit B_{12}
Dosage: 10-15 mll twice daily in milk orally
Packing: 100 ml and 450 ml bottles

(iii) Name: Ciplex - C (Cadila)
Composition: 5 ml contains vit. B_1-3.75 mg' nicotinamide 37.5 mg; vit B_6-nicotinamide 37.5 mg; vit B_6-0.62 mg; D-panthenol-1.25 mg; vit B_{12}-6.25 mcg vit B_2-1.25 mg, and vit C - 5 mg
Dosage: @ 2.5-6 ml daily
Packing: 500 ml and 5 litre jar

(iv) Name: Cal-D-plus (Cadila)
Composition: 10 ml contains 0.833 g calcium gluconate; vit D_3 - 1,200 IU vit B_{12} - 16.7 mcg; stomach extract - 3.3 mg; available iron - 167 mg
Dosage: 10 mll twice daily
Packing: 100 ml and 1,000 ml

(v) Name: Incremin syrup (Lederle) vitamin B_1, B_6, B_{12}, lyusine with iron tonic, appetite stimulant 1 TSF BID
Packing: 175 ml

Other preparation available include Hyclvit (Akelvi), Kecal (ACI), Keliplex (Keepharma) (ACI), Kentab (Alved), Conciplex (Concept), Neocalcium (Vesper), Ostocalcium B_{12} (Glaxo), Stressnil (Vasper), Toconex (Blue cross) and Vitatone (Cadila). Liv - 52 drops, syrup, powder and tablets (Himalaya), vitazyme, codliver oil or shark liver oil, hepatoglobin, haem up gems, Livò-vet Syurup and vi-Syne ral Syrup, Soyal powder (FDC) Pronutrin (CFL) Vitbin complex (FDC) Vitapet, Nutri liv Calcinol syrup F, Osopan.

(e) Dog biscuits/meals

(i) Name: Royal Dog discuits (Royal)
Packing: 350 g and 700 g packs

(ii) Name: Glenand dog biscuits (Glenand)
Packing: 400 g, 1,000 g and 5,000 g packs

(iii) Name: Priya dog biscuits (Priya)
Packing: 275 g packs
Others: Threptin (Raptakas), Nutribix, Nutricoat, Nutripet-pet meal (Pet care)

13. ANAESTHETIC AND PREMEDICATION AGENTS

Please see Chapter 12

(i) Name: Gesicain Vet solution (SG -Pharma)
Composition: Lignocaine HCl as local infiltration agent
Dosage: 1-2 ml for local infiltration
Packing: 1%, 2% and 2% with adrenaline 30 ml vials.

(ii) Name: Intraval sodium (M & B)
Composition: Thiopentone B vet C injection
Dosage: 30 mg/kg BW by I/V route
Packing: 25 x 0.5 g ampoules and 25 x 1 gm ampoules

(iii) Name: Ketamine hydrochloride
Composition: 100 mg/ml of Ketamine HCl
Dosage: 25 mg/kg BW, in cats only by I/M route
Packing: 5 ml, 10 ml vials

(iv) Name: Novocain Vet (Hoechst)
Composition: Procaine HCl
Dosage: 2-3 ml for conduction anaesthesia
Packing: 30 ml RC vial

(v) Name: Pethidine injection (Dey's)
Composition: 50 mg and 100 mg pethidine HCl
Administration: I/M or I/V or orally or S/C route
Dosage: Pack 100 x 1 ml ampoules (50 mg), 100 x 2 ml (100 mg) ampoules

(vi) Name: Siquil (Sarabhai)
Composition: Each ml contains triflupromazine HCl 20 mg
Dosage: Dog - 1-2 mg/kg BW, I/V and 2-4 mg by I/M route
Packing: 5 ml

(vii) Name: Atropine sulphate (BAIF)
Dosage: 30-100 mcg/kg BW, S/C, I/M or I/V
Packing: 10 ml viall

(viii) Name: Xylocain injection, topical jelly ointment (Astra-TDL)
Others: Ketnin - 50 (Thenis Chemicals), Glycopyrrotate (Khandelwal), Thiopent (Trikaa), Dropidol, Xylocaine etc. (Astra-IDL)

14. INFUSION AND PLASMA EXTENDERS (FLUID THERAPY)

Please see chapter 12

(i) Dextrose injection - prepared by various firms
2.5% 500 ml (MCGaw)
5% 540 ml (Bayer and Mount Mettur)
10% 540 ml (Mount Metter and Dey's)
20% 540 ml (Mount Mettur etc.)

(ii) Name: Dextran (Rallis)
Composition: 6% Dextran in NSS or 5% dextrose

Packing: 540 ml bottle

(iii) Dextrose with sodium chloride prepared by different companies

(iv) Name: Haemaceel (Hoechst) polymer from gelatin (Equivalent to 0.63 g N); 3.5 g electrolytes and water

Packing: 500 ml polypack

(v) Mannitol injection (Mcgaw and Mount Mettur)

(vi) Name: Ringer lactate injection (Mount Mettur and McGaw)

Composition: 0.31 g sodium lactate; 0.6 gm sodium chloride; pot chloride USP - 30 mg; Cal Chloride USP - 20 mg per 100 ml

Packing: 540 ml and 500 ml respectively

Others: Others are oral electrolytes, Dextral (Ethicare), Electral (FDC), Emlyte (M.M.Labs), Medilyts (Medicare), Sodium chloride soln. 0.45%, 0.9%, 5%, 20%, Unisodilact (Unichem), Wintrolipos 10%, (Win-Medicare)

15. HORMONES

(i) Name: Chorulon (Inter care international)

Composition: 1500 IU/ml of chorionic Gonadotrophin B. Vet C

Administration: Injected I/M

Dosage: 1,500 IU vial with 5 ml solvent. Bitches - 100-500 IU daily or alternate day. Male same dose twice weekly.

Female: Promotes ovulation, Formation of Corpus leuteum, maintenance of pregnancy.

Male: Promotes testosteron production

(ii) Name: Follugon (Intercare International)

Composition: 1,000 IU serum gonadotrophin B. Vet C. Dosage I/M, S/C twice weekly, 50-200 IU/weeks.

Female: Stimulate growth and ovulation ovary

Male: Stimulate testis growth

Packing: 1,000 IU with 5 ml diluent in a pack of 5 + 5 ml

(iii) Name: Secrodyl injection (Allenburys)

Composition: 5 mg of megestrol acetate and 0.03 mg ethynylesterdiol per ml

Administration: By I/M injection

Packing: 1 ml ampoules; also tablets\

For secondary amenorrhoea of short duration

(iv) Name: Testanon - 25 (Organon)

Composition: 25 mg/ml Testosteron propionate

Administration: I/M

Packing: 3 x 1 ml ampoules; 50 x 1 ml ampoules

For delayed puberty, eunuchism infertility in male

(v) Name: Proluton Depot (German Remedies)

Composition: Hydroxy progesterone - 125 mg, 250 mg/ml and 540 mg/2 ml

Packing:	125 mg; 10 × 1 ml, 250 mg; 10 × 1 ml, 250 mg; 10 × 1 ml; 540 mg; 5 ml, 2 ml For recurrent and threatened abortion
(vi) Name:	Aquaviron injection (Nicholes)
Composition:	Free testosterone 25 mg/ml
Indications:	Male - hypogonadism, delayed puberty, premature senility, organic impotence
Packing:	By I/M 1 ml ampoules
(vii) Name:	Duphaston (Duphar)
Composition:	Dydrogesterone, 5 mg
Indications:	Dysmenorrhoea, threatened abortion, endometritis, infertility, premenstual syndroms
Packing:	10 tablets
(viii) Name:	Orgametril (Organon)
Composition:	Lynestrenol, 5 mg
Indications:	Dysfunctional uterine bleeding, postponement of menstruation, endometritis
Packing:	10 tablets
(ix) Name:	Osterone (Lyka)
Composition:	Progesterone 25 mg, oestradial benzoate, 2.5 mg/ml
Indications:	Amenorrhoea, habitual and threatened abortion
Packing:	1 ml ampoules
(x) Name:	Testophos (Mac)
Composition:	Methyl testosterone 0.1 mg, vit E 0.75 mg, phoselits, 100 mg, yohimbine HCl 1 mg, Ext. colae, 50 mg, muriae pumae, 5 mg
Indications:	To stimulates, improve the sexual desire and performance. To over come weakness and fatigue in male
Packing:	40 draques
Others:	Restore, Sustanon - 100, Miscogen, Lyneral, Ledogal, Regestone etc.

16. ANTISEPTIC MOUTH WASH

(i) Name:	Hexidine mouth ringe (Indo)
Composition:	Chlorhexidine gluconate BP 0.2% W/V diluted in water in the ratio of 1 : 2 parts and used as mouth wash
Packing:	100 ml
(ii) Name:	Listerine mouth wash (Warner)
Composition:	Methyl salicylate and thymol 0.06% each, benzoic acid 0.03%, euclyptol N.F. 0.09%, menthol 0.04%, boric acid 2.35% and alcohol 25-27% V/V
Use:	For mouth wash as antiseptic
Packing:	85 ml, 200 ml, and 400 ml
(iii) Name:	Odine 1 and 10 (ACI)
Composition:	1 and 10% W/V povine iodine USP
Use:	Mouth wash for all dental problems
Packing:	10% - 100 mll and for 1% 450 ml bottle

(iv) Name: G-32 (Alarsin)
Composition: Gingivitis, glossitis, and stomatitis
Dosage: 2 tablets/day
Administration: Apply in the whole oral cavity for 3-5 days

(v) Name: Stolin gum astringent (Group Pharmaceuticals)
Composition: Povidone iodine 1%; tannic acid 2%; zinc phenosulphonate 0.8%; thymol 0.5%; methnol 0.5%; glycerine Q.S.
Uses: Gingivitis, bleeding and painful gums to prevent infecction of gum, pyrrhoea
Application: To be gently massaged on affected area of gum
Others: Tantum, Vidone

17. ANTIALLERGIC DRUGS

(i) Name: Avil (Hoechst)
Composition: Pheniramine maleate
Uses: For allergy, dermatitis, urticaria
Dosage: 0.5 to 1.0 ml I/M or I/V
Packing: 10 ml vials

(ii) Name: Phenergan (M & B)
Composition: Promethazine HCl
Uses: For antihistaminic therapy
Dosage: 0.5-10 ml I/M
Packing: 2 x 5 ml ampoules

(iii) Name: Foristal (Ciba Geigy)
Composition: Dimethindene maleate 1 mg
Indications: Allergic dermatitis, pruritis and ocular allergic conditions
Dosage: 1 tablet BID orally
Packing: Strip of 10 tablets

(iv) Name: Foristal lintabs (Ciba-Geigy)
Composition: Dimethindene maleate 2.5 mg
Packing: Strip of 10 tablets

(v) Name: Kenamine (Sarabhai)
Composition: Triamcinolon 1.25 mg; carbinoxamine maleate 2 mg
Uses: Used in allergic condition, angioneurotic oedema and drug reactions
Dosage: 1 tablet BID orally
Packing: Strip of 10 tablets

(vi) Name: Perideca (MSD)
Composition: Dexamethasone 0.25 mg; Cyprohepatadine HCl 4 mg
Indications: Allergic disorders
Dosage: 1 tablet BID
Packing: Strip of 10 tablets

(vii) Name: Vegecort (Himalaya)
Indications: Allergic dermatitis, itching, exudate, inflammation, loss of hair urticaria and mange

	Dosage:	1 tablet 3-4 times a day
	Packing:	Strip of 100 tablets
(viii)	Name:	Anthisan (M & B)
	Composition:	5% solution of mepyramine maleate
	Indications:	Antihistaminic, anaphylactic shock, allergic skin conditions
	Dosage:	1-5 ml I/M (2.5% solution) at 8-12 hour intervals for maximum 3 days
	Packing:	2 x 10 ml ampoules
(ix)	Name:	Chloril (TTK)
	Composition:	Chlorphenaramine maleate IP 10 mg
	Indications:	Anaphylactic shock, pruritis, urticaria, dermatitis, eczema and antihistaminic
	Dosage:	5-10 mg I/M
	Packing:	10 ml vials
	Others:	Actidil, Actelong, Cynbi, Dilosyn, epasulfol-AA, Incidal, Mebryl etc.

18. CORTICOSTERIOD AND RELATED DRUGS

(Avoided in diabetes melitus, T.B., hypertension, peptic ulcers), Ranal dysfunction) glaucoma

(i)	Name:	Betnesol (Glaxo)
	Composition:	4 mg betamethasone sodium phosphate/ml
	Uses:	Anaphylaxis, toxaemia
	Dosage:	1 ml daily for 3 days I/M or I/V
	Packing:	1 ml ampoules
(ii)	Name:	Betacortril tablet (Pfizer)
	Composition:	Betamethasone 0.5 mg
	Indications:	Allergic and autoimmune disorders
	Packing:	10 tablets
(iii)	Name:	Betacortril injection (Pfizer)
	Composition:	4 mg betamethasone sodium phosphate 1 ml
	Indications:	Immune disorders, acute and severe allergic inflammatory conditions
	Packing:	2 ml ampoules
(iv)	Name:	Cambison (Hoechst)
	Composition:	Each g contains prednisolone I.P. 5 g; neomycin HCl 1.6 mg; surfen 3.0 mg
	Indications:	Inflammatory reactions, pruritis, external Otitis and acute and subacute dermatitis
	applications:	Applied 1-3 times daily locally
	Packing:	5 g tube
(v)	Name:	Dexona (Cadila)
	Composition:	4 mg dexamethasone phosphate
	Indications:	Inflammation of respiratory, urogenital tract, arthritis, shock, pregnancy, toxaemia, induction of parturition and local inflammation
	Dosage:	2-4 mg daily I/M
(vi)	Name:	Hostacortin - H (Hoechst)
	Composition:	10 mg prednisolone/ml
	Indications:	Allergic and inflammatory conditions, rheumatoid arthritis

Dosage: 10-30 mg I/M
Packing: 10 ml vials

(vii) Name: Kena cort (Sarabhai)
Composition: Triamcinolone 1 mg, 4 mg and 8 mg
Indications: Allergic conditions and rheumatoid arthritis
Packing: Strip of 10 tablet of 1 and 4 mg and strip of 6 tablets for 8 mg; also available in injection of 10 mg triancinolone/ml

(viii) Name: Pedso (ACI)
Composition: Each ml contains prednisolone IP 10 mg; benzyl alcohol IP 1% W/V
Indications: All allergic and inflammatory conditions and insect bites also
Dosage: 10-30 mg daily I/M for 3-4 days

(ix) Name: Vetalog (Sarabhai)
Composition: 6 mg triamcinolone acetonide/ml
Indications: Allergic dermatitis, arthritis, tendosynovitis
Dosage: 0.1 to 0.2 mg/kg BW, I/M or S/C
Packing: 5 ml vials

(x) Name: Curadex (Concept)
Composition: Each ml contains dexamethasone, 4 mg; sodium phosphate
Indications: Arthritis, pregnancy toxaemia, induction of parturition synovitis, eczema, shock, all allergic and inflammatory conditions
Dosage: 0.5-2 mg I/M or I/V daily
Packing: 2 and 5 ml vials

C. STANDARD DRUGS IN CANINE PRACTICE: DOSAGE AND ROUTE OF ADMINISTRATION

Drug	*Dose (per kg body weight)*	*Route of administration*	*Frequency*
1	*2*	*3*	*4*
Acetaminophen	7-12 mg	Oral	Repeat after 12 hours
Acetazolamide	6-9 mg	Oral	Repeat after 8 hours
ACTH	2 unit	IM	Sid
Albendazole	20-30 mg	Oral	Repeat after 12 hours
Aluminium hydroxide	20-40 mg	Oral	BID
Aminophylline	10 mg	Oral	Repeat after 12 hours
Ammonium chloride	200 mg	Oral	Repeat after 8 hours
Amoxicillin	11 mg	Oral	Repeat after 12 hours
Amphotericin B	0.15-0.5 mg	IV	SID on alternate days
Ampicillin	10-12 mg	Oral	Repeat after 6 hours
	5-10 mg	IV, IM	Repeat after 6 hours
Amproliuim	110-220 mg	In feed	SID
Apomorphine	0.08 mg	IM, SC	Once

(Contd.)

Drug	*Dose (per kg body weight)*	*Route of administration*	*Frequency*
1	*2*	*3*	*4*
Aprindine	1-2 mg	Oral	Repeat after 8 hours
	100 microgram/kg/min	IV	Continuous infusion
Arecoline acetarsal	5 mg	Oral	Once
Aspirin	10 mg	Oral	Repeat after 12 hours
Atropine	0.04 mg	IV, SC	Repeat after 12 hours
Betamethasone	0.15 mg	IM	Once
Bismuth subsalicylate	15-30 ml	Oral	Repeat after 6 hours
Bunamidine	25-50 mg	Oral	Once
Butamisole	2.4 mg	SC	Once
Buterphanol	0.05-0.1 mg	SC	Repeat after 8 hours
Calcitonin	4-8 IU	IM	Repeat after 12 hours
Calcium carbonate	100 mg	Oral	SID
Calcium EDTA	25 mg	IV	Repeat after 6 hours
Calcium gluconate	50-150 mg	IV slowly	According to circumstances
Calcium lactate	0.5-2.0 gm	In feed	SID
Captopril	1-2 mg	Oral	Repeat after 8 hours
Carbenicillin	15-50 mg	IV	Repeat after 6 hours
Castor oil	5-25 ml	Oral	According to circumstances
Cefamandole	25 mg	IM, IV	Repeat after 6 hours
Cefazoline	20-25 mg	IM, IV	Repeat 4-6 hours
Cephradine	20 mg	Oral	Repeat after 6 hours
	10 mg	IM, IV	Repeat after 6 hours
Cephadroxial	10 mg	Oral	Repeat after 12 hours
Cephalexin	10-30 mg	Oral	Repeat after 8 hours
Cephalothin	25-35 mg	IV, IM, SC	Repeat after 6-8 hours
Chloramphenicol	28-50 mg	Oral, IM, IV	Repeat after 8 hours
Chlorothiazide	28-40 mg	Oral	Repeat after 12 hours
Chlorpheniramine	1 mg	Oral	Repeat after 12 hours
Chlorpromazine	3 mg	Oral	Repeat after 12 hours
	0.5 mg	IV or IM	Repeat after 12 hours
Chlorpropamide	10-40 mg	Oral	SID
Cimetidine	10 mg	Oral	Repeat after 8 hours
	5 mg	IV	Repeat after 12 hours
Clindamycin palmitate	3 mg	Oral	Repeat after 6 hours
Clindamycin phosphate	5 mg	IV, IM	Repeat after 8 hours
Cloxacillin	10 mg	Oral, IM	Repeat after 6 hours
Codeine	2 mg	Oral	Repeat after 6 hours
Colistin	10 mg	Oral	Repeat after 6 hours
Colistimethate	1-2 mg	IM, IV	Repeat after 12 hours
Danthron	35 mg	Oral	As per requirement
Dantrolene	1-5 mg	Oral	Repeat after 8 hours
Dapsone	1 mg	Oral	Repeat after 12 hours
Dasmopressin acetate	1 drop	Intranasally or conjunctival sac	Repeat after 8 hours

(Contd.)

Drug	*Dose (per kg body weight)*	*Route of administration*	*Frequency*
1	*2*	*3*	*4*
Dexamethasone	0.25 mg	IV, IM	Once
Dextroamphetamine	0.2-1.3 mg	Oral	SID
Dextromethorphan	1-2 mg	Oral	Repeat after 6 hours
Diazepam (anticonvulsant)	1 mg	IV	As per requirement
Diazepam (anxiolyutic)	0.25 mg	Oral	Repeat after 8 hours
Diazoxide	10 mg	Oral	Repeat after 12 hours
Dichlorophen	300 mg	Oral	Once
Dichlorphenamide	2-5 mg	Oral	Repeat after 8 hours
Dichlorvos	11 mg	Oral	Once
Dicloxacillin	10-25 mg	Oral, IM	Repeat after 8 hours
Diethylcarbamazine (Prevent ascarids)	10 mg	Oral	SID
Diethylcarbamazine (Tret. ascardis and Filariasis)	50-100 mg	Oral	In 3 divided doses for 30-45 days
Diethyl stilbestrol	0.5 mg	IM	Once
	0.1-1.0 mg total	Oral	SID
Digoxin	0.22 mg	Oral, tabs	Repeat after 12 hours
	0.18 mg	Oral	Repeat after 12 hours
Dimenhydrinate	8 mg	Oral	Repeat after 8 hours
Dimercaprol	6 mg	IM	Repeat after 8 hours
Diphenhydramine	4 mg	Oral	Repeat after 8 hours
Diphenidol	1 mg	IM, IV	Repeat after 8 hours
Diphenoxylate	0.063 mg	Oral	Repeat after 8 hours
Diphenylthiocarbazone	70 mg	PO	Repeat after 8 hours
Dipyrone	25 mg	IM	Repeat after 8 hours
Disophenol	0.22 ml	SC	Once
Disopyramide	7-30 mg	Oral	Repeat after 2 hours
Dithiazanine iodide	22 mg	Oral	SID for 7 days
Dopamine	10 microgram/min.	IV	Continuous infusion
Doxapram	2-5 mg	IV	Once
Doxycycline	5 mg	Oral	Repeat after 12 hours
Ephedrine	2-4 mg	Oral	Repeat after 8 hours
Epinephrine	10 microgram	IM, IV	As per requirement
Erythromycin	10-20 mg	Oral	SID for 3 days
Flucytosine	50 mg	Oral	SID for 3 days
Flucytosine	25-38 mg	Oral	Repeat after 6 hours
Fludrocortisone	0.2-1.0 mg total	Oral	Repeat after 6 hours
Flumethasone	0.05-0.25 mg total	Oral, IV, IM	SID
FSH	0.75 mg	IM	SID
Framycetin	20 mg	Oral	Repeat after 6 hours
Furosemide	2-4 mg	Oral	Repeat after 8 hours
	2-8 mg	IV	Repeat after 6 hours
Gentamycin	5 mg	IV, IM	Repeat after 12 hours

(Contd.)

Drug	Dose (per kg body weight)	Route of administration	Frequency
1	2	3	4
Glibenclamide	0.2 mg	Oral	SID
Glipizide	0.25-0.5 mg	Oral	Repeat after 12 hours
Glucagon	0.03 mg	IV	As per requirement
Glycerin	1-1.5 mg	Oral	Repeat after 6 hours
Glycobiarsol	220 mg	Oral	SID
Glycopyrrolate	0.01 mg	Oral	SID
Gonadotrophin-releasing hormone	60-200 microgram total dose	IM	Once
Griseofulvin	60-100 mg	Oral	SID
Growth hormone	5-10 unit	IM	Every other day, 5-15 treat ments
Haloperidol	0.02 mg	IM	Repeat after 12 hours
Heparin	500 unit	SC, IV	Repeat after 8 hours
Human chorionic gonadotropin	100-200 IU	IM	SID
Hydralazine	1 mg	Oral	Repeat after 12 hours
Hydrochlorothiazide	2-4 mg	Oral	Repeat after 12 hours
Hydrocortisone	5 mg	Oral, IM, IV	Repeat after 12 hours
Imidocarb dipropionate	5 mg	SC	Once
Insulin (protamine zinc)	1 unit	SC	SID
Insulin (regular)	o.25 mg	IM	As per requirement
Isoproterenol	0.01 mg	IV	As per requirement
Isosorbide dinitrate	1 mg	Oral	Repeat after 6 hours
Kanamycin	5-15 mg	IM, IV, SC	Repeat after 6-8 hours
Kaolin-pectin	1-2 ml	Oral	Repeat after 6 hours
Levamisole	11 mg	Oral	SID for 6-12 days
Lidocaine	4 mg	IV	Initial bolus continuopus
	50 microgam/min	IV	infusion
Lidocaine	6 mg	IM	Repeat after 1 hours
Lincomycin	15-25 mg	Oral	Repeat after 12 hours
	10 mg	IV, IM	Repeat after 12 hours
Lithium citrate	7 mg	Oral	Repeat after 8 hours
Magnesium hydroxide	5-30 ml	Oral	As per requirement
Magnesium sulfate	10-25 g	Oral	As per requirement
Mebendazole	20 mg	Oral	SID for 3 days
Medroxyprogesterone	10 mg	IM, SC	Once
Magestrol acetate	1-2 mg	Oral	SID
Meperidine	10 mg	IM	As per requirement
Metaproterenol	0.5 mg	Oral	Repeat after 6 hours
Metaraminol	100 microgm	IV, IM	As per requirement
Methicillin	20 mg	IV, IM	Repeat after 6 hours
Methionine	0.2-1.0 g	Oral	Repeat after 8 hours
Methylprednisolone	2-4 mg	Oral	SID

(Contd.)

Drug	Dose (per kg body weight)	Route of administration	Frequency
1	2	3	4
Methylprednisolone	1 mg	Oral, IM	SID
Metac lopramide	0.5 mg	Oral	Repeat after 6 hours
Metronidazole	60 mg	Oral	SID
Mibolerone	3 microgm	Oral	SID
Miconazole	10 mg	IV	Repeat after 8 hours
Milrinone	1 mg	Oral	Repeat after 8 hours
Minocycline	5 mg	Oral	Repeat after 12 hours
Mitotane (Lysodren)	50 mg	Oral	SID
Morphine	0.25 mg	IM	Repeat after 5 hours
Nafcillin	25 mg	Oral, IV, IM	Repeat after 6 hours
Nalidixic acid	3 mg	Oral	Repeat after 6 hours
Nalorphine	1 mg	IV	As per requirement
Naloxone	40 microgram	IV	As per requirement
Nandrolone decanoate	1-1.5 mg	IM	Weekly
Neomycine	20 mg	Oral	Repeat after 6 hours
Neostigmine	0.02 mg	IM	Repeat after 8 hours
Niclosamide	71.4 mg	Oral	Once
Nitrofurantoin	4 mg	Oral	Repeat after 8 hours
	3 mg	IM	Repeat after 8 hours
Nitroprusside sodium	1-5 microgram/min	IV	Continuous Infusion
Niscapine	0.5-1.0 mg	Oral	Repeat after 8 hours
Nystatin	100,000 U	Oral	Repeat after 6 hours
Polymixin B	2 mg (20,000 U)	IM	Repeat after 12 hours
Potassium chloride	5-15 mEq	Oral	SID
Pralidoxine	10-50 mg	IM, IV	As per requirement
Prednisolone	1 mg	Oral, IM	SID
Prednisone	0.5 mg	Oral	SID
Primidone	11-22 mg	Oral	Repeat after 8 hours
Procainamide	8-10 mg	IM	Repeat after 4 hours
Prochlorperazine	0.13 mg	IM	Repeat after 6 hours
Promazine	3-4 mg	IM, IV	SID
Promethazine	2 mg	Oral	SID
Propantheline	0.5-1 rng	Oral	Repeat after 8 hours
Proranolol	5-40 mg	Oral	Repeat after 6 hours
	0.5-1.5 mg	Oral	SID
Prostaglandin F2 tromethamine	250 microgm	IV slowly	SID
Psyllium	3-10 g	In feed	SID
Pyrantel	5 mg	Oral	Once
Pyrimethamine	0.5-1.0 mg	Oral	SID
Oxacillin	10-15 mg	Oral, IV, IM	Repeat after 6 hours
Oxymorphone	0.03-0.05 mg	IM	Repeat after 6 hours
Oxytocin	5-10 U	IV, IM	15-30 min

(Contd.)

Drug	*Dose (per kg body weight)*	*Route of administration*	*Frequency*
1	*2*	*3*	*4*
Paregoric	3-15 ml	Oral	Repeat after 6 hours
Penicillamine	10-15 mg	Oral	Repeat after 12 hours
Penicillin G (Na or K)	20,00-40,000 U	IV, IM, SC	Repeat after 4 hours
Penicilline G (Procaine)	20,00 U	IM	Repeat after 12 hours
Pentobarbital (Sedation)	2-4 mg	Oral	Repeat after 6 hours
Petrolatum, liquid	5-30 ml	Oral	As per requirement
Phenobarbital (anticon-vulsant)	2 mg/kg	Oral	Repeat after 12 hours
Phenobarbital (sedation)	2 mg	Oral	Repeat after 6-12 hours
Phenylbutazone	20 mg	Oral	Repeat after 8 hours
Phenylephrine	0.15	IV	As per requirement
Phenylpropanolamine	3 mg	Oral	Repeat after 12 hours
Phenytoin	30 mg	Oral	Repeat after 8 hours
	10 mg	IV	Repeat after 8 hours
Phthalofyne	180 mg	Oral	Once
Piperazine	20-30 mg	Oral	Once
Pitressin	1-2 U	SC	Repeat after 4-6 hours
Pitressin sannate	1-2 U	SC, IM	Repeat after 36-72 hours
Quinacrine	50-100 mg total	Oral	Repeat after 12 hours
Quinidine	6-20 mg	Oral	Repeat after 8 hours
Sodium EDTA	25-75 mg	IV	Continuous infusion
Spectinomycin	5-10 mg	IM	Repeat after 12 hours
Spironolactone	2-4 mg	Oral	SID
Streptomycin	10 mg	IM, SC	Repeat after 6 hours
Streptpzotocin	14.5 mg	IV	SID infusion
Sulfadiazine	110 mg	Oral	Repeat after 12 hours
Sulfadiazine-trime thoprim	30 mg	Oral	Repeat after 12 hours
Sulfadimethoxine	25 mg	Oral, IV, IM	SID
Sulfamethizole	50 mg	Oral	Repeat after 8 hours
Sulfasalazine	15 mg	Oral	Repeat after 6 hours
Sulfisoxazole	50 mg	Oral	Repeat after 8 hours
Styrypyridium-diethyl-carbamazine	5.5 mg	Oral	Once
Terbutaline	10 microgm	SC	Repeat after 4 hours
	30 microgm	Oral	Repeat after 8 hours
Testosterone propionate	2.5 mg	IM	Once
Tetrachloroethyline	0.22 ml	Oral	Once
Tetraccycline	25 mg	Oral	Repeat after 8 hours
	5-10 mg	IV	Repeat after 12 hours
Theophylline	5-7	Oral	Repeat after 8 hours
Thiabendazole	25 mg	In feed	Repeat after 12 hours

(Contd.)

Drug	*Dose (per kg body weight)*	*Route of administration*	*Frequency*
1	*2*	*3*	*4*
Thiacetarsamide	2.2 mg	IV	'Repeat after 12 hours, 2 days
Thiamine	2 mg	Oral	SID
Thyroid, dessicated	15-20 mg	Oral	SID
Thyroxin	20-32 microgm	Oral	SID
Ticarcillin	20 mg	IM, IV	Repeat after 8 hours
Tobramycin	1 mg	IV, IM	Repeat after 8 hours
Tocainide	75 mg	Oral	Repeat after 8 hours
Toluene	0.22 ml	Oral	Once
Triamcinolone	0.25 mg	Oral, IM	SID
Triamterene	1-2 mg	Oral	Repeat after 12 hours
Triflupromazine	0.2 mg	Oral	Repeat after 8 hours
Triflupromazine	0.2 mg	Oral	Repeat after 12 hours
Triidothyronine	4.4 microgm	Oral	Repeat after 8 hours
Trimethobenzamide	4 mg	IM	Repeat after 6 hours
Tylosin	5-10 mg	IV, IM	Repeat after 12 hours
	10 mg	Oral	Repeat after 8 hours
Valproic acid	50 mg	Oral	Repeat after 8 hours
Vancomycin	10 mg	Oral, IV	Repeat after 6-8 hours
Verapamil	0.1 mg	IV	Repeat after 8 hours
Vinblastine	0.05 mg	IV	Weekly
Vincristine	0.01-0.025 mg max. dose 1.5 mg	IV	Every 4-7 days
Vitamin D	80-160 IU	Oral	SID for 7 days
Vitamin K_1	1.1 mg	Oral, SC	Repeat after 8 hours

Appendix-6

COMMON TERMS USED IN DOG KEEPING

AKC	:	American Kennel Club used world wide for classification.
Action	:	Forward movement style of dog.
Almond eyes	:	Eyes that resemble almonds in shape but not so common.
Angulation	:	Describing the conformation of a particular joint such as the elbo.
Apple head	:	A convex or dome-shaped forehead.
Apron	:	Longer hair on the chest, at the base of the neck, making a frill in some dogs.
Bad mouth	:	Faulty dentition - teeth may be absent or fail to meet correctly or irregular shape.
Bandy legs	:	Either of legs that bow abnormally outwards which change the normal structure.
Barking	:	Common vice of dog.
Barrel	:	The rounded body shape due to ribs in some breeds of dogs.
Barrel hocks	:	Hock joints that are directed outwards, results in the feet to point inwards. Sometimes termed 'spread hocks'.
Bat ears	:	Ears are wide at the base and rounded at the tip, with the ear canals directed forwards. It is a characteristic feature of the French Bulldog.
Bay	:	Howling call of a hound in pursuit.
Beard	:	Long thick hair on the lower jaw. It is also called beard dog.
Benched	:	Show dogs are placed on benches, and secured by special chains.
Belton	:	A white body coat densely flecked with coloured hair.
BIS	:	'Best in Show' award, conferred on the best winner of all the breed winners in a competition or in dog show.
Bird dog	:	A dog trained for hunting especially for birds.
Bitch	:	A female dog.
Blanket	:	Colour of the saddle area in hounds is known as blanket.
Blaze	:	A white stripe running down in face, usually between the eyes.
Bloom	:	Glossy appearance of a healthy coat is termed as bloom.
Blue belton	:	Blue flecking on a white background, typicallly associated with English Setters is termed blue belton.

BOB	:	'Best of Breed' award by a society of dog show.
Bone	:	Strong, muscular legs mostly found in hunting dogs.
Bossy	:	More development of shoulder muscles.
Bracelets	:	Rings of hair remaining on the legs mostly seen in Lowchens and Poodles in show clip.
Brisket	:	Area of the body under the chest, between the forelimbs termed as brisket.
Bite	:	Act of cutting with teeth.
BKC	:	British Kennel Club used world wide for classification.
Blue Merle	:	A body coat of grey and black hair giving blue appearance.
Brace	:	A pair of dogs.
Breeching	:	Tan-coloured hair on the medial side of thighs.
Brindle	:	Mixed coat of light and dark hair forming irregular strips.
Broken-coated	:	Wire-haired or rough-body coat.
Brood bitch	:	Pedigree female kept for breeding.
Brush	:	Bushy tail, same as in fox.
Butterfly nose	:	A partially pigmented nose.
Button ear	:	An ear with forward folding tip placed close to the skull.
Burr	:	Inner surface of the ear is called burr.
Canid	:	Member of the genus Canis, e.g. wolves (canine family).
Canines	:	Long, pointed teeth next to the incisors, present on both jaws as in dogs.
CC	:	Challenge award certificate at KC Championship Show for best entries of both sexes of a specific breed of dog.
CD	:	Companion Dog - a suffix given by the AKC for a dog that has achieved the minimum points score in Novic Classes at a specific number of shows. It is also used for canine distemper disease.
Ch Champion	:	A prefix used to indicate a winner of three Challenge certificates, under separate judges in Britain, or the accumulation of a specific number of points in other countries also.
Cheeky	:	Rounded, thickish and protruding cheeks of either sex.
China eye	:	A clear blue eye is known as china eye.
Chiselled	:	Describing a head with a clear-cut appearance, especially below the eyes.
Choke chain	:	A collar around the dog's neck correctly applied, should loosen or tighten, depending on the handler's grip.
Chops	:	Jowls, mostly significant in the Bulldog.
Clip	:	Trimming of the coat, particularly significant in Poodles and other long hair dogs.
Clipping	:	Front legs are hit by the hind when the dog moves.
Cloddy	:	Low, thickset and relatively heavy dog.
Coarse	:	Unrefined; a dog of poor quality and unrefined.
Coat Foot	:	Short, round and compact foot with highly arched toes.
Cobby	:	Short-bodied compact animal.
Condition	:	General state of health, from its overall performance.
Coupling	:	Part of body between fore and rear legs.
Covering ground	:	Stride, involving fore and hindlimbs in dog.
Cow hocked	:	A deformity of hind legs in which the hock joints are turned inward and feet to turn outwards.

Crabbing : Sideways movement.

Crank tail : A tail carried low or downward.

Crest : Uppermost arched part of the neck; also the hair present on the head of a Chinese Crested Dog termed as crest.

Cropping : Cutting of the ear leathers to make the ears remain erect.

Crossbred : Offspring from the mating of two different breeds of dog.

Croup : Part of the back nearest to the tail region.

Crown : The top of the skull between the ears.

Culotte : Relatively long hair at the back of the thighs in certain breeds.

Cur : A mongrel or local breed.

Crying : Noise made due to pain.

Cryptorchid : Male in which testicles are not descended in the scrotum.

Dew claw : Rudimentary additional toes.

Dewlap : Loose skin under the throat and neck.

Dock : Amputation of tail.

Dog : An individual of common domestic dog without the differentiation of age and sex.

Double coat : Body coat comprising woolly undercoat and long coarse outer guard hair.

Down in pasterns : Weakness of the metacarpus, causing the feet to be at an angle from the fore-limbs, rather than in a relatively straight line.

Drag : A scent trail laid by dragging a strong smelling lure, later to be followed by hounds in lieu of a fox.

Drop ears : Long pendulous ears hanging close to the head.

Dry neck : Taut skin.

Dual Champion or Bench and field Champion : Both working and show winner in any dog show.

Duddley nose : Light brown nose.

Ectropion : Eyelids directed outwards.

Entropion : Eyelids directed inwards towards the eye.

Even bite : Both rows of incisor teeth meet directly.

Ewe neck : Concave neck.

Fall : Hair which overhangs the face as in some toy breeds.

Feathering : Tufts of long hair on ears, legs and tail.

Fiddle : Front feet turned in, while the elbows are turned out.

Flag : Long tail or hair thereon.

Flews : Pendulous inner angles of upper lips.

Flush : Driving birds or animals from cover.

Foul colour : Untypical marking or colour.

Front : Part of the body visible when viewed from the front.

Furnishings : Long hair on the foreface.

Furrow : Line running from the centre of the skull to the stop.

Gait : Leg movement categorized into types, including the wald, trot and gallop.

Gay tail : Tail carried over the back.

Grizzled dog : Bluish-grey colour dog.
Guard hair : Longish hair which conceal the undercoat.
Gun-barrel front : Straight forelimbs.
Gun-shy : A pet which is nervous of the sound or sight of guns.
Hackless : Hair on the neck and back erected when the dog feels threatened.
Hackney action : Lifting of the forelegs high in an abnormal manner.
Handler : Person responsible for the dog in the show ring or at a field trial or at training.
Hard-mounted : A dog which marks retrieved game with its teeth.
Hair Foot : An elongated narrow foot.
Hariequin : Black or blue patches on white colour; associated with Great Danes.
Harsh coat : Stiff and wiry coat.
Heat : A term applied to a bitch which is reproductively active, i.e. in season.
Height : Shoulder height, measured from the ground to the withers in a vertical line.
Hock : First joint of hind leg above the foot.
Inbreeding : Mating of dogs which are closely related, such as dam to son or brother sister.
Incisors : Teeth at the front of the mouth between the canines.
In season : Bitch in heat.
ICD : Indian classification of dog.
Jowls : Fleshy part of the lips, and jaws.
KCI : Kennel Club of India.
Leathers : Ear flaps.
Line-breeding : Breeding of related stock together.
Lippy : More development or overhanging of the lips.
Litter : A term for the puppies resulting from one whelping or delivery.
Loaded shoulders : Unusual excessive development of shoulder muscles.
Lock up or tie : Third stage of mating when male and female are joined sexually in tail to tail position.
Loins : Extend from the last ribs to the hind-quarters.
Lumbar : Excess musculature.
Lurcher : Crossbreed hound dog.
Mane : Long hair on and around the neck, resembling that with a lion.
Merle : Combination of blue, grey and black colours.
Milk teeth : Deciduous teeth or temporary teeth.
Miscellaneous Class: A class for breeds that cannot be shown competitively in order AKC classes.
Molar : Teeth with relatively large surface areas, at the back of the mouth.
Molera : Faulty ossification of the skull.
Mongrel : Undefined street dogs.
Muzzle : Region of the face in front of eyes.
Nick : A beneficial mating.
Occciput : A bony protuberance at the posterior of the skull.
Ottertail : A tail which is thick at its base, round and showing no feathering, with hair divided on the underside.

Outcross	:	Mating of a dog and bitch which are unrelated but of the same breed.
Overshot	:	Upper incisors protrude past those of the lower jaw.
Pace	:	Legs on one side of the body move before those on the other.
Pack	:	A number of hounds kept specifically for hunting.
Pad	:	Tough yet vascular covering of the base of the foot, soles or pad.
Paper foot	:	Thin-soled, flat foot.
Parent club	:	National Breed club.
Particolour	:	Variegated patching on the body.
Pasterns	:	Part of the foreleg extending from the carpus to the digits.
Patella	:	Knee cap help in proper movement of legs.
Pedigree	:	Ancestry of a particular individual.
Pencilling	:	Black line present on tan-coloured toes.
Pig eye	:	Abnormally small eye.
Pigeon-toed	:	Toes point inwards towards the midline.
Pile	:	Thick undercoat of a dog.
Plume	:	Fringe of hair on the tails of breeds such as setters.
Point	:	Rigid posture adopted by a hunting dog to reveal the location of prey.
Points	:	Colour of the hair on the legs, face, ears and tail.
Poke	:	Carriage of the neck at an abnormally low angle.
Pompon	:	Circular tuft of hair at the end of the tail, mostly in Poodles.
Prefix	:	Name of the kennel where the dog was bred, which appears in front of the dog's individual name.
Premolars	:	Teeth located between the canines and molars.
Prick ear	:	Pointed and angular erect ear.
Pup or Puppies	:	Young ones of dog.
Quality	:	A reflection of the dog's conformation and character.
Rangy	:	Tall, long body.
Rag tail	:	A tail with hair absent from the tip.
Ribbed up	:	Long, well-angled ribs.
Ring	:	Area where dogs are judged for their performance.
Ring tail	:	Tail carried high, almost forming a circle.
Roached back	:	Curved back.
Roan	:	A mixture of red and white (red roan) or black and white (blue roan) hair in body coat.
Roman nose	:	Nose with a high ridge whose point turns down.
Rose ear	:	Small-sized ear folding away from the front to expose the inner surface.
Ruff	:	Long and relatively thick hair around the neck.
Sable	:	A bright black hair lacing in lighter coat.
Sabre tail	:	Tail in the shape of a semicircle.
Saddle back	:	Excessively long back.
Scissor bite	:	Upper incisors overlap their lower counterparts when the jaw is closed.
Screw Tail	:	A tail which is short and twisted.
Self-coloured	:	Of one colour only.

Semi-prick : Ears carried erect, with tips pointing forwards.

Service : Mating of the bitch of a dog.

Set-up : Dog displayed in the show ring.

Smooth coat : A body coat containing small coloured patches on white coat.

Snipy : Weak, thin muzzle.

Spay : To prevent bitches from breeding, by surgery.

Splashed : Patches of white contrasting with a solid colour.

Splay foot : Toes spread wide apart.

Squirrel Tail : Tail carried upright, falling quite flat over the back.

Standard : Breed description specified by the governing canine authority.

Staring coat : A coat in poor condition.

Stern : Tail of a hound or other sporting dog.

Stilted : Gait associated with a straight-hocked dog.

Stop : Point between the eyes where the nasal bone and skull meet.

Straight-hocked : Insufficient angulation at the hocks.

Stud dog : An uncastrated male used for breeding.

Symmetry : All parts of the dog are in proportion.

Team : More than two working dogs is termed as team.

Terrier front : Straight profile at the front.

Texture : Describes the type of coat.

Throaty : Excessive skin below the throat.

Ticked : A body coat containing small colloured patches on white coat.

Tongue : Call of hounds when they are on a trail.

Top knot : A tuft of long hair on the poll of the head.

Topline : Profile extending from the withers to the tail.

Tricolour : A body coat of three colours usually white, black and tan.

Tulipear : An erect ear with a slightly curved tip.

Trace : Dark stripe along the back, characteristic of pugs.

Trail : Follow by meash of a scent.

Trim : Grooming which involves clipping or plucking.

Type : Qualities specified for the breed in its official standard.

Undercoat : Soft, insulating hair under the top coat.

Undershot : A shorter upper jaw or longer lower jaw and overlapped upper incisors by lower incisors.

Wall eye : One or both eye balls with pale, white or colourless iris. It is also called pearl eye, glass eye or figh eye.

Wheaten : Yellowish-fawn colour.

Whelping : Process of delivery or parturition.

Wire haired : A body coat of hard and wiry hair.

Appendix-7

COMMON NAMES OF PET

1. Audy
2. Appu
3. Aksha
4. Aonex
5. Abu
6. Abbey
7. Abba
8. Alex
9. Allen
10. Andy
11. Boxer
12. Buff
13. Buffo
14. Booty
15. Bounder
16. Brandy
17. Bosky
18. Boxy
19. Bully
20. Bhura
21. Bhuri
22. Brownie
23. Blackie
24. Bonny
25. Butten
26. Candy
27. Canter
28. Casper
29. Caper
30. Cofee
31. Cupid
32. Cooksy
33. Cadbury
34. Cuddly
35. Cuddles
36. Cool
37. Crox
38. Cranker
39. Champs
40. Campa
41. Chetu
42. Chemalee
43. Chena
44. Cheenu
45. Champion
46. Carier
47. Devil
48. Drake
49. Dumbo
50. Dingle
51. Dan
52. Danny
53. Danger
54. Dolby
55. Dexter
56. Dane
57. Duke
58. Dusty
59. Chuni
60. Dewy
61. Dalor
62. Daboo
63. Dablu
64. Doby
65. Donny
66. Dicky
67. Dap
68. Dapgua
69. Eshan
70. Eera
71. Eugene
72. Epta
73. Fluffy
74. Fancy
75. Frosty
76. Fanny
77. Flash
78. Feeler
79. Francy
80. Foffy
81. Gumer
82. Golf
83. Grundy
84. Gundo
85. Grumpy
86. Gamps
87. Game
88. Gammy
89. Gapur
90. Guju
91. Goldie
92. Gola
93. Hooray
94. Hamps
95. Hans
96. Hunter
97. Hepty
98. Huff
99. Helly
100. Heera
101. Haria
102. Hema
103. Honey
104. Inky
105. Inka
106. Lirish
107. Lonex
108. Licy

109. Imp
110. Ina
111. Jack
112. Jacky
113. Jackson
114. Jeff
115. Jerry
116. Jean
117. Jox
118. Jana
119. Jewy
120. Julie
121. Juna
122. Jimmy
123. Jandu
124. Johny
125. Jhabra
126. Jhabu
127. John
128. Jetley
129. Jojo
130. Jona
131. Jinny
132. Jung
133. Joom
134. Joon
135. Kasper
136. Kucker
137. Krax
138. Kroper
139. Krazy
140. Kooksy
141. Knight
142. Kinker
143. Killer
144. Kalu
145. Kabra
146. Katy
147. Kesari
148. Karjan
149. Kalia
150. Kallo
151. Kitty
152. Lamby
153. Loner
154. Loren
155. Lanty
156. Lana
157. Lumpy
158. Lotta
159. Lick
160. Lean
161. Leena
162. Lalita
163. Laila
164. Lallu
165. Lucky
166. Loty
167. Lussy
168. Luna
169. Lann
170. Mark
171. Max
172. Muller
173. Miller
174. Mandy
175. Mink
176. Money
177. Memo
178. Moti
179. Mack
180. Mickey
181. Meena
182. Mickloo
183. Mini
184. Mikka
185. Manty
186. Nelco
187. Notty
188. Nod
189. Noddy
190. Nono
191. Nimp
192. Norax
193. Nanmi
194. Noorie
195. Nimbi
196. Nina
197. Nanha
198. Oona
199. Onkar
200. Orkey
201. Opy
202. Oscar
203. Oua
204. Olhy
205. Olva
206. Olya
207. Panther
208. Pixie
209. Pinky
210. Pirate
211. Puma
212. Prance
213. Prank
214. Peter
215. Pappu
216. Pansy
217. Panchho
218. Poochi
219. Pony
220. Peggy
221. Poxy
222. Punch
223. Quintex
224. Quniten
225. Queeny
226. Quinx
227. Queen
228. Rick
229. Ricky
230. Rocky
231. Rex
232. Rumy
233. Rusty
234. Rumpy
235. Roller
236. Randy
237. Rinky
238. Ranker
239. Raja
240. Rani
241. Ranjha
242. Raju
243. Rimjhim
244. Rinka
245. Reshma
246. Stony
247. Stumpy
248. Sticker
249. Shade
250. Shana
251. Sona
252. Soni
253. Snoopy
254. Snooty
255. Shopy
256. Showy
257. Snowy
258. Snow
259. Sinner
260. Slander
261. Scamper
262. Sharp
263. Sheka
264. Sinker
265. Suzy
266. Softy
267. Seema
268. Sunnel
269. Sydney
270. Sunny
271. Shiny
272. Shafer

273. Sherry
274. Shera
275. Shivu
276. Sweta
277. Timmy
278. Typsy
279. Tobu
280. Tubby
281. Trox
282. Trinker
283. Tommy
284. Tony
285. Tuna
286. Tanner
287. Tangy
288. Toffee
289. Timsy
290. Toto
291. Tingler
292. Tippy
293. Tinku
294. Tito
295. Tipu
296. Tiny
297. Tulu
298. Tina
299. Tan
300. Tiger
301. Urana
302. Uranus
303. Ura
304. Una
305. Umpty
306. Ullo
307. Venu
308. Veru
309. Vicky
310. Vack
311. Vicking
312. Victor
313. Van
314. Wicker
315. Wicky
316. Wolf
317. Wolfy
318. Woof
319. Wink
320. Woolhy
321. Whisker
322. Whisky
323. Wander
324. Wandy
325. Whitey
326. Xorax
327. Xono
328. Xollo
329. Xandu
330. Xaner
331. Zena
332. Zaner
333. Zingy
334. Zuma
335. Zoblo
336. Zany
337. Zeba
338. Zebu
339. Zoro
340. Zar
341. Zack
342. Zumpy
343. Zono
344. Zobo
345. Zippy

INDEX

CBS OUTSTANDING BOOKS